HF DAVIS LIBRARY COAST COMMUNITY COLLEGE

970.48 M222d
Dog soldiers, bear men, and buffalo women;
a study of the societies and cults of the Plains
Indians.
CCC120256

D0722745

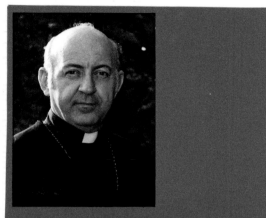

ABOUT THE AUTHOR

Thomas E. Mails leads a full and rich life as a minister, an author and an artist.

He attended the California College of Arts and Crafts, was an engineering officer with the United States Coast Guard in World War II and was for seven years an architectural designer in the Seattle and San Francisco areas. Graduated from Luther Theological Seminary in St. Paul, Minnesota, he became a minister and is presently pastor of Christ the Victor Lutheran Church in Pomona, California. He is the author of eighteen books concerned with religion and, as evidence of another facet of his busy life, has paintings and drawings in many private collections.

Mr. Mails has been interested in Indians—their culture, their religion, their public and private lives, their crafts—for many years and, at one time, had a large collection of Indian artifacts; these have served him well as "models" for his paintings and drawings. He has had several one-man shows of these pictures—at the Jamison Galleries in Santa Fe, New Mexico, and at the Southwest Museum and the Biltmore Galleries, both in Los Angeles.

Mr. Mails's previous book on Indians was the well-received *The Mystic Warriors of the Plains*. He is at work on two more, *The People Called Apaches* and *The Sun Dance*.

First page: *Member of Crow cult wearing grizzly bear claw medicine necklace, with beaded medicine ring hung in background. Rings like this were carried to war as protective devices.* Left: *Ponca warrior wearing typical Sun Dance costume of the Southeastern Plains area. He carries an eagle bone whistle and a hoop covered with spruce or sage and adorned with eagle and owl feathers.* Below: *Comanche war shield cover hung with golden eagle feathers and showing the variety of carrying loops employed.* Next page: *Member of the Blackfoots Blood tribe Black-soldier society carrying society club and staff and wearing painted war shirt adorned with rolled ermine tails and hair locks.*

DOG SOLDIERS, BEAR MEN AND BUFFALO WOMEN

DOG SOLDIERS, BEAR MEN AND BUFFALO WOMEN

A Study of the Societies and Cults of the Plains Indians

written and illustrated by
Thomas E. Mails

A Rutledge Book
Prentice-Hall, Inc.
Englewood Cliffs, N.J.

Q
970.48
M222d
1973

To Dr. Carl S. Dentzel, director of the Southwest Museum,
Highland Park, Los Angeles

Library of Congress Catalog Card Number: 73-1829
ISBN: 013-217216-X
Copyright 1973 in all countries of the International Copyright Union by
  Prentice-Hall, Inc. All rights reserved including the right of reproduction in whole
  or in part
Prepared and produced by Rutledge Books, 17 East 45th Street, New York, N.Y. 10017
Published in 1973 by Prentice-Hall, Inc., Englewood Cliffs, N.J.
Printed in Italy by Mondadori, Verona

S27520

Library
Colby Community Junior College
Colby. Kansas

CONTENTS

FOREWORD

From the time of the discovery of America until today, people everywhere have been interested in the aboriginal inhabitants of the North, Central and South Americas. Of the many nations that make up the Western Hemisphere, none has had more interesting natives than the United States. The American Indian and his significant ways of life reflect many patterns of culture. From the time of the first contact with the Red Men of the New World, artists have been fascinated with Indians.

During the seventeenth, eighteenth and nineteenth centuries, many scholarly works appeared in most European languages relating to the Indians of North, Central and South America. These significant works were usually generously filled with drawings, engravings and colored plates of Indians in their native habitat. Great attention was paid to clothing, implements, customs, warfare, ceremonies and all other aspects reflecting strange new ways of life. The artist became one of the most useful interpreters of native peoples.

With the establishment of the United States of America and its pageant of progress from the Atlantic to the Pacific in the nineteenth century, the Indian became an important catalyst in history. As population moved from east to west, a great wealth of literature was created concerning exploration, settlement and development. The Westward Movement counted many outstanding artists in its stimulating progress: great ethnohistorical artists such as Titian R. Peale, Samuel Seymour, George Catlin, Karl Bodmer, Alfred Jacob Miller, Rudolf Friedrich Kurtz, Henrich Mollhausen, Carl Wimar, Otto Lewis, Frederic Remington and Charles M. Russell.

These artists were exceptionally gifted men who sensed the meaning and drama of the frontier and the New West. They appreciated the place of the Indians and worked diligently to portray and preserve for posterity the changing ways of life and what once seemed to be "the Vanishing American." Besides being artists, they were also anthropologists interested in and recording archaeology, ethnology, folklore and history. The twentieth century has not produced many artists that follow this tradition. Thomas Mails is one of the few that can equal them. He and his work are in the great tradition. Besides being a truly gifted artist, he sees, feels and appreciates the Indians he paints as an enlightened anthropologist does.

Among contemporary artists and interpreters of American Indian life, the Reverend Thomas E. Mails is foremost. His knowledge of and appreciation for Indian ways are outstanding. He is sensitive to the Indian ways of life, respecting the cultural, philosophical and religious traditions reflected in the many tribes he has studied and portrayed.

The Reverend Thomas E. Mails's oils, charcoal studies and pen and-ink sketches of the American Indian very strongly yet sensitively depict their highly detailed themes of ceremonial and home life. His brush style and technique produce classical forms of figures convincing in character and expressiveness of American Indian living. The artist is profoundly interested in the people he depicts and is moved by the culture he esteems. His creative writings and paintings reflect this.

Carl Schaefer Dentzel, Director
Southwest Museum
Los Angeles, California

Dr. Dentzel, an authority on the culture of aboriginal America, has written, edited and annotated a number of publications on the subject; he is president of the Cultural Heritage Board of the City of Los Angeles.

PREFACE

During their prime period of existence, between the historic years of A.D. 1750 and A.D. 1850, the Plains Indian nations achieved a way of life that was replete with sophistication and richness in its every dimension: religion, heritage, tradition, government, family life, social life, crafts, hunting skills and warfare. Along with these accomplishments came a profusion of splendid ceremonies, costumes and regalia ranking with the finest the world has ever seen. The greater part of these were directly associated with the warrior societies, civil societies and cults.

Learning about these Plains organizations is a consummate pleasure. Yet it is a joy that until now has been shared in the main by anthropologists, avid students of Indian lore and those Indians whose hearts have remained rooted in the rich old ways. It deserves a broader audience—among the Indian nations themselves and the non-Indians, both of whom are now especially sensitive to the fact that because we concentrated on justice and injustice, we have gone blindly by the very core of a great people who have much to offer the world of our time.

I wish, in view of the many enjoyable years I have spent in researching and preparing this material, I could say it is all original. Yet anyone should recognize that that is not possible. The Indians who actually belonged to the societies and cults, plus all eyewitnesses, have passed on; even those with secondhand knowledge have gone. In fact, by the time the first White anthropologists recognized the importance of these groups and went among the Indians from 1870 to 1930 to learn what they could about them, it was often impossible to obtain more than hearsay accounts concerning their activities. Now and then an actual member of a defunct order would be located. Sometimes several older people who could each add a piece of information would be discovered. Some societies, whose nature had by then become social, still existed. Eventually a general overview of the Plains organizations was painstakingly pieced together and filtered over a long period of time into ethnological publications and numerous books of a more general nature. Of late, a few experts have done some work among individual tribes that has contributed worthwhile information.

My offering lies in the introductory chapters and in the organization, condensation and interpretation of the information regarding the societies of specific tribes that exists, together with the addition of illustrations taken and adapted mainly from museum collections and from ancient photographs and drawings, in order to make a comprehensive presentation for both student and popular consumption.

In admitting that my sources are not entirely original, fairness demands that I gratefully acknowledge in advance the distinguished men and women who labored so long, and under such difficult circumstances, in the field to produce the societal and cultural literature of the Plains Indians. Naturally, too, the materials they authored are listed in the bibliography at the back of this book. The dates associated here with their names are the publication dates of their efforts, but readers should bear in mind that publication followed—in some instances, at least—twenty or more years of active research among and about the Indians. For example, Grinnell's work concerning the Cheyenne was published in 1923, yet he was among them as early as 1890 and studied them constantly thereafter for the balance of his life. The last of Edward Curtis's stupendous forty-volume work of accounts and photographs was published in 1930, but he began it in the field in 1898.

The authorities and their fields are:

Arapaho: James Mooney, 1893; Althea Bass, 1966.
Arikara: Edward S. Curtis, 1909; Robert H. Lowie, 1915; Frances Densmore, 1918.
Assiniboine: Edwin T. Denig, 1893; Robert H. Lowie, 1909; Michael S. Kennedy, 1961.
Blackfoots: George B. Grinnell, 1901; Edward S. Curtis, 1909; Walter McClintock, 1910; Clark Wissler, 1913; John C. Ewers, 1954.
Cheyenne: George B. Grinnell, 1923; George A. Dorsey, 1905; Robert H. Lowie, 1910; E. Adamson Hoebel and Karl N. Llewellyn, 1941; Margot Liberty, 1967; Peter J. Powell, 1969.
Comanche: Ernest Wallace, 1952.
Crow: Edward S. Curtis, 1909; Frank B. Linderman, 1915; Robert H. Lowie, 1916; William Wildschut, 1960.
Gros Ventre: Edward S. Curtis, 1909.
Hidatsa: Edward S. Curtis, 1909; Robert H. Lowie, 1915.
Kiowa: James Mooney, 1897; Robert H. Lowie, 1916.
Mandan: George Catlin, 1842; Edward S. Curtis, 1909; Robert H. Lowie, 1915; Alfred W. Bowers, 1950.
Ojibway: Alanson Skinner, 1914.
Omaha: George A. Dorsey, 1905; Alice C. Fletcher, 1911; Alanson Skinner, 1920.
Pawnee: James R. Murie, 1914.
Ponca: George A. Dorsey, 1915; W. W. Newcomb, Jr., 1961; James A. Howard, 1965.
Shoshone: Robert H. Lowie, 1909.
Sioux: Edward S. Curtis, 1909; Clark Wissler, 1912; Frances Densmore, 1918; Joseph Epes Brown, 1953; Royal B. Hassrick, 1964; Helen H. Blish, 1967.
Ute: Robert H. Lowie, 1915.

Beyond this, my utmost gratitude must be extended to the American Museum of Natural History, New York, for permission to illustrate their outstanding collection of Plains society artifacts; to the Museum of the American Indian, Heye Foundation, New York, for the privilege of inspecting their artifacts; to the Southwest Museum, Los Angeles, California—and particularly to its gracious director, Dr. Carl S. Dentzel —for permission to make extensive use of its artifacts, photographic collection and library; to the Denver Public Library, Denver, Colorado, for permission to use its photographs; to the Gilcrease Institute, Tulsa, Oklahoma, for permission to photograph its artifacts and to use its library. To properly credit the photographs and artifacts used and adapted, an abbreviation indicating the source will be placed in parentheses after each caption. Where no letters are found, the drawings are original. The abbreviations will be as follows: American Museum of Natural History (AMNH); Museum of the American Indian (MAI); Southwest Museum (SM); Gilcrease Institute (GI); Denver Public Library (DPL); Field Columbian Museum (FCM).

My deepest appreciation goes also to Glenn Harrison for his outstanding photographs of my illustrations; to J. R. Eyerman for the superb transparencies from which the color plates are made; to Gardner/Fulmer Lithograph of Buena Park, California, for their sensitive work with the negatives for the black and white illustrations; to my agent and friend Clyde Vandeburg for his constant optimism and encouragement of my work; to Wilbur F. Eastman, Jr., and Dennis Fawcett of Prentice-Hall for their boundless enthusiasm for the book, a factor of inestimable value to an author, and to my daughter Allison, whose research and typing skills reduced my workload by a significant degree and made my production schedules achievable.

1
THE ORIGIN OF THE SOCIETIES AND CULTS

One summer day during the year 1890, a tall, imposing Sioux warrior named Kills Two joined his assembled people in the celebration of their annual summer festival, which, until it was forbidden by the United States government, had been known as the Sun Dance. Kills Two's appearance was so striking that an alert White photographer named D. F. Barry snapped his picture and thus recorded it for posterity.

Already in 1890, Kills Two's costume included some evidences of the changes that had come about as a result of White contacts and the permanent reservation period. Since his hair was cut short, a gaudily beaded headband helped to hold his deer-tail roach headdress and his head feathers in place. The top half of a suit of long underwear, dyed yellow, covered his upper body and arms. He also wore brightly colored trade ribbons, and strings of metal bells hung on straps that passed down the sides of his legs to the ankles. Round trade mirrors, attached to his breechclout, glinted in the sun as he moved about.

Besides these, however, he had slipped over his head in poncho fashion an opulent otter skin collar, trimmed at its lower edge with the beautiful porcupine quillwork native to the ancient Plains Indians alone. It, too, was decorated with round trade mirrors, yet it was also a continuance of the collars that had identified influential Sioux warrior-society members for untold centuries. Every Indian knew that.

Over Kills Two's left shoulder was a braided rope of sweetgrass, whose use as sacred incense and sublime fragrance had carried the prayers of the Sioux up to God since the beginning of time. To such ropes were often tied the medicine items that linked the warrior to his Creator in conscious dependence. Now and then a heavy buffalo skull would be secured to such a rope and carried for hours on a man's back in return for Divine favors already granted.

On his back at waist level, Kills Two wore a circular crow bustle of golden eagle and hawk feathers and, secured to the back of his neck, a smaller circlet of matching feathers. Such bustles could be worn only by men who had earned them through outstanding accomplishments on horse raids and in battle.

Fur bands of mountain-lion winter coat hair were wrapped about his wrists, quilled armbands were on his upper arms and what appears to be a narrow wolf skin band was around his neck. Each was a medicine helper of great magnitude.

Kills Two's entire face was painted with a stunningly bold design. His eyes were narrowed and penetrating. His expression indicated that he was thinking only of war and of revenge—yet in his right hand was another cord of braided sweetgrass, a rattle and a pipestem. Therefore, those who were able to read such signs would explain that Kills Two had come to dance the Sacred Pipe Dance of Peace, whose purpose was to put an end to the dissension between warring peoples. If only those non-Indians who saw Kills Two and others like him that day had known the true nature of the people, if only they had tried to understand, who can guess how different a most regrettable history of White–Indian relationships might have been? Or, to put it in a slightly different but more current form, if the attempt to understand is made now, perhaps that history can finally be altered.

Assuredly, the look in Kills Two's eyes and the significance of his regalia indicated pride in his position and heritage. Plainly he was willing to stand with his people for what they were. But just as cer-

Opposite: *Kills Two* (DP̄L).

THE GREAT PLAINS

12

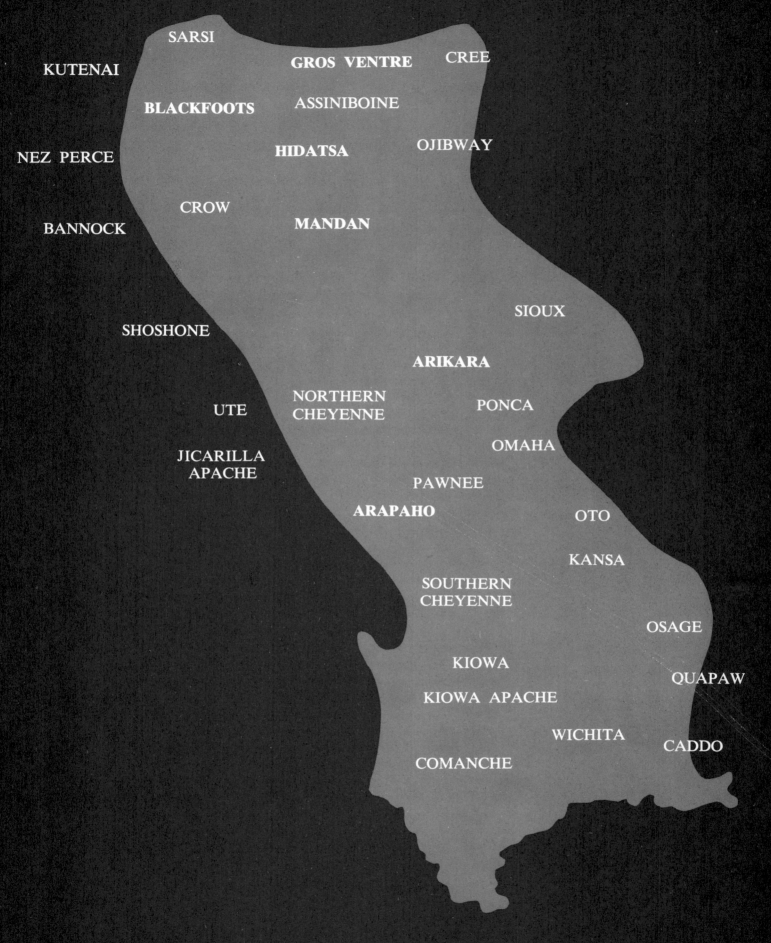

SARSI

KUTENAI

GROS VENTRE

CREE

BLACKFOOTS

ASSINIBOINE

NEZ PERCE

HIDATSA

OJIBWAY

BANNOCK

CROW

MANDAN

SHOSHONE

SIOUX

ARIKARA

UTE

NORTHERN
CHEYENNE

PONCA

OMAHA

JICARILLA
APACHE

PAWNEE

ARAPAHO

OTO

KANSA

SOUTHERN
CHEYENNE

OSAGE

KIOWA

QUAPAW

KIOWA APACHE

WICHITA

CADDO

COMANCHE

13

Map of Great Plains area showing approximate locations of tribes during years 1750– 1850.

*Hidatsa warrior wearing horned, ermine bonnet, with earth lodge and corn-drying rack
in background* (SM).

tainly, the look in his eyes was really that of perplexity over his inability to make the non-Indian spectators understand that the Sioux and all the other Indian nations were something vastly more and different from what they were thought to be by non-Indians.

The picture merely represents a momentary encounter between a venerable Indian warrior and a perceptive White photographer. Then drums began to boom a short distance away and singers commenced an ancient song. Kills Two moved off to join them without so much as a backward glance. But history of no small magnitude had been standing there within him, his costume, paint and society regalia, and it is a history well worth knowing.

During the historic period that began in the eighteenth century, there were thirty-five Indian nations dwelling on the Great Plains of North America. Twenty-six of these are known today as the Plains nations proper:

Sarsi	In addition to those listed on the left, there were several nations living in the Rocky Mountain and western Plateau areas that made occasional forays onto the Plains to hunt buffalo and to war defensively against some of the Plains nations proper. These also adopted a substantial part of the typical Plains culture. They are known as "marginal tribes":
Blackfoot	
Cree	
Ojibway	
Gros Ventre	
Assiniboine	
Crow	
Hidatsa	
Mandan	Beaver
Arikara	Kutenai
Sioux	Nez Percé
Shoshone	Northern Shoshone
Arapaho	Ute
Cheyenne	Jicarilla Apache
Ponca	Lipan Apache
Pawnee	
Omaha	In the Southeast there were two other marginal tribes:
Oto	
Kansa	Quapaw
Iowa	Caddo
Missouri	
Osage	
Kiowa	
Kiowa Apache	
Wichita	
Comanche	

While all the nations used the familiar hide tipi for dwellings as they followed the ever-migrating buffalo, eight of the tribes dwelt for the greater part of the year in earth or grass lodges. These Indians are known in literature as "semisedentary peoples," or the "stationary village tribes." The earth lodges were forty to fifty feet in diameter, with walls and ceilings constructed of posts and beams covered with earth and grass. These were used by the Mandan, the Arikara, the Hidatsa, the Pawnee and the Omaha peoples. The grass lodges consisted of a pole frame covered with grass thatching. They were from fifteen to twenty feet wide and from thirty to a hundred feet in length. These were built by the Caddo, the Wichita and the Osage.

In the main, the semisedentary peoples were as oriented toward farming as they were toward hunting. They raised sizable annual crops

16

of maize, beans, squash, pumpkins and sunflower seeds and stayed close to the villages during the planting and harvesting seasons. At other times of the year, a majority of the people would move out to hunt buffalo, carrying their tipis with them on dog- and horse-drawn travois just as the nomadic nations did on a year-round basis. Because of their agricultural base, the permanent villages became natural trade centers for most of the Plains nations, who followed regular land and river routes to them at certain seasons every year.

While the Indians of the Plains hunted many kinds of animals, such as elk, deer, pronghorn and mountain sheep, their very existence was dependent on the Plains bison, most often called the buffalo. Not only did the bison supply most of the meat for their diet, its every part was used in fashioning their equipment, in building their homes and most of the furnishings, in making storage containers and, in combination with wood, in constructing weapons and riding gear.

By what the Indians felt was Divine providence, the erratic but seasonal migrations of the huge bison herds brought the tribes a steady source of almost everything they needed to live comfortably. Conservative estimates indicate that more than 60 million of the animals once roamed the Plains. And these were divided in such a way that herds were moving either circularly or north or south through the north, central and southern portions of the Plains at all times. No one knows for certain what made them move—perhaps it was because of the changes in weather that affected the grass; perhaps it was simply habit. The Indians themselves believed it was God who sent the buffalo in response to their ceremonial buffalo "calls."

The general life-way of the Plains Indians can be described by picking it up at any point on the calendar and pursuing it until it returns to that point a year later. However, since the Indians counted their years in terms of so many "winters," I will follow their pattern and begin with the winter season.

When the first light snow began to fall on a given area of the Plains, the tribes in that area would scurry about to make a final hunt, trying to lay in stores of meat, mainly buffalo, sufficient to carry them through the better part of the winter. This done, the stationary village tribes would settle down for the season, and the various migrating bands who until now had been going their separate ways would pack their belongings and move from all directions toward a wintering area selected at the great tribal encampment the previous spring. Here they would remain from perhaps late November until early May.

Winters were often terrible on the Plains. The snow was deep, the wind howled and the temperature dropped as low as forty degrees below zero. Yet with adequate fuel supplies, the skin tipis remained fairly comfortable, and with the family lodges closely bunched in a random pattern, there was time and opportunity for warm fellowship and the industrious pursuit of crafts. Men spent the days repairing weapons and gear and making such new items as were needed. Women adorned hides, fashioned containers, cooked, tended the babies and gossiped. Children and youths did the absolutely necessary chores and spent the rest of the time playing winter games and getting away with as much mischief as they could. At night the older people gathered in small groups to tell stories and dance, and the young people courted one another. The children came to watch and to listen, and it was on these cozy winter evenings around a warm fire that the great heritage

Blackfoot village (SM).

of the nation was passed down from generation to generation. In this oral teaching, the warrior societies, which were made up of the most renowned warriors of the tribe, played a central role. They not only related the legends of their orders as the protectors of the tribe, they were living legends in themselves, and their impact upon receptive young minds was phenomenal.

For the most part, the frequency of warring and horse-raiding activities lessened considerably in the winter. Nevertheless, offensive-minded groups did venture forth as weather permitted, and every tribe remained on the alert for an attack or a horse raid. During these periods the society members functioned as well-qualified guards who patrolled the camp and watched for enemies. If it appeared that food supplies might run short during a long winter, small hunting parties were sent out by the camp chiefs to search for game. Otherwise, hunting was at a minimum.

The coming of spring spurred the entire tribe into fresh activity. As soon as the ground was passable, each nomadic nation moved to a suitable location for a great encampment. Here the first significant ceremonies were held, the new chiefs chosen and the warrior societies reorganized in preparation for the new year. Everyone observed the cultic rituals now, and prophets strained for encouraging guidance from Above to lift the people's vision and spirits. The tribal chiefs met with the camp chiefs and the new leaders of the warrior societies to plan the tribe's migrations for the new year. This was true of both the stationary and the nomadic tribes, for while the nomads would move constantly, the permanent village people also had hunting and war excursions to arrange.

This done, the stationary peoples began their planting ceremonies and the great camps of the nomadic peoples broke up into their many divisions, which then moved off into designated areas of the home country to follow the wind and the buffalo. For the most part, the bands, which were communities of primarily unrelated families, and the clans, which were communities of related people, became the controllers of their own destiny. They moved along their designated routes, changing campsites every four days or so, and they made their own decisions as to whether to go out on hunts, horse raids or war parties in defense of their home country.

Sometime in midsummer, the bands and clans assembled again for a tribal encampment. At that time the great religious ceremonies were held, with the awesome Sun Dance as the climax. This was the Plains nations' monumental rite of thanksgiving to God, and as some of the societies filled the role of policemen to ensure order among the jubilant thousands assembled and others held their ceremonies to admit candidates, the array of magnificent costumes and regalia, together with the ritual dancing, was enough to dazzle the senses. It was the legendary society members, after all, who wore the most fantastic outfits of the Plains Indians and who carried the most holy regalia. Every society group played its part to the hilt, and in the end some of the members sacrificed themselves heroically by hanging from the rawhide thongs attached to the center pole of the Sun lodge. The purpose of this ceremony was but to give a token of their profound and obviously sincere thanks to God for providing for their needs through the centuries and to ensure that they could expect the same from Him in the years to come.

The Sun Dance was usually followed by a glorious buffalo hunt in

An assembled group of great warriors from various nations, showing magnificence of clothing and warbonnets at peak of cultural development. Feathers are golden eagle, horn bonnets are covered with ermine and rolled ermine tails cascade down warriors' backs (SM).

which the entire tribe participated. This ensured the best use of the herds and guaranteed that every family would receive a fair share of the kill. The societies served as police to monitor this hunt, making certain that all the traditional regulations regarding it were followed to the letter.

Then the stationary peoples turned their thoughts toward harvest, and the nomadic bands and clans went their separate ways again to wander and hunt as they pleased, to trade with other tribes now and then, to war and raid, to ply their industries of tanning, painting, quilling and beadwork and to defend themselves against enemy attacks as necessary. Later they would say to their White conquerors, "You measure time, we enjoyed it."

Of course, this is only the most general and superficial account of the life-way of the Plains Indians. Such an examination becomes truly interesting and significant as one catches the spirit of the people and decides to delve deeper.

According to the Indians, all societies and cults originated in a legend, a vision or a dream. In other words, however practical the orders eventually proved themselves to be, no human being simply decided that such and such a group would serve a useful purpose and then organized it on that basis. To have done so would have eliminated or at least violated the holy aspect of the societies that brought them immediate acceptance, for while Divine guidance in such instances was never questioned, the plainly human decisions made by Plains people in all strata of life were always matters for discussion. Because of this

21

Blackfoot Sun Dance lodge in background, Bull Child as Weather Dancer (SM).

Blackfoot Sun Dance ceremony—Fasting Woman in her ceremonial clothing (SM).

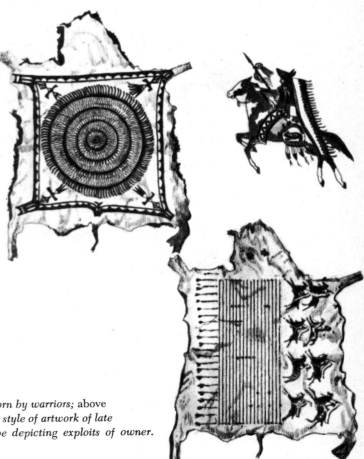

Above left: *Painted buffalo hide robe, warbonnet pattern worn by warriors; above right: Copy of Indian pictographic drawing showing typical style of artwork of late nineteenth century; below right: Quilled and painted robe depicting exploits of owner.*

attitude, a man's purely human decision would never have given rise to a society.

To say that a society originated in a legend (or myth) meant that in the most ancient days of the tribe, one or more of its members had encountered a supernatural being, who, acting as an intermediary for God, issued specific instructions as to the formation of the group or groups in question. In Indian understandings, such beginnings were never symbolic or mythical in the sense of their being imagined occurrences. They were historical events that accompanied the creation and evolution of man and that took place so far back in time as to defy any of the White man's dogged practicality in seeking to prove or disprove them. Their effectiveness within the life-way was all the certification of authenticity the Indian needed, for he believed that one who attempts to prove God is only caught in the awesome trap of seeking to reduce Him to purely human levels of comprehension.

Sometimes, as in the case of the Blackfoots, only one or two of the many societies in a tribe might have originated in a legend, with the rest having found their beginnings in a vision or dream. In another instance, the Cheyenne considered a single legend to be the source of every society but one in their tribe.

Thus, according to Edward S. Curtis, the Blackfoots accounted for the Horn society with the following myths:

> A chief of the first people had two wives, the one an industrious worker, the other his favorite, who performed no labor. On a day while the worker was gathering wood, she heard something singing. She looked about, but could see nothing. Yet it seemed to be very close. Her eye fell on a small stone lying on a roll of old buffalo-hair; it was singing: "Woman, take me. I am supernatural." She wrapped it in the hair, placed it in the bosom of her dress, and returned to the lodge. To her husband, the chief, she said, "Go round the camp and find a small piece of buffalo-fat, if you can." The tribe was starving. So he made a search, and found a piece of fat in the lodge of the beaver medicine-man. This the woman mixed with a bit of brown earth-paint and daubed the stone with it. That night she laid the stone on the buffalo-hair in the center of the lodge, and began to sing, and the people whom the chief at her bidding had invited joined in the songs. All night they sang, and the next morning the people beheld many buffalo around the camp. The woman imparted to the men the wisdom she had learned from the stone, and under her direction they built the first buffalo-fall. She gave the stone to her husband, and it became known as iniskim, the buffalo-stone.

> After the buffalo-fall was completed, the chief selected a young man, who, properly instructed, started out to drive the buffalo between the lines of brush and stones. He gradually herded them in, and then the people rushed from their concealment behind the heaps of brush and stones, and so frightened the buffalo that they hurried themselves over the edge of the cliff. The young man now sat on the brink of the precipice and looked on while the others killed the buffalo. In the corral the animals were running about in a circle, while on the outside men were shooting them down with stone-pointed arrows. The chief remained in his lodge, and the best portions of the meat were taken to him, because it was his duty to feed all who came to his home.

> During the winter a young man was driving the buffalo into the runway, when a cow became buried in a snow-drift. With the bit of brush in his hand he prodded the cow, causing her to jump forward and struggle out of the drift. Once free, she galloped away and escaped. On the second night following, as he sat in the chief's lodge listening to the songs of the buffalo-stones (for he was again to drive the herd), a strange boy entered,

sat beside him, and said, "Father, my mother wishes to see you."

The young man went out with the boy and found a woman sitting in the brush. He said: "You do not belong to this camp. Whence did you come? What are you?"

"It is true," she answered, "I do not belong here. That time you drove the buffalo, I was the cow in the snow-drift, and you prodded me with a stick. This is our son, and I have come to you with him. There is only one reason I have come to you. This boy keeps saying, 'Why do you not show me my father?' I have told him, 'You have no father among the buffalo. We will go find him.' So we have come, and now you and we must live together. One thing I ask of you: if you ever become angry with me, do not strike me with fire."

The young man took the woman to his lodge, and she was his wife. One night the wind blew, and the lodge was filled with smoke. He sent her out to fix the smoke-flaps, but she could not arrange them effectually, and in sudden anger he seized a stick from the fire and struck her with it. The woman and the boy at once leaped up, rushed out of the lodge, and appeared immediately as buffalo galloping away. He followed them. The calf stopped occasionally and waited for him, but the cow would force him to go on, saying, "Your father did not treat us well." After a time the calf came back to him, and said, "Father, my mother says you had better go back." So the young man returned to the camp. Days passed, and thinking his wife must have overcome her resentment, he started out to find her. He arrived at the village of the buffalo-people. When he had found his wife, she told him that the buffalo chief had decreed that he must undergo a series of tests and demonstrate his worthiness to have a wife of the buffalo-people. So for many days he remained in their camp, and when he had successfully pointed out his son under various difficult circumstances, the chief gave him the dance of the buffalo calves and permitted him to take his wife and child back to his own people, among whom he organized the Tail society, in imitation of the dance of the calves.[1]

A man married a Buffalo. She ran away and rejoined her herd. He followed her. The Buffalo chief came galloping up to him as if to gore him. But the man stood fast and declared he would not depart without his wife. The chief retired, and another came up in the same threatening way. Four times this happened. Then the chief said, "If you can identify your son four times among the dancing calves, you may have him and your wife." So the man entered the camp.

His son secretly came to him and said: "In the first dance one of my ears will be drooping, and so you will know me. In the second I shall have one eye closed; in the third I shall limp." So three times the man identified his son. For the fourth dance, however, he had no sign. He could not tell which calf was his son; he made a mistake. The old Buffalo thereupon stampeded and trampled him to death. There was nothing left of him. The Buffalo went away.

With his father the man had left his medicine-robe, a buffalo-skin with the horns attached. This he used in curing the sick. He had told his father why he was going away, and if something happened to him his father would know it by the robe. Lying on his pallet, the father heard the rumbling bellow of a buffalo. He said to his wife: "The robe has made a noise. It means that something is happening to our son. He is killed. Let us look for him." He had the small hoop and shafts used in the game itsiwan. They made ready for a journey. After four motions he threw the wheel to the ground. It rolled away. They walked beside it. Sometimes it would stop where the young man had stepped in water. The man would throw it again. Wherever the young man had stepped in water or stopped to drink, the wheel stopped. At last it stopped in a place where the grass over a large space had been trampled by buffalo. The old man picked it up and threw it down with four movements. It went a little way and came back in a circle to the center of the plot. Four times it did this. Then the man knew his son had gone no farther.

He searched for some sign, and at last found a bit of hair and a long-bone partially covered with earth. He said: "Let us see what we can do for our son. Give me the robe." He spread it on the ground and wrapped the hair and the bone in it. He laid the bundle down. He raised it, and called his son, 'Aiakatsi (gambler), we are going to gamble!' He spat on the hoop, and with four motions dropped it to the ground. It rolled in a circle, and the robe stirred. His son got up, alive. He told them that the Buffalo had said that if he could defeat them in a fight, he should recover his wife. So he was going to fight the Buffalo. He covered himself with the medicine-robe. He threw himself on the ground and rolled like a buffalo, and grunted. He stood up, a Buffalo. He pawed the earth. They saw a large bull coming. Behind him was the herd. The two bulls charged. Neither could succeed in goring the other. After a long struggle the young man was weary. Just then he recognized his wife standing by. He implored her help. She ran up and gored her Buffalo husband, making a long gash in his flank. He retreated, and Aiakatsi ran forward and gored him to death. The Buffalo chief told him that since he had won he could take his wife and his son home. The Buffalo became a human woman, the calf a boy. They went home, and the young man founded the Horn society, to perpetuate the dance of the buffalo calves.[2]

Cheyenne societies as a whole are attributed to a legendary holy girl who founded the Cheyenne governmental structure. According to a story received by E. Adamson Hoebel, while the Cheyenne were wandering about the country in ancient times, one family left the main band to travel alone. After a number of strange mishaps and experiences, the now-orphaned children of the family were finally granted visitations by a series of supernatural animals and people who endowed the girl with "power" to direct the Cheyenne in the setting up of both the tribal council of the forty-four chiefs and the four chiefs of each of the societies.[3]

The regalia and rituals were given to the societies by Sweet Medicine, the mythological culture hero of the Cheyenne who dates back to about 1000 B.C. According to one of several slightly different versions, Sweet Medicine was an odd Cheyenne youth with peculiar habits. On one occasion during the first years of his marriage, he traveled with his wife to the Sacred Mountain, home of the holy ones, in the Black Hills area. There he became a pupil of a certain personified great spirit, who was instructing selected wise men from among all the peoples of the earth. The teacher presented four sacred arrows to Sweet Medicine and instructed him in great detail as to their care and use. Two of the arrows had power over human beings, and the other two had power over animals. Thus the arrows would become the means of supernatural grace that would ensure the survival of the Cheyenne. He also gave Sweet Medicine instruction in the ceremonies and regalia of the societies, and the young man returned home to deliver the arrows and the information to the Cheyenne people.

Since many of the visions and dreams that led to the creation of various societies are included in the chapters to come, which deal with the individual nations, at this point it will be necessary only to consider how such visions and dreams came into being and why they were followed.

Clearly the Plains people took their religion very seriously, viewing their existence as fully dependent upon God. It follows naturally that they would seek His guidance and blessing in all their under-

takings, calling upon the various celestial, natural and animal bodies or beings they believed served Him as mediums of communication.[4] Nevertheless, many non-Indian authors seem reluctant to use the term *God* when they write of the Plains Indians. They will go so far as to mention "a Spirit Who Rules the Universe," who is thus superior to the lesser spirits ruling individual things such as Summer, Health and the like; the wisdom of the lower spirits lay in the "working" or managing of things rather than in their creativity.[5] Yet so long as the Pawnee, Ponca, Arapaho, Sioux and Crow holy men were resoundingly clear in defining their god as identical with the God of Scripture, I find it extremely difficult to believe there would be a serious gap between their position and that of the Cheyenne or any other tribe of the Plains. In example, the eminent Cheyenne informant John Stands In Timber, born in 1884, speaks of a specific Creator and sets forth a number of creation accounts.[6] I stress this only because I shall continue to mention "God" as the primary source to which the Plains people turned for strength and enlightenment and it is only fair to report that others differ.[7]

Some readers may well be troubled by a confrontation with the religious aspect of the Plains people, and thus wish to pass by the subject. However much I respect their feelings, it is just not possible to do so, for the Indian nations of America cannot be properly understood apart from their faith. In whatever manner one may interpret the religious beliefs of the Indians, trust in the supernatural permeated their lives in the way that water fills a sponge. They were literally soaked with it, and it played an essential part in all but their most in-

27

Sioux warrior with full tail headdress praying to God at sacred medicine ring with buffalo skulls placed in center (SM).

consequential thoughts, words and deeds. In the chapters to follow, I will return to a discussion of their religious views wherever it becomes appropriate, and I must trust the readers to understand why I do so.

Although individual details varied, many religious practices were observed throughout all the nations. Dwellings were oriented with the doorway toward the east so that a person awakened to the rising sun in the consciousness that God was sending daylight, warmth, growth and enlightenment to him to begin the new day. Individual prayers followed, expressing thanksgiving for past, present and future blessings and for the fresh opportunities now before each person. A confession of responsibility to others was made, as were sacrifices consisting of bits of valuable materials revealing the true gratitude of the supplicant. After this the day began, wherein man reverently walked a sacred path among all the things of earth, each of which had life, and under the heavens in which the supernatural powers dwelt. Frequently repeated ceremonies reinforced the focus of the entire concept, so that while each man worshipped in his own way part of the time, he also gathered with others to express a mutual faith in and dependence upon the One above. Each of the nations had its own name for Him, yet the different titles did not matter, for He was to all intents and purposes the same everywhere.

Just a few random statements in evidence . . .

From Crow chief Plenty Coups, 1848–1932:

"I am old and am living an unnatural life. I know that I am standing on the brink of the life that nobody knows all about, and I am anxious to go to my Father, Ah-badt-dadt-deah, to live again as men were intended to live, even in this world." . . . Ah-badt-dadt-deah literally translated means the one who made all things. . . . "We kept the laws we made and lived our religion." . . . There is never any shadow of doubt in these expressions by old Indians concerning death and a future life. They do not merely imply belief, but carry the positive declaration, "I know!" [8]

From Sioux holy man Black Elk, 1863–1950:

"Our Grandfather, Wakan-Tanka, You are everything, and yet above everything. You are first. You have always been. . . . You are the truth. . . . our Father, Wakan-Tanka, has made His will known to us here on earth, and we must always do that which he wishes if we would walk the sacred path. . . . You are the source of everything. . . . You are the One who watches over and sustains all life." [9]

From Arapaho Carl Sweezy, 1881–1953:

It was then that our chief Left Hand went to Agent Stouch to give him a better understanding of our plight. Left Hand, an orator and a leader in all things, made him see that our Man-Above and his God were the same, and that we differed only in the way we worshipped. [10]

And finally, a list of the ancient commandments of the Ponca tribe:

Have one God.
Do not kill one another.
Do not steal from one another.
Be kind to one another.
Do not talk about each other.
Do not be stingy.
Have respect for the Sacred Pipe. [11]

When considering the societies and cults of the Indians, the reader should recognize that no such thing as a purely secular institution existed among the Plains people, for every thought and action was permeated by their religious view. Each group had its sacred bundle. Dances were enacted in brackets of sacred numbers, with each set of movements usually repeated four times. Then too, sacred taboos were an integral part of every act, for it was believed that unless each part of a ceremony was done at its proper time and in its correct way, a serious misfortune would befall the offenders. Persons who consider such beliefs to be nothing more than primitive superstition should bear in mind that attendant omens frequently came true in astonishing ways, even though they may have done so partially because a mind conditioned toward disaster can lead to the very calamity itself.

An example of how the Indians viewed such things is the Blackfoot tale of a White agency employee who, in rounding up his cattle, saw the sacred tobacco plot. In ignorance of their taboo against looking at it, he did so and then reported to the Indians that the crop was doing well. Shortly thereafter his horse stumbled in a badger hole, throwing him off, and he was killed. The Indians regarded this as just another vindication of their belief that intruding upon the "dwarfs" who tended the tobacco plot was fatal! [12]

Walter McClintock, who was privileged to witness the ceremonies of the Blackfoot nations in a most personal way from 1895 to 1925, fully caught the attitude of the people when he said, "It is difficult for one of the white race to realize the deep solemnity with which the Indians opened the sacred Bundle. To them it was a moment of deepest reverence and religious feeling." [13]

One should never demean the part religion played in the Plains way of life. All too often an attempt is made to reduce Indian beliefs to simple sun worship and superstition. Or, wherever accounts of their practices reveal a similarity to the Jewish or Christian ways, some are quick to attribute such things to contact with the Whites. The Whites did give the Indians information that helped them to comprehend some of their old ways, but the understandings imparted were just that— insights into ancient customs rather than newly acquired knowledge. The accounts of Indian informants simply do not bear out the contention that Whites brought true religion to America.[14] It had been here since the beginning, and the fact that some practices differed from the imported religion does not disprove it. The eminent Plains authority Clark Wissler agrees, and in a qualified way so does the equally well-informed John C. Ewers.[15]

The Indians simply practiced a monotheist "natural" religion as compared to the specific information and religion available to Orientals, Asians and Europeans through the Bible. And natural religion was clearly acceptable to God in those geographic areas where no other form was possible. In Rom. 1:20, we are told: "Ever since the creation of the world his invisible nature, namely, his eternal power and deity, has been clearly perceived in the things that have been made." This perception was acknowledged and seen wherever men worshipped and served the Creator, wherever men made no images of God and knew that He alone was truth, wherever the life-way of the people corresponded to what is taught in Scripture. That of the Plains Indians did.[16]

To speak of natural religion in the Plains sense is to speak of a people who recognized themselves as but one segment of a vast creation, whose every part contained life both in itself and in the nature of its ongoing relationship with God. In effect, He gave each object and animal true life by working through it to accomplish His eternal goals.[17]

Therefore everything had its assigned purpose and fulfilled its role as it carried out that purpose. Furthermore, its assignment was never a selfish one in that it existed for itself alone. Everything helped others out in the way God had planned, thus serving as the channels through which God transmitted Divine grace to the earth.[18]

For instance, an eagle, lord of the air and symbol of the sun and wind, was blessed with superb skills. Yet some of these, those appropriate for man's use, could be obtained by man when he captured the bird or some part of it in a ritual way and carried it thereafter in a medicine bundle or appended it to his body or costume. Naturally, the transfer of "power" or abilities was not automatic. It also required diligent practice at imitation of the bird, constant prayers, meditation on the fact, an exemplary life and submission acceptable enough for God to work with.[19]

John Stands In Timber explained how the other beings assisted men even, or perhaps one should say primarily, in war:

> There were other things used in that battle, especially by those who wanted to fight in the front. White Shield told me about being instructed that morning by his father Spotted Wolf; he had a warbonnet that came from his grandfather, and a mounted swallow, the kind that hang around rocks. Spotted Wolf had him stand his horse in water for a certain length of time. Then he got dirt from the creek bottom and used it to touch the horse's shoulders and head, and White Shield's also. He had a lot of instructions to follow. There were many ways to perform ceremonies on the body. The warriors depended on being protected by the power that came from them. They could ride close to the soldiers and not be harmed. Some were wonderful medicines, like the mounted hawk of Brave Wolf's that he was given after fasting [vision-seeking] at Bear Butte. He would tie it onto the back lock of his hair and ride into a fight whistling with a bone whistle. Sometimes on a charge that bird came to life and whistled too, when they came close to the enemy in hand to hand fighting. Many mentioned that bird. On the other hand, a man without power of some kind did not go in close that way. He did not dare.[20]

The uniformity of such beliefs even among enemies on the Plains is affirmed by Plenty Coups when he reports that during an engagement with the Sioux

> we fell in behind them and gave them something to think about besides our friends ahead. But suddenly we saw them turn and ride toward us until they were nearly in range. Then they split into two parties, riding past us out of range, with many more coming—all doing as they had done, avoiding us altogether. They might easily have ridden us down, but they feared my medicine! It was very strong that day, and if my horse had not been so gunshy, I might have taken more scalps than the one I got.[21]

Even rocks played their medicine role by transferring unique abilities and by teaching men of the eternal nature of God. A turtle symbolized human longevity. Sweet-smelling grasses and herbs were fragrances fit to be burned; the smoke carried acceptable prayers up to God. As people walked along a sacred path, everything contacted was entitled to respect, deference and preservation because of the role it played. Sometimes, in response, a wolf, a buffalo, a badger or even a rock might speak to a man by word or action to transmit a message from Above concerning the man's habits and well-being. This was not a miracle, but to be expected, for that is the way God is.

31

Opposite: Crow holy man wearing full golden eagle on head; opposite right: Hidatsa or Mandan offering thanks to One above after successful catch at eagle pit (SM).

If created things were regarded as channels of Divine grace by the Indians, they considered themselves, as the principal beings who alone could make rational decisions, to be so to a greater degree. Subsequent chapters will emphasize and spell out this truth in many ways, but certain factors concerning it should be mentioned here. God expected every man to serve Him, and the Indian understanding of how this was done fits very well what one learns in the Bible. To be an effective servant among men and other created objects required a concentrated effort to rid oneself of those things about a man that would tend to frustrate the will of the One above. Selfishness, willfulness, hate and doubt had to be put aside. To accomplish this, the Indians evolved a program of practices that removed the barriers and "hollowed them out" until they were like a smooth tube through which the Creator and preserver could act with maximum effectiveness. Accomplishments thereafter on any occasion were never their own doing, and even the recipients understood the "way" so well as to give the credit for blessings received to the proper source rather than to the instrument. If a man deserved praise at all, it was for his willingness and sacrificial attempt to be used rather than for what resulted. And, if failures occurred, the blame was always attributed to the human instrument, for it was obviously due to some error on his part; God never made a mistake.

When the foregoing philosophy is applied to the performance of a society ceremonial, it can be seen that except for purely social occa-

32

Above left: Golden Eagle head used as Blackfoot war medicine (AMNH); below left: Blackfoot warrior wearing eagle head as war medicine (SM); right: Plains Cree necklace decorated with white ermine skin, bell and beaded ring—believed to protect the wearer from bullet wounds (AMNH).

sions, strange and wonderful powers beyond those of ordinary human beings were at work in the midst of those persons assembled. Understandably, each part of the ritual exacted a profound emotional reaction from the performers and the spectators—even though most Whites may have missed that truth when they observed the ceremonials without understanding.

It can be said that in the Indian way of existence, all life was in balance, for the people sought to bend and to move in harmony with other living things. There was a reverence for life and a reverence for death. One could not separate the life from the way, for the way was in itself what made the life rich and productive. The tense is past, since I write primarily of ways which were rooted in antiquity, but the essence of it all still applies to those Indian peoples who are governing themselves by the ancient religious principles. Some of this spirit can be found on and off the reservations today, although the years of deprivation have eroded precious customs to a serious degree. (In this regard, I strongly recommend the reading of two superb publications: *The Sacred Pipe*, Black Elk's account of the seven rites of the Oglala Sioux, recorded and edited by Joseph Epes Brown, and *The Spiritual Legacy of the American Indian*, by Joseph Epes Brown. Complete information regarding these is given in the bibliography.)

Accordingly, one must learn to read between the lines when confronted by the sometimes brief and cryptic records of the Plains society organizations. It should not be necessary for an author to continually point out the religious significance of various aspects of a ceremonial performance. It is there; with enough contemplation it can be seen.

It should be also borne in mind when considering the societies that one moves immediately into a secret world, where non-Indians do well to shift about at least with respect and more properly with reverence. The functions of the societies and cults were so holy and personal that the Plains people hesitated to expose any of their details to an outsider's view. Moreover, the abusive and intolerant attitudes of most Whites caused them to hide whatever precious customs they could for a long time, and only the few Whites who treated the Indians as worthwhile human beings were finally permitted to share enough of the secrets to pass on a small part of the majestic story.

Vision-seeking was an absolute must in the life-way of the Plains people. A young man was hard pressed to enter upon his career as a warrior without one; some did so, but with great trepidation, and sought a vision all the more fervently at every opportunity because of it. The vision was vital because it brought the seeker the insights and assistance he needed for wisdom and survival. The preparations for vision-seeking varied from tribe to tribe, but they were extensive and commenced with utmost solemnity. The advice of both holy men and prominent men was sought, helpers were procured to assist in the proceedings, there were sweat-lodge purification ceremonies, fastings, incense-burnings, bathings, prayers, painting with white clay for purity, sacrifices of personal property and, finally, journeys alone to perilous places where the actual vision was "lamented for" or "cried after" over periods lasting from one to four days and nights.

In the end, the seeker hoped, God would bless him by sending a vision in which mystic beings such as dwarfs would speak of his future and in which birds, animals, rocks, herbs and the like would present themselves as his helper companions or "medicine" to guarantee his future success.[22]

Once an effective vision was received and interpreted, the latter often being done by an elder or a holy man of the tribe, the seeker moved into his adult responsibilities and toward the future with maximum confidence. His mental preparation now matched the physical conditioning that had attended his youthful years. Subsequent visions might be sought as life's changes called for further information, but seldom did any later enlightenment significantly alter the course established by the initial encounter with God.[23]

The later visions might, however, bring information concerning the founding or formation of a new society; such guidance might involve either the originating of an order or the instructions as to the borrowing and altering of a society from another tribe. In these instances, the unfolding of the vision by word or action when the seeker returned to the camp was accepted as "gospel" by fellow tribesmen, for it assuredly was God himself who bade them follow the plan set forth. Thus, no matter who had the dream, man or woman, provided that the person was of exemplary character, the experience was in itself self-authenticating. And if it included the birth of a new or borrowed society, that order was begun and took its place at an acceptable level among the groups already in existence.

Most definitely, the vision concept itself led to those dreams in which the ceremonies and regalia of some societies were received. A people whose religious inclinations were such as I have described and whose imagination was excited and intensified by the vision concept would naturally dream at the level of a vision. They would no more dream of ordinary things than non-Indians do when their entire beings have been whetted by active minds and stimulating circumstances.

In many instances, dreams occurred under circumstances not unlike those that had attended the preparation for and reception of a vision. A warrior who had girded himself for war by the traditional methods, which inspired him and fostered resoluteness, might fight a brief but frantic battle, be wounded and left for dead on the battlefield. As he lay in agony and delirium for several days, he might have a strange but wonderful dream in which he was confronted by the usual "messengers" and instructed to return home and form a society. The dream was equivalent to a command from God, and upon his successful return to his village, the dream was told and the society begun. The dream of a woman who was captured and then escaped might have the same impact and result. Either instance and others of like nature were acceptable for the founding of a society.

Frances Densmore puts this very well:

> The obligation of a dream was as binding as the necessity of fulfilling a vow, and disregard of either was said to be punished by the forces of nature, usually by a stroke of lightning. Dreams were sought by the Sioux, but it was recognized that the dream would correspond to the character of the man. Thus it was said that "a young man would not be great in mind so his dream would not be like that of a chief; it would be ordinary in kind, yet he would have to do whatever the dream directed him to do." The first obligation of a dream was usually its announcement to the tribe. This was by means of a performance which indicated the nature of the dream and allied the man to others who had similar dreams. If the dream were connected with the sacred stones, or with herbs or animals concerned in the treatment of the sick, it was considered obligatory that the man avail himself of the supernatural aid vouchsafed to him in the dream, and arrange his life in accordance with it.[24]

Naturally, there was not room for an unlimited number of organizations, so at some convenient point in history visions and dreams regarding societies either were ignored or ceased to occur. After all, the fulfillment of a need usually brings an end to the pursuit of it.

The vast majority of cults also resulted from visions and dreams, and under the same kinds of circumstances as those just described. Not everyone distinguishes between cults and societies, but I feel it is important to do so, as there are broad differences between the two.

With certain exceptions, societies had fixed numbers of members and careful rules about participation: the songs, ceremonies and regalia were traditional, as was the structuring of leadership. Societies were reorganized each year. Memberships were bought and sold and, in the case of the age-graded orders, at regular intervals. Societies played an important role in government. Only the founder of the order had to have his particular vision to begin it; the other members did not have the same dream. Men might be led by a vision to join a certain society, but most joined by being asked, by personal selection or by climbing the steps of the age-graded ladder along with the rest of their age group. Societies also served as camp police. None of these things were true of the cults.

The cults were loose associations of individuals who banded together on the basis of all having dreamed or having had a vision of the same "helper" bird, animal, sacred stone or celestial being. Most could be joined by both men and women who qualified. They did not follow their cult leaders in the same way the society members followed theirs, and cult costumes and appendages were personal, based upon the dream or vision of the individual involved. There were no set periods for membership in a cult; a person might belong to one for his entire life if his "power" remained productive, or he might abruptly leave the association if his "power" appeared to be blunted or lost because of one or more failures.

The cults were occupied mainly with the control of nature and the healing of mind and body. They consisted of both priests and doctors, and their function in the life of the community was always concerned with the physical and mental well-being of the people. While any vision-seeker might return home with an animal or bird "helper" to be employed primarily for his own guidance and protection, the cultist used his helper or helpers mainly for the welfare of the tribe as a whole. This is not to say that the cult member failed to benefit by it personally. On the contrary, he often did, through payments received for services, by the prestige that came with success and by the protective powers bestowed by his helper.

In a typical instance, the Sioux considered a dream of the thunderbird to be the greatest honor that could come to a man from a supernatural source; consequently, the obligation of this dream was heavier than that of any other.[25] In Sioux lore the thunderbirds were great birds in the sky. They were encompassed by the clouds and could cause great destruction on the earth. A man who dreamed of the thunderbirds could command the powers of the sky to assist him in his undertakings. His behavior thereafter in the village was to act the "backwards" fool before people, and he was often described as a clown.[26] To anyone who did not understand, the posture was misleading, for only one who had much power could afford to act the fool and his reverse actions in fact emphasized the truth of what he could do when he wanted to.

There was a Sioux ceremony of public humiliation, called Heyó ka Ká ga, which every thunderbird dreamer had to lead once, after he had received his dream and was ready to begin his career. The others who had already done this were expected to join him in the ceremony, which was held any time after the thunderstorms had begun in the spring. Intention to perform the rite was signified by the dreamer's placing costly gifts on top of his tipi poles as an offering to the thunderbirds. A ragged tipi was then erected within the camp circle, and the leader and other performers dressed in the poorest possible garments. During the first part of the ceremony the leader was jeered by the spectators. Then the thunderbird dreamers related their dreams to the people, the leader speaking last. To conclude the occasion, meat was placed in a pot of boiling water and the dreamers were ordered to remove it with their bare hands. (It was on these occasions that herbs were tested to prevent and treat scalding. These were mixed with water and rubbed on the hands and arms. Some worked very well.)

This was a ceremony designed to teach "a great lesson," for while ignorant people laughed at the foolish men and their strange actions, truly intelligent members of the tribe regarded the ceremony with great reverence, for it spoke profoundly of the way of supernatural things.[27]

To dream of a small stone was regarded as a sign of some import, indicating that the dreamer, by fulfilling the requirement of his dream, would become possessed by supernatural power. In the exercise of this power, he would be able to use the sacred stones to cure sickness, predict future events and tell the location of objects beyond the range of his natural vision.[28]

Dreams concerning animals were especially coveted by all the tribes, for the dreamer then took on the special abilities of the dreamed-about animal, plus an extraordinary resistance to injury in war. Of course, each animal had its own characteristics and disposition. It followed then that while no one man or group could obtain enough animal power to cover all tribal needs, the sum of the various dreamers combined to make an awesome force against enemies of every kind. In most of these dreams, the animal told the dreamer that he had been selected to represent that animal in life. The challenge was taken most seriously, and dreamers never hesitated to prove it. For example, a Sioux named Brave Buffalo was told in a dream by the buffalo that he would live to the age of 102. To demonstrate his faith in their promise, he covered himself with a buffalo hide and invited his relatives to see whether they could hurt him with their arrows. They filled the hide with shafts, but none of them penetrated his skin. He did not die in war, either.[29]

Whatever their origins in legends, visions or dreams, the evolution of the various societies and cults was by no means accidental, for they came to fill an important and practical place in the life-way of the Plains people. The need for most of them was in itself undoubtedly the factor that led each founder to the point where he engaged in the legend or had his vision or dream. Saying that societies and cults were practical does not in any way deny that they originated with God, for He is more inclined to lead men into practical solutions to the needs of life than He is to foster luxuries. As it is stated in the Sermon on the Mount, He knows our needs, and the rest of the Bible reveals that He sometimes answers those needs in the most wondrous of ways.

Four kinds of orders came into existence on the Plains. Most of this book will be devoted to an amplification of each type as it was found within the various tribes, but in summary they were:

1. The warrior societies.
   a. Age-graded. In this scheme all the young men of a tribe as a group entered the first of a series of societies, doing so at whatever age the tribe had established as sufficient to begin a career as a defender and policeman of the tribe. The group then proceeded up the ladder of societies by selling and purchasing ceremonies and regalia at regular intervals of four years or so.
   b. Non-graded. In this scheme a man who had come of age and was ready to be a defender and policeman could enter any of the societies of the tribe, either by choice or by responding to an invitation. He usually remained in his chosen order for the length of his career as a warrior, although he might shift to another under certain circumstances.
2. The religious societies. These consisted of certain older men who had survived their battle years and, being of proven ability, now banded together in accordance with individual tribal custom to serve the people as influential holy men and counselors.
3. The women's societies.
   a. Cultic groups. These were made up of women whose dreams led them to participate in orders whose rituals related primarily to the buffalo, to other animals and to the raising of crops. They shared in buffalo "calling" to draw the herds close to the camps, in rites ensuring good crops and abundant kills and in performances designed to sponsor

Sioux thunderbird dreamers extracting meat from boiling liquid with bare hands.

Cheyenne Women's Guild members. Left: Quillworker; right: Tanning skins (SM).

fertility among the many animals the Indians depended upon so completely for food, housing and clothing. Some were prayer groups.

b. Craft guilds. Women who belonged to these were especially gifted in the arts of the tribes, such as tanning, painting, quilling and beading. The women considered these orders to be as important as the men's societies. They had ceremonies designed to receive candidates and to accompany certain important tasks. (See the chapter on the Cheyenne tribe for an example.)

c. Women's war societies. There are only scattered and brief references to these, with little further information than the references themselves contain.[30] Wives often accompanied men to war in order to cook, to provide company and sometimes to fight. Since this was a perilous task, it is more than reasonable to assume that such women would be permitted to band themselves into an honor society with rituals forbidden to others. (See the chapter on the Ponca tribe for specific examples.)

4. The cults. Each of these was made up of men—and sometimes of women, as well—who had dreamed of the same objects, ranging from stars to stones to animals and birds. Non-Indians would refer to this as dreaming of animate and inanimate objects, but since the Indians believed that everything possessed life, there was no such thing as an inanimate object in their view. The dream endowed the dreamer with a certain power from Above that could be put to personal and tribal use through rituals and medicine practices.

A listing of the societies and cults is given at the back of the book showing which categories were employed by the different nations. The list will also serve as an index of sorts by indicating the pages on which each group is described. The equivalent Indian names for the societies are not included. These are not used in the main text either since most non-Indians could neither interpret nor pronounce them—nor could Indians do this for tribes other than their own. Those Indians who are familiar with the Indian titles within their own tribes will make the necessary translation even though English is used.

2
THE NATURE OF THE WARRIOR SOCIETIES

The warrior societies were the most dominant bodies in number and influence, and as such deserve the greatest consideration. They are most often referred to as military, police or protective organizations, but this is an oversimplification of their place in the life-way of the people. In the broader sense, they:

- preserved order in the camp
- preserved order during camp moves
- preserved order during hunts
- punished offenders against the public welfare
- guarded the camp against possible surprise attacks by an enemy, both at the camp and while moving
- kept the camp informed at all times as to the movements of the buffalo herds
- fostered intersociety rivalry to cultivate bravery and a military spirit among themselves and among the boys, who needed a living example of their future responsibilities
- took the commanding and most dangerous places in battle
- ministered to the desires of members for social recreation through feasts and dances
- served as keepers and reminders of the tribe's heritage and traditions
- played a unique intermediary role in government by serving as the active but temporary dispensers of authority
- served as creative display centers where recognition was given for honors earned by warriors and women's guild workers for tasks well done on behalf of the tribe

In something of a complement to this mixture of secular and religious responsibility, the Plains cults acted as more specialized units of grace—mediums through which God dispensed His supernatural power to the people in circumscribed areas for instruction, healing, prophecy, assurance and hope.

While the functions of the warrior societies were numerous, they can really be subdivided into three major categories and titles according to which the various activities can be grouped. No one of these categories took precedence over the others, for each was of equal importance in the life-way of the Indians.

THE SOCIETIES AS POLICE

Throughout the book the reader will notice many references to the disciplinary actions performed by the different societies as they exercised their role of police. The severity of some of these actions may trouble those unacquainted with the role the orders played, and it may be helpful if I explain that aspect here.

The people of the Plains lived in a dramatic, volatile climate. The nature of the geographic area itself was such that existence was always in tender balance, for weather changes were swift and severe and the animal, bird and reptile inhabitants seemed to reflect the elements in their attitudes. Added to this was the intense pressure caused by the coming of the Spanish and other Europeans. The Spanish mistreatment of the Indians bred in reaction a climate of rivalry and bitterness among the Southern tribes. The White fur traders in the Northwest and Northeast had the same effect on the nations of those areas. Then with colonization the kettle really began to boil. The White settlements moved steadily inward toward the Plains. Eastern tribes were subjugated and relocated time and again. To escape, as many as were able moved westward, and the pressure this migration put on each tribe it encountered caused the tribes first to strike back in anger, then to retreat like the others before the ominous tide. The stacking up of peoples turned what had once been occasional quarrels into vicious struggles. Tempers flared and the war spirit rose and subsided in regular patterns.

Some tribes had been on the Plains for centuries before the rest came. These were few in number and relatively contented. As the Woodlands tribes spilled into the area and began grasping for territory, each set of newcomers forcing others to shift again, survival took on a new tone. Now the nations had to contend not only with the elements but also with each other. Tribal languages, customs and the varying pressures made an overall unity impossible. A few nations would unite for a time now and then, but for the most part each was on its own.

The introduction of the horse, which began about A.D. 1620 and continued through 1800, brought the entire situation into a tenuous balance. Now the strikes at one another during survival campaigns could be made more swiftly; the horse became prize booty, for movement was easier, and the hunting of the valuable buffalo was transformed almost into a sport. Affluence came about for the first time, and the crafts flourished. Then the White tide began to lap at the edges of the Plains, and the old story commenced again—only now there was no place to go, so the nations turned to meet what they eventually came to realize were hopeless odds. Battle victories were only temporary, epidemics of disease struck, and when the Plains' mobile storehouse, the fabulous bison, was systematically wiped out by White hunters, the last being killed in the north in 1886, it was the end. Long before that various tribes had been moved onto one miserable reservation after another in a sad, successive process of mistreatment that began about 1820 and continued inexorably thereafter until 1890.

The real tragedy was that the Indians knew they didn't need the entire country. After all, they were few in number. They would gladly have given much of it up, and did. But the Whites always demanded whatever ground the Indians were on, and peace was not to be had. Broken treaties were the ghastliest part of it all. Nearly 150 were pushed through and then broken by the Whites. An Indian spokesman expressed it well recently when he said (and government documents bear him out) "the Whites kept only one promise: to take our land."

It was within this cauldron of pressure that the warrior, or war, societies, many of which were of ancient vintage, altered their nature and came to the fore. With emotions constantly provoked to fever pitch, the people needed to be controlled; they required a visible source of hope, and they needed periodic releases from tension. The societies became the fundamental answer to all three.

They policed the people, and they did it in a remarkably sophisticated way. Most of the tribes had a number of warrior societies, commonly ranging from four to twelve societies per tribe. A given order's membership numbered from ten to more than a hundred. Some authoritarian structures were simple, others were complex. For governmental purposes, there were civil chiefs, camp chiefs and society leaders who together made the basic decisions regarding the general activities of a tribe.

Civil chiefs were men of proven leadership ability in war and at home. But actual dictatorships were rare, almost nonexistent, and in most instances a civil chief in disfavor could be deposed more easily than he could be elected. Few held such power, or were so respected, as to have their commands instantly obeyed. In addition, the tribes had traditional oral codes rather than written rules, allowing each problem to be handled as an individual case. Therefore discussion of a situation was common practice before the disposition of a problem was made.

It was important, too, for civil chiefs to avoid direct blame for the way in which a situation was handled, for while most decisions were affirmed and little was said in consequence, a single serious error could bring dissension to a tribe and ruin to a career. Therefore the warrior societies were called upon to fill a judicial role. Each season the civil chief or council of chiefs appointed one or more of the orders to become the intermediary instrument of maintaining discipline, either within the great tribal encampments or within the nation that had split up for subsistence purposes during the good-weather months. It worked out amazingly well, for a given society seldom served for more than one year at a time, being replaced by another unit the following spring or at the onset of the first tribal assembly. This meant that the authority of any order was limited to its period of duty and that whatever its members meted out in the way of punishment, they were in turn subject to when they were replaced by the next society.

The temporary order could also strike more severely when the occasion demanded it, however. While a permanent police force would have been likely to curry favor and to live with its decisions in a most personal way, the rotation pattern avoided this. By the same token, police performance was tempered by the fact that the members of an order always approached their tasks in the consciousness of ordinary citizenship and of what it was like to live under authority.

The societies did not, in any event, have control over every function of the people. Their role was carefully circumscribed by tradition and need, and when they were appointed for their season of duty, the civil chiefs were quick to remind them of this.

In essence, their work was connected with those matters wherein the general welfare of the camp or of the people as a whole was concerned. They punished offenders against the public good who chose to violate tribal codes, they patrolled the start and the conduct of the hunts to see that everyone received an equal opportunity to obtain his share of the meat and they served as camp sentinels, guarding against both enemy attacks and hot-tempered or adventurous young men of their own camp if they attempted to go on vengeance raids when it seemed to the civil chiefs that such actions were ill timed. Other specific examples of police function will be discussed later in the book.

It should be borne in mind, however, that in each instance of police action, the turbulent days demanded the severe curtailment of any individual conduct that might tend to jeopardize the camp or tribe. It was important to keep tempers under control, and as the days became more difficult under White pressures, a kind of rare sharing of the hardships became the only answer to the survival of some. The people understood this, and painful as it may have been at times, they knew that the society police performed their thankless duties for the good and longevity of them all.

The commonest Plains way of teaching a lesson was by providing an example. For instance, children were not punished directly by the administering of a whipping; but they were taught what to expect when they came of age, for the police societies carried out their punishments of adults in public view whenever possible. Frequently, time was allowed between the seizing of an offender and the administration of the penalty so that parents would have an opportunity to bring their children to the place of justice to see it happen. The system was even more effective, of course, for the watching adults, who would know they could expect the same treatment if they violated the rules.

With this philosophy in mind, one can better understand why the punishments often took dramatic forms such as apparently savage attacks by an entire warrior society upon a single individual, his possessions sometimes being cut to ribbons and his valuable horses destroyed. This was always the price a culprit paid for breaking the hunting rules. Punishment for murders brought anything from ostracism through instant and permanent banishment from the camp to the exacting of the killer's life. Yet the very drama of most punishments by far masked a subtle truth. More often than not, an awesome flurry of activity, accompanied by sounds intended to impress the spectators' minds, hid the fact that little real damage was being done to the culprit himself. The man or woman might be pushed around. His shirt or tipi skin might suffer a few superficial rips or cuts. An easily replaced blanket might be torn to bits with great fanfare as it was tossed in the air from man to man. The threat was more severe than the action; the bark was worse than the bite. And it is indeed a little sad that Indian informants, sensing that the Whites wanted to believe the worst of them, could manage to convince so many authors to repeat for White audiences grisly facts about Plains punishment that were seldom a description of the average or usual instance.

Given the nomadic, migratory habits of the Plains Indians, a natural question tends to rise regarding the activities of the various orders over the course of a year. As is repeatedly pointed out in literature, societies were reorganized in the early spring. When the first great tribal encampment took place, a given number of groups were assigned to duty as camp police for that and the subsequent important functions of the year. What happened, however, when the great camp broke up into the various bands and clans that then went their different ways to hunt between assemblies? Did certain society units stay together, or were members of a given order spread throughout the tribe? Generally, the latter was true. So then, since orders continued to function, how did they do so?

The answer is found in the variety of names that Indian sources have called societies possessing the same rituals and regalia but simultaneously in different places—such as the Doves, the Pigeons and the Mosquitoes of the Blackfoots. Obviously, enough members of some orders were a part of each band to manage to carry out organized police duties, to maintain their rituals and to encourage the military spirit of the people. Therefore each village could have a part of a certain society that it would identify by a slightly different title from the others. Some societies might not have any members in one band but would have enough for an effective unit in another. Beyond that, there were known instances when the members of a society were called by their herald to gather for police work, such as for a large raid or a battle. By no accident, the various and socially minded bands

frequently crossed paths as they moved and would spend a few days together in happy celebration before continuing. These were always prime opportunities for the society members to be together in the fellowship they so richly enjoyed. Besides, winter always brought a period of close assembly, and the members of the organizations were then near enough for frequent contact.

THE SOCIETIES AS MILITARY UNITS

A major purpose of the societies was to foster a military spirit among themselves and the rest of the tribe, since war was a matter of survival. Here again, the Plains people revealed a surprising maturity in their manner of accomplishing the task.

The societies were the war force of the tribe. Every man whose age made him eligible for the responsibility of being a defender of his tribe and land was expected to make his choice among the available orders in the non-graded tribal scheme or to start up the ladder at the appropriate point in the age-graded complex.

The vital question is what they did once they had become a part of it all. Future chapters will be devoted to the regalia and the ceremonial practices of the best-known tribes, but the societies' military function and practices were virtually the same across the Plains.

Within the units themselves the ceremonial and organizational structures provided the basic impetus toward a military spirit. The ceremonies by their very nature called upon the members to reverently act out their traditional roles and to treat their regalia with the solemnity due the "power" it brought forth. Officers were selected

46

Above: *Crow warriors counting coup on Sioux in battle.*
Opposite: *Blackfoot warrior counting coup in Sun Dance lodge* (SM).

according to their victories upon the field of battle and by their proven leadership there. The course of rising to power was firmly established, and a man who wished to reach the available heights within the tribe knew how it must be done. Not surprisingly, the society members drew upon the "powers" of their order with every fiber of their being so as to obtain the utmost benefit from it. These were not considered selfish actions, for in the end the camp and tribe always benefited more from such achievements than did the man himself.

To advance the military spirit still further, the orders became natural rivals in achieving the common good, plus the rewards such efforts brought. To the greatest defenders went the highest honors and the richest spoils. It was the acknowledged front-runner who was called upon to perform the prominent duties in connection with the great Sun Dance and other tribal celebrations. The members recounted their coups before the rest. It was the leading unit that provided the new civil chiefs when important positions had to be filled. It was the number-one society of the day whose meeting lodge gained the most prominent place at the center of the camp. These were the men whose counsel was sought in peace and war. Association with them brought attendant status. Their celebrations were always the biggest and the

49

Above: *Sioux Crow Owner society member on way to meeting.* Opposite:
Sioux sash-wearer with lance planted in ground and prepared to fight to the death (SM).

best. Candidates flocked to them before the others. The system led to greater effort from the other societies; and in the end, fortunes always changed to provide a new champion for a time.

While, as Robert H. Lowie says in speaking of the Crow Indians, "more often than not discretion seems to be the better part of valor," it is understandable that the call to heroism on the battlefield would become a prime factor in the society scheme.[1] The tenuous nature of the home country has already been mentioned, and the maintenance of a territory sufficient to survive in was essential. The phrase "this is our land" became dear to an extraordinary degree to the Plains nations. And, when a sash-wearer drove his lance through the sash and into the ground to anchor himself there in the midst of a tumultuous encounter with the enemy, that spot represented his precious land. From there he was forbidden to retreat until released by the traditional rules of his tribe.

When a society officer or member strode or rode around the camp in his regalia, he spread pride, determination and hope wherever he went. As a sign of these feelings, the gifts of food and other goods he sometimes demanded from camp members were furnished without rancor. Most of all his presence had a telling effect upon the boys, and from their accounts they literally burned within to be old enough to join one of the societies. At night during the fair-weather periods of the year, the less-secret ceremonials of an order were conducted with the tipi sides rolled up just enough to let the mesmerized boys who crowded about outside see the blazing fires, the splendidly costumed and painted members and most of all the power-filled regalia placed about the lodge. Once the booming drums began, the singers joined in, the rattles commenced to rattle and the dancers shifted and turned close by the crackling flames, it was almost an unbearable thing to be just a boy. Many a solemn vow was made by a little fellow on such an occasion, which was later kept to the letter. As boys know the names, numbers and records of sports figures today, the boys of the Plains knew every man and every detail of the societies of his tribe. He also knew their records and traditions and, by the time he was a youth, could recite them at will.

During the winter months, when the bands were camped in close proximity to one another along the rivers and lakes, the societies continued to promote the military spirit. During this season their most renowned officers would gather the young men of the tribe into their lodges to teach them by oral tradition of the beginnings of each society and of its proud history down through the years. These were quieter nights than those of the summer months, and they engendered a different attitude, which offered a more complete picture to the attentive listeners. At such times, lessons were also taught about the society role as camp police, what it meant and why it was so important, and discussions followed to cement the instructions in receptive minds. All in all, the society–youth encounter was a warm association which delicately combined the spirit and the mystery so necessary to a wholesome growing experience.

THE SOCIETIES AS SOCIAL UNITS

One would expect that the tensions of maintaining status would soon become intolerable without the release of social discourse so common to all civilizations. In recognition of this, the societies became one

Opposite: *Sioux Crow Owner society member wearing buffalo horn bonnet, raven around neck, carrying otter-skin-wrapped lance, leading highly trained war horse.*

of the major outlets for pure fun. During the peaceful times, which grew rarer with every passing day after 1850, the societies performed as many ceremonial rites as possible outdoors. On such occasions the entire camp became the audience, either collecting around the dancers or following along behind them in a happy mood as the members paraded about the camp. Before the Whites came, the outdoor rites always culminated in sumptuous feasts so long as sufficient supplies were still available, and everyone contributed to the festivities.

A standard part of many of these public ceremonies was the inclusion of events that permitted the audiences to participate in the activities. For instance, in the Blackfoots' dance of the Bears, boys were allowed to throw horse dung at the bears to agitate them. In the Flies ceremony of the Gros Ventre, the members rushed about seeking to scratch the excited spectators with sticks that had thorns pushed through them like nails. At a point in one ceremony or another, the members of a number of societies fired blunt arrows at their dodging audiences. The Gros Ventre Crazy Society members shot war arrows with steel points straight up into the air and then stood their ground to show their bravery while the crowd scattered madly in every direction to get out of the way. During the annual summer dance, the Blackfoots Ugly Horns prowled about the camp in terrifying costumes to frighten children into good behavior.

In evidence of their rapture over the conduct of the societies in general, boys formed groups of friends into miniature copies of one order or another and spent their days diligently seeking to emulate their heroes. The great Crow chief Plenty Coups spoke at length to Frank B. Linderman about the profound effect the warrior societies had had on him as a boy and also of how he and his companions played their very hearts out in imitation of the older men.[2]

Along with the activities mentioned, the societies served the usual club purposes of providing the members with a place to find companionship, a place to manufacture and restore weapons by exercising a combination of talents and a place to which to retreat when the burdens of family life became such that an exodus from conflict seemed wise.

It appears that whenever possible, society members rode together, hunted together, fought the enemy together and celebrated together.

Opposite: *Blackfoot boy wearing ermine costume imitating father's Brave Dog clothing and regalia. Horn society members in background* (SM).
Below: *Blackfoot Brave Dog society performing ceremonial dance* (SM).

Sioux youth named White Bull in dance costume, including roach headdress, bear claw necklace and hair-pipe bone breastplate (DPL).

Blackfoot society members training together to rescue wounded comrade during battle. Full war outfits are worn to simulate actual conditions—although bonnets and clothing were put on only when time permitted before the enemy was engaged.

Blackfoot society members returning from a successful horse raid.

Understandably, unusual bonds of friendship were often formed between warriors under such circumstances. Both Sioux and Omaha informants tell of tribal rites for the "making of brothers," which bound two men together in a lifelong relationship that was considered closer than a blood relationship. The rites were performed when the men involved had shared an experience in which the deliverance of one or both bordered on the miraculous. Such instances were taken as indications from Above that the two men were to be cemented together in a special way from then on.[3]

The personal bond between society members was, of course, always broader than that between a pair of members. A number of old photographs, particularly those of the Blackfoots, show small groups of men carrying the same regalia riding out to scout the countryside on raiding and war days and also traveling together to view and to contemplate their dear and beautiful homeland during the moments of peace.

In summary, it is clear that the warrior societies evolved as the hubs of the life-way of the Plains people. They provided a source of control, fostered and answered the need for a military spirit and became the social centers during the historic period when they ascended to prominence.

In contrast to all these positive aspects, Plenty Coups suggests that they were an "Achilles' heel" of sorts in light of the cooperation necessary for the effective unification of tribal affairs. "These secret societies possessed great influence over their members, so much that I believe them in a measure responsible even today [1930] for the lack of unity that sometimes presents itself in the administration of tribal affairs."[4] Of course, he spoke as a chief and may have been expressing the difficulties he sometimes had with them in conducting the duties of his office.

Blackfoot society members enjoying home country during peaceful times (SM).

3
SOCIETY
REGALIA

Every society had its ceremonies, songs, dances, paint customs, costume and pieces of equipment that identified it and distinguished it from all the others. These will be treated in detail as each society is considered in the following chapters, but since the drawings of the ceremonials and costumes will often include specifics that might be overlooked or that are too small to be noticed, it may help to discuss some of the more common equipment here. By "common" I mean those found in slightly varying forms among many of the orders of the Plains and which in each instance served similar purposes. In studying them, it should be understood that while the designer of each item always had in mind its visual effect upon others, no piece of equipment or apparel was ever fashioned for a purely decorative purpose.[1]

In the first place, no founder of a society ever presumed to take credit for the regalia of his order. That was given to him in the legend, dream or vision that came from the One above. The size, the shape and the finishing of each piece was established during either the first supernatural encounter or subsequent ones, and no founder dared to deviate from his instructions lest calamity befall him. It is true that, as has already been suggested, common regalia emerged, but Indian informants would explain this as simply being the result of God's consistent guidance in given areas of life and of the fact that the Indians were working in each instance with the same basic materials, which on the Plains were relatively few. In substance, though, each piece was a holy item that reminded its bearer of his true source of power and of his responsibilities as a servant among men of that power.

Second, the regalia served as a mute teacher and transmitter of the tribal heritage for both the society members and the rest of the people. Since traditional forms and patterns were employed in its fashioning, each piece conveyed a sometimes astoundingly detailed message to those who wore it and to those who saw it. One could tell the nature and inclinations of a person by what he wore and when he wore it. The full regalia spelled out the origin and contemporary function of each group, and its use in ceremonials was so well known to the people that even the simplest traditional gestures and sounds while wearing it presented a total story. Non-Indians often wonder why the Plains songs and ceremonies were short and repetitious. It was because of the fact that both participants and spectators were so personally acquainted with the performer that they could fill in the details themselves. The repetition was for emphasis, and the brevity allowed those who shared in the event to become involved as they were permitted to finish the portrayal, which was in truth a picture, on their own.[2] Indians at ceremonials were often seen with one hand placed over their mouths in the typical expression of wonder so common to the people of the Plains nations. It was because of their awe at seeing so much in what to non-Indians often seemed to be so little.

Third, because of the direct association with God, when a man went through the painting of his body and the donning of his regalia, he was no longer the exact self of daily life, but a transformed being, or a man made anew. This transformation lasted for the duration of a given ceremony and also took place whenever the regalia in whole or in part was employed—such as while on police duty or in war.[3] Accordingly, there were customary personal preparations for this, such as prayers, sacrifices, vows and the sweat-lodge ceremony, which took

Above: *Framework of sweat-lodge showing placement of buffalo skull;* below: *Blackfoot sweat-lodge covered with hides and blankets* (SM).

place outside the society complex or ceremonial and preceded even the finishing touches themselves. Beyond this, the counsel of a holy man or woman was often sought to ensure that all wisdom and tradition, society and tribal, were rigidly followed. Some orders turned to certain experienced men within their own group for this advice; those without such convenient helpers went outside to anyone in the tribe who could serve the purpose. Sometimes they obtained medicine in the form of certain songs or herbal preparations or even rented or purchased a part of the counselor's medicine bundle in order to ensure success in a performance or raid.

Participants used the sweat-lodge ceremony to rid themselves of their "channel" obstructing ignorance that hindered God's desire to work through them, and which the lodge symbolized when it was covered over and they sat praying in blackness with the intense heat burning away at sinful bodies and minds. Every part of the lodge, its plan and the items connected with it, such as a buffalo skull and an outer fire to heat the rocks, had a holy purpose in accomplishing forgiveness and cleansing. And, when the sacred four coverings and uncoverings of the lodge had been made, the people believed themselves freed from the human blindness that had until that time caused them to do the unfortunate things men and women do on earth. Such resultant mercies never lasted beyond the period or situation to which they were addressed, and the preparation had to be repeated again and again on other days, so that the people remained close to and dependent upon God at all times.[4]

Function and appearance held an important place in the making

61

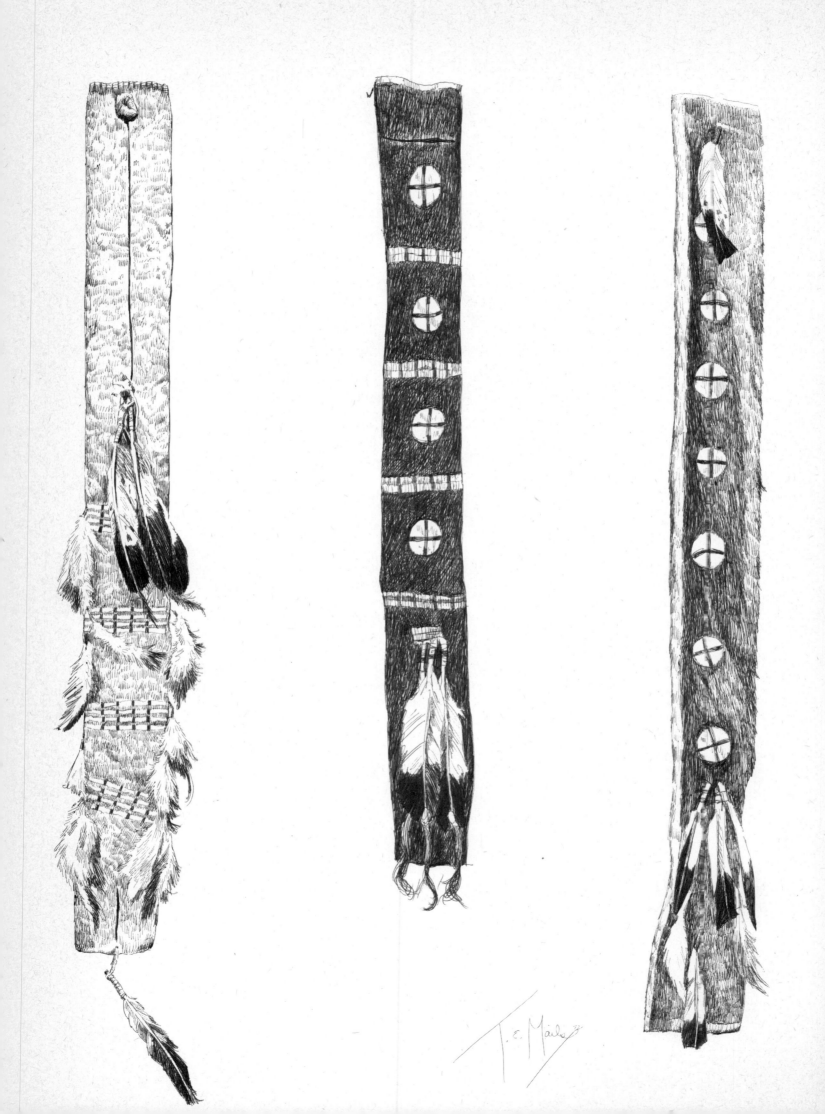

of regalia, though they were secondary to the religious considerations. Since everything had to be movable, both for ceremonial purposes and for travel, as the camps shifted from place to place continually during all but the winter months, weight and storage convenience were vital factors. Those who have the privilege of handling Plains items today are repeatedly astonished at both their lightness and compactness, or perhaps I should say compactability. Except for war shirts, leggings and dresses, which were sometimes made of very heavy, thick elk skins adorned with beading, everything else a man or woman wore or carried was feather-light and could be handled all day on foot or on horseback without causing fatigue. Furthermore, it could be folded a hundred times into a surprisingly small bundle and then spread out again in perfect condition. The ingenuity with which items were designed for both transportability and continued use excites the utmost admiration. Durability was also a factor in choosing the materials employed for regalia. Almost every piece was required to stand up under active use in camp, on the march and on the battlefield. Some of the society staffs and lances did have to be remade each year or when a transfer of ownership took place, but this was because the wooden shaft would lose the strength and resiliency so vitally necessary in the encounter with the enemy.

One of the major purposes of this book is to illustrate and describe society regalia. Very little of this important Plains equipment has ever been made available in print, yet references to the societies and their functions are included in nearly every publication that mentions Plains Indians. The reader is cautioned, however, that all too few of the pieces actually survived the turbulent White–Indian war years. In fact, when the societies began to phase out during the early reservation period, some of them disappearing as early as 1850, most of the regalia quickly vanished. There was never much of it anyway from a relative point of view, for while there were many societies, only the officers bore the pretentious pieces of gear. Then too, important emblems were often handed down through a succession of owners, so that when items became worn they were eventually disposed of by methods not disclosed. Some of the best may have been buried with their owners, since that was a Plains custom in warrior burials.

What is illustrated here, though, will be the most comprehensive display of society regalia included in a book to date. As such, it is important that I mention again my primary source, the American Museum of Natural History in New York City. Their display of Plains artifacts includes, at least at present, a magnificent show of society regalia. By some good fortune, certain men of note associated with the museum, such as Dr. Clark Wissler and Robert H. Lowie, both curators of anthropology who have written extensive and detailed descriptions of many societies, made certain that the museum either obtained these rare pieces or made models of some if the originals were not available, and most of them have become an ongoing part of the museum's spectacular display. Other sources have made smaller contributions, and some items I have included were held in the hands of their owners while photographs were taken in the late nineteenth century.

Perhaps the best-known piece of society regalia, although most people have never seen one even in a photograph, is the society sash. It is familiar because of its noble associations; that is, those who wore it were men of proven courage who were willing to attach themselves

Opposite: *Arapaho society sashes.* Left: *Red-dyed hide with grass bands—described in text* (AMNH); middle: *Black-dyed hide with rawhide targets and grass bands* (Smithsonian); right: *Mountain-lion sash with rawhide targets* (Smithsonian).

to the ground by it in the midst of a titanic battle and to remain there fighting to the death if necessary. These sashes are sometimes described in literature as dog-soldier sashes, or dog-ropes. Yet neither description is a good one. There were specific societies whose names did not include the title *dog* whose officers also wore the sashes. The term *dog-rope* is misleading because it implies that a rope literally was used, when in fact the "rope" was only the conventional sash.

Sashes were fashioned of various materials. The earliest ones were made of animal hide; sometimes buffalo hide was used, but other animal skins such as elk and deer were also employed. During the years of contact with Whites, red and blue wool trade cloth called *stroud* became a popular sash material. The hide sashes were themselves often colored by smoking, dyeing or painting.

Sashes were made in different lengths and widths. Informants report that the most common length ranged from six to eight feet, and the usual width was from six to eight inches. Lowie, however, discovered that at least one Crow society, the Muddy Hands, made a sash twelve feet long and five inches wide.[5] Even when worn by a man mounted on horseback, this one hung clear to the ground. One can only assume that its purpose was to provide the wearer with greater mobility than the shorter sashes would permit when the bearer was anchored during a battle.

In addition to the basic coloring of the sash, various symbols were appended in the form of quilled or grass lines, painted hide targets, feathers, bits of animal fur and lichen. Each of these would be placed on the sash in such a way as to tell an important story.

Two styles of sashes were made, one that hung down the middle of the back and had a slit near the top through which the head was inserted, and another that was fashioned into more of a loop at the top so that it could be worn over the right shoulder and under the left.

Sashes were secured to the ground during a battle by two means. Some had a small slit cut in the lower end, and a lance was driven through this into the earth to fix it in place. Others had an approximately six-inch-long wooden pin attached to the bottom edge by a twisted rawhide thong, and this was either pushed into the ground from the end of the sash or punched through a hole at the sash bottom.

The Arapaho made some of the finest society sashes, and fortunately a few of them were collected and preserved. There is a superb specimen in the Museum of Natural History in New York, which I will compare to a similar one of my own in order to detail the features of an Arapaho over-the-head type dating from A.D. 1825 to 1850. Mine was sold by Little Left Hand to W. R. Black of Watonga, Oklahoma, on March 26, 1926. Left Hand's thumbprint is affixed to a certified statement, which declares it to be "one old sash made from Buffalo hide and feathers and is to by knolage to be over one hundred years old. This old time sash is used in what we call the Dog clan."

The sash is five feet ten and one-half inches long and six and one-half inches wide. The tanned hide is painted on the decorated side with dull red paint of the type commonly applied to sacred objects. The slit for the head begins three inches down from the top and is twenty-one inches long. The slit for the lance at the lower end begins two and one-half inches up from the bottom and is six inches long.

A most interesting feature is the use of what appears to be sweetgrass, rather than quilling, for part of the marking. The very top of the

64

Opposite: *Society regalia.* From Left to right: *Crow Hammer society staff; Crow Muddy Hands society sash; Crow Fox and Lumpwood society short straight staff; Sioux Strong Heart society rattle (AMNH); Crow Fox and Lumpwood hooked staff.*

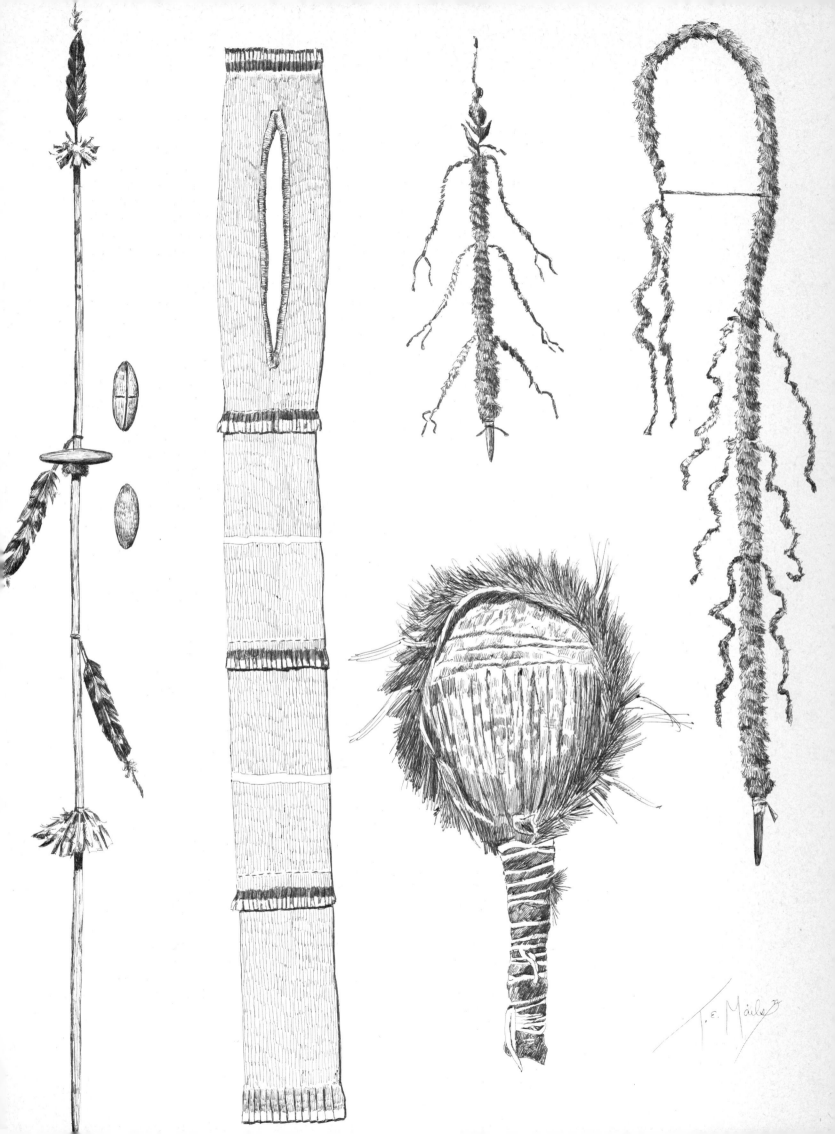

sash is cut into twenty strips, each three-eighths of an inch wide and a half an inch long, which are wrapped with the grass in its natural dull yellow color. On the lower half of the sash are four sets of grass bands consisting of four lines each. The grass is its natural color except for four black-dyed lines on each row. It is beautifully applied in the traditional quilling manner, with two parallel sinew threads first laid across the sash horizontally and the grass then wrapped vertically around these with the ends tucked under. No grass shows on the back side of the sash. A note on the sash at the American Museum of Natural History states that the four banks of lines represented the four divisions of a normal human life and that the eagle feathers were believed to endow the wearer with speed in battle. Their note also says that the sash was worn "over the shoulder." However, it is not that type, but they have a properly mounted one on an Arapaho figure in another display case.

The museum sash has a large hide knot tied at the upper end of the head slit. Mine has a mottled eagle feather there, instead, attached by a thong whose end is pulled through the quill butt. This feather would hang down the middle of the chest when the sash was worn. The museum sash has three golden eagle tail feathers hung in an assemblage at the base. My sash has three beautifully matched tail feathers also, plus four short, sliced hawk feathers, two eagle down feathers and a plume feather dyed red with its quill wrapped with blue beads. There are also four plume feathers attached by thongs along each side of the sash, with the attachment being made at the end of the top row of each bank of grass strips. At the very bottom of the museum sash, a full-sized eagle tail feather is attached by a thong. My sash has a plume, or "breath feather," that is secured in the same way.

The next most familiar piece of society equipment was the staff, or lance, called a "spear" by some—improperly, since it was seldom thrown. This was made in two varieties. There was the straight lance, which was either full sized, meaning it was seven or eight feet in length, or short, which was about four feet in length. Lances were straight shafts with points of stone or metal attached. If there was no point, the lance was more properly called a staff, for in battle it could be used only as a coup, or "honor counting," stick to touch an opponent. There was also the hooked staff or lance. This was fashioned like a shepherd's crook, and it ranged in length from four to a majestic ten feet, depending on the society. To make a hooked staff, either one end of the shaft was bent over or a bent piece of wood was tied to the straight shaft and then held in place by a cross-tie of buckskin. Their different types of lances and staffs were one of the means used to distinguish the ranking officers of the societies from one another.

The finishing of both types of the lances and staffs varied with the society. In most instances, the most "powerful" types of animal skins, such as otter and wolf, were cut into long strips, four inches or so in width, and then wound in spiral fashion along virtually the entire length of the shaft. White swan skin with the fluff left on was a favorite wrapping material. The winding was secured by thongs tied around the lance shaft at regular intervals. Beyond this, there were dangling strips of skin, feathers, hair-locks, scalps, horse-tails and many other kinds of appendages to add grace to the lance—although none of these things could be added by society members in other than the accepted traditional patterns. Fur-covered hides were not the

S27520

only wrapping material employed for lances. Some, such as orders among the Crow, Kiowa and Sioux, wrapped their lances with strips of dyed buckskin in alternating colors to give a striped effect.

Society lances and staffs were intended for ceremonial purposes, but they were also carried to war and used in combat—sometimes to secure the owner in place by his sash. In most instances, however, only the society officers carried these lances. Therefore a war party loaded with lances included many made, for the most part, simply for purposes extending from buffalo hunting to battle. An experienced observer can tell the difference between society and other lances, the first indication of the society lance being its rich fur wrapping.

Since the wood used for the lance shafts became brittle in time and might snap in a critical situation, the precious fur windings were usually removed at intervals, preserved and later placed on new shafts. At the least, this was always done when societies reorganized in the spring.

In addition to the use of hooked staffs by societies, it was the custom of some tribes, such as the Crows, to make staffs in the field out of green limbs. This was done to designate lieutenants appointed by a war chief to assist him when the size of a battle required their help. Men qualified for such duty commonly carried with them on trips strips of otter or wolf skin for wrapping purposes so as to be prepared for such emergencies.

Besides the lances, some societies employed the flag. The shaft was fashioned of a straight round wooden staff from seven to nine feet in length. A long row of feathers was secured, each by the butt of its

67

Sioux war party showing society markings on horses and different kinds of regalia— hooked staff, flag, bow-lance, lance and three coup sticks. The war chief is in the front, and the staff bearer is his assistant (SM).

quill, to a strip of hide (later replaced by trade felt), which was then
either wrapped around the shaft and fixed there with thongs or tied at
intervals to the shaft so that the loose parts of the felt tended to hang
gracefully away from the shaft. Some flags had lance points attached
and others did not, depending upon the order's traditions. Both kinds
were carried to war.

Once again, not all flags seen in photographs are society flags.
Any warrior who had earned enough coup honors could make a flag
after his bonnet was completed. A war chief often called upon a flag
bearer to flank him in a big battle so that warriors could more easily
spot him and receive his commands.

An interesting side feature of the Plains life-way, showing the
esteem in which a warrior held his wife and children, was that at
celebrations and ceremonials the warrior's wife was frequently permitted to carry his lance or flag. This enabled her to share in his accomplishments and thus to exhibit mutual pride. The Crows made a
beautiful kind of hide case, which was painted, fringed and otherwise
adorned, in which to carry the lance. The lance head was inserted in
the case, and when the family moved to a tribal assembly or to the
camp center for a ceremony or celebration, the children often had the
great honor of carrying their father's lance, which was inserted at an
angle through a cinch strap with the cased end protruding above the
horse and behind the rider.

The members of many orders wore society belts. All of these were
of about the same size but were made of different materials and finished in several ways. A typical belt was anywhere from ten to four-

68

Above: *Crow girls escorting father to celebration, with girl in background carrying father's
lance in lance case.* Opposite: *Arapaho society belts.* Top: *Drum (Lance Men) society belt
described in detail in|text (AMNH); bottom: belt with buffalo tails (Smithsonian).*

teen inches in width and long enough to go around the owner's waist.

The belts worn by the youngest men in the age-graded societies were simple and made of relatively low-grade materials, such as dog skin with the hair left on. Belts worn by members of the upper grades were richer and involved far more symbolism. For example, a museum hide-belt worn by an ordinary member of the Arapaho Drum society is painted with six green crosses that represented to the tribe "our father, the Morning Star." Four green vertical lines indicate the four days of the Drum society ceremony. Green lines along the top of the belt represent a straight path and a good life, and the serrations or notches cut along the entire bottom edge indicate clouds. Besides the paint there are nine bunches of cut black feathers hanging from the belt. The museum caption gives no indication of what the feathers meant to the society. Other Arapaho belts had such decoration as three buffalo tails hung from the front.

Both women and men wore society belts, and I have illustrated several of these. The Arapaho women wrapped the belts around their backs and tied them in front because of special ties used, while Arapaho men wrapped theirs around the front and tied them in back. It is not known, however, whether these methods were standard practice on the Plains.

Another common piece of society regalia was the rattle. But these were so individual in design that each must be described in the context of the order that used it. The same condition must apply to other items such as eagle bone whistles, bow-lances and headdresses.

Individual painting styles will also be treated tribe by tribe, but some remark should be made here about the color sources and about the nature of painting itself. It has already been mentioned that a man who was painted, whether by someone else or by himself, underwent a transformation. He was changed, no longer the same man. Therefore it is essential to recognize that while the painting of a man's body conveyed a message to others, it was also a process whereby the warrior began to focus his own being upon his "powers" and upon what he was to become in an intensified way for the time being. Hence the "bear face" painting, which included colors and marks to symbolize the bear, was in truth a vital part of a ritual that actually converted the warrior into one. Once the regalia was put on or carried, the paint applied and the ritual begun, the Bear member was no longer a man, but a bear-man. And in a battle, he even fought more like a bear than like a man. Perhaps it would be more accurate to say that he fought as would a bear who inhabited a man's body. Likewise a Crow scout who daubed his body with white clay to make himself look like a wolf was actually psyching himself into becoming one. How else could he concentrate on the attributes of the animal?

Now and then I have read comments by White authors to the effect that Indians painted themselves to look as "hideous" as possible. Yet nothing I've learned from the Indians themselves substantiates this. It is true that for other than ceremonial purposes, it was permissible for a person to paint himself with an individual selection of colors and patterns expressive of his vision or dream history. That is, the paint conveyed a message to and about the man. Yet even then the types of application were so standardized as to be read even by enemy tribes. In evidence, Plenty Coups tells of an encounter with a Sioux warrior wherein he "saw he was a fine man, and that he had spent the night in

70

Opposite: *Illustrations showing how carefully body paint was applied.* Left: *Cheyenne Sun Dancer;* right: *Arapaho Sun Dancer* (SM).

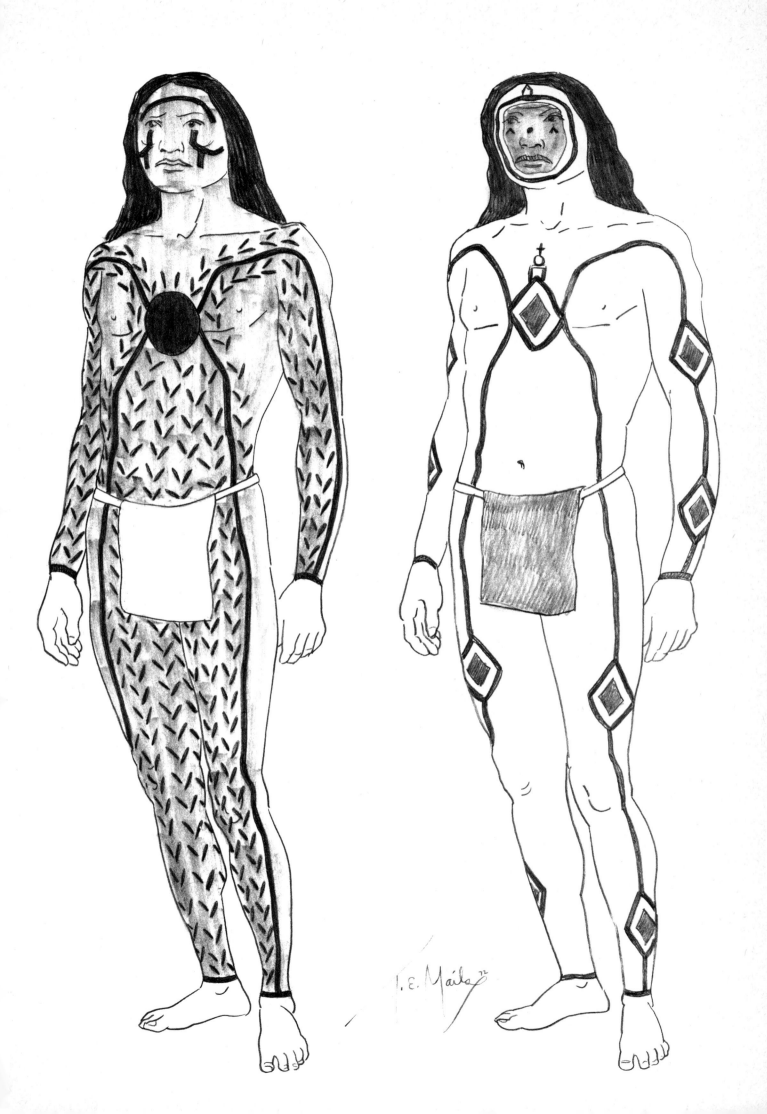

dancing. I knew this because his shoulders were painted red, his face yellow, with little lines of red over his eyes." Obviously, the Crow was familiar with the differences between ceremonial and social painting, even within the Sioux.

The data in later chapters will show that informants are in total agreement that paint customs for society members were traditional and constant. In some instances, the members were allowed to vary their paint according to personal tastes, yet even this practice was a tradition within the group itself and its use was circumscribed.

Alice Fletcher reports that while the young men of the Omaha nation "used merely fanciful designs," the "men generally painted their faces or bodies in accordance with dreams or in representation of some achievement or honor." Further: "When going to battle, on the surround at the tribal buffalo hunt, when taking part in the Hédewachi ceremony, at the races, at the Hethú sha society, and the Pebble society, the painting on their faces and bodies had a serious significance, partaking of the nature of an appeal or prayer. Except with very young men, painting could hardly be called strictly an adornment."[6] Again: "A man frequently painted his horse to represent a valorous act in which the man had won honors, or he might paint the animal in a manner intended as a symbolic representation of a vision. Such a decoration partook of the nature of a prayer."[7]

The Cheyenne, the Arapaho and other tribes had traditional designs that were to be used by the pledgers during the Sun Dance ceremonies. St. Clair discovered a considerable complexity in the body-painting of the Wind River Shoshone.

Some wolf-dancers had realistic representations of a bear or snake below their breasts, standing for bear- or snake-medicine; a sun-dancer had a similar painting of a buffalo. Right angles, or angular horseshoes, represent horse tracks; wavy lines extending along the entire length of the arms and legs symbolize the rainbow; short lines, horizontal, curved, oblique or vertical, indicate people killed; and painted hands record hand-to-hand encounters with the enemy.[8]

Among the Crows, black paint was applied to the face to convey mourning. When a Sioux used black, it meant that the fires of revenge had burned out in his heart, and he was now repentant. The well-known artist E. A. Burbank says, "Most White people assume that the Indians smeared their war paint on indiscriminately, but the truth is that each daub has a significance, as does each feather an Indian wears."[9]

For colors, the Indians turned to nature. In the earliest days, they used only a few earth tones, such as black, red, brown and yellow, which were derived from clays. Authorities suspect that the blues, the greens and the more subtle tones came later. It is well known that the Indians responded in absolute delight when traders brought commercial colors to the Plains. Gifts of vermilion were made to the Assiniboines before 1776. By the mid-1800s, a blazing array of additional pigments was available, such as various reds, yellows, green, blue, lamp black and Chinese white.

The Blackfoot Indians are known to have made green paint from the vegetable coloring found in dried water plants; Lewis and Clark found a green earth paint among the Rocky Mountain Indians; the Cheyenne used gum-covered cottonwood tree buds to make a brown.

73

Opposite: *Sioux warrior, named Charging Thunder, wearing robe with pictographic paintings showing war accomplishments and religious symbols (Densmore,* Teton Sioux Music).

A quick overview of native color sources for various parts of the Plains is as follows:

Green: dried water plants; algae; earth; boiled rotten wood; copper ores
Yellow: clay; buffalo gallstones; bullberries; pine-tree moss; boiled vine roots
Blue: duck droppings; blue mud; boiled rotten wood
Brown: cottonwood buds; clays
Red: powdered earth; clays; rocks containing oxides of iron; boiled roots
Black: charcoal; yellow earth and tallow—combined with a mixture of maple bast and leaves and roasted
White: chalklike earth; clays; ground kaolin

Body paint was applied in one of two ways. The first was to rub grease made from buffalo back fat into the palms and then onto the face and body. The greasy hands were dipped into the bag of powdered paint and rubbed on the areas to be painted. A slightly different method was to mix the fat and the paint together in the palm of one hand and then to apply it with the thumb and forefinger of the other.

Burbank found it a common and alternate practice for Indians to lay the dry paint on their tongues, moisten it and then use a narrow stick to transfer it to their bodies or hair. Sometimes the Indians mixed the paint with water and smeared it on their faces with their fingers.[11]

Whatever paint colors were derived from, they were always dried, powdered and then stored in small buckskin bags, which were then closed by a drawstring or a thong tie. Toilet kits were a standard part of an Indian's equipment. These pouches, worn on necklaces or hung from belts, contained small bags of paint, tallow or fat; some mixing bowls, such as seashells or small rocks with hollowed areas; and little pointed sticks. Whenever possible—in trade days—a mirror was carried.

The society members also painted their regalia, using the same symbolism and good taste as was employed in their body painting. Going beyond the regalia, a man might also paint his favorite war and buffalo horses. The Sioux and Cheyenne were particularly noted for their spectacular designs, and pictographic drawings provide excellent records of them. Since few of the actual horses bearing society designs were, for understandable reasons, available to White photographers, I have illustrated some that I did find and have reproduced a few pictographs by placing the patterns on living horses in a way that I hope will give a better representation of how they really looked. Once again, each design had its meaning, so that the painting done on horses had the same forethought and purpose as the painting on a man or his regalia. Decoration in itself was always the lesser concern.

Of course, materials other than paint were employed to embellish the regalia. Porcupine quills, beads, shells, grass, buttons, feathers and other items all came into play. The captions for the drawings will indicate most of these as the different artifacts are treated in the book.

We can turn now to a consideration of the specifics of the various societies. Unfortunately, records are not so complete as to offer a comprehensive picture of the orders of every tribe—indeed, there are no accounts whatsoever of the orders of some nations. We are therefore limited to the best examples available. Fortunately, both the age-graded and non-graded schemes are well represented in literature, and these provide superb illustrations of the society situation as it existed on the Plains for the nations that made it a part of their way of life.

74

Opposite: *Painted horses, Blackfoot.* Top: *Medicine symbols for snake and lightning, which imparted their powers to the horse;* bottom: *Typical society symbols—symbols on flanks identify the society, marks on chest pray for hail to fall on enemy, stripes on nose count war honors.*

4

THE AGE-GRADED SOCIETIES

THE BLACKFOOTS AS EXAMPLE

The question of how the age-graded societies (as opposed to the non-graded) came into being among certain of the Plains tribes has not been answered to the satisfaction of many authorities. In his brilliant treatment of the Assiniboines, Robert H. Lowie sifted through the research of anthropologists, and struggled mightily to deal with the question, though when he was through, the problem was almost as muddied as it had been before.

In summary, Lowie concludes that the age societies of the Plains were by no means simple age classes; few of them were pure in this respect, containing mixtures of some age-graded orders with non-graded groups in patterns that varied from tribe to tribe. He feels that the system of age classification did indicate a single point of origin, possibly beginning with the village tribes of the upper Missouri area, the Mandan, Hidatsa and Arikara. However, the changes that took place as this form of structure spread from tribe to tribe were such that "their historical development can no longer be traced in detail." Further, it was clear that the age societies of even a single type that became common to several nations, such as the Kit-foxes, did not conform to one ceremonial type. "Ceremonially, age-societies cannot be separated from 'religious' or other forms of organization occurring either in the same or in other tribes." In the end, Lowie simply decides that future wholesale comparisons of either orders or societies should be eliminated "in favor of an intensive comparative study of well-defined single traits. Each series, as well as each society, will then appear, to some extent, as a unique historical product determined by specifically tribal factors." [1]

It is at this point that I find myself in serious disagreement with previous conclusions as to the true origin of the societies, age-graded or otherwise. It should be clear that in my view encounters with supernatural forces were what brought the societies into being. This does not mean that I deny a geographic center of origin for some of the societies—which then spread out to become a series, of which one by the same name existed in several tribes. However, the more ancient the concept of origin, the more valid my premise becomes. My difference with Lowie and others is simply this: They refer to the societies and cults as "uniquely historical products"; I prefer to think of them as "uniquely theological products," spelled out as all such products are upon the historical plane with God acting in history on man's behalf. Age-grading was "the way" for some, rather than the consequence of an analysis of their needs, and non-grading was "the way" for others. No one dared violate the principle once it had been traditionally established, and a mixture of the two types resulted naturally in most tribes. It is by no means surprising that any pursuit by anthropologists of a purely age-graded system was doomed to failure from the start.

Why then do I separate the age-graded type, as represented by the Blackfoots, in this chapter from the non-graded discussed in the following chapter? Simply because the age system is slightly different from the non-graded one and because it has become a standard and somewhat helpful approach among researchers to do so.

The Blackfoots were a confederation of three large tribes occupying a huge slice of the northwestern portion of the Plains, together with an even bigger chunk of southern Canada. Estimates of their numbers

Opposite: *Renowned Blackfoot chief sitting in place of honor in Sun Dance lodge, wearing ermine horned headdress and war shirt trimmed with ermine tails (SM).*

vary from 15,000 to 30,000 at their peak growth point in 1780, with 15,000 being the favored figure.

The confederation consisted of three divisions, the Blackfoot, the Bloods and the Piegans, each group comprising about one third of the total population. They were among the earliest migrants to the Plains, having moved there from the North or Northwest long before any contact with Whites.

The Blackfoots were a restless and aggressive people, intelligent, handsome, superb hunters and warriors. They were constantly at war in historical times with the Cree, the Assiniboine, the Sioux, the Crows, the Flatheads and the Kutenai, even on occasion making swift and destructive raids on tribes further south.

The three divisions were essentially independent politically, yet they acted in concert whenever it was necessary to repel invaders or put a neighbor in his place by an offensive thrust. Writers always point out that the Blackfoots were feared by early Indians and Whites alike. All too often they neglect to add that when such people as Walter McClintock, who truly respected their life-way, came to live among them, the visitors were treated with the utmost courtesy and permitted to share in the most intimate secrets of the tribe. Accordingly, these privileged men were able to describe the Blackfoots' rich ceremonial ways and their fabulous clothing and regalia, which assuredly equaled that of the Crows and was perhaps the finest on the entire Plains.

Because they were among the more thoroughly studied and photographed nations, the Blackfoot tribes serve particularly well to portray what were known as the age-graded societies. These actually existed among only six of the Plains nations: the Blackfoot, the Mandan, the Hidatsa, the Arikara, the Arapaho and the Gros Ventre. (Lowie is not even willing to include the Arikara.)

The men of the three Blackfoot tribes (properly known as Blackfoots), the Blackfeet, the Bloods and the Piegans, were organized into a number of warrior societies, in each of which the membership was determined by age. A fifteen- to nineteen-year-old youth could belong only to a certain society associated with his age group, and a nineteen- to twenty-three-year-old person could belong only to the next higher society, and so on. Each society had its own name, which was descriptive of its function, but as a group they were known among the Blackfoots as the All Comrades.

Virtually all the following material regarding the Blackfoot tribes has been taken and interwoven from the writings of three authors: Edward S. Curtis, *The North American Indian,* vols. 6 (1911) and 18 (1928); Clark Wissler, *Societies and Dance Associations of the Blackfoot Indians,* American Museum of Natural History Anthropological Papers, vol. 11 (1913); Walter McClintock, *The Old North Trail* (1910) and *Old Indian Trails* (1923). This being the case, rather than to end nearly every sentence with a footnote, I include only a random selection to indicate the author's comments I feel are most important in any given section of the Blackfoot chapter. Those who would like to make comparisons of source material should obtain the works of the three authors, for they are more comprehensive than my own and thus will provide greater insights.

It has been a complicated project for researchers to establish firm lists of the warrior societies for any of the Blackfoot tribes. In 1913,

Opposite: *Blackfoot Grass Dancers seated during intermission. Notice hair decorations and paint-loaded hair. The paint is white and yellow (SM).*

Clark Wissler set forth the following as the societies of the three Black-foot groups:

Piegan	Blood	Blackfeet
Pigeons		
Mosquitoes	Mosquitoes	Mosquitoes
		Bees
		Prairie-chickens
		Crows
Braves	All-brave dogs	All-brave dogs
		Bad-horns
All-brave dogs	Braves	Black-soldiers
Front-tails	Black-soldiers	Braves
Raven-bearers	Raven-bearers	Raven-bearers
Dogs	Dogs	Dogs
Kit-foxes	Horns	Horns
Catchers	Catchers	Catchers
Bulls	Bulls	Bulls
		Kit-foxes
	Matoki (women)	Matoki (women)[2]

Beginning with the youngest group and ranging by age upward to the society made up of the oldest men, Curtis records two different lists

82

Blackfoot Grass Dancers (SM).

of society names as existing among the Piegans:

1. Doves
   Flies
   Braves
   All Brave Dogs
   Tails
   Raven Bearers
   Dogs
   Kit-foxes
   Catchers
   Bulls [3]

2. Pigeons
   Mosquitoes
   Braves
   Reckless Dogs
   Tails
   Raven Carriers
   Kit-foxes
   Soldiers
   Bulls [4]

For the Blackfeet he set forth the following sequence:

Bees
Prairie-chickens
Reckless Dogs
Braves (matsiiks)
Raven Carriers
Black Soldiers
Ugly Horns
Dogs
Soldiers
Kit-foxes
Bulls [5]

Complicating these differences further, McClintock gives as his Blackfoot list (implying that the three tribal divisions used identical names) the following:

Doves (or youths)
Mosquitoes (men who went to war)
Braves (or tried warriors)
Brave Dogs (Crazy or Mad Dogs)
Kit-foxes
Bulls [6]

Actually there are several possible reasons for the differences in the lists. The societies were often in a state of transformation: societies might begin in one tribe and later be adopted by another; different names were often used to describe identical groups; some societies ceased to exist before others; not all Indian society names were translatable into English, so that a discussion between Indians and Whites might be about "Flies" in one circumstance and "Mosquitoes" in another, yet actually be about the same group. Also, two or more societies often merged into one as circumstances required and at other times a group split up, so that the given number of orders in one or all divisions might change from year to year. The Flies, Braves and All Brave Dogs are known to have existed in 1854. The Tails became obsolete about 1865. The Braves and Reckless Dogs were still active among the Piegan in 1925, as were the Raven Carriers, the Dogs and the Horns among the Bloods, the Raven Carriers having been revived about 1920. By 1925, the Bulls had been defunct for so long that many elderly informants were unaware such a society had ever existed. Actually, Blackfoot informants never did agree as to either the number or the sequence of the societies.

Careful analysis of the Blackfoot confederation situation has determined that the following societies were known to have existed at one time or another during the historical period of the orders:

Doves
Flies
Pigeons
Mosquitoes
Braves
Brave Dogs
Raven Bearers
Dogs
Kit-foxes
Black Soldiers
Soldiers
Bulls
Tails
Ugly Horns
Catchers
Horns

The precise position of the last five groups on the ladder of progression cannot be established at this late date, but the Kit-foxes plus the Bulls and those following them in the list appear to have been made up of older men. Curtis believes that the societies of the Doves, possibly the Flies, and the Bulls were introduced after the others had become associated with the All Comrades; hence these three were probably not a part of the system. He also felt that the Kit-foxes, the Catchers and the Bulls probably did not perform police duty.[7]

In addition to the age-graded societies, the Blackfoot tribes had a Buffalo Cow society, which was a women's cult; a Bear cult; a Tobacco society; and a Medicine Pipe society. These were open to people of all ages except children, and their existence was an independent one. Their origin, ceremonies and place in the life-way will be set forth following the treatment of the Blackfoot age societies, and like the latter their counterparts were found among most of the nations of the Plains.

The All Comrades societies were the dominating factor in the tribal confederation, and indeed even the power of a tribal head chief depended largely on his cooperation with them. When a tribal council was called by the head chief, not only the lesser civil chiefs and head men of the bands but also the chiefs of the societies were summoned. The more general functions of the societies were primarily to preserve order in all circumstances and to punish offenders against the public welfare whenever necessary. They protected the camp by guarding against possible surprise by an enemy. When a band was moving to a new campsite, the members of the warrior societies rode ahead, at the sides and in the rear to protect the others. The societies took turns checking on the movements of the buffalo herds so as to know where they could be found for tribal hunts. A spirited rivalry among the orders reinforced the military spirit so essential on the Plains, and their feasts and dances provided both their members and the rest of the people an additional form of social recreation. All these services were most actively performed by the groups composed of warriors in the full vigor of youth or middle age, but the activities of those orders made up of the more elderly men, such as the Kit-foxes, the Catchers and the Bulls were centered in religious ceremonies.[8]

When the various bands of each tribe left their winter quarters to assemble for the great tribal encampment in the spring, the head chief invited band chiefs and the leaders of the societies to a feast at which they discussed the general route of the coming summer's travel as they followed or intercepted the buffalo. An understanding and agreement having been reached, the head chief appointed two or three of the younger societies to be the camp police for the season; and whenever the entire tribe gathered for special occasions such as the Sun Dance, the leaders of each society thus honored joined their lodges into one double lodge in a place near the center of the camp. These lodges became the headquarters of the orders on duty and were the place where their feasts, ceremonials and councils were held. Theoretically, the societies chosen to preserve order were subject to the dictates of the tribal chief, yet their duties were so clearly defined and understood that they were mainly their own masters. Usually the societies served in annual rotation, although an order experiencing particular success in war or horse raids sometimes served for successive years.

When the tribe separated into bands to go their individual ways, the chiefs of the orders named as guardians of the public welfare joined the camp chiefs in selecting the camping places along the general route previously agreed upon; differences of opinion were settled by a vote of all the involved chiefs. The daylight assignments of the society members, a few of which were now in each band, have already been mentioned. On a typical evening when no tribal ceremony or celebration was taking place, the soldiers on duty became especially alert as

Opposite: *Sentinels meeting at edge of Blackfoot camp—entire division of nation has gathered for Sun Dance ceremony.*

darkness fell and shouted warnings that all should remain in their lodges insofar as possible after nightfall. The men of the order then took turns keeping watch over the camp until sunrise, each man patrolling a portion of the camp-circle. When there was a tribal encampment, a society member guarded that area in which his own band dwelt, stopping at the edge of his section to meet the sentinel of the next band and exchange information with him.

Since horse-stealing raids by enemies were almost always carried out at night, if a man was seen among the horses, it was standard procedure for the guards to rush at him. If he ran away, they shot to kill him, the presumption being that he was an enemy, but if he ran toward the camp, it usually turned out that he was a youth who was testing his abilities by cutting horses loose as a joke. If he were caught, he was only beaten for his clumsiness and sent home in disgrace without his robe.

Day and night, in camp and on the march, mounted or afoot, the soldiers on duty carried their lances or other emblems, which were as much their identification as their weapons. Like the policemen of other Plains tribes, the Blackfoot orders always sought to prevent the individual from jeopardizing the public good in camp and during the hunts. Sometimes their punishment of an especially obstinate disrupter was to force him to march at the head of the camp column, under guard, to show by example that the soldiers were to be obeyed by all, else the same would happen to them.[9]

Each order of the All Comrades had as a member an old man whom they called Big Comrade. He served as their herald, and his duty was to ride through the camp making announcements of concern to the members, such as an order from their leader to assemble for a council or ceremony or to search for buffalo or the enemy or to inform the people of the results of such events and expeditions. Each Big Comrade held office indefinitely, advancing with his age-group of warriors as they passed from grade to grade through the system. The members of each society elected one of their own group to the office of chief, usually choosing one who had demonstrated his capability in war and hunting and was therefore wealthy because of what he had earned in prizes and been given as gifts.

Memberships were always bought and sold, and the initiation ceremonies were held in succession when the great summer camp was made. Beginning with young men about fifteen years of age, and thus old enough to go to war, the regalia, the songs, the dances and the other traditions comprising the ceremonies and rules of each Blackfoot society were purchased from the members of the age group just above it, the young men acting collectively to do so as a group but receiving their regalia and instruction individually, although at approximately the same time and place. Thus a young man, in company with others in his own age bracket, first purchased his membership in the youngest society, and after a given number of years bought membership with the entire body in the next grade, and so continued until at last he acquired the rights of the oldest order. After selling its society membership to those coming up, a group was without a place in the All Comrades until they obtained the ritual and regalia of the next higher grade.[10]

When a group was old enough to join the next higher society, each man visited one of those whose place he wished to assume. He offered a pipe, which was filled and ready to smoke, and the other asked in feigned innocence his desire. "I want your clothes," was the standard

Opposite top: *Regalia of Blackfoot Yellow Pigeons;* bottom: *Full front and partial rear views of Bear member of Pigeon society. He wears a wide belt of bear skin, which is not visible in the sketch (after drawings by Blackfoot informant, AMNH).*

reply. The older warrior then smoked the pipe, prayed for his successor and returned the pipe. The other smoked it and gave it back. When at last it was smoked out, the elder returned it for the last time and his visitor departed. The candidates were summoned shortly thereafter to the higher order's double lodge, where all the members were already assembled. Each seller clothed and painted his successor, and then everyone danced. In a few of the societies the seller is said to have cohabited with his successor's wife. Curtis declares it was "certainly the case with the Bulls, and at a Horn society lodge of the Bloods," for he had seen it happen.[11] In rare cases a man joined a society in fulfillment of a vow made in illness, but in the usual instance he joined a society and passed through the regular sequence at the specified intervals.

It is not known whether these exchanges occurred at exact and measured age intervals. Some informants insisted they did, reporting that the interval was four years. Others said that four years were spent in each of the societies after the Braves. Two men spent three years each in the Flies, Braves and All Brave Dogs, and in later years men sometimes made a step up after a year or two and even skipped a grade. Yet several Blackfoots declared they could not recall a summer in which any two societies disposed of their rights; and since there were more than four societies, two exchanges would have taken place in some one year if four full years were actually spent in each order. The ceremonies of all the societies for the transfer of a ritual from one group to another lasted four days and four nights, but the dances held on other occasions never lasted more than a day.

While it was not always the case among the various societies of the Plains, among the Blackfoot, women had the status of lay members of the societies in which their husbands were active. They took no part in the dancing but assisted in the singing. Unmarried women were sometimes asked to join the Pigeons, taking the place of retiring Pigeon women who wished to drop out of the order and perhaps marry members of an older group. In such cases the Pigeon men collected the price traditionally paid to the women whose important places were being taken.

By 1925, there were numerous "societies" among the Blackfoot, such as the High Hat, the Eagle Feather, the Cree, the Horse Racers and the Bronco Busters, which held dances simply for amusement. Even the old societies still existing had lost their purpose and force and had nothing in common with the former system, being merely groups of dancers. The Grass Dance was in a somewhat different class from the rest. It had been obtained from the Sioux, among whom it was said to have originated in the dream of a man who slept near a flock of prairie chickens. He dreamed that they were dancing and that the prairie-chicken leader instructed him in their dance.

THE BLACKFOOT WARRIOR SOCIETIES

The Doves Society

The Doves were the latest formed of the Blackfoot age societies. The organization originated among the South Piegan in 1855 or 1856. Shortly after that, some of the Blackfeet people visited them, brought back their ceremony and began to practice it. Then the Bloods borrowed it from the Blackfeet. Even the place where the Doves' first dance was held

Opposite: *Blackfoot society regalia.* Top: *Dog skin belt worn by an officer of the Pigeon society, which ranked lowest in the scheme;* bottom: *Pipe used by a Blood woman in the transfer ceremony for the Horn society (AMNH).*

89

was remembered. There was a certain "high hill" where they once went to feast and prepare for their dance. After that, the Blackfoot people called it Dove Hill.

Indian informants said that the Dove society was originated by a man named Change Camp, who had had a dream wherein a group of doves gave him the dance. They told him to gather all the young men and boys who were without power in the tribe. If they would band themselves together and follow the doves' directions, they would become strong and everyone would fear them.[12]

As the society evolved, all Blackfoot youths of about fifteen years became eligible for membership, and graduation from membership in this organization to the next higher grade followed the procedure of the other age societies. In the early summer of each year, those who were coming of age met, elected their own chief and notified those who were already Doves of their wish to join the organization. The members of the society then gathered in their society lodge and spent a day in dancing and feasting. The next day they went in a body to a double lodge which had been erected by the candidates, who followed them in. Upon entering the lodge, each new man gave one of the Doves a smoke of his pipe and a present. The members accepted these and bestowed upon the candidates the standard bows and arrows which each Dove carried as his society insignia. Then each veteran painted a candidate as he himself was painted, for each man had his own style of decoration and power. When all had been painted, the members sang their three society songs. Then the candidates filed outside the lodge and sat down in such a way as to form an elongated arch with its opening toward the east.

Six or more of the best singers among the veterans then sat in a concentric curve within the arch and began beating on a stiff rawhide and singing the other Dove songs. Now the new members arose and danced, each holding a drawn bow and arrow in his hands and carrying a quiver full of arrows on his back. A young unmarried woman, chosen for her virtue and goodness before the initiation ceremonies began, also held a bow and arrows and assisted in the singing. Each song was repeated many times for the benefit of the candidates, after which the new members rushed outside the camp, shooting at the ground or at any unlucky dogs that happened in their way. After some time they returned to the double lodge, deposited their insignia and went home. The same ritual was repeated for the next three days, the new members painting themselves in the double lodge while the former members sang for them at the dance. The Dove dance itself always lasted about a day. It was held at any time during the summer that the members wished, and the double lodge was always pitched for the occasion in the center of the camp. Authorities say that the last dance of the Doves was held about 1874.[13]

McClintock reports that the Doves held their traditional ceremonies outdoors, usually in the early morning. They had eight officers and an indefinite number of members. The leader wore an eagle feather on the back of his head, and his face and body were painted red. There were four Yellow Doves who wore only breechclouts and painted their bodies yellow. These carried bows and arrows made of serviceberry wood, and their quivers were fashioned from the yellow skins of buffalo calves. Contrary to the initiation ceremony arrangement, they seated themselves in a circle and sang in unison, some beating time on

Opposite top: *Knob-headed staff of the Bee society decorated with bells and feathers;* bottom: *Positions of members of the Pigeon society during a ceremony (after drawings by Blackfoot informants, AMNH).*

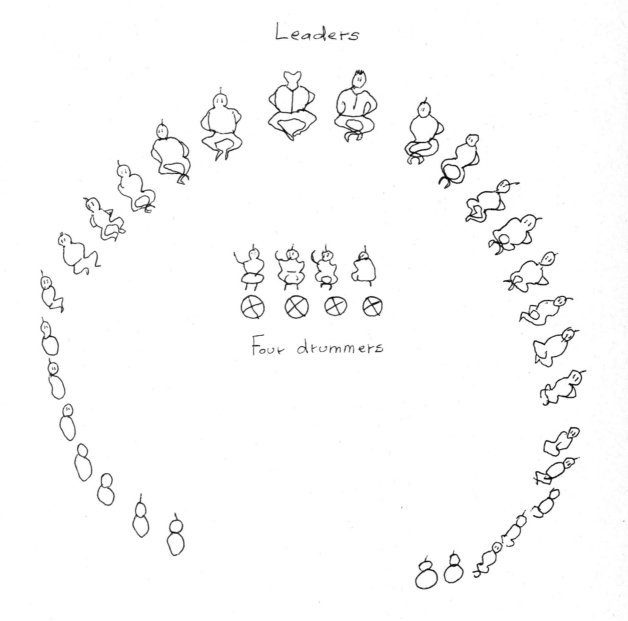

Leaders

Four drummers

Two Bears

T. E. Mails '74

their bows with arrows and others drumming on the sides of their drums with plain sticks.

As a form of training for war, the Doves played risky games in the camps. If a prominent chief did not do as they said, they sought continually to annoy him and others by playing every trick they could devise. A favorite one, when buffalo paunches were still used for water bags, was to lie in ambush and, when they saw a woman returning from the river with her water bags filled, shoot arrows into them so that the water would leak out. If she became angry, they only made her more furious by seeking to destroy the bags! If a woman were going out to pick berries and they ordered her not to do so, her disobedience meant that they would await her return, attempt to surprise her and spill her berries. At other times they took long willow sticks and ran ahead to beat the berries from the bushes where she hoped to work. Of course, the women knew the society's nature and sought to outwit the boys, all of which made the contest more interesting.[14]

The Doves always took into their society one woman who liked to dig roots and pick berries so that they could count on an abundance for their feasts during the berry season.

It was said that the head chief of the camp, and even the powerful societies, overlooked the games or excused them by explaining that since the Doves were young and foolish and would do anything to have their own way, it was bad to oppose them. What they meant was that they understood that daring and testing were both forms of preparation for a young man to take his rightful place as a defender and preserver of his people. Under such circumstances, a certain license was both right and good.

The Flies Society

Before the formation of the Doves, the Flies were the youngest of the Blackfoot age societies, although this order was of later origin than all the others and in the beginning was not considered to be a warrior society. Once the Doves had been organized, the Flies consisted of youths about twenty years of age. The lay members painted themselves red and yellow, with stripes across their noses and eyes, and wore buffalo robes with the hair side out. Each man had a claw of a hawk or an eagle tied to his wrist to represent the fly's nose or beak and wore a downy eagle feather at the back of his head in the scalp-lock. The chief of the Flies wore an eagle tail feather in his hair and a yellow buffalo robe and had his face and body painted like the others.

In performing their ceremonial dance, the Flies knelt on the ground in a circle around their singers. They covered themselves with their buffalo robes, put their heads to the ground and began grunting like buffalo bulls. Then they sang four songs, leaped up, threw off their robes and rushed about the camp scratching everyone they could catch with their hawk or eagle claws. The people pretended great fear and ran hastily into their tipis to get out of their way. Like the initiation ceremony of the Doves, the candidate ritual of the Flies lasted four days, while on other occasions they danced for only a single day. Their final dance was celebrated about the year 1872.

The society that was known as the Flies in one area was known as the Mosquitoes in another. The original dream remembered by the

Blackfoot informants was associated with that insect. As the story went:

There was once a man who hunted in a place where there were many mosquitoes. They came in swarms and stung him so badly that he wondered if they were going to kill him. He took off his clothes and lay down on the ground. The mosquitoes quickly covered him and bit him until he lost all feeling. Then he heard strange voices singing:

> *Mosquitoes, mosquitoes, get together, get together;*
> *Mosquitoes, get together.*
> *Our friend is nearly dead!*

He saw mosquitoes having a dance. They sat in a circle and sang; they jumped up and down, springing this way and that, always dancing in the direction of the sun. Some were red and others yellow. They had claws attached to their wrists and long plumes hanging from their heads. He heard a voice say:
"Brother, because you were so generous and let us drink freely from your body, we give you the society of mosquitoes and make you the leader."
Then that man came safely home and started the Society of Mosquitoes. The members wore buffalo robes with the hair side outward. Some painted themselves red and others yellow, with stripes across nose and eyes. They wore plumes in their hair and eagle claws attached to their wrists to represent the bills of mosquitoes.[15]

Wissler gives the organization and numbers of the Mosquitoes as follows:

Leader (1)	Old men comrades (4)
Yellow Mosquitoes (4)	Single men comrades (1 to 2)
Mosquitoes (x)	Drummers (4)

Brave Dogs society marching. Notice that son of leader is included at left and that his outfit is an ermine-adorned imitation of his father's, all part of inspiring the boy for the future (SM).

93

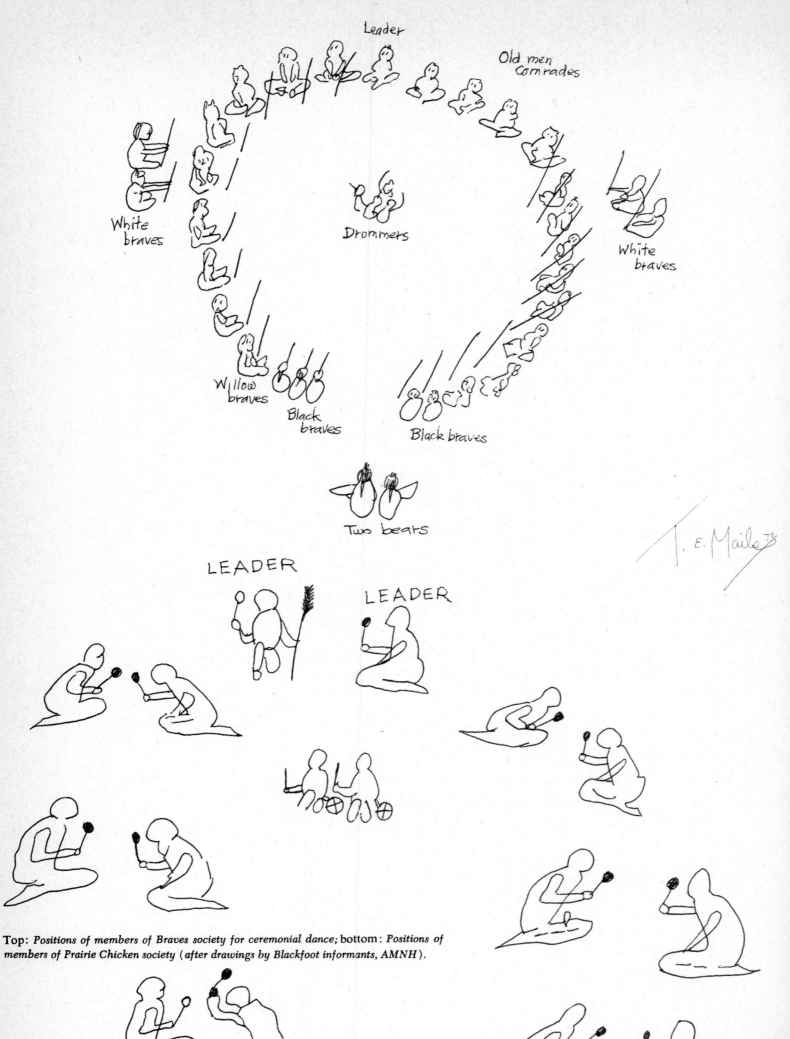

Top: *Positions of members of Braves society for ceremonial dance; bottom: Positions of members of Prairie Chicken society (after drawings by Blackfoot informants, AMNH).*

The leader wore an eagle tail feather on his head. His face and body were painted red with a black band across at the level of the bridge of the nose. He wore a buffalo robe, with the hair side out.

The four yellow Mosquitoes were each painted yellow with a red band across the nose. They wore feathers in their hair and robes with the hair side out. On each wrist was tied an eagle claw, representing the mosquito's bill.

The Mosquitoes painted themselves red and wore eagle plume feathers in their hair, but otherwise they dressed in the same manner as the yellow Mosquitoes.

The old men comrades wore their regular clothing during the ceremony and had no special regalia. The single men comrades dressed like the Mosquitoes.[16]

When those who went by the name Mosquitoes gave their dance, they sat in a circle with the drummers in the center. The leader took his place at the head, or north side, of the group and the yellow-robed Mosquitoes stood on both sides of him. As they danced, they waved their robes like wings, hovering close together and pushing one another, all the while imitating the movements of mosquitoes. Now and then they pretended to alight by sitting down and making the buzzing sound of mosquitoes. They always danced this way four times and then scattered in all directions through the camp, like the Flies, scratching anyone they met with their eagle claws and always being especially pleased to find a man wearing minimal clothing. Unlike the Flies, it did no good to run from the Mosquitoes, for the insects followed people into their lodges as the miserable creatures always do and scratched them all the harder! On the other hand, it was said that those who offered themselves were not especially hurt "because if a mosquito is left alone, its bite does little harm."[17] The import of the dance is clear: Enemies who left the Blackfoot nations alone would suffer only a little at the hands of the troublesome Mosquitoes, but those who resisted would pay a bitter price. It was more of the mental preparation so necessary to survival on the Plains.

The Braves, or All-Tried Warriors, Society
Wissler's list for the Braves was as follows:

Leader (1)	Braves (x)
Willow Brave (1)	Old men comrades (4)
White Braves (4)	Single men comrades (4)
Black Braves (4)	Drummers (4)[18]
Bear Braves (4)	

In the last half of the nineteenth century, the Braves were the most powerful of all the men's societies. They originated in the early history of the tribe by a man who had had what was called "a strong dream." He had seen a band of fierce, loyal dogs and noticed the way they behaved. Like the dogs, the Braves watched over the camps and helped the civil chiefs keep order. Members stated that they punished men and women who quarreled and sometimes killed people who disobeyed their orders. Whenever the camp was to move, the Braves marched around beating their drums and singing, each member carrying a knife, a bow and a quiver filled with arrows. That night they curled up on the ground at the center of the camp, "like dogs." The next day the tribe moved on, while the society members remained be-

95

Regalia of Blackfoot Braves society. Top left: *Lance of the White Braves;* top right: *Leader's lance;* bottom: *Willow Brave's staff* (AMNH).

hind and ate the food that was left. Then, like dogs again, they followed slowly along after the others, entering the new camp after all the lodges had been pitched and the fires were going.[19]

On camp or tribal buffalo hunts, the society was considered to be the guardian of the herds. If the buffalo were frightened off by someone who disobeyed orders, the Braves would track him down, take away his horse and weapons, destroy his clothes and whip him. As a lesson for all who might do likewise, the offender was then sent back to camp naked and afoot.[20] The Braves were also the official buffalo scouts. Once a herd had been located, they moved the tribe in its direction. The Braves reaped what they sowed, for men who moved up from the Flies to join the society of Braves were mature warriors in the prime of life and they were expected to face danger whenever it came. They could never retreat or pass the responsibility to others.

Whenever the Braves wished to hold their ceremony, they placed their huge society lodge in the center of camp and began the ritual early the next morning. The society leader wore a coyote skin for a headdress, with the tail hanging down behind. He was called Wolfskin Man, and he carried a small bulb rattle and a short, straight lance decorated with four pairs of feathers. He wore a war shirt, fringed with weasel or hair-locks, and leggings. The right half of his face was painted blue, the left red; black bands were around his wrists. The officer next in rank, called Willow Brave, carried a willow branch to the end of which were tied yellow plumes, and he wore a hairless robe to which were attached buffalo hooves which rattled when he danced.

The leader sat on the ground, and thirty feet or so to the east and the west of him sat four men who were known as White Braves. These had bone whistles and white-painted lances, decorated with feathers and sage stuck into the ground in front of them. They carried eagle feathers. Their bodies were painted white, and four black or yellow stripes were painted across their noses and eyes. Two black marks were painted across the arms, the thighs and the calves.

Two other members, who were called Water Braves, were painted black; they carried animal bladders on their backs for water pails and hide bags for back-fat and pemmican. Four Black Braves sat thirty yards to the north of the leader. These carried black-painted lances, had their bodies painted black and had black stripes across their faces. Each one had a bag on his back called a water pail. Southeast of the leader sat a man called Brush Brave. He represented a herder and wore a robe consisting of a piece of old lodge cover. He carried a bundle of brush and in dancing acted as if he were driving a herd toward a buffalo jump.

Two other men, called Grizzly Bear Braves, carried bows and arrows instead of lances. They had their faces painted in such a manner so as to awe the spectators; their bodies were covered with red, and on their faces was the bear sign—black streaks down over the eyes and at each corner of the mouth. They wore their front hair cut short and made it stand straight up by loading it with paint. They had fringed shirts made from the smoked tops of old skin lodges, belts of bear skin and leg bands of bear skin with bear claws attached; for headdresses they wore strips of otter skin with bears' ears and two claws attached to look like double ears. They sat twenty-five yards to the east of the leader.

The lay members were known as Red Braves. They carried red

Opposite: *Blackfoot Brave Dog society Grizzly-bear wearing perforated shirt and bear headdress band.* Above: *Back view;* below: *Front view* (SM).

lances and painted their bodies red. Each had an eagle bone whistle. Curtis states that a Hudson's Bay dagger was used for the lance head and that the lance shaft was wrapped with bright cloth (red) and ornamented at intervals with feathers.[21]

Whenever they danced, the Braves went outside the society lodge and sat in an ellipse or half-circle with four drummers in the center. Then each Bear placed his lance upright in the ground in front of himself.

Accounts by different informants show in an interesting way how the dance varied within the camps or divisions. According to one, the two Bear Braves began the rite by covering themselves with robes as if they were bears lying in a den. Then the leader began dancing, blowing his bone whistle as a signal for the others to join him. They dropped their robes and followed, blowing bone whistles and bearing their lances. Leaning forward, they danced slowly around in a circle, holding their lances near the ground and acting like dogs looking for places to lie down. The white-painted Braves drove the others before them with their lances but stopped as soon as the two Water Braves appeared. Then came the brave with the willow staff, who could not stop dancing until the two Grizzly Bear Braves appeared. The Bears danced only when they felt like it. Until then they lay lazily in their den and acted as they pleased. Sometimes the spectators threw things at them to try to make them dance. When they were ready, they rose slowly, holding their hands bent over the way bears hold their paws. They also danced leaning over, hopping along in short jumps with their feet together as bears do. Now and then they aimed their bows and arrows at the other dancers, driving them back to their seats. To close the ceremony, the two Bears scattered the crowd by pretending that they were going to shoot at them with real arrows, but they always shot over their heads instead. Then the entire society ran in the direction of the arrows, at the same time removing their moccasins and throwing them away to show how the ceremony had filled them with resistance to pain.[22]

They returned within a short time and marched through the camp, singing the society song and briskly shouting out orders to the people. It was their custom on such occasions to take anything they wanted in the way of food as they marched, even food being cooked in a kettle, "as dogs do." Some made a habit of stopping to dance at the lodges of prominent chiefs, who were expected to give them presents of food and clothing. If people troubled them in any way, the Bear Braves shot at them with blunt arrows.

Another informant reported that two songs were used alternately, four times each. During the four repetitions of the first song, the Grizzly Bear Braves came forward and made the members rise and dance, after which they returned to their stations and sat down. During the four repetitions of the second song, everyone danced, including the Grizzly Bear Braves, who imitated bears in their actions. As they danced, the Bears held arrows aloft. At the end of the fourth repetition, each Grizzly shot a single blunt arrow straight up into the air, whereupon all the people ran in mock terror while the Braves stood fast in the midst of the falling shafts, demonstrating their fearlessness in war or trials. When the arrows had landed, two of the Black Braves picked them up and put them into the bags on their backs. Then the Braves scattered in all directions, running outside the camp circle, removing their moccasins, leaving them there and then singing as they returned swiftly to the camp to their own tipis. Now the people rushed to find the moccasins, for to do so was considered good luck. Meantime the Grizzlies went running about the camp, taking whatever food they could find and giving it to the helpers, who carried it to the double lodge where a great feast was held lasting into the night. According to Curtis, the last dance of the Braves was held in 1877.[23]

The Brave Dogs, or the Crazy or Mad Dogs, Society
The organization of the Brave Dogs society according to Wissler was as follows:

Leader (1)	Old men comrades (4)
Assistant leaders—horsemen (2)	Single men comrades (2)
Bear-all-brave-dogs (2)	Drummers (4)
All-brave-dogs (20)	

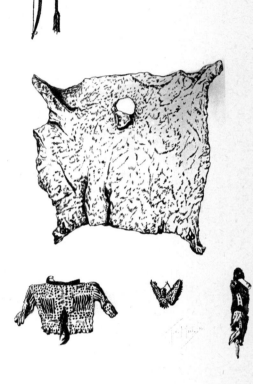

This society is said to have been founded by two renowned Gros Ventre chiefs who killed enemies in battle by riding them down with their horses. When a certain powerful Gros Ventre society refused to permit one of the chiefs to join it, he became so angry that he gave the secrets of his society, the Brave Dogs, to White Calf, the head chief of the Piegans. As the society evolved thereafter, its members gained a reputation for such bravery that people were reluctant to oppose them. As a prelude to their ceremonies, they let the camp know they were going to dance by marching around and singing their society song. The parade was led by a mounted herald and the society's two assistant head men, known as Mounted Men, who rode horses and represented the Gros Ventre chiefs who had originated the society. Their horses were painted on the flanks, necks and faces with symbols indicating the war honors of the riders. Every so often the members paused at the lodge of a chief and danced there until he presented them with food.

The Brave Dogs were often appointed to serve as the police during great tribal encampments. At such times their function was to preserve order and to punish offenders. They also saw that all tipis were located in their proper places and that the entire camp was symmetrically formed.[24]

In its dances and ceremonies, the order cultivated a resolute military spirit and, at the same time, ministered to the social desires of the members. The society employed three lodges, which were grouped together in a large open space near the center of the camp circle. There was one large lodge and two smaller ones whose doors were placed together so that they opened into one another. All feasts, councils and ceremonies were held here, and within these they stored their weapons and regalia in preparation for parades and dances.[25]

In their parades through camp, it was their custom to go by twos, dressed in full costume, accompanied by drummers, shaking their society rattles and singing in unison. Now and then they stopped and, turning about, faced the drummers, danced backward and forward awhile, then reversed and moved on. The leader might well have his small son at his side as a part of the boy's training, and he would be dressed in a costume like his father's. The Piegan Brave Dog head man wore a war shirt of deerskin hung with rolled weasel tails and a large coyote skin, like a poncho, with his head thrust through a slit in the middle so that the long black-tipped tail hung down his back and nearly touched the ground. His nose, mouth and chin were painted red, which was "coyote" painting. This painting was sometimes spoken of as "eating raw meat." In explanation, it was said that when a coyote had been

99

Regalia of a Black Bear Brave. Top: Bow and arrows; middle: Robe with hole and flap; bottom left: Gashed and perforated shirt; middle: Gashed and fringed moccasins; right: Belt of bear skin with bear tail attached (AMNH).

Four drummers

Leader

Mounted Man

Mounted Man

Two bears

100   Above left: *Positions of the Brave-Dogs for a ceremony before the tipi of a head man;*
above right: *Headdress band of a Bear All-Brave-Dog made of bear skin with ears and
two claws attached, plus a curved wooden fan;* middle: *Armband of bear skin with bear
claw attached;* bottom: *Rear view of costumes and hair styles of Brave Dogs leader on
right, two Bears in middle (after drawings by Blackfoot informants, AMNH).*

eating, his face usually was red with blood. Also, he usually got his meat whenever he looked for it. According to society tradition, this head man carried a rattle in his right hand and a blanket over his left arm. To his left marched a distinguished chief in a horned headdress, wearing also a weasel tail war shirt with a large beaded disk mounted on the chest. This chief was also one of the society's four "old men comrades." The other three wore eagle feathers on the backs of their heads. Their duties in the society were to advise in the various ceremonies, to act as heralds and make announcements about the society to the camp and to call the group together whenever a meeting was desired.[26]

McClintock states that two of the members were known as Grizzly Bears. These imitated the actions of bears and always attracted the most attention. They alone carried bows and arrows. Their faces were painted with what was called the "bear-face pattern," which consisted of a coating of red with long black marks placed at the corners of the mouth to represent tusks and vertical black lines across the eyes. They wore headdresses of bear skin, with the bear's ears left on, and two bear claws stood upright on top for horns. They also used armbands of bear skin with a single claw attached. For clothing they wore short-sleeved fringed shirts made of tanned skins and painted red on each shoulder. They also wore breechclouts and beaded belts with stabber-type knives and sheaths. The exposed lower parts of their bodies were painted with various bright colors.[27]

The lay members of the society wore their best regular clothing. Many came from the most prominent families and had fine costumes. When parading, they always carried the society rattle in the right hand and a blanket over the left arm. Their faces were painted either half red or with individual designs corresponding to those on their rattles. The rattles were regarded as ceremonial objects, and if a member wanted to withdraw from the society, he would sell his rattle in ceremonial fashion.[28] The typical rattle was very small, with a wooden handle wrapped with a spiral of hide and with a hide head to which beads and feathers were appended. The feathers were those of the eagle, the owl, the woodpecker and other birds known as good fighters.

Four drummers walked in the rear of the parade line, wearing blankets tied about their waists so that their arms would be free for drumming. These were also good singers, and they led the members in their songs. Each carried a sacred buffalo-hide shield decorated with eagle feathers and the famous war-bridle of the society known as the "horse-medicine." The latter was always taken to war and on raids because of its protective power and to buffalo hunts to increase the speed and surefootedness of their fast buffalo horses. A sacred quirt and a cluster of eagle feathers went with the bridle, and the assemblage of pieces, which made up the society's medicine bundle, was believed to ensure success in taking horses from enemies, in catching wild horses and in horse-racing—by causing a rival horse to falter and lose.[29]

In their public dance, the Brave Dogs seated themselves in a cere-monial circle, with the drummers in the center, the "old men comrades" on the left, the Grizzly Bears on the right and the lay members in between. Then the members arose from their places, and the two mounted men rode around the circle in opposite directions, slowly forc-ing the dancers toward the center and then pretending to ride them down. This was done because the Gros Ventre founders of the society had ridden down enemies in that way. After this, all the members who

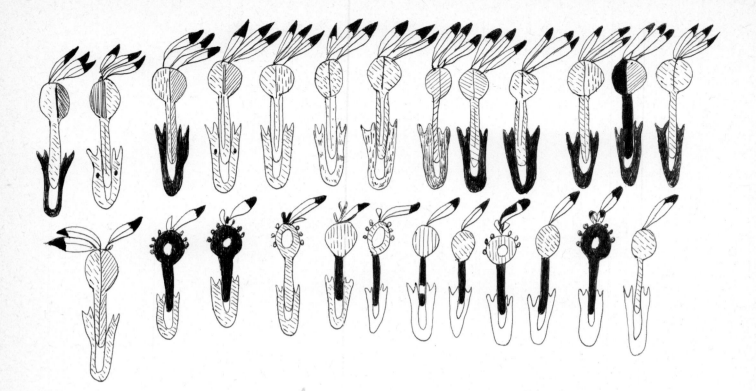

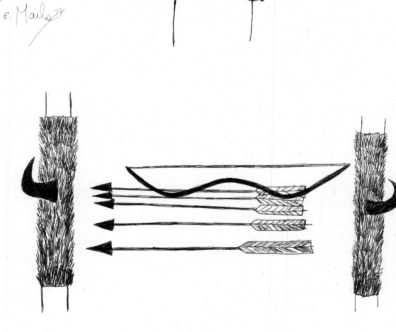

Regalia of the Blackfoot Brave-Dogs. Above: *Twenty-five types of rattles of the equipment of a Bear—colors, blue (vertical lines), green (right oblique), red (left oblique) and black; below left: Bear wearing bear skin belt; above right: Bear claw headband and arrows (after drawing by Blackfoot informant, AMNH).*
Opposite: *Blackfoot Brave-Dog society member carrying typical society rattle. Notice smallness of actual rattle (SM).*

had unhorsed an enemy in battle seized the mounted men and pulled them roughly down from their horses. Then they all danced together. To conclude the dance, they held their rattles and drums at arm's length above their heads, shouted in unison and then seated themselves. Then came the inevitable feast at which the prominent men made speeches; and all sang together, accompanied by the drums.

McClintock was privileged to see the interior of the Brave Dog tipis and the way they cared for their society costumes and sacred bundles. The medicine bundle was tied to one lodge pole. From another pole hung a single society rattle, which was regarded as a ceremonial object. To a center pole was fastened a banner decorated with black-tipped strips of ermine, a warbonnet of eagle feathers, the buffalo-hide shield and a weasel tail hung shirt and leggings, which in themselves were looked upon as a medicine bundle.[30]

During the annual Sun Dance ceremonies, the prestigious Brave Dog members were privileged to hang their weapons and regalia on the center pole of the Sun lodge and to sit in rows before it in a prominent place reserved for them. Then they performed their dances and rituals and recounted for the assembled people the brave coups they had performed as warriors. After this, they sang war songs accompanied by the beating of drums, took part in a feast and passed around a medicine pipe for everyone to smoke.

On at least one evening during such great occasions, the Brave Dogs would emerge from their tipis dressed in their spectacular costumes and parade through the camp to the beating of drums, singing in unison and shaking their rattles. A crowd of their women and children would follow proudly and join in the singing as the herald rode in advance of all and announced in a loud voice that a dance would be given that night in their big society lodge to which the people were invited. As night would descend, their lodges would begin to glow like great candles with the light from their roaring fires. The steady drumbeat would grow louder and louder and louder as excited men, women and children would come from all parts of the camp and crowd into the big dance lodge until it was jammed.

Then would begin the shrill war-whoops and singing, while the rhythmical beating of the drums would increase in volume until it reached a thundering climax; then, with accompanying shouts from the singers, the drums would suddenly cease, only to begin, rise and fall again and again.

On such occasions the three lodges were opened and placed together as one. The dancers looked gigantic and ominous as the red glow of the fire reflected on their painted bodies and faces. Most of them wore only breechclouts and moccasins. Some blew eagle bone whistles while others alternately sang and gave sharp war-whoops. The leader was distinguished from the rest by the large coyote skin he wore, while four of the dancers had their bodies painted with white clay to represent gray wolves and carried long sticks decorated with eagle feathers. They would circle round and round the other dancers, in imitation of wolves driving buffalo. The two Grizzly Bear members sat in a shallow hole, which symbolized a den, wearing their bear's paint and outfits and acting lazy and lolling about, while the spectators would throw things at them to make them dance. Finally, after the four gray-wolf dancers had rounded up the buffalo dancers and were closing in on them, the two Grizzly Bears would wake up. Slowly and deliberately, like bears,

104

Opposite: *Famous Blackfoot straight-up eagle feather headdress similar to those worn by members of Bulls society and others.* Left: *Rear view of Brave Dog leader with full wolf or coyote skins hanging down back;* right: *front view of bonnet with rows of brass tacks on brow band and ermine pendants (SM).*

they would rise and join the members to help drive back the wolves, after which they would return to their den. This dramatic maneuver was repeated the sacred four times, to the utter delight of the crowd. The dance continued well into the night. At its end there was a feast of serviceberry soup, and the members would march through the reeling camp singing their famous society song:

> It is bad to live to be old
> better to die young
> fighting bravely
> in battle.[31]

The Brave Dogs society made such an impression that its rituals were still being performed in the early twentieth century, and the Blackfoot nations remember it with pride today. Curtis states that the last exchange of the songs and regalia of the Brave Dogs took place in 1877. Those who purchased these still owned them and held their dance in the summer of 1925, when "there were about twenty-five members, all old men." [32]

The Raven Bearer Society
The organization of the Raven Bearer society according to Wissler was as follows:

Leader (1)	Raven-bearers (40 to 100)
Assistant leader (1)	Pipe-keeper (1)
Black-raven-bearer (1)	Drummers (4)[33]

The Raven society came into being when a certain war party went on foot to confront the Crees. Although old men seldom went on such expeditions, according to the informants, "in the battle an old man was shot in the leg, and his fleeing companions abandoned him." After lying unconscious for many days, he awoke and saw a flock of ravens flying above him. Then he heard one singing in a bush next to him. This raven spoke to him, telling him he would be safe and would not die. Then it called to the other ravens, telling them all to come together and dance. As the ravens gathered in a circle, the raven chief, who carried a special flag with feathers, said, "You see how we are doing. When you go home, do likewise." As the old man watched in spellbound fascination the ravens became like men and sang and danced. Afterward, the raven spokesman told him that when anyone was sick, he could be made well simply by promising to join the society. The old man himself was now well enough to return home, and when he arrived there, he secured the necessary feathers, made the costumes and staffs and organized the Raven Bearer society.[34]

The feather-bedecked flag carried by each ordinary member of the Raven Bearers had a strip of alternately red and black trade cloth, six or eight inches wide and about eight feet long, attached by one of its longer edges to a wooden staff. Along the opposite edge of the cloth, the feathers of the raven, the hawk, the owl, the eagle and other birds of prey were strung by their quills at right angles to its length. Each man also carried a rawhide rattle and some arrows, but no bow. The chief carried a buffalo hide rattle and had a full raven skin on his head. Its wings were decorated with strips of porcupine quillwork, and a strip of red flannel hung from its beak like a tongue. He also wore a

106

Opposite: *Skin of a raven worn on the head by one of the leaders of the Blackfoot Raven Bearer society (AMNH).*

peculiar necklace made of imitation bear's claws carved from buffalo hooves or horn. He wore either a coyote skin or a large gray wolf skin, which was slit in the middle so that it slipped over his head and permitted the wolf's head to hang on his chest. Two other leaders were distinguished from the rank and file by their regalia: The staff of one was wrapped with black cloth and decorated with scalps and that of the other was painted red and decorated with eagle tail feathers like those of the regular members. The bearer of the black staff painted his face red and then covered it with white dots to represent the raven's excrement.[35]

To conduct their ceremony, the Raven Bearers sat down and planted their staffs upright in the ground before the group. The two leaders sat apart from the others. As a dance song was begun, all rose to their feet, took up their staffs and danced. They faced inward and held their staffs pointed upward and forward, all the while imitating the croaking of ravens. The leaders then turned about, and the others followed their example, dancing in the same manner while facing outward. Then they sat down. The singers, however, continued to sing, and after a short pause the dance was repeated. Again they sat while other songs were sung without dancing. The ritual was repeated for four days. To end each day's performance, the members would retire to their double society lodge and, seating themselves, once more thrust the staffs into the ground, leaving them there when they arose and went home. The ceremony of the Raven Bearers was last transferred to a younger group about 1874, although those who purchased it at that time were still performing their dance as late as 1890.[36]

The Dogs Society
The Dogs society organization was as follows:

Black-dog (1)	Old men comrades (2)
Assistant leader (1)	Single men comrades (3 to 4)
Black-dancers (2)	Pipe-keeper (1)[37]
Dogs (40)	

The identifying mark of the Dogs was their society sash. In the latter part of the nineteenth century, it consisted of a strip of red trade cloth about eight inches wide and seven feet long. It was adorned with four rows of eagle feathers sewn on in horizontal banks, had hair fringes and had a slit at the top through which the wearer could put his head. The sash trailed behind him as he walked and was hung in front of him when he sat. It was called "a dog rope." The Dogs also wore a close-fitting hood made from the smoke-blackened top of a tipi and covered with owl feathers. A tail which was lined with red cloth, covered with owl feathers and hung to approximately the middle of the wearer's back was attached to it. Their rattles consisted of rounded sticks covered with tanned deerskin and strung along one side with small dew claws or trade tin cones. The lay members painted themselves by first coating their faces with yellow and then scratching downward through the wet paint with their fingers slightly separated, thus producing vertical lines. The dance leader applied black paint in the same manner. He wore a black sash.[38]

During their ceremonies for a change of leadership, leader-to-be was seated at the right end of a curved line of members and his black "rope" was fastened to the ground either by an arrow or by a wooden

Opposite: Blackfoot Raven Bearer members, flag carrier on left and leader wearing raven on right.

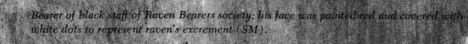

Bearer of black staff of Raven Bearers society; his face was painted red and covered with white dots to represent raven's excrement (SM).

picket pin driven through its lower end. Performances began with a repetition of the scouting songs, while the Dogs shook their rattles to mark time. This continued until the "black rope" leader-elect sent a messenger to call his most attractive wife. She came immediately, accompanied by as many relatives as possible bearing gifts. The wife and presents were given to the leader he was replacing, who then pulled up the stake and released him. The new leader then moved along the line, drawing his fellow members one by one to their feet, and dancing began. Although the dance-ritual pattern of the Dogs remained the same on all occasions, the giving away of the wife was done on only the first day of the four-day ceremony for transferring leadership. Also, other dances were only a day in length. The society sold its rights for the last time about 1860 and became obsolete a few years later.[39]

Until its demise, the members of the order were expected to show the type of bravery so typical of the sash-wearers of all the Plains tribes. They were to secure themselves by the sashes in any engagement wherein the war party or tribe's survival was in question. There they were to stand and fight until they either died or were victorious.

The Kit-fox Society

The Kit-fox society was one of the societies formed earliest by the Blackfoot. Wissler speaks of it as "an extinct Piegan society still regarded as very powerful and dangerous to speak of." [40] It originated in the dream of a man named Elk Tongue, who dreamed about a kit-fox while he was on a war expedition against the Shoshone Indians.

In his dream, the fox invited him into its den, where the chief of the foxes was seated with his mate beside him. On one side of the den were two straight lances wrapped with skins and fringed with feathers and on the other side were two curved lances wrapped with swan skin and adorned with feathers. The foxes showed Elk Tongue their dance and how to dress for it. He was told always to wear a fox skin on his back and to use it for his medicine. Before he left the den, he was directed to gather some of the young men and to form the society of Kit-foxes, instructing them how to dress and dance. If they would practice these things and kill foxes only to obtain the skins for medicine, they would benefit. However, it would mean very bad luck for them to harm a fox for any other reason.

Before Elk Tongue died, he passed the fox skin medicine on to his son, telling him the story of its origin and the secrets of the ceremony. After that, the power of the fox skin was handed down to other leaders over many years, and the members of the society kept the tradition by teaching their children never to harm a kit-fox.

According to Curtis, the Kit-fox society has not existed since the smallpox epidemic of 1841, when all the members except one died, and he "took his medicine to the Horn society." This explains the assertion of a Piegan who told Curtis that the Piegan Kit-fox society was the equivalent of the Horn society of the Bloods and the Blackfeet.[41] The Kit-fox society was unique in that the wives of members played a more important part in it than in the other orders, for they were practically members.

The lay members carried curved staffs wound with strips of otter skin. They wore otter skin anklets, plus the usual leggings, shirts and moccasins, and they painted their faces and bodies red. Their leader wore a headdress fashioned from the skin of a kit-fox. Four eagle tail

113

Opposite: *Regalia of Blackfoot Dog society member.* **Top**: *Rattle, sixteen inches long with tin cones; middle: Headdress of owl and hawk feathers; right: Sash of over-the-shoulder type with hawk and eagle feathers (AMNH).*

feathers were stuck up on top and one at the tip of the tail. The whole skin was daubed with red paint. Brass buttons formed the eyes of the fox. His body was painted red, and he had a blue band on each wrist and on his face. Another officer carried a ten-foot-long curved staff wrapped with strips of swan skin, from which all but the down feathers had been removed. It had four otter skin ties, and four pairs of eagle feathers were appended. Two other leaders carried bows and arrows in quivers made of mountain-lion skin. When the people were moving camp, the Kit-foxes sometimes rode in a body, with the officer bearing the swan skin staff crossing and recrossing in front of them.[42]

To purchase the songs and equipment of the Kit-foxes, the Dogs entered the double lodge where they were in session and gave each Fox member a filled pipe. When all had smoked, the Dogs returned to their tipis, gathered presents and, with the help of their wives, carried them to the Kit-fox lodge. The candidates, with their wives just behind them, sat in a row in front of the Kit-fox members, whose wives also sat behind them. The Kit-fox men painted the Dogs, who then moved back out of the way while the Kit-fox women painted the wives of the Dog society. Then the members filed out of the lodge and sat down in the usual incomplete ellipse. The initiates formed a concentric curve around the singers, the wives seated once again behind their husbands and the wives of the Kit-foxes seated behind the women each had painted. The candidates planted their staffs in the ground before them. The leader (or chief) sat in the middle of the curving line of members, and on each side of him was one of the two who carried the quiver made of mountain-lion skin. One song was sung, and as the second song began, they chewed a certain herb, spit on their hands, rose and made four pretended efforts to draw their staffs out of the ground. As the song ended, they pulled them out and began to dance while a third song was started.[43] Curtis states that four nights were spent dancing in this fashion in the double lodge, "but there were no rites for the daytime." [44] However, McClintock's report differs, declaring that for four days and four nights they sat inside their double lodge, painting and dressing themselves, singing and making ready, appearing outside their dance-lodge only at night, "but on the fifth day they came out and marched through the camp."

On this occasion the leader wore a fox skin cap with the fox head in front, the ears left on top and the rest of the skin hanging down the back, with small bells attached to the tail. He carried a bow and arrows, which were painted green; his body was painted red and his face was painted green, "all to look as frightful as possible and make people afraid." [45]

The second officer in rank was called the White-Circle Man. He carried a spectacular, long, curved lance, which was wrapped with white swan skin and had white eagle feathers attached at intervals along its length. The next officer in rank carried a curved lance that was wrapped with otter skin and had black and red feathers appended to it. All the other members carried straight lances decorated with feathers with lance points at one end and also small pipes that were painted red. All painted their faces and wore eagle feathers at the backs of their heads. Wide bands of otter skin with small bells attached were worn on the legs.

In their marches through the camp, the society formed themselves

Opposite: *Blackfoot society regalia.* Left: *Holy offerings of Horn and Ma'toki societies left on dance field (notice that fur has been stripped from hooked staffs)*; middle: *Flag of Raven Bearer society*; right: *Hooked staff of Kit-fox society* (AMNH).

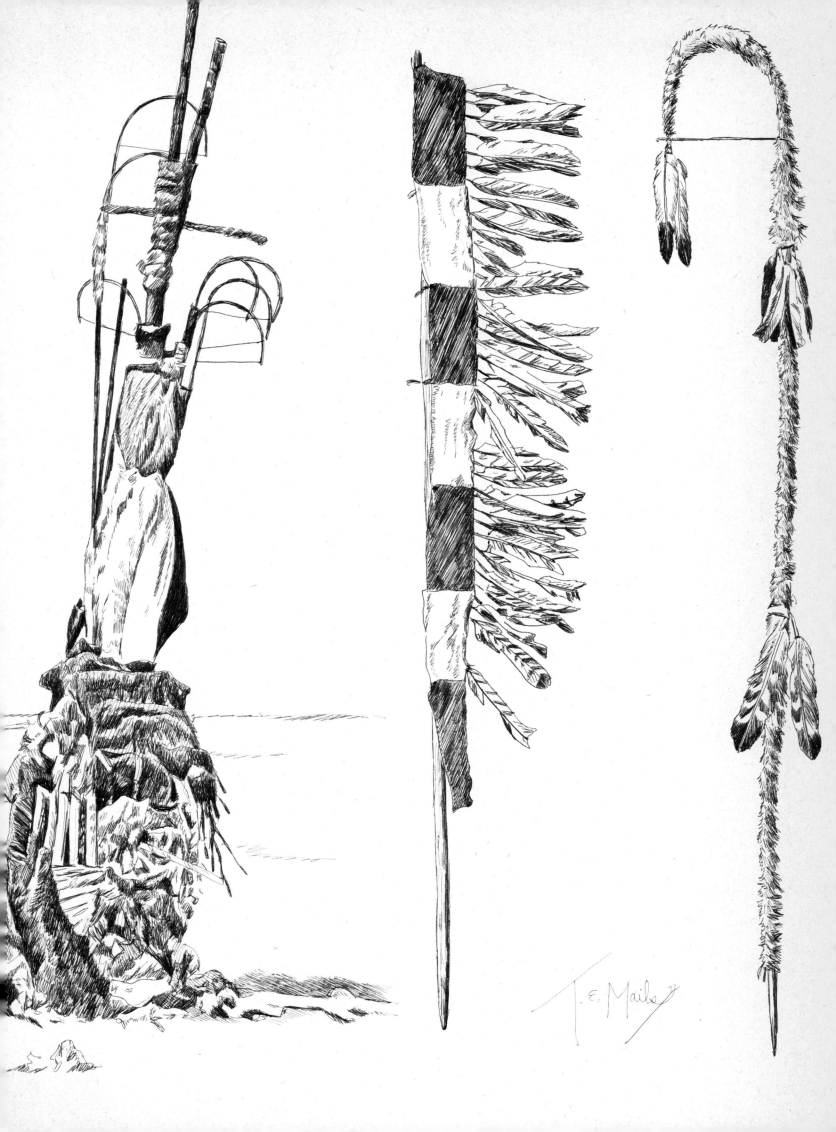

in the shape of a fox head. The chief represented the nose. The second and third men were the eyes and the other members completed the head of the fox.

To begin their dance, they sat in lines, with the regular members in the first line. If any were withdrawing from the society or giving up their lances to new members, they sat in the second line, with all the wives of the members behind them. When the drumming began, their leaders danced first and the other officers followed. After them came the other members carrying their lances. Since kit-foxes run together, the men danced in pairs, making short, even jumps with feet close together, all the while imitating the movements of a fox, barking and darting about, first in one direction, then in another. The two officer assistants danced between the lines, barking and swinging their curved lances. They never moved in a straight line because a fox never does. By this means, the fox either eludes his pursuers or throws his prey off guard. So, too, they fought this way in a battle in the belief that it would bring the success a fox had in capturing his intended victim.

To conclude each segment of the ceremony, the leader would shout, "It is enough." The dancing would then cease and the members return to their seats. After a short rest they would begin again, repeating the same dance until the usual sacred series of four had been finished.

The Black Soldiers Society (Bloods)

Like most of the societies, the Black Soldiers originated in the dream of a Blackfoot man. For regalia, each member wore a narrow headband made of wolf skin with an upright tail feather attached to each side of it, plus wolf skin anklets and wristbands. His entire body was painted red, and wide black bands were drawn across the forehead and the chin. Two vertical black lines representing wolf's teeth were painted on the cheeks. Each man carried a long staff with a lance point at one end. It was painted red, and wolf skin strips were appended to it at intervals. In addition, the leader wore a wolf skin draped across his shoulders, and he carried a flat wooden club, which was beveled at the head end and had a single feather attached.[46]

In performing their ceremony, the Black Soldiers grouped themselves in a round mass and turned slowly in a circle, with the leader placed outside the others and proceeding in the opposite direction. The members shook their lances in a threatening manner, moving with high, awkward steps and barking like wolves at the completion of each song.

This society often served as camp police during the large annual encampments, and they were noted for their severe treatment of members who failed in their responsibilities to the order. For example, if a member were absent from a ceremony, the rest danced four times, making stabbing motions with their lances in the direction of his tipi. Then they mounted an attack upon it and cut to pieces everything that belonged to him—tipi, clothing and whatever else was there. As in other instances of discipline, this kind of treatment is astonishing to those cultures not subject to such stringent rules or expectations. However, it becomes immediately understandable when one considers that the Plains tribes lived in circumstances that de-

116

Opposite: *Member of Blood Black Soldier society wearing wolf skin headband and carrying society club (SM).*

manded unity and sacrifices for the good and longevity of all. The Black Soldiers achieved their best results as camp police by setting an example among themselves, and the people understood that the orders of the group were not to be taken lightly.

If the Black Soldiers had cautioned the people against leaving camp during dangerous times or when a buffalo hunt was about to be held, they immediately pursued anyone who disobeyed, and if he were caught, they cut up his clothing and other possessions. In one of the unusual exceptions of Indian law, however, if the pursued had fought from an entrenchment during a battle and was now surrounded by Black Soldiers, he could dismount and draw a circular line on the ground around himself. Once he had done this, no one could enter the symbolic entrenchment save a warrior who had performed a similar feat in battle. Even then, if such a one were present and came to the attack, the besieged had only to roll his blanket into a bundle and toss it to his opponent. If he did this, the Black Soldiers would simply withdraw without molesting him in any way. In another exception, the pursued could take refuge in a stream or lake, since wolves, which the Black Soldiers represented, detested water. In such instances, no one could come after him except a warrior who had performed the rare feat of having killed an enemy in the water. Again, if the pursued escaped into a tipi, only one who had entered a tipi to kill an enemy or to capture war prizes could follow him, and even in this instance the soldier could only take and destroy the man's blanket.[47]

Hence, while elderly informants invariably reported with great positiveness that the "soldiers would cut everything—tipi, clothing, medicine-robe, anything," [48] closer questioning revealed that eyewitnesses were able to recall only a single instance when anything of the kind had happened to persons other than members of the society. On this occasion a Soldier who had once entered an enemy lodge followed a fugitive into a tipi, brought out his blanket and tossed it to his companions, who then cut it up. The pursued himself was still not molested in any way. However, the Black Soldiers were seen flinging a member into the water because he had failed to attend a society meeting, and they were frequently observed in the process of destroying the tipi and personal effects of negligent members. Curtis believes that "in view of the various means provided for the escape of non-members and the frequency of punishment meted out to members, it appears that these latter occasions were deliberately arranged for the purpose of impressing the populace." But the informants have vigorously denied that this was the case. When they were asked to explain how any member could be such a fool as to risk the loss of so much property that was both valuable and difficult to replace, they replied that sometimes a man did not want to dance and deliberately absented himself out of personal pique. "An Indian whose feelings have been injured, whose pride has been assaulted, takes little account of consequences." [49]

The Black Soldier society ceased to exist soon after the Royal Canadian Mounted Police issued an order that the Black Soldiers were no longer to have the right of punishment. They continued to hold their annual dance for a short period after that but terminated all activities about 1890.

118

Opposite: Blackfoot warrior in typical dress of lay members of many societies, wearing painted shirt and beaded hair bows and carrying pipe and shield (SM).

The Soldier Society

The Soldier society was something of an enigma in the society scheme, for while it performed a kind of policing activity, it was primarily a healing order and not a military unit as such. Indeed, its role was unique, for it appears also to have served as an instrument of fulfillment in the performance of a warrior's vows. Informants have explained that the Soldier society functioned in some ways like the Black Soldiers, yet the members were even more severe in their disciplinary proceedings, going so far as to strike their victims with clubs and axes to maintain order.

The emblems of the society were kept in a bundle. These included pointed yellow punishment sticks hung with calves' hooves and a calf tail taken from a yellow-colored buffalo, a long pipe and a bow and arrows. When the members pursued a disobedient tribesman, they carried the sticks and used them to strike him. When the order danced, the society leader and an assistant were keepers of the pipe, and another warrior and his assistant were in charge of the bow and arrows. Each member carried one of the punishment sticks, holding it in front of himself and moving it up and down in a pumping motion of supplication to draw the healing powers of God down to earth.[50]

The healing aspect of the society is revealed in its general practices. A man could join the Soldiers and by so doing might obtain supernatural assistance in his own or a relative's recovery from illness. He joined by purchasing one of the sticks from a member, or he could take technical possession of the bundle or any part of it by paying a heavy price to the leader.[51]

The Blackfoot people learned to be cautious about absenting themselves from the Soldier society summer dances. Usually they completed their tasks early in the morning so that when the Soldiers began their dance unexpectedly, as the order always did, they would not be caught away from camp and later be punished for it.[52]

Sometimes a member of a wealthy family would publicly vow that if he recovered from sickness, he would permit the Soldiers to destroy his personal clothing as a sacrifice of thanksgiving. The following summer, when the Soldiers were dancing, he would dress in his best clothing, put his finest blanket on his horse and stand with the horse near the dancers. After the fourth dance, the Soldiers would rush upon him and pretend to tear his garments from him, apparently utterly destroying these and the horse blanket. Having done this, they would run about wildly, threatening the properly astonished spectators with their sticks and pretending that they were cutting the clothing of various men. Some Blackfoot informants gave investigators the impression that the Soldiers literally ruined the clothing of their victims. Under questioning, however, they admitted that they had never seen anyone truly abused in such a way. They had seen the Soldiers take hold of a man and rough him up a bit, swinging him into the air and pulling at his shirt, but without really damaging it. They also reported having seen two young men who had made the sacrifice-vow set upon by the Soldiers, who did not cut but tore their blankets down the middle and ripped their shirts without actually tearing them off. Curtis tells us that the same means of escape was provided for fugitives from the Soldiers as was available to those fleeing from the Black Soldiers.[53]

Again, while the societies were often said to destroy property in

120

a purely wanton manner, the truth indicates that something less occurred in most instances. A flagrant violation of the tribe's unwritten
codes was quickly and severely dealt with, but this was the exception
rather than the rule, for the people were too intelligent to do otherwise. After all, homes and apparel were not easily replaced, and care-
less destruction could work severe hardships on a family. The societies
did as much as was necessary for the well-being of the individual
villages and tribe. Otherwise, the punishment was symbolic rather
than real, a method of training rather than a torment.

The Bulls Society

The society of Bulls was not a part of the series of organizations known
as the All Comrades. It was an independent company of older men
who banded together without regard to their previous affiliation with
the various societies of the All Comrades. It was formed about 1820
by a man who, while hunting in the mountains, had had a dream in
which he saw a certain kind of dance. On his return he fashioned the
necessary insignia, sold it to a number of old men and instructed
them in the songs and dance.[54]

Some of the members wore the unique Blackfoot style of upright
warbonnet, which consisted of a broad headband covered with ermine
or other material from which the feathers stood straight up. Others
wore the conventional type of warbonnet with a tail of feathers attached, representing the backbone of the buffalo. Still others wore
horn bonnets formed of the scalp skin of the buffalo with the horns
still attached, although the horns were shortened by cutting off the
base. All members of the order wore buffalo robes with the hair side
exposed. These were painted with white earth in spots to represent
mud. Two of the men wearing the horned caps used robes made of
the rough skins of aged bulls; these were known as Scabby Bulls. The
leader wore a headband of straight-up eagle feathers to which a small
arrow shaft, without a point, was attached in such a manner that it
lay straight across his forehead. From the arrow, pieces of weasel
skin were hung like fringe to about the level of the eyes, and at each
end of the shaft was an eagle down-feather dyed red.[55]

When the Bulls were ready to dance, an announcement of this
fact was made to the people, whereupon everyone except the Bulls
then moved about a mile way. The Bulls remained behind in their
lodges, which were located by a lake or stream. After dressing and
painting, they lay in random order near the water with their robes
drawn over their shoulders, as buffalo lie. The two Scabby Bulls lay
on the ground behind the rest of the "herd." A distinguished young
man, previously appointed by the leader to the duty of "driving in
the buffalo," rode up, dismounted at a distance, approached cau-
tiously and threw a stone into the water. At this, the Bulls leaped to
their feet as if frightened but in a moment lay down again. Then the
young herder gathered a number of buffalo chips, lighted them and
placed them in the water so that they floated along with their smoke
drifting toward the Bulls, who now began to show signs of uneasiness
and fright over the strange scent. Still they stayed where they were.

Finally the herder mounted his horse and rode near, shouting at
the top of his voice. Then the Bulls rose to their feet and began to
move away, mimicking as they did so the actions of uneasy buffalo.
The driver rode from side to side to keep them in a compact herd, not

Blackfoot society regalia. Above: Headdress worn in Bull society; left: Otter-skin cap with quill-wrapped feathers and four pieces of tree fungus growth attached; right: Leader's straight-up warbonnet with weasel tail fringe and an arrow placed straight across the front. It was called "the bonnet which was struck by an arrow"; after Bull society was discontinued, it was used a great deal in war. Below left: Headdress used by Horn society, with arrow sticking straight out in front; below right: Staffs carried by Horns—a yellow-painted flag about seven feet long and a hooked staff borne by mounted members (after drawings by Blackfoot informant, AMNH).

moving too rapidly lest they stampede, and finally brought them to the camp, exactly as a herd of real animals was moved into the funneling heaps of stones that led to a buffalo-jump. As they reached the camp, the youth rode in front of them and led the way to the place in its center where the dance was to occur. Now the people surrounded the "buffalo," and the herder recounted four of his coups, giving a present to a needy old person as each was related. After this he reported where he had found the buffalo and how he had driven them in. Squatting on the ground under their robes, the Bulls now began to sing their four songs, and when at last the dance-song was reached, they arose and danced, imitating again the movements of buffalo.[56]

The society had only a brief span of life, for the Bulls gave their last performance of the drama of driving the buffalo herd about 1842. On that occasion an elderly member named Fox Louse fell as they moved toward the camp. He regained his feet and followed the others but died a short time later. This caused the deeply religious men to regard the dance of the Bulls with suspicion, and it was never repeated. In retrospect it can be seen as a primarily religious group whose function was buffalo calling, in order to ensure the availability of the animals for the many purposes to which they were put.[57]

The Tail Society

According to Wissler, the organization of the Tails was as follows:

Leaders (2)	Pipe-keeper (1)
Front-tails (x)	Drummers (4)
Old men comrades (?)	Women members (?)[58]
Single men comrades (?)	

Curtis states that the Bulls and the Tails originated when a woman was carried away from her camp by a buffalo to a buffalo village. There were two society lodges at the village, and the buffalo, after removing their coats, were "just like humans." Here her captor made her his wife and revealed to her all the secrets of the societies. She remained there about a year, and being instructed to return and tell her people about this, she came home and introduced the two orders.[59]

Another and more detailed account reports that the Tail society originated in the earliest days of the Blackfoot nations. Its source was a tribal myth in which a woman whose people were starving found a talking buffalo stone. By following its instructions regarding certain rituals and songs, a buffalo herd was "called" to the camp and the famine was ended. The woman also learned how to plan and execute the first buffalo piskun and jump and imparted this valuable knowledge to the tribe. Heaps of brush and rocks were to be placed at intervals to form two long lines funneling in a V shape toward a corral in the case of the piskun and toward the edge of a fifteen- to twenty-foot-high cliff for the jump, sometimes called "a buffalo fall." The buffalo herds were to be driven into the funnel's mouth and then goaded down its length by people hiding behind the rock heaps. They were to jump up as the herd passed them, shouting and waving buffalo robes until at last the terrified animals were swept into the corral or over the cliff and fell to the ground below. Some would be killed outright by the fall, and those that survived were dispatched with arrows, clubs or knives.[60]

Considering the nature of the myth, it is doubtful that the Tails

were ever a purely military society, and the lack of details available regarding regalia tends to bear this out. It may have been an important buffalo-calling society, whose spiritual dances were employed at specific times each year to "call" the buffalo close to the camps and thus to ensure an adequate food supply for the people. Its last ceremony took place in 1874, two years before the Custer battle and ten years before the buffalo herds were entirely eliminated in the northern Plains.

The leaders of the order wore buffalo horn headdresses and belts with buffalo tails attached to the backs. A regular member of the Tails wore moccasins, leggings, a shirt, otter skin legbands decorated with quills and bells, a broad belt with a buffalo tail attached to the back of it and horizontally in his hair an eagle tail-feather trimmed with quills and small bells. The belts were the chief regalia from which they took their name. An appendage on the right side was formed by wrapping a seven-inch stick with the skins of two buffalo tails. This was bound around the middle with red cloth and had white and blue beading. A fringe of buckskin, weasel fur, red cloth and bells was added. The ends of the sash hung down on the left side. The members' faces were painted yellow, with horizontal stripes of red across the eyes and mouth. Bodies were black with lines drawn through the paint. White dots were placed on the face and joints.[61]

To begin their ceremony the members sat in the ellipse formation characteristic of all the Blackfoot societies. The singers chanted a praying song, and as the first dance-song was begun, the other members rose to their feet. They remained facing in with one foot slightly advanced and, in imitation of buffalo calves, threw the weight of their bodies back and forth from one foot to the other without lifting their feet from the ground. Then they turned outward and duplicated the shifting action, then back to the original position at the beginning of the repetition of the song. After four such changes the dancers sat down. A brief pause separated the second dance-song from the first. The second time the Tails rose and danced in a double column, the men standing shoulder to shoulder and in this manner circling round a group of singers until they returned to their original positions. Now they turned about and danced backward but in the same direction as before. The two movements were repeated, and following another pause the same song and dance were used again four times. Pauses and dances were duplicated until they had been performed sixteen times in all and the dancers had passed sixteen times around their group of singers.[62] The members then retired to their respective lodges, fully satisfied that the Creator would respond by blessing their people with an adequate supply of buffalo for the time being.

The supernatural buffalo stone, which had in truth "found" the woman—as the One above always does those who need Him and seek Him—was a most unusual kind of rock, for its shape was remarkably like that of a buffalo. Several of these stones were "discovered" by members of the different Blackfoot tribes over the years, and each stone was greatly venerated thereafter as a special messenger or servant of God, to be used in calling ceremonies. Informants say that most were found in riverbeds, although they are less smooth than one might expect coming from that source. Once discovered, a stone was rubbed with sacred red paint and placed in a medicine bundle. Its owner undoubtedly joined the Tail society at that time if an earlier dream or vision had not already led him to become a member.

125

Opposite left: *Regalia and paint of Blackfoot Front Tail society member;* right: *Sketch of Front Tail and dancing order of society (after drawings by Blackfoot informants, AMNH).*

The Ugly Horn, or Bad-Horn or Blackfeet, Society

The Ugly Horn society passed out of existence before mid-nineteenth century, and little is known of its actual practices and makeup. It too began with the dream of a Blackfoot warrior, who apparently was concerned about the matter of proper child-rearing. It had two leaders who wore fringed leggings, a fringed, ill-fitting garment shaped like a woman's dress and fringed moccasins, all of which were made from a smoke-blackened tipi cover. Joined to the dress with thongs was a large, loose-fitting head hood. This was fringed at the bottom and provided with white-ringed circular holes for the eyes and mouth. It also had two large, earlike flaps at its sides, and these were the "ugly horns" from which the society took its name. Each leader possessed a wooden staff that was wrapped with blackened tipi cover material. Along one side of the staff were hung a number of buffalo hooves that served as rattles. The lay members wore breechclouts, moccasins and a broad headband made from a black tipi cover or any skin they preferred. A feather was inserted in the band at each side. Their bodies were painted whatever color they desired.

During their annual summer dance the leaders went about the camp in their awesome outfits, frightening children into good behavior.[63] Their function was similar to that of the Hopi Ogre Kachina, who comes once a year and threatens to carry the children away to the San Francisco peaks unless they remain obedient to their parents. In each instance the parent intercedes to request another year's good grace because of the child's apparent capabilities as a son or daughter. In effect, the occasion cements the bond between parent and child and fosters a sense of responsibility on the part of each.

The Catcher Society

Wissler's list for the organization of the Catchers is as follows:

Leaders (2)	Catchers (x)
Pipe men (2)	Drummers (4)
Tomahawk men (2)	Women members (x)[64]

This society existed among only the Piegans and was the next grade above the Kit-foxes. Each Catcher carried a round, red-painted club of cherry wood about thirty inches long and two and a half inches in diameter, to the lower end of which were attached a dangling tail feather of the hawk or eagle and a buffalo hoof for a rattle. An eagle feather, with a bit of otter skin attached to it, was thrust at an angle through the hair at the back of the head. The members' war shirts were painted red. In addition to the clubs, two officers carried ash pipestems about thirty inches long decorated with eagle downfeathers; and two others carried a quiver filled with arrows. Two young men chosen to be the order's messengers were keepers of tomahawk-pipes.[65] Prince Maximilian, who explored the Plains in the early 1800s, says each carried a wooden club with hooves of the buffalo cow hanging from the handle.[66] They also wore buffalo robes like capes, with a large beaded cross in the middle.

When they were ready to become Catchers, the Kit-foxes took possession of the two largest lodges they could find and pitched them as a double lodge in the center of the camp-circle. The Catchers and the Dogs assembled in the lodge, and one of the Dogs gave a pipe to each

126

Opposite: Blackfeet Ugly Horn Society member. **Top right:** *Depiction of hood based on description set forth in text. Full figure is taken from old photograph and shows a different style of hood with a single huge buffalo horn mounted on the front. The society staff is thrust into the ground at the member's right side.*

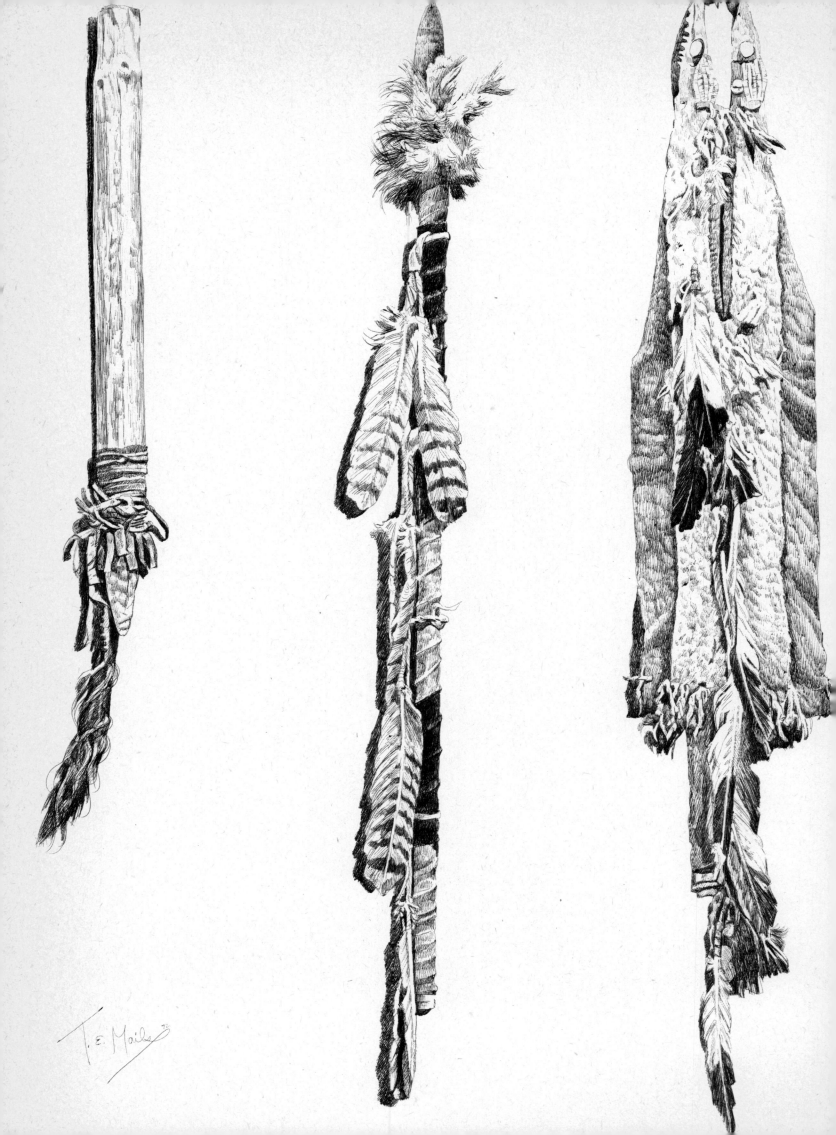

Catcher. After the smoke, the Dog was painted by the Catcher. Once instruction in songs and dancing had been given, all filed outside and sat down in the usual ellipse formation. The new members rose to their feet and danced four times facing inward, then outward, then inward and outward again. As the fourth dance ended, the spectators hurriedly scattered, for if anyone were caught by a Catcher, his robe might be torn to pieces. For night meetings the society assembled in the double lodge in response to an invitation to a feast by one of the several women belonging to the order. There they sang and danced. The usual four days and four nights were given over to the ceremonies that attended the purchase of the society's regalia and songs, but on other occasions their dance was finished in a day. The last transfer ceremony took place about 1850, when the Piegans sold their rights to a party of Bloods. Shortly thereafter the Catcher society passed from view. But the pipes were still cared for and rituals occasionally demonstrated.[67]

The Horn Society (Bloods)

The Horn society was a religious cult rather than an age society. Its members were older warriors whose achievements had given them a standing of religious veneration. People believed that they had the power to cause death if they wished, and they were feared because of it.[68]

Two leaders wore shirts and leggings trimmed with eagle tails and bonnets with horns and tails. One of these had a small arrow sticking straight out in front. He was the leader for all the society dances.

In the club's earliest days the two members next in rank wore buffalo horn headdresses with a large horn mounted on the front or with a front and two side horns. Later, these same members wore a spectacular bonnet whose cap was covered with white ermine and hung with rows of long, rolled ermine tails as side pendants. Contrary to the usual Plains bonnet, which had a circle of feathers, the Horn headdress had a single row of tail feathers running over the top of the cap to represent the buffalo's back. Horsehair tips were added in cascades to the feathers, a red plume feather was placed at the front of the row and a rectangular piece of trade cloth finished off the back. Curtis states that the "weasel-tails were arranged in imitation of horns," but examples of the bonnet do not support his contention.[69] One lower officer wore a shirt, leggings and a cap made of swan skin. He carried a seven-foot staff, painted yellow and sharpened at one end. A strip of flannel in sections of black and white was attached to the staff. Each of two mounted men wore four owl feathers in his hair and carried a hooked lance about eight feet long. One lance was wrapped with otter skin and the other with white swan skin.

Membership applications began with a vow made during illness. Later the pledger visited any Horn member, saying that he was sick and had made a promise that if he were healed, he would take the man's place. The other's regalia, which included a headdress, moccasins, leggings, a robe, paint, sweetgrass incense, a pipe and a staff that was curved at the upper end, wrapped with otter fur or swan skin and dangled feathers from its shaft and crook, was purchased with proper ritual for a number of horses. The new member took immediate possession and participated in the next meeting of the Horns. He and his predecessor avoided meeting for a time thereafter, and the displaced member was not allowed to watch him dance. The reason for

Opposite: Blackfoot society regalia. Left: Wooden emblem of Catcher society; middle: Short lance carried by leader of Braves society; right: War sash of dog skin mounted on red flannel and decorated with feathers, strips of weasel skin, bells, beaded disks and quill-wrapped strips of buffalo hide (AMNH).

this was that the first time they met officially, the seller had to be paid a suitable sum, which took time to accumulate. Once this was done, they were known as "friends."

All Horn members were supposed always to tell the truth, and when a man joined the order, he was required to smoke the Horn pipe as a pledge of future right-living. Each Horn member possessed such a pipe and smoked it at ceremonies thereafter. It was a short pipe with a stone head, to which the braid of the sweetgrass mentioned earlier was tied. This pipe was a central object in the elaborate transfer-of-membership ceremony.[70]

In 1925, there were still fifty active members of the order. Women participated in the ceremonies, but informants would not explain what they did. The provision that a membership could be acquired only by displacing another member meant that the total number of members never grew larger.

As with all deeply religious societies, the Horns evolved a detailed and ritualistic scheme of life and teachings to which every member subscribed. Among these were to love all and speak evil of none; to strike none in the tribe lest he be killed; never to strike the head of an animal in butchering it, for that might react like a blow on the striker's own skull, causing headache and perhaps death. In smoking they were not to tamp the burning tobacco with their finger, for that might make their eyes sore; no one was to break an animal's spine, for that would cause lameness in one's own back; no one was to pass before a Horn while he was smoking lest the member's eyes become sore; no one was ever to burn the hair of a human being or a beast in the fire of the tipi lest it cause dizziness and insanity; in the lodge, they were not to stir cooking food with a knife lest their teeth loosen and fall out; they were not to eat waterfowl, for it might cause a sore face; they were not to burn feathers in their tipi, because that could cause catastrophe.[71]

Because of its members' exemplary life, the Horn society was charged with the duty of selecting, bringing in and raising the important center pole for the Sun Dance lodge. In cutting the tree, they always prayed that it would fall straight and that the crotch would not be broken. And, as if to show the truth of their relationship with God, no such calamity ever occurred during their years of service. The Horns observed their sacred ceremonies in the summer when the berries were ripe, always erecting a large lodge in the very center of the

131

Opposite: *Blackfoot Horn society member wearing splendid ermine bonnet of Horns, carrying Horn transfer ceremony pipe and standing in front of painted Horn double lodge* (*Artifacts from AMNH*). Above: *Double lodge of Blackfoot Horn society* (*SM*).

camp, and the members usually slept there. As soon as the sun pole was raised, they took down their lodge and at that time became the masters, or leaders, of the ceremony.[72]

The Horn dance was an imitation of the actions of buffalo calves; its performance was the action that transmitted the healing from God to those who then were healed and kept their vows thereafter by joining the society. According to informants, the Horn society was founded by a women's society named the *Ma'toki,* which means "Buffalo Cows," a religious cult of women comparable to the Horns,[73] who danced once a year at the time of the Sun Dance. Like the Horns and other societies, memberships in the Buffalo Cows were transferred in a four-day ceremony. Certain male members of this organization were called Scabby Bulls.

As usual, the Blackfoots had a detailed myth pertaining to the origin of the Horns. It related how a man married a Buffalo Cow who ran away and rejoined her herd. Later the cow became a human being and her buffalo-calf son became a boy, whereupon they returned home and the young man founded the Horn society to perpetuate the dance of the buffalo calves.

Four Scabby Bulls wore bonnets with horns and robes of cow skin, hair side out. Others wore feather bonnets covered with soft bird feathers. The leader wore a snake bonnet, made from a tube-shaped hide headband. It was painted yellow with a zigzag line beaded on it. A branch of plumes extended at each side.

The Bear Cult

The Bear society was founded by a young man who was said to have "lived among the Bears." Two of its members, called Bear Braves, wore bear-skin sashes, to which were appended ornaments of bear claws and eagle tail-feathers. Pieces of bear skin were placed at the sides of the head to represent ears, and two black lines were drawn downward from the eyes to represent the bear's teeth. The result was a beautiful creation. There were four leaders, who were called White Braves. Each of these carried a bone whistle and a short lance, which had a broad steel knife mounted on a wooden staff. Owl feathers were tied to the shaft immediately below the point, and eagle tail feathers were tied at the butt end. Two members were known as One Black Bags, and they carried pemmican bags. All the others were called Red Braves. Each Red Brave had a knife lashed to a staff, which itself was wrapped with red trade cloth. The White Braves carried staffs that were tied in four places with strips of swan skin. All the staffs were straight and pointed so that they could be planted in the ground. Each Bear Brave possessed two arrows, one pointed and the other having bear hair tied at one end and covered with sinew.[74]

In giving a public performance, the society members made four circular motions with the pointed arrows in the direction of the clockwise movement of the sun and then shot the other arrows high into the air. Anyone who was hit as the arrows fell would become a Bear member. To begin the dance, the Bears sat on the east side of the ellipse, the White Braves on the south and all the others facing the Bear Braves. The Red Braves and the Black Bags planted their staffs in the ground, while the White Braves implanted short, forked sticks, on which their spears rested at an angle. All the Bears sat with bowed heads, their bodies covered with buffalo robes the hair sides of which were turned in.

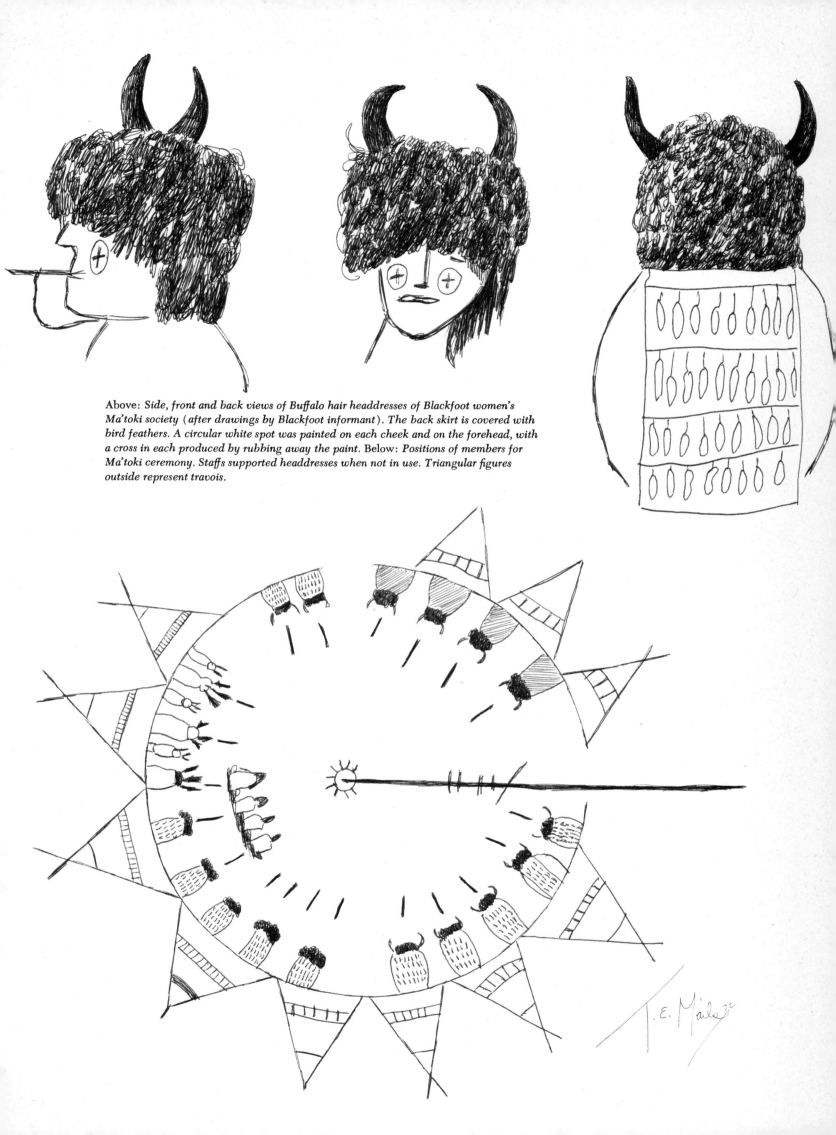

Above: Side, front and back views of Buffalo hair headdresses of Blackfoot women's Ma'toki society (after drawings by Blackfoot informant). The back skirt is covered with bird feathers. A circular white spot was painted on each cheek and on the forehead, with a cross in each produced by rubbing away the paint. Below: Positions of members for Ma'toki ceremony. Staffs supported headdresses when not in use. Triangular figures outside represent travois.

When the singing started, young male spectators ran around the group and pelted the Bears with dry horse dung. At this the Bears dropped their robes and sprang to their knees like angry bears, holding their hands beside their ears and growling ominously. Then they sat down again and covered themselves with the buffalo robes. Now the boys assaulted them again, and they jumped up, took their bows and arrows and danced single file in a circle. Following this, the White Braves rose and danced in their places, blowing their bone whistles. Now everyone else danced in their places while the Bear Braves moved vigorously to the left, passing the White Braves and proceeding out in front of the main body, at the same time pretending to shoot their arrows at the feet of the Red Braves and Black Bags, thus forcing them back. Then the White Braves danced forward in such a way so as to pass behind the main body and to force it forward to the original position from which it had retreated before the threats of the Bears. When the Bear Braves reached their own original positions, they shot their arrows into the air and sat down.

_ A pile of food was placed in the center of the dance circle, but no one could eat before the Bears had given the signal. This was done when the Bears rushed upon the Black Bags, seized their pemmican and returned to their seats to devour it greedily. Then they circulated among the members and the spectators and distributed food to everyone. Tradition allowed a member's relative to come and dance beside him, after which the relative had to give something away.[75]

According to Curtis, this cult was still active in 1925. Its purpose, of course, was the gathering and dissemination of bear power from above. The bear was a great healing agent, and Bear members usually possessed healing abilities.

Differing somewhat with Curtis, John C. Ewers states that "the nineteenth-century Blackfeet appeared to lack any Bear Cult group organization." [76] He did discover evidences of cult paraphernalia and certain ceremonial functions similar to those of the Assiniboine Bear cults spread among the Pigeons, Braves and All Brave Dogs societies. The Blackfoot tribes possessed several bear-knife bundles, and their owners carried these to war to be employed in battle. The bear knife was a splendid creation, usually of the stabber type with a huge, broad, double-edged blade and with either a large flat wooden handle or one made from a bear's jaw with the teeth remaining. The bundles were subject to purchase and were passed on with traditional ceremonies. Bear power for healing and war was transferred with the knife bundle, and the owner was required to paint the buyer's face red, making scratch marks on his cheeks by drawing the fingers through the wet paint. Black lines were then added to represent the bear's teeth. Wissler claimed that the Bears also gave the purchaser a bear lance and two tipis painted with bear designs.[77]

Blackfoot Bear cult members wore the unique bear shirt that was perforated with either round or diamond-shaped holes and had cut-fringe edges. The Blackfoot shirt did not have a flap at the front like that of the Assiniboines, but the outfit of a Bear member of the Braves society included a robe with a flap cut in it. Several McClintock photographs picture men wearing the perforated Bear shirt so that its details can be plainly seen.

The Tobacco Society
Like the Crows, the Blackfoots had a sacred Tobacco society and a

Opposite: *Member of Blackfoot Ma'toki, or Buffalo Women, society—for comparison with drawings by Blackfoot informants of the society (SM).*

keeper of its important Beaver medicine bundle. The Blackfoots believed that tobacco was given to them at the same time as the Beaver bundle by the chief of the Beavers. The seeds themselves were sacred because they came from the "Dwarf People," who looked after the crops of tobacco. All year long the Blackfoot families sought to keep the little dwarfs in good humor by giving them presents of clothing and food, which were left outside the tipi with a prayer to the Dwarf People to look after the tobacco crop.

In May of each year the tribe established a temporary camp near the site selected for the tobacco garden. For this purpose the Blackfoots always chose an isolated place near a stream or river where the land was fertile. The Beaver ceremony was performed in the spring when the tobacco seeds were planted, because that was the time when beavers were accustomed to leaving their winter dens. A large double lodge was erected some distance from the main camp, and the members of the Tobacco society were called upon to assemble there about dusk. The entire population attended the ceremony, for it was considered most unlucky to be absent. With great ceremony, the custodian's wife opened the bundle, removed its otter skin and tied it to a long pole, which she then leaned against the outer tipi wall so that the skin hung down from the peak like a pennant. After this the members danced, each holding a stick, the crooked root-end of which was encased in a small moccasin. These sticks were not kept from year to year but were prepared anew each season and left standing after the ceremony like sentinels overlooking the tobacco garden. The ritual continued through the night, and just before dawn the tired people

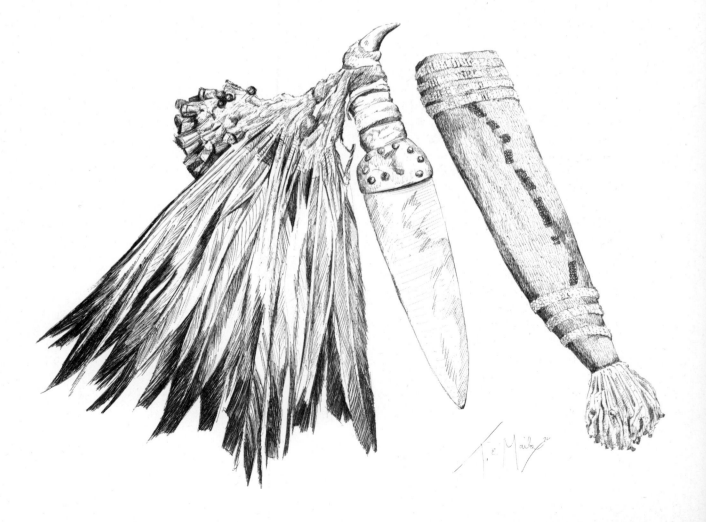

136

Opposite: *The Blackfoot bear knife. It has a double-edged blade and a wooden handle with a section of bear's jaw and teeth attached, plus a pendant of feathers and bells. The hide case is dyed red and has seven bands of blue beads wrapped around it* (Whitney Gallery of Western Art, Cody, Wyoming). Above: *Blackfoot Bear brave standing near Bear lodge of the Bloods* (SM).

feasted. Outside the lodge was a group of young men dressed in their finest clothing, each bearing a long pole to which, near the pointed end, was attached an important article, such as a feather headdress or a medicine object. At the words "Come, wet your sticks!" each one in turn thrust the pointed end of his pole through the doorway. The society members stuck pieces of meat on the poles, after which the youths withdrew them and feasted in a symbolic sharing of all things with the peoples of the Blackfoot nation.[78]

Then everyone slept. Later in the day the entire society membership, with most of the camp following, went to the place where the tobacco was to be planted. The custodian of the bundle led the parade, walking slowly, singing and praying for a bumper crop of the tobacco so necessary for ceremonies. He carried with him a whole beaver skin, a beaver skin headdress and some sticks. Arriving at the chosen location, he placed some sticks on the ground and prayed that the people would have good luck and not cause an uncontrollable grass fire in preparing the garden. Touching a match to some punk, he then lighted a bunch of dry grass and started a fire. The others formed a line about the rectangular space and prepared to stamp out the flames at the plot's edge. When the plot was burned off, all returned to their lodges and slept again.[79]

Later, tobacco seed, chokeberries, serviceberries and the dung of buffalo, elk and deer were placed in a rawhide bag filled with water and allowed to soak. That night was spent in singing and dancing and mixing the seed. Early in the morning, the members marched to the plot and readied the ground for planting. The bearer of the mixed bag of seed and fertilizer placed it on the ground; then the custodian of the Beaver bundle held it up to God and prayed to the man who first acquired the sacred bundle in ancient times from Beaver Old Man, pleading for good luck with the seed. While singing, praying and burning sweetgrass as incense, he made a number of holes in a line with a stick, and when he had finished the song, he bade the others do the same. Each society member planted his own strip in the plot and placed an identifying stake at each end of his row. Finally the custodian called for the children to run back and forth across the plot. It gave them an opportunity to share in the important ceremony, but since it was believed that one who fell while doing this would not live long, they were careful not to fall. Informants said that before it was planted, the ground was carefully covered with the dung of deer, antelope and mountain sheep. This made the tobacco grow fast because these animals were swift runners. The dung of the slow-moving elk and moose was never used.[80]

The planting finished, everyone returned to the double lodge, took it down and moved about halfway back to the main camp. No one was supposed to stay to watch the Dwarf People work, for anyone who saw them was sure to die. They remained here for three days, at which time all except the Tobacco members themselves returned to the main camp. Then the members assembled in the Tobacco lodge for the closing ceremony. Outside the lodge were two young men mounted on swift horses. After appropriate songs, ten sticks were given to them and they were told to ride as fast as possible without looking back. They raced toward the tobacco plot, dismounted at the top of a hill overlooking it and planted the sticks in a line pointing toward it. One stick represented the custodian of the medicine bundle;

the others stood for his fellow society members. These remained there as protectors of the crop. To each stick was attached a tiny moccasin, a bead necklace, a tobacco bag and a small pipe. When the two youths returned to the lodge, the members struck it and went back to their homes.

In August, the members met again to sing and dance, after which they dispatched a young man to the tobacco plot to report on its condition. The members went to a hill from which they could observe him. If he walked back and forth, they knew all was going well and went to look at the crop themselves. Any member whose part of the crop was not flourishing was always depressed, for this portended sickness and perhaps even death in his family. While assembled there, they sang and prayed in preparation for gathering the crop. The seed and some of the leaves were placed in the Beaver bundle at this time.

Most of the tobacco harvested from the crop was preserved for use in the ceremonies performed when the bundle was opened, and a member seldom used this ceremonial tobacco for ordinary smoking. Each person kept his own harvest, however, and when the society assembled brought a small portion to the leader for use in the rites.[81] Even for ceremonial purposes the Indians did not use their tobacco straight but mixed it with certain bark or leaves common to the different areas to give it a better taste and aroma. This was acceptable, since the smoke and its fragrance were prime transporters of prayers to God. The Blackfoot mixed their tobacco with bearberry leaves, and the result was called *kinnekinnick*.

Ownership of the Beaver bundle could be purchased for a steep price as the result of a vow. If a man made such a vow, the owner could not keep the bundle and was required to transfer the songs, prayers, dances and movements that made up the Beaver ceremony. It took an excellent memory to remember it all. Sometimes the owner's wife took part in the ceremony, and relatives who contributed to the purchase price might also own shares in the bundle. The bundle itself was kept at the back of the owner's lodge and was taken out of the lodge only when the camp moved.

The duties of the owner of the Beaver bundle did not end with either the ceremonial planting or the harvesting, for he was believed, like beavers, to have the power to forecast the weather. So he was expected to observe the moon and read the signs in the sky, advising the camp chiefs of his determinations. If the camp lacked food in winter, the bundle owner brought out his bundle and charmed the buffalo to the camp. Anyone who was ill could make a vow in return for healing, and the Beaver ceremony would be given on their behalf. For this service, they were required to pay the owner whatever they could afford. If, in a dry season, the tobacco garden needed rain, the owner took the otter skin from the bundle and tied it to a long pole, where it floated in the wind and was sure to bring rain.

There were also stringent rules of conduct to be observed by the bundle owner, and misfortune was sure to result if these were not kept to the letter. For example, he might not eat a beaver or strike a dog or kill any of the birds or animals that were represented in the bundle. He might not beat his wife without first singing the appropriate song, and even then she could avoid the discipline by singing in reply a certain defense song. There were many other such rules—enough to make one wonder whether the job was worth having. It was, though,

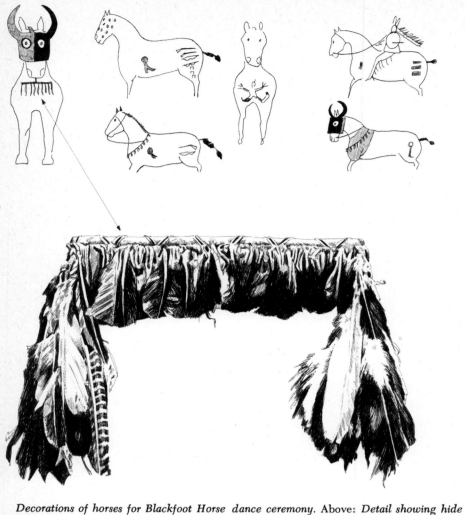

Decorations of horses for Blackfoot Horse dance ceremony. Above: Detail showing hide horse bonnet, one side painted red, the other blue; horse wearing cross-bar stick-bridle (bridle is illustrated in greater detail below). Such bridles were believed to make the horse swift and surefooted and to protect its owner from the enemy (AMNH); painted symbols on the horses record war and raid accomplishments of their owners (after drawings by Blackfoot informants, AMNH).

140

Arikara Young Buffalo society member.

for it brought good fortune to both the family and the tribe and gave the owner's family a prominent position in the tribe.

The Medicine Pipe Society

Informants said the Medicine Pipe "was given to the Blackfeet long ago, when the thunder struck down a man." [82] While the man lay on the ground, the Thunder Chief appeared in a vision. He showed the man a fabulous pipe, which he gave him and told him to make another like it. It was wrapped with rawhide and decorated with feathers and the white winter skins of weasels. Every spring when the first thunder was heard, the pipe was to be brought forth and held up to God. He also instructed him to make a medicine bundle containing the skins of many animals and birds to go with the pipe. Whenever any of the Blackfeet people were ill or dying thereafter, a vow had to be made and a certain ceremonial given with a feast. The sick would then be restored to health.

Later a grizzly bear appeared to the same man and gave him his skin to wrap around the bundle, because it was larger than the skins of other animals. [83] The bear also instructed the man in the details of the transfer ceremony of the bundle. It was to be done stealthily and just before daybreak, when bears are on the move, so that the new owner would be taken by surprise. Once a man was caught and offered the pipe, he dared not refuse it but must accept and smoke it, else death would surely result—for no one dared to turn away from a grizzly bear!

Keeping the bundle was a demanding and expensive proposition, and after a man had held it a few years, he was more than ready to give it up. In any case the maximum term expected by the tribe was four years. The replacement member was difficult to secure, because the society could afford to receive only prominent men who could pay for the pipe and then give the customary feasts and ceremonials. In fairness, it was always made known when a new member was to be taken in, so that those who were unwilling were given an opportunity to sleep away from their lodges while the new man was being sought. [84]

When the society representatives went looking for the new man at night, they kept at it until dawn if necessary. They carried the pipe and usually tried to catch a prominent chief in his lodge.

The owl was featured in the Pipe ceremonial because he was a bird of the night. As the society members sought the new member, they sang owl songs and prayed softly to the owl to help them catch their victim in a deep sleep. [85]

Once a man had been caught, pandemonium reigned in the camp. Drums were beaten, and there was shouting and singing to awaken everyone. A herald called everyone to come, bearing food and gifts, to the lodge of the new owner of the bundle. Meanwhile the former owner of the pipe marched through the camp with the new owner, the latter carrying the pipe. Behind them came their wives, carrying the Medicine Pipe bundle and its tripod, and after these the drummers with the rest of the society and their wives.

It made a grand parade, which ended at the new owner's lodge. Before entering, the group paused to perform certain rites, then the society members slowly entered and took traditional places around the lodge. The women deposited the bundle on its tripod rack at the back of the lodge. The new owner was dressed in the ceremonial outfit that went with the transfer of the bundle. This consisted of a headband of buffalo hide and a feather in the hair, a beaded skin shirt which was fringed with hair and ermine locks, beaded leggings fringed with ermine tails, moccasins and a blanket decorated with red marks to represent stars. In addition to the clothes, the former owner also gave the new man the horse, saddle, bridle, quirt and lariat that went with the sacred Medicine Pipe. The former owner's wife also gave an expensive outfit to the new owner's wife, which was to be worn only during the Pipe ceremonials.

The spectators crowded about outside the lodge, generously leaving a tremendous variety of expensive gifts. These were presented to the new owner, who gave them in turn to the former owner as his fee for transferring the pipe.[86]

In the actual transfer ceremony, the bundle was opened with utmost reverence, and as each piece of animal or bird skin was taken from it and given to the new owner, the transfer was accompanied by traditional songs, gestures and dances designed to empower the new owner with the desirable characteristics of that animal or bird. In essence, marvelous imitations were given of many creatures: the grizzly bear, the thunderbird, the swan, the antelope, the crane, the duck, the goose, the owl, the buffalo, the muskrat and the bee.

The ceremony lasted all day. At sunset the former owner led the new owner and his wife from the lodge and, facing the four directions in turn, chanted proverbial songs about what the new owner could learn from each direction. After this, he instructed them in the countless and demanding rules that must be observed by the keeper of the Pipe. In all, the ceremonial instructions went on for four days. During this period the new pair of owners fasted and sought dreams at night during which special instructions and blessings might be given by God.

In addition to these Blackfoot groups covered in detail, there were several ceremonial organizations whose membership was open to both sexes. Each of them had its own regalia and ceremonies, and membership was purchased.

McClintock refers to the Crow-Water society, whose members were able to cure the sick and who reputedly became wealthy because of their renown.[87]

Wissler mentions four other ceremonial groups and seven types of dance gatherings:

The Black-tailed Deer Dance, whose purpose was to ensure good deer hunting. It was similar to the Elk cult of the Sioux.

The Ghost Dance for the Spirits of the Dead, whose rite consisted of a dance to which the spirits of the dead were invited.

The All-smoking ceremony.

The Stick-game Dance, which was a late import and in which a set of stick-game pieces became a medicine bundle.

The Hair-parters or Grass Dance, which was primarily a social function.

The Horse Dance, which was perhaps more appropriately entitled the War Dance since its purpose was to arouse the people for war.

The Scalp or Victory Dance, which was held on the return of a successful war expedition and in which anyone could participate.

The Kissing Dance, which was purely social.

The Tea Dance, which was also social.

The Begging Dance, which was social.

The Night Singers.[88]

5

THE ARIKARA

The Arikara, Hidatsa and Mandan nations were located in close proximity to one another on the upper Missouri River and their national life-ways were virtually identical. Their life-style centered in hunting, farming, conducting ceremonies and trading intertribally. Their stationary villages, which were of the permanent lodge type, became in fact the main exchange centers for the commerce of most of the northern Plains tribes. Through these strategic hubs, the tribes from all parts of North America traded goods with one another, for the great rivers were the foremost arteries of movement and commerce.

The Arikara nation numbered approximately 3,000 persons in 1780. Its origin has been traced only as far back as an early home on the southwestern Plains, when they were a division of the Skidi Pawnee. When they parted, the Pawnees settled on the Loup River in Nebraska, while the Arikaras moved steadily north until they reached the Missouri River at a point just above the present city of Omaha. Later they moved to the vicinity of the Cannonball, Cheyenne and Grand rivers. Eventually they became the most northern tribe of the Caddoan linguistic family.

The name *Arikara* means "horn" or "elk." It refers specifically to the ancient tribal manner of dressing the hair, wherein it was the custom for both sexes to wear two pieces of bone on their heads, one placed vertically on each side of a central crest of hair.

However, because the Arikara were most influential in spreading agricultural knowledge among the nations of the upper Missouri, other tribes identified them with corn, or "maize." When talking in sign language, others referred to them by imitating the gnawing of a cob of corn.

When the Arikara migrated north, they carried with them a special kind of corn, whose ears were quite small but very nutritious. Other tribes obtained the seed kernels from them for their own plantings, while those whose ground conditions would not permit them to grow it, or whose life-style was so mobile as to make farming impossible, came to the stationary villages to obtain corn in trade for furs and other items.

Each spring the Arikara and their permanent village neighbors planted a new maize crop. Understandably, it played a vital role in their life-way. It was their staple food, it had superb trade value and it became a central factor in their religious practices. They referred to maize as "Mother," for it was the life-giver, and they held numerous annual ceremonies concerning it to ensure its reproduction. The finest ears were always preserved for ceremonial purposes, and the holy men of the tribe were charged with watching over some ears that had been carefully guarded for generations by their ancestors.

The Arikara hunted buffalo and other animals, as did all Plains tribes—particularly in the winter, for once the corn and other crops such as beans, squash and sunflower seeds were planted in the spring, most of the men stayed close to their villages to cultivate and guard the planted areas.

The traditional style of Plains warfare came to the Arikara as it did to all tribes. The nearby Sioux, in particular, assaulted their settlements time and again, and the ruins of many stationary villages have been found. Some of these disagreements had their origins in trade disputes, others in territorial arguments. Eventually the Arikara, hard pressed by White settlements, rose up in fury and were nearly eradicated in consequence. Diseases introduced by the Whites completed the job of rendering the Arikara virtually powerless.

The tribal enemies of the Arikara included the Wichita, the Comanche, the Kiowa, the Cheyenne, the Crow and the Sioux. Even the sedentary tribes sharing their life-way, the Mandans and the Hidatsas, were often at war with them, and until a late truce was established among the three, Arikara warriors claimed that every man, Indian and White, was their enemy.

At the time of their separation from the Skidi Pawnee, the Arikara were a substantial tribe with ten subdivisions. Yet when Lewis and Clark visited them in 1805, they numbered only 2,600. In 1871, their population was only 1,000; in 1888, it was 500; by 1907, they had decreased to 389 destitute souls.

One can appreciate why the Arikara societies would come into being and play a dominant role in their tribal scheme and why also there would be a two-pronged thrust to each of the groups. The societies were age-graded, and their main activities were religious and military. Indeed, most of the thirteen age groups were known more for their religious practices than they were for their military actions. Only three of the thirteen had military activity as their main function. According to Curtis, a fourteenth division was composed of three women's societies. One group, known as the Goose Women, performed certain mystic ceremonies designed to ensure bumper corn crops and to entice buffalo to the villages. A second group, called White Buffalo Cow Women, had a special annual ritual to lure or "call" the buffalo toward the villages for easier hunting. A third women's group was the Otter society.

In Arikara government, the tribal chief, or leader, was always a member of the "Abandoned" band. Each of the other nine bands had a head chief and three subordinate chiefs who together formed a council for the nation. The commands of the council and individual chiefs were always enforced by the Black-mouth society, which had a chapter in each band.

According to Curtis, the Arikara male societies were as follows:

> The Shin Ravens. The name of this society for young men was derived from its dance in which raven feathers hung from slits in the boy's shins.
> The Foolish Dogs
> The Black Mouths
> The Buffalo Bulls
> The Straight-heads
> The Young Dogs
> The Chippewas
> The Half-moons. Their name came from the practice of trimming their hair in the shape of a half-moon.
> The Ravens
> The Thumpers. Their name came from their characteristic of beating the ground with one foot as they danced.
> The Speckled. These painted themselves with dots of different colors.
> The Feet-aparts. These danced with their feet spread apart.
> The Cut-throats [1]

Of these, the Black Mouths, the Half-moons and the Chippewas were the only purely military societies.

After Lowie considered the various older though limited records available on the Arikara, he compiled the following list, which he felt was in accord with what his informants told him during a brief visit he made to the Arikara between longer visits to the Hidatsa and Mandan:

Men's Societies	Women's Societies
Young Dogs	River Snake
Straight-head	Goose
Buffalo	
Young Buffalo	
Black Mouths	
Grass Dance	
Cut-hairs	
Fox	
Hot Dance	
Cut-throat	
Crazy Horse	
Crow	
Hopping	
Chippewa	
Foolish People	
Buffalo Calling [2]	

Lowie also describes the men's and women's societies of the Arikara in considerable detail, and the following information regarding these orders is a condensation of his work: *Societies of the Arikara Indians,* American Museum of Natural History, 2: 8 (1915).

Edward S. Curtis devoted most of his attention to the Arikara Medicine Fraternity, and his work provides the primary source material for my description of that cult: Edward S. Curtis, *The North American Indian,* 5: 64–100.

The Young Dogs' Society
The main emblem of the Young Dog order consisted of a sash of blue cloth edged with white, which was about ten inches wide and worn passed around the neck to make a loop. To this, a length of red cloth was attached so that altogether it reached to the ankles of the wearer, though it did not touch the ground. These sashes were always manufactured by the older members of the organization who, as sponsors for the new men, painted and dressed them as well.

A candidate received one of the sashes first and then was taken to the society lodge to complete the initiation rite. Every member had a rattle made from a stick about a foot long, covered with hide, decorated with a feather at one end and attached with buffalo dew claws. To each candidate was given a quill-wrapped buckskin string for the suspension of his whistle and a coyote skin belt to tie around his waist. Owl feathers tied in a bunch were attached to the crown of his head.

Members' bodies were painted red, with a black band that went around each wrist. A curved black line was drawn from the center of the forehead down each side of the face to make an oval. A vertical line was drawn on the center of the forehead and the chin. Smaller lines were placed on the cheeks horizontally.

Not all members dressed alike. A few glued a piece of white weasel skin to magpie feathers and attached these in regular bonnet fashion to a buckskin cap with an eagle feather roach. Most, however, wore only owl feathers.

New members joined war parties, and the "fathers" who had sold them their regalia always prayed they would not be killed. They were instructed to be generous with horses captured from the enemy, giving them away to whomever they met first on their return. This was so that they would grow in prestige "and be noticed by the people."

Public parades of the organization were led by an officer wearing a black sash and carrying a pipe and by another also bearing a pipe but wearing the regular sash. A third officer remained in the rear with a quirt to see that all members joined in the march.

The Straight-head Society
The members of the Straight-head order were noted people of various ages. There was no particular costume; everyone wore the best he had. The name of the society was derived from the lack of a horned headdress, such as formed the emblem of a similar society, the Young Buffalo.

The leaders carried fancy pipe pouches. The regular members bore bows, guns and other weapons. Dances were performed both inside and outside the lodge. Two brave men, whose horses had been killed or wounded in battle, covered themselves with white paint and touched over it here and there with red clay to show that they had been shot. They rode their horses outside the line of dancing members and dismounted from time to time to join briefly in the performance.

The primary aim of the society was to aid the poor. If, during a dance, a member saw a poor man, he would present him with a horse or a shirt, while a poor woman might receive a buffalo robe. When a large feast was held, all the old people and orphans came as spectators and the food was distributed among them.

The Buffalo Society
This Buffalo order had many traits in common with the Straight-head. The emblem of the society was a headdress worn by each member. It consisted of a cap made from the head and horns of a buffalo, and it extended over the wearer's eyebrows. One member wore, in addition to this cap, a mask of buffalo hide with the mane on. It was provided with eye slits and a mouth opening. Although it was a separate piece, the mask was attached to the headdress so that the whole appeared to be one piece. Hair hung down from the jaw. This mask was usually given after some deliberation to the bravest man in the order. He also carried a lance with a point at one end and feathers clipped as though for fletching arrows at the other. The entire lance was wrapped with dyed horsehair. The mask-wearer did not join the rest in dancing but remained by himself. He was often referred to as "the Crazy Buffalo."

The Young Buffalo Society
Members of the Young Buffalo society bore lances; each wore a buffalo horn headdress trimmed with concentric tiers of eagle feathers. Each also carried a bone whistle covered with quillwork and a gourd rattle with a wrist loop. The order was short-lived, for when the Grass Dance was introduced, many members left to join the new society.

The Black Mouths Society
The Black Mouths were the guards of the village. In the winter the buffalo were easily frightened away by the echo of tree-chopping; consequently, the society forbade the cutting of trees. If anyone disobeyed after the order had been issued, the Black Mouths beat him.

If he took his punishment in the proper spirit, the society gave him presents, even horses, lest he harbor ill feeling against them.

Two officers carried lances wrapped with otter skin. A stuffed crow was tied to the upper end. There were two gourd rattle carriers and two pipe-keepers. The costume varied, but the upper part of the face was painted red and the lower part black.

The Cut Hairs Society

The Cut Hairs order received its name from the fact that the members cut a small section of hair on each side of their heads in the shape of a half-moon. In addition to being specially cut, the hair was combed up stiff in the center and switches were worn in the back. Owl feathers, with eagle feathers in the center, were attached above the switches. All members wore shell breast-ornaments. Horn shells were strung together in rows and attached to a strip of hide, which was placed on each side of the head. The shirt worn was generally of white muslin, with red flannel around the sleeves and shoulders and along the border.

There were two lance bearers in the society. The shafts were wrapped with red cloth, and swan, owl and crow feathers were added for decoration. If one of the lance men was in battle, he stuck his lance in the ground and stayed there until a fellow tribesman pulled it out and ran away with it. The lance bearer was required to follow. The lance men continued in office as long as they pleased but could give up the lance at any time if they had served with honor. Then a replacement was selected.

Two other officers acted as leader and pipe bearer respectively. In dancing, the Cut Hairs sometimes imitated horses and pawed the ground; they also swung their arms in imitation of horses' legs. This group sometimes performed the Bear dance. On such occasions one man wore a bear skin robe fastened with an arrow.

The Fox Society

For a public parade, the leader of the Fox society carried a pipe, the mouthpiece of which was held in front of him. The man next to him carried a doubly bent bow-lance. To each end of this were attached pigeon-hawk legs with the claws on. The whole bow was decorated with beadwork and red cloth. The rattler generally wore no shirt and had pink paint all over his arms and face; he drew his fingers over the painted surface and put red paint on the spots thus marked. His necklace consisted of the whole of a fleshed cow skin, the tail sticking out at the back of the head. He also wore wristbands.

In dancing, once the music started, everyone rose, and as the tempo of the music increased, all put their hands in front of their waists and bent down, making noises in imitation of birds. Then they stood up straight again.

One informant said that members wore their hair roached in the center with most of the rest of the head shaved. On each side a little hair was braided, and long strings of beads, shells and weasel skin were attached to the braids. A mixture of red paint and white clay was painted on the shaved parts of the head. A black cloth was tied around the head. A belt was also worn to which two young fox or coyote skins were attached at the sides. Between them was attached either a weasel skin or a bunch of eagle feathers. The necklace consisted of a string of trade-brass objects of half-moon shape.

The Hot Dance Society

The members of the Hot Dance society put their arms into a container of boiling water to take out meat and carry it on their shoulders. They imitated turkeys and wore headdresses of turkey feathers. Sometimes the hair was dressed so that it suggested a turkey in the back. Tail feathers were attached to look like a turkey's tail.

On rare occasions the Hot Dancers performed the Elk dance. For this they used a long whistle. From the elbows and knees downward, they painted themselves with dark paint, and likewise from the collarbone to the chest. The rest of the body was painted yellow, with patches of white. White clay was daubed round the eyes. Sometimes they painted themselves in imitation of bears, sometimes to resemble crows.

The Cut-throat Society

Members of the Cut-throat society dressed as well as possible. The hair was braided in front and tied with a strip of otter skin or red cloth. A space in the back was left for the attachment of a switch, which was decorated with perforated tin-disk ornaments. Bangs of hair were cut to shade the forehead. The breechclout was generally long and made of white trade broadcloth.

The Crazy Horse Society

Candidates for admission to the Crazy Horse society were permitted to witness all the society dances from midwinter until spring in order to learn the correct way of performing them. Then the Crazy Horses surrendered their memberships.

Among the insignia of the organization were two exceptionally long bow-lances. The officers carrying these wore their hair loose on one side and braided on the other; a circlet of crow feathers was attached to the side of the loose hair. At both ends of the bow, eagle claws and a strip of wool or buffalo skin were attached. The entire length of the bow was decorated with beadwork, and at either side of the grip there was a ring of crow feathers, which was duplicated at some distance toward the ends. At the very ends were eagle feathers.

The Crow Society

Members of the Crow society wore buckskin leggings but no shirt. Members cut the front of their hair square; two braids were also cut in this fashion, and to the end of the braidstrings, shells were attached. A long switch hung down in the back. Usually, brass armbands were worn. Some members painted their foreheads, but the manner of painting was immaterial. There were four lances, which were stuck up in the center of the lodge. Two of these were wrapped with broadcloth and decorated with crow feathers. The other two were hooked and were wrapped with otter skin; at the end of the straight part an eagle feather was attached so that it stood erect. Below the hook there were several twisted strips of otter skin placed at intervals.

In their dance the members alternately stamped each foot; they held a bow or other weapon in the left hand and struck out with the arm of the same side. Two of the bravest members were mounted on horses. One of them cut out the effigy of a person in rawhide and attached it to his horse's neck. The rider wore only a breechclout and painted his face and body with white clay. He would also add red to his mouth to indicate bleeding from a wound received in battle. The hide effigy represented an enemy. The second horseman had two such images on his horse. At the sound of the drum, the horsemen headed off the members and turned them to begin their dance.

The Hopping Society

The Hopping society was a society for boys about fifteen years old, who were joined by a few men who knew the songs. For music, skin rattles decorated with hawk feathers were used. Whistles were worn suspended from the neck. The hair was clipped in front, and two braids were cut off square at the end. On one side of the top of the head was attached a small crow ornament, with night-owl feathers arranged in a disk. Only breechclouts were worn. In dancing, the members stamped each foot alternately on the ground. Sometimes the society had horse parades as well.

The Chippewa Society

Most of the members of the Chippewa order wore fringed buckskin leggings. Stripes on the legs symbolized war exploits. Black paint with yellow and speckles indicated participation in many battles, the black spots representing bullets. Wigs were secured on the head by means of red flannel, and the hair was worn loose in the back. The whole of a slit weasel skin was tied immediately above the wig, and from the other end there was suspended a strip of buckskin. The face was painted with specks of white clay and yellow paint. Some men wore a feather in their hair.

During a dance the members held a weapon in the left hand and shook bells with the right. They stooped over, throwing the head back and extending their weapons. There were two bow-lances in the order similar to those of the Crazy Horses but shorter. At both ends of the bow there was a bunch of weasel tails, with three bear gut strings hanging down from them. The whole bow was wrapped with bear gut. The bowstring was loose and had eagle plumes attached at the ends.

The River Snake Society

The River Snake women's order was noted for its generosity in aiding the men's societies. Its regalia consisted of a headband of braided grass, wrapped in front with beaded cloth. Five straws and an eagle feather were thrust obliquely through the band in front. When a meeting was to be held, a crier made an announcement to that effect. Then women of all ages unbraided their hair and combed it so that it hung loose down the back. Most of them put on dresses of goat skin. The headbands were kept in the dance lodge, strung on a rope between two poles. Members painted their faces red from the corner of the eyes to the ears, with a little paint below the cheeks. Their dance was in imitation of snakes with the performers zigzagging in a long line.

The Goose Society

The emblem of the Goose women's group was a headband made of the rolled skin of a goose neck, with the head left on. Otherwise the members wore regular clothing. During a dance the women walked about in a circle, sidestepping. Each carried a bundle of sage enclosing a partly visible ear of corn. The seeds of these ears were to be planted for the next year's crop; at the close of the performance they were laid on the ground.

A woman inherited membership through her mother. A girl entering the organization was expected to take good care of the garden work; she was asked to join if she had distinguished herself in this line. She still paid for the honor of being admitted. The society gave her instruction in caring for the fields.

The Arikara declared that the Father in heaven had instructed them to perform the planting and cultivating ceremonies of the Goose society. In the founding myth, a Goose spoke to the Arikara as follows: "I will go to the edge of the big rivers. When it is time for you to prepare something for me to eat, I shall return. When I shall have come back, you may proceed with your garden work, and you will be sure of success." That is why the geese always came in the spring, when the sowing began, and why they departed after the harvest.[3]

It should be mentioned that Maximilian spoke of a Fox society as existing among the Arikara about 1833.[4]

While relatively little is known about the regalia and ceremonies of most of the Arikara societies, considerably more has been recorded about the prestigious Medicine Fraternity. It was made up of nine groups:

The Ghosts
The Black-tail Deer
The Shedding (Buffalo)
The Swamp Bird
The Principal Medicine
The Big Foot (Duck)
The Moon, also called Owl
The Mother Night, also called Young Dog
The Bear [5]

When the Medicine Fraternity assembled for ceremonials in the huge medicine lodge, which measured about seventy feet in diameter, each of the nine groups took fixed positions along the walls of the lodge according to ancient traditions. Beginning at the post directly south from the southeastern center post, the first four groups sat in the southern half of the lodge and the last four in the northern half. The Principal Medicine, which consisted of four men who represented the marsh inhabitants—the beaver, the otter, the muskrat and the swamp-owl—sat between the other groups in the extreme rear of the lodge upon a slightly elevated square of earth. Directly above the head of each Principal Medicine man hung a long ceremonial bundle, which had an outer wrapping of buffalo skin and five large gourd rattles fastened at intervals at right angles to its length. These were four of the ten ancient bundles originally given, one to each band of the tribe, by "Mother," and each contained the stuffed skins of various creatures connected with the mythic emergence and migrations of the Arikara people.

The annual ceremony, which began at the time of the ripening of squashes and continued until autumn, consisted largely of magic performances. Their purpose is not difficult to understand, for they symbolized God's ability to produce the needs of the tribe out of nothing year after year. Each order of medicine men had its unique songs and feats of magic. Each night of the ceremony might be devoted to the performance of a single trick or set of tricks.

Every afternoon the group members, appropriately painted in accordance with the manner prescribed by their medicine, danced and marched about a special cedar tree and stone in front of the lodge, at the same time singing and calling upon the Wonderful Grandmother, the mythic leader of the people, and the Wonderful Grandfather, the supreme God, represented by the cedar and the stone.

A typical trick performed by each of the orders went as follows: The leader of the Ghosts would stand up, hold a human skull at arm's length above his head and then appear to swallow it. He would then lie, face downward, on the floor while another Ghost covered him with a buffalo robe. Then, as the leader rose to his feet, the skull would reappear and could be seen lying on the ground.

As the Black-tail Deer stood in a row and sang, one of them would run swiftly outside, climb to the roof of the lodge and give a shrill whistle. From a distance would come the answer of a real elk, which was then called closer and closer by the continued whistling of the Black-tail Deer medicine man.

The Buffalo men would place a buffalo skull beside the southwestern center post. Then as all of them danced on the opposite side of the fire in imitation of the buffalo the skull would seem, incredibly, to bellow like a great buffalo bull.

Dancers performing in Arikara Medicine ceremony (SM).

The Swamp Bird men would stand in a row and sing their special songs for a long time. After this they would race outside and run several circles around the cedar. Then they would reenter the lodge, rush out again, leap into the river and return to the lodge with each man holding two large, wriggling fish in his hands!

The Big Foot order wore a unique necklace of duck bills strung on otter skin. In performing one of their magic tricks, the men would run to the water's edge and bring back a number of rushes. A holy woman would stick these into the earth near the lodge fireplace to symbolize the marsh where ducks nested. A second virtuous woman would be given their necklaces, which she would hold out to the north and then throw among the rushes. Immediately a sound would be heard like that of the quacking of the spirit duck, which was believed to dwell within the body of the leader. When the fire had died down, he would pass through it to the opposite side of the fireplace, imitating as he did so the actions of a duck. Observers heard the sound of a large flock of ducks quacking and even the flapping of their wings against the surface of the water.[6]

The Moon men would spread a robe beside the fire. When the fire had died down, the leader would raise the robe and swing it several times through the air. Then a golden light like the rays of the

moon would be seen streaming down through the smoke-hole.

An even more spectacular trick was performed by the same order. They would begin it by spreading a mat of dry rushes on the ground. After this, the leader would paint a broad black circle around his face and other circles about his wrists and ankles, finishing with a black spot on his chest. Sticks were set vertically in the ground and the rush mat was thrown over them to form a miniature lodge. Carrying a whistle and a small drum, the leader would then crawl into the tiny lodge. When he was inside, the fire-keeper would set the mat afire. It would blaze fiercely, and everybody would shout in excitement! Yet when the little lodge was entirely consumed, no trace of the medicine man could be found. Still, those spectators who went immediately to the river would see him emerging from the water, blowing his whistle, beating his drum and staggering as if exhausted. Supported by fellow Moon medicine men, he would enter the lodge and sit beside the fire, saying, "I have traveled far. I have learned that we are going to have good crops and many buffalo."

The Arikara said there was once a time when Moon medicine was greatly feared and shunned by initiates. It seems that a man and his son, having entered the little rush lodge together, failed to return. It was supposed that upon entering the earth, as they were assumed to do to escape the heat and fire, they had encountered a thick wall of rock that held them prisoners in spite of three days of medicine-making in their behalf. A possible explanation suggested by Curtis is that the father and son, having in the usual manner made their escape unnoticed from the rush lodge, were set upon at the river's edge and killed or captured by enemies lying in wait.[7]

The Mother Night men would paint themselves spectacularly with red paint on their legs, black paint on their bodies and red spots over a coat of black on their faces. Then they would place a large round stone, painted red, behind them, and the youthful wife of a younger member was invited to come forward; her hair was then loosened and brushed, and her face painted. She would reach behind them and touch the stone, whereupon all the members of the order would join in rolling it into the fireplace. The keeper was told to build a great fire, and when the painted stone was red-hot, the young woman's husband, who had been rubbed with special medicine herbs by the leader and encouraged to fear nothing, would leap upon it and dance. In reality, he touched his feet to the hot stone as little as he could manage, aiding himself in this by holding crutchlike in each hand a stout staff. Usually the flames only singed his eyebrows and skin, for he would quickly leap on through the fire to the opposite side where the leader would immediately rub him with a profusion of moist herbs.

In yet another magic act, the Mother Night medicine men would paint a huge earthen vessel red, decorate it with four feathers and place it beside the fire. As the keeper stoked the fire, the men of the order would sing while the performer danced around the fire. All the other Medicine Fraternity men in the lodge would gather about in a circle, crying, "Hurry! Hurry!" At this point a woman would place in her mouth a pinch of pulverized willow-root mixed with an unidentified root, take a sip of water and spray it on the feet and legs of the dancer. He would then step into the heated jar, supporting himself once again with the two staffs, and quickly leap out again. He would dance a few moments, and the leader would rub his body with medicine herbs.

For a third trick, the Night men chief would load a gun with powder, bullet and wadding. His helper would dance around the fire and, holding the gun aloft, would fire it. Then he would dance again, holding the muzzle down, whereupon bullet, powder and wadding would roll out upon the ground.

Once the Bear men had sung their traditional songs, one of them, who was covered by a full bear skin, would dash madly back and forth across the lodge. Stopping in front of a square of earth that served as an altar, he would place his hands to his mouth and kick the ground. When he dropped his hands, long bear teeth would protrude from his mouth. As the other Bear men beat a drum and sang, another Bear would run off to one side. Some of the strongest men in the lodge were then called upon to throw him to the ground and hold him. Taking a knife, they would then pretend to cut off his foreleg, and either a stuffed foreleg or an object resembling one would suddenly be thrown in front of the main Bear group. They in turn would hurl it across the lodge to the Ghosts, while everyone cried "Hurry! Hurry! Put it back!" At this point one of the Bear medicine men would return it to the prostrate Bear and supposedly reunite it to his body.

The Principal Medicine men brought in a large tree-top, whose butt was about four inches in diameter, and placed it upright in the ground in front of the square of earth. The Beaver medicine man would then dance around the fire with his beaver skin in his hand. After some time he would hold its nose to the tree, and the tree would fall, seemingly gnawed in two by the dead Beaver. For another trick the Principal Medicine order would call a boy from the crowd, remove his moccasins and leggings and stretch him out on the ground. One

155

Opposite: *Bear Dancers performing during Arikara Medicine ceremony* (SM).

of the men would then press the sharpened point of a long piece of ashwood against the sole of the boy's foot, causing it to disappear deeply into his foot. Then the Beaver medicine man would miraculously heal the wound by withdrawing the stick and leaving no sign of a wound, for his medicine mended even broken limbs! On another occasion the leader of the Principal Medicine would step forward and stretch out his buffalo robe. As the people moved back, he would shake his robe violently, and the gourds tied to the bundles hanging above the platform would be heard to rattle by everyone present.[8]

The Medicine Fraternity always had several initiates who were carefully selected by the members to perform certain menial labors. After a successful probationary term, these servants were offered the privilege of buying the medicine of any order and thus becoming a member. If the invitation was accepted, a man first offered a pipe of tobacco to the sacred cedar, lamenting while he did so. Then he entered the medicine lodge and offered the pipe first to the firekeeper, then to each group in order, beginning with the Ghosts. When he arrived at the group he wished to join, he held out the pipe to their leader, but the head medicine man always clenched his hands as if unwilling to accept it. The aspirant was expected to force them open and thrust the pipe between them, an act taken as a sign that he was firm in his intention to be initiated.

The pipe was then smoked in turn by each of the men in the lodge. The novice was stripped and hurriedly painted, and the painter received his clothing in payment. Medicine herbs were then rubbed over his entire body, and he was given a drink made of roots. From this time forward he assisted in the singing so that he might learn the numerous songs of his order, and he was given some small part in each performance of tricks. He became, in effect, a servant to his particular group instead of to the entire fraternity. As time passed, he was given further instruction in the performance of his order's medicine tricks, and for each new lesson a fee was levied. There was no attempt to help the beginner become adept at once. The initiation became an enjoyable contest between the older members and the initiates, the latter seeking to be taught as much as possible immediately, the former bargaining for the amount of the payment, parting with their wondrous secrets only after much persuasion and many promises.[9]

When the leader of a group of the Medicine Fraternity died, the one who had learned the most from him became his natural successor. Understandably, the number of members for each group remained small and varied from order to order. It seems to have been from four to six, though Curtis feels each must have been considerably larger in the early days of Arikara history.[10]

Because of their deeply spiritual nature, the Arikara, as well the other permanent village nations, enacted their religious views in such a way as to make them a living part of their ongoing history. Keeping all factors in delicate balance, they designed their ceremonials to be both profound, as the worship of God deserved, and entertaining, so as to relieve the tension that prolonged solemnity can bring to both audiences and performers. Ceremonials also maintained a tantalizing balance between secrecy and public display.

The Arikara developed their summer-long medicine ceremony to such a point of excellence and productivity that tribes from the whole of the northern Plains were influenced by it, coming from far

Opposite: *Buffalo Dancers performing during Arikara Medicine ceremony* (SM).

and near to observe and imitate their activity. It was generally believed that the Arikara Medicine Fraternity was a special channel used by God to mediate His supernatural powers. Irrespective of the tendency of non-Indians to put down the rites as superstition, until the Arikara were decimated by the Whites through wars and diseases, their tribal life was rich and successful in most respects. While one might be tempted to question how effective that remarkable medicine ceremony was in the light of the ultimate destruction of the Arikara, one might bear in mind that the ceremony was totally suppressed by White agency officials about 1885, so that it could no longer be used. Holy medicine assuredly has no effect when it isn't practiced.

Those who would appreciate a detailed description of the profound summer ceremony can find it in Curtis, *The North American Indian*, 5: 70–76. To illustrate the spiritualism of the Arikara, however, a few things can be excerpted from the account, which was published in 1909.

The ceremony was held in the early spring before the planting season. It began with the opening of one of the powerful medicine bundles said to have been left with the several bands by Mother (the Corn). The opening was accompanied by a repetition of the myth of the genesis and migration of the Arikara, and this was followed by a dramatic enactment in the nature of a prayer for bounteous crops.

Then a second bundle, which contained the skins of animals, birds, fish and ears of corn, was opened. "In the words of the Arikara: 'Mother has undone her belt. Her feet are placed on the earth, that she may understand we are praying to the Supreme Deity and struggling to help ourselves by planting corn and other things that grow. We pray for rain and moisture, that we may have good crops.'"

After this, the people of the tribe offered meaningful sacrifices of material things to God, and ceremonies commenced, which were in themselves detailed and sophisticated prayers to God. In this there was much pantomime and symbolism, portrayed in graceful body movements and dancing.

The first actions were followed by ceremonies that expressed heartfelt and emotional assurance that having asked God for His favors, they would be granted. The corn was envisioned as growing already. The corn would give strength; they would conquer the enemy.

At this point a cedar tree, brought from faraway hills and made sacred by ceremonies attending its cutting, was reverently carried into the village and deposited on the ground, whereupon it was literally buried with offerings. Now infants and children were brought to the holy men for consecration. "While repeating a prayer the priests brushed each child from head to foot with a bunch of sage, thus symbolically driving away all evil from it. This ceremonial blessing of children, analogous to infant baptism, is universal with the Indians of the Northern Plains, its observance being a part of nearly every Sun Dance and other important ceremony." When the blessings were finished, the tree was carried into the lodge and laid on the ground with its base toward the altar. It was then painted red, and eagle feathers were tied at its topmost twig "as Mother had directed."

While the tree ceremony was taking place, the different medicine groups painted themselves carefully according to ancient sacred formulas. Then each group danced in front of the lodge four times, a prescribed holy number that brought maximum results in ceremonial accomplishment, and entered the lodge. After a while the entire Medicine Fraternity emerged to engage in a simulated contest with two bears and two buffalo, each of whom blew an eagle bone whistle and wore the rich skins of those animals, decorated with splendid arrangements of beads and feathers. To touch any of the "animals" was to gain its medicine strength and finally to break its power so as to symbolize man's superiority over it. In conclusion, the tree was carried from the lodge and planted in the ground in front of the lodge next to the stone, which symbolized God in His eternal nature.

In the evening all the members of the fraternity painted their entire bodies with white clay to indicate purity, as a prayer for forgiveness from God. Drums were beaten and songs sung to drive away illness. This endeavor could be expected to be successful now that proper purification and an expression of total dependence upon God had taken place. Exuberant dancing around a roaring fire followed, with the men crowding as close to the leaping flames as possible for further purification and in the persistent pursuit of health. After all, healthy minds and bodies were believed essential to an ideal life.

All in all, the Summer Medicine ceremony was a stunning performance and one that was repeated with traditional variations day after day throughout the summer season by the Medicine Fraternity. At the same time, the rest of the Arikara nation, greatly comforted by the monumental intercession with God on their behalf, went about the regular business of daily life.

6

THE HIDATSA

Once closely related to the Crow, the Hidatsa separated from them and located close to the Mandan and Arikara, while the Crows moved to the Rocky Mountains. After their affiliation with the Mandan and Arikara, the Hidatsa adopted many of their customs and religious beliefs. The Mandans called them the *Minitari*, which meant "they crossed the water." They too were nearly exterminated by smallpox. In 1780, they numbered 2,500; in 1804, they were down to 2,100; in 1900, their population was less than 300.

The society lists of Curtis and Maximilian differ considerably:

Curtis [1]	Maximilian [2]
Fox-band	Stone-hammers
Small dog	Lumpwoods
Dog-band	Crow
Scraped Wood	Kit-foxes
Owners of stone-hammers	Little-dogs
Raven-band	Dogs
Crazy-dog	Half-shaved heads
Half-shorn	Enemies (Black-mouths)
Lumpwood	Bulls
Crow	Ravens
Bull-band	
Black-mouth	
Wood-root	

Added to these are the women's groups, which consisted of at least the following:

Buffalo-cow-women
Goose
River-women

Lowie's list is different still: [3]

Men's Societies	*Women's Societies*
Notched stick	Skunk women
Stone hammers	Enemy women
Hot dancers	Goose
Kit-fox	Old women
Lumpwoods	Gun
Crow	River women
Little dogs	Cheyenne women
Half-shaved heads	White buffalo cow
Black-mouths, or Soldiers	
Crazy dogs	
Ravens	
Dogs	
Buffalo bulls	

While Curtis gives only a summary account of the Hidatsan societies, we are again indebted to Robert H. Lowie for his extensive details concerning the individual orders, found in *Societies of the Hidatsa and Mandan*, American Museum of Natural History, 2 (1913). The following is, for the most part, adapted from that data.

The Lumpwood Society
The Lumpwood society had a close association with the buffalo. In-

162

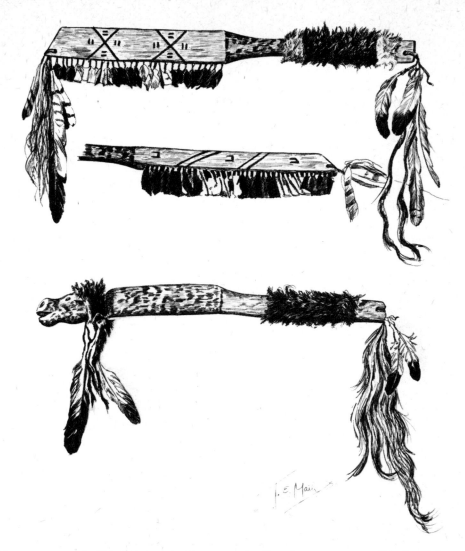

formants said the Lumpwoods were inclined to pray to the buffalo
for good luck and constructed pens (piskuns) into which they would
drive the herds. When one of their "ancestors" went out on the prairie
to fast, he took his knobbed stick with him and it revealed four songs
to him, by which he was able to lure buffalo into the pen.

The rank and file carried unknobbed sticks with representations
of animal faces of different kinds. One was that of a bear, and the man
carrying it was expected to advance against an enemy standing at bay.
When they paraded, one of these sticks was carried by an officer. The
American Museum of Natural History collection includes one of these
stunning pieces. The twenty-four-inch-long stick is rounded, with a
carved buffalo head at the front end and a dyed horsehair pendant
attached to the handle. Buffalo-hair wrappings are also mounted at each
end of the stick, as are hangings of eagle feathers.

Each member wore an ornament of weasel skin strips decorated
with beads and shells on the back of his head. They also wore crowns
of bear gut; at the tying place, on the right side, two hawk feathers
were attached. Certain individual variations in costume were due to
the member's visions. Thus, one having had a revelation from a buffalo
painted a large horn on the back of his robe, with the point toward
the right. For the same reason, some members used wooden whistles
while others used eagle bone.

Two of the Lumpwood officers also carried a thirty-inch-long club
of marvelous design. It was a flat board with rounded edges, some
four inches in width except for the handle, which was round and
burned over. On one side the flat part of the club was painted with

163

*Regalia of Hidatsa Lumpwood society: Clubs carried by officers—marks represent
war honors.*

four diagonal green lines representing honor marks and three angular green horse tracks. On the other side was an X denoting the striking of an enemy. A row of about thirty cut raven feathers, each two-and-a-half inches long, was attached to the board with a thong fed through the quills. They represented scalps. A cluster of eight hawk feathers, plus an eagle tail feather and purple horsehair, was tied to the head of the club. A twenty-inch purple horse-tail and a cluster of grayish white feathers were attached loosely to the club handle.

The leader wore moccasins, the heels of which were painted red to symbolize the enemy's blood. Near the ankle a wolf tail was tied to the moccasin; at the near end this tail was wrapped with red cloth and buckskin, while at the other end shortened raven wing feathers were attached. Since the raven wings represented a scalp, only men who had scalped an enemy were privileged to use them for decoration; a man who had caught an enemy with his hands might both use the raven feathers and redden his moccasins. Antelope leggings with gull-wing quillwork decorations were worn, and a band of rawhide was tied around the knee. A breechclout was worn, and to the left side of the belt was attached a bunch of bison tails cut short at the bottom and hanging down to the muscle of the lower leg.

Four officers carried bow-lances, the heads of which represented a buffalo's sharp horns. One of the lances was double-headed and represented a young bull moving quickly in a fight; it was borne by the drum carrier. When marching, the officers always carried their bow-lances in their left hands so that the points slanted toward the right. The bow was about six feet in length, painted a light pink, bent in the center and at the top, and bore a slanting lance head of sheet iron. The square bottom of the head was fixed in the split end of the bow by means of a buckskin string and was cut into four times on each side. The incisions were intended to lacerate the enemy. One man painted the four inches at the tip of the lance head red in order to show that he had struck an enemy. His bow was decorated on both sides with an incised, uncolored lightning line. The bow had glued to it several fleshed birds and parts of birds—bluebirds, red woodpeckers, ducks, etc.—and was decorated with bunches of feathers. The bow-string was of the kind of thread used for snares and supported a number of fine eagle plumes placed at intervals along its length.

Two officers carried hooked staffs wrapped with otter skin and decorated with feathers and strips of skin. Two others carried straight staffs wrapped with wolf skin, with eagle feathers at the top; the upper halves were painted red. Two whippers had quirts, occasionally wrapped with fox skin. When young men hesitated to dance, these officers whipped them to make them take part.

After a lengthy transaction to purchase the Lumpwoods' memberships, the new members paraded around the village. They were led by the new leader, followed by the first bow-lance officer. Next came a number of lay members bearing their sticks; behind them marched the second bow-lance carrier, some more rank and file and, in the middle of the procession, the owner of the knobbed stick, followed by ordinary members, the third lance-carrier, more lay members, the member with the bear-face stick, the drum carrier and the second flat-board carrier at the rear. The single-file procession was supposed to represent a herd of buffalo.

Between ceremonies the wooden staffs were hung up in a bunch in a member's lodge. In dancing, members put their hands behind them, letting their hands rest on their rumps.

The Stone Hammer Society

Even more regal than the pieces just mentioned was the staff of the Hidatsa Stone Hammer society. The straight central staff was about six feet long, with two slim willow branches tied at the upper end and forking or curving off to each side. The branches were peeled at four-inch intervals to form stripes. Eagle or hawk feathers were attached in pairs to the head of the staff and to the ends of the willow forks. A cluster of wolf fur strips and several eagle wing-feathers were hung from the butt end of the staff. Just below the point where the staff forked, a brown-stone hammerhead was mounted on the staff, which had been thrust through a hole in the stone. A six-pointed star was engraved on one side of the stone head and a moon on the other side. Except for the stone, the entire straight staff was then wrapped with wolf fur. The Stone Hammer society is said to have been formed by a man who learned in a vision from supernatural beings the songs, dances and regalia of the Hammers.

In one of several accounts given by Hidatsa informants regarding the purchase of this society by a younger group, one of the sticks with the stone emblem was set in the ground and the buyers were obliged to heap up property four times the height of the stone. In this transaction the buyers were assisted by the Lumpwoods.

The consummation of the purchase was followed by a parade through the village and then a public performance of the dance, during which several of the sellers acted as musicians. In dancing, the boys formed a circle and began to move clockwise, holding their hammer wands in their left hands. At one point in the ceremony, the spectators pelted the dancers with mud. While being pelted, they held their emblems over their shoulders. The object was to strengthen the resistance of the Stone Hammers in preparation for war.

Some members painted their faces with white clay to represent the stone used for the hammer. A few painted one side of the face red to symbolize the sun, others used yellow or black paint over the entire face.

Though mere boys, the order members did their best to distinguish themselves in battle, regarding themselves as made of "stone" and thus unafraid of the enemy. Their war song was as follows:

> I am on the earth
> just for a little while;
> when there is a fight
> I must die.

A distinctive and enjoyable game of the society was to steal food from the village lodges. Before it could be done, a public announcement had to be made to spice the contest. If caught then, a heavy ransom was paid for the member's release.

The Notched Stick Society

Members of the Notched Stick society, declared by some to have been the lowest of the men's orders, derived their name from an unusual musical instrument used in their ceremonies. The instrument was a large piece of wood over three feet long called a "rasp." It was

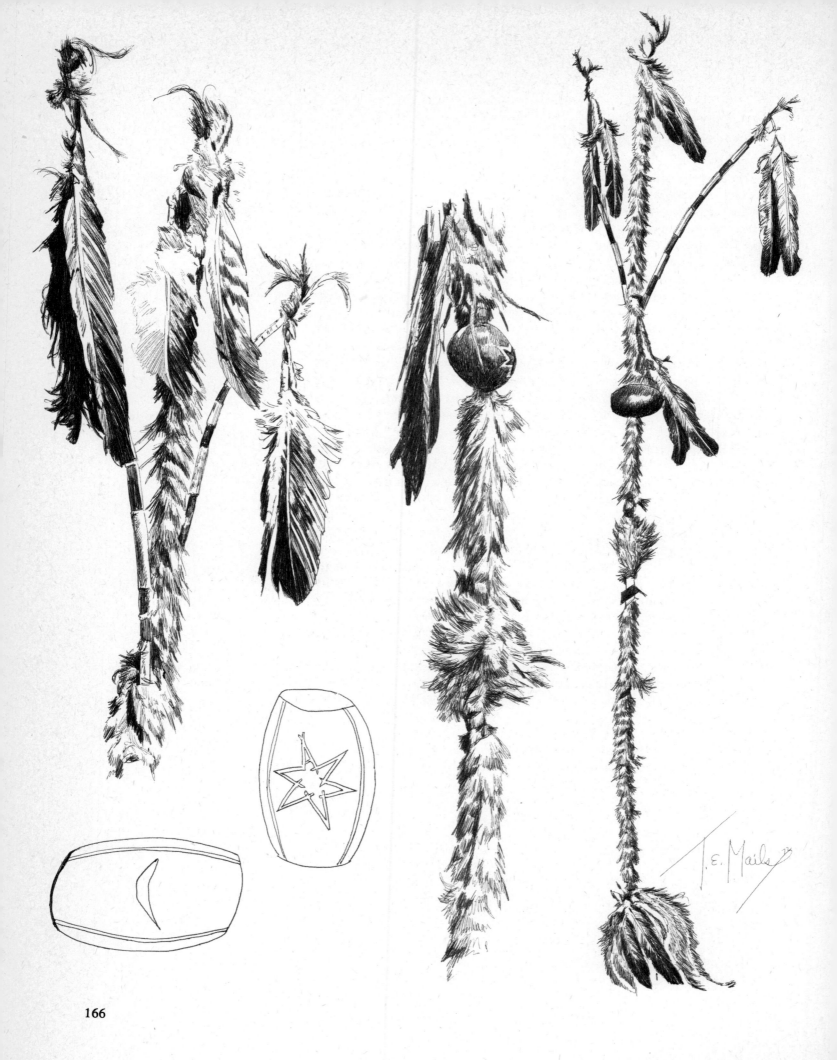

carved at one end to represent a snake's head, tapered to a point at the opposite end and notched along the top edge to signify a snake's backbone. In most tribes, to play one, such as the Ute did in their Bear dance, the performer rested the head at an angle from his body on a gourd or piece of rawhide that was placed on the ground and served as a resonator. He then drew a stick or a bone back and forth along the notches, keeping time. At meetings the Hidatsa propped their rasp up on two forked sticks and sometimes ran the ash-wood stick across its notches while it was in this position. One informant said the Hidatsa stick was rubbed only downward.[4]

When young men were ready to buy the society, a great deal of property—robes, quillwork and eagle feathers—was collected for the sellers and food was presented each of them on four successive nights. On these evenings four songs were sung, then the meeting broke up. The fourth night the sellers instructed their "sons" in how to rub the notched stick, which was placed on a pile about two feet high so as to be seen by everyone present. The buyers then gave a gift for each symbolic part of the stick, such as its eye, head or back. After this, a feast followed and the buyers received their regalia from the sellers. For this each purchaser paid a horse, a gun, an eagle feather or the like. Only one man got the notched stick; he was also the one in whose lodge the members met.

The Dog Society

In perhaps the most regal portrayal of a society member on record, Carl Bodmer painted a Hidatsa Dog society member in his full regalia. His face and body are painted red, and lines by the mouth indicate canine teeth. Most captivating of all is the man's huge, unusual head-dress, which consists of a sunburst of long, dark, narrow magpie feathers, looking something like a rocket when it explodes, plus a single row of turkey or hawk feathers that runs over the center of the crown and rear of the bonnet like a giant fan. Each of these feathers is topped with a weasel tuft, and a large eagle plume-feather stands upright at the front of the fan. The Dog dancer wears an over-the-head society sash of red trade cloth. He also wears an eagle bone whistle around his neck similar in design to that of the Arapaho Dog soldier. Besides the whistle itself, there are long side-hangings of quill-wrapped thongs, which fall similar to fringe when they are worn. The Hidatsa warrior carries a small rattle fashioned from a slim stick. It is bent or hooked at the forward end and covered with hide, to which is attached a row of dew claws. The dancer also carries one of the famous horn bows made by some Plains tribes. For clothing he wears only leggings, which have quilled legbands and painted horizontal stripes. The leggings are hair-fringed. Fox tails trail from the heels of his moccasins.

Each regular member wore the eagle bone whistle suspended from his neck by means of a buckskin string decorated with quillwork. Their headdress consisted of owl feathers with one or two eagle feathers in the middle. All carried rattles similar to the one just described.

The Dogs "behaved backwards," acting in a manner contrary to what was said or expressed. This was true even in battle, and to indicate to one that he should go forward against the enemy, he had to be told to flee.

In a public parade the members marched in single file, except for the Real Dogs, who walked abreast. The Dogs had a saying: "Who-

167

Opposite: *Staff and hammer of Hidatsa Stone Hammer society. Hammer details show celestial symbols etched into sides of hammer head (AMNH).*

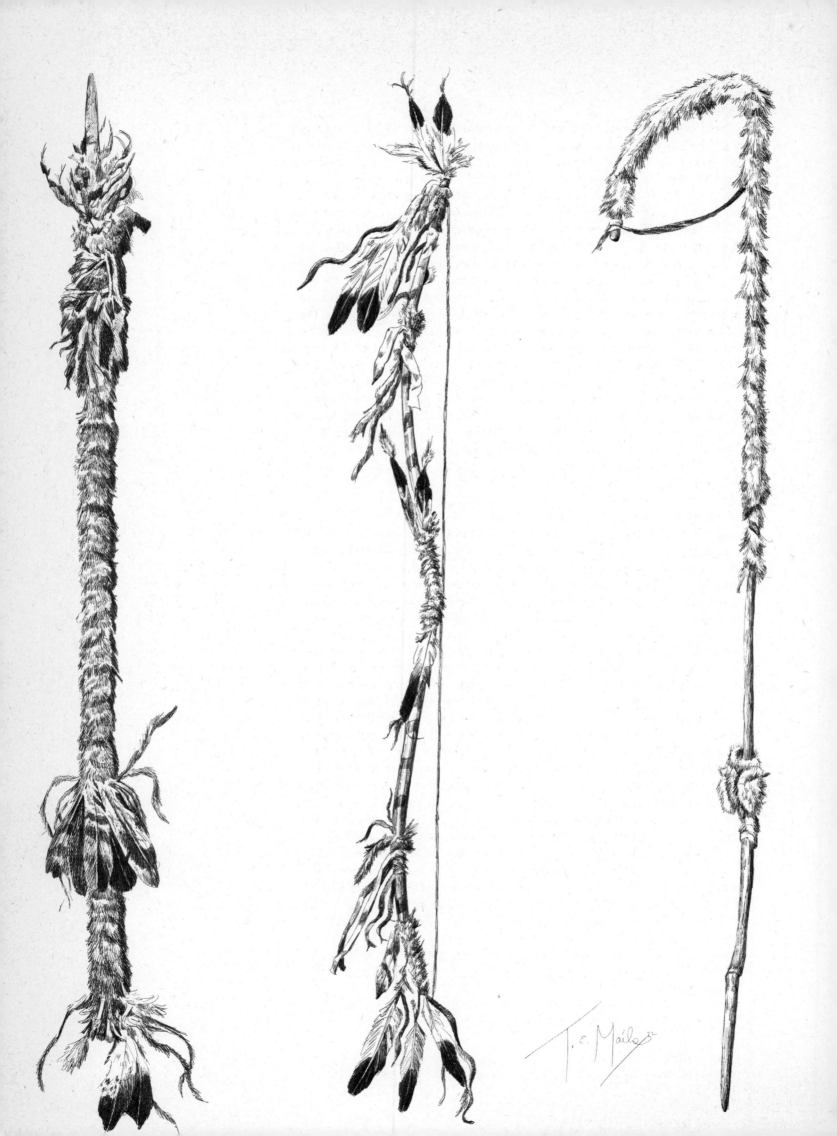

ever kills a Sioux or strikes the first coup shall be feasted by us." Those who did so were accordingly entertained by the society.

The Black Mouth Society

The Hidatsa Black Mouths consisted of middle-aged men who alone exercised police control in their villages. Two officers carried lances and two headmen known as rattlers had rattles. In dancing, the membership divided into two lines facing each other, with the rattlers standing between them. The latter two would begin to sing and shake their rattles, and as they danced, they would cross each other's path.

The officers' emblems were known as raven-lances. Each lance was blackened, and the head was normally carried pointing upward. Below the head was a bunch of owl wing feathers, to which strips of otter skin were attached; and fastened to these were some raven wing feathers. This decorative arrangement appeared at three points on the lance. A strip of otter skin was wrapped spirally around the shaft, which remained partly exposed. At the bottom of the lance was a raven head with its bill pointing downward. The tail of a raven was fastened to the head. The lance carriers were not elected. If a man's father happened to have a raven-lance, the buyer automatically became an officer through purchasing an officer's membership.

In battle, if the enemy pursued the Hidatsa, a raven-lance carrier was expected to sing his song, invert his emblem and plant it in the ground. Until someone pulled the lance out for him, he could not retreat. If the rescuer was not a member of the society, he removed all decoration from the emblem and returned only the bare shaft with the lance head. The officer was then required to go to the man from whom he had purchased the lance and have him decorate it once more. If the seller had died, another member of the former group was approached for the same purpose.

Each of two other officers carried a flat-stemmed pipe, red on one side and black on the other, decorated with quillwork and a dyed horse-tail. These men were expected to mediate quarrels and preserve peace in the tribe. The black and red colors represented night and day, bad will and good will, respectively. All the spirits were represented by the pipe. The members prayed to the pipe, asking that their children should live to grow up and that there should be plenty of buffalo.

In addition to acting as a camp police force, the Black Mouths tried to effect a reconciliation whenever some difficulty arose in the tribe or between friendly tribes.

The rattlers' rattles were made of rawhide. They were shaken not from left to right but back and forth. One informant mentioned two "death-men," one of whom wore a red bonnet and the other a white one. During a battle each one led half the Soldiers, who in turn were followed by the Fox society. The death-men could retreat only when wounded in the chest or back. Each of the rank and file members carried a club consisting of a knife blade set in a wooden stick near the turn of the tapering bent end.[5]

The Black Mouths painted the lower part of the face black and drew a slanting line from the forehead across the face. Their public parade was led by one of the raven-lance officers, the other bringing up the rear. Directly behind the first lancer and just in front of the second marched the two rattlers. The pipe bearers occupied the

Opposite: *Hidatsa society regalia.* Left: *Staff carried by officer of Black Mouths;* middle: *Bow-lance of Lumpwoods;* right: *Hooked staff of Foxes* (AMNH).

center of the line, separated or immediately followed by the herald of the organization.

The Half-shaved Head Society

The Half-shaved Head society originated with the Crows, but the Hidatsa name came from a vision in which the founder saw a buffalo bull with its hair shaved off. Accordingly, the man shaved half his head, and as he was known to be a very brave warrior, the subsequent members of the order adopted the shaving custom by which they afterwards became known.

The leader had a war club with a solid yellow stone and a buffalo tail attached to the end of the handle. Half the stone was painted red, the remainder with white clay. His face was painted red all over, and on the left side a tail of old spotted eagle feathers was made to stand erect. The hairs of a buffalo mane were strung together for a necklace, which was painted half red and half white.

In their parade, men who were dressed alike walked together. Several horsemen were in the group, wearing sacred feathers and honor marks on their heads. The horse-tails were turned up and shortened by tying. An informant said that in later years the shaving custom ceased. Instead, the members wore their hair loose on one side and tied on the other to give the appearance of no hair being there.

The leader carried a hooked stick called a "white stick" but painted red; it was wrapped with wolf skin, and pairs of wolf skin strips, each about a foot long, hung down from three points on the shaft. The last man in line bore a similar lance wrapped with otter skin. Two other officers had bow-spears resembling those of the Lumpwoods, except that red cloth took the place of bear gut. A weasel skin with the head was wrapped around the grip of the bow so that the head was above the holder's fingers. Above the weasel a mallard skin was glued to the bow, and above it the skin of the neck of a woodpecker and the skin of a yellow bird, a white bird and another mallard. A symmetrical arrangement of skins was made below the weasel skin. To four points on the bow, eagle tail feathers were attached; the sides of the bow, throughout its length, were decorated with magpie feathers. These bow-lances were buried with their owners.

The Hot Dance Society

Like its Arikara counterpart, the Hot Dance group took its name from the peculiar performance of the members, who plunged their hands into hot water to extract meat from a pot—which, of course, indicated their bravery as warriors. The ceremony originated in a vision in which dancers, wearing raven skins tied to the backs of their belts, rubbed a certain kind of weed on their hands and arms and plunged them into boiling water without injury. The weed had been given to the visionary.

There were five officers. Of the two head men, one painted a red lightning line on both legs and arms and across the chest. The other painted a red sun on his chest in front and a red new moon on his back. Two other officers, also decorated with lightning lines and a new-moon design, bore pipes. Two men wore raven skins fastened on their backs.

The Kit-fox Society

According to Maximilian, when the members of the Kit-fox paraded, they wore otter and wolf skins. One informant said they wore belts edged with eagle feathers and decorated with three kit-fox skins, one in the rear and one on either side. Their bodies were painted yellow or pink, and all members wore a rawhide or cloth headband decorated with a number of kit-fox jawbones, which were sometimes painted yellow or pink. This was similar to one worn by the Mandans. At one time some of the members shaved their heads on the sides so as to leave a central roach and one lock in front. Others used hair styles that somewhat imitated the roach. At the back of the head some members wore a bunch of feathers painted red. A necklace made of a whole skin of a raven, with the bill and the tail tied together, is also mentioned.

One leader carried a hooked staff, wrapped with wolf skin and decorated at four points with pairs of wolf skin strips—one pair at the end of the hook and the others at points on the shaft. The upper half of the stick was painted red. The other leaders' staffs were similar but wrapped with otter skin. Two carried straight staffs, which were long, wrapped with black and red cloth and decorated at the top with two erect eagle feathers. Two rattlers carried rawhide rattles. Later on these were made of tin cans with stones enclosed.

In battle the hooked-stick men would sing a certain song as an indication of their next move, which was to plant their lances in the ground. The rank and file then prepared to aid them, for regardless of danger the officers could not flee unless their lances were removed by a fellow tribesman.

The Crow Society
Little is known about the Crow group. Its regalia resembled that of the Little Dogs and the Dogs. There were four sash-wearers and a whipper. Rattles were used in dances, and the dance resembled that of the Crazy Dogs.

The Little Dogs Society
The dogs originated the Little Dog society. Its myth of origin speaks of their approaching an Hidatsa village, howling like wolves but at the same time simulating sounds of the human voice. When the villagers went out to see them, they found them transformed into human shape and wearing the regalia of Little Dog officers. The dogs said, "This will help you to live with greater ease and to enjoy yourselves."

Each of the Little Dogs wore two society sashes of skin or blue or red cloth. They slipped over the head by means of a slit, crossed the chest and trailed down to the ground; in the center of the back they were decorated with bunches of owl feathers, which were regarded as sacred objects. Some say the sashes were common to all members, others say only the four officers wore them.

One of the sash-wearers said that in battle he would sing his song, raise his sash, slip it on and then spur his horse straight into the enemy's lines—knowing full well that his action focused the foe's attention on him.

One officer bore an elk horn whip. He was expected to be the last man to flee the battlefield. If the Hidatsa were pursued by an enemy, it was the whipper's duty to dismount and give aid to those wounded or in danger. If he were killed, another man took his place.

Besides the sashes, Maximilian mentions a feather ornament worn

171

on the back of the head. This was a circlet of raven feathers, with an eagle feather in the center. The members wore switches, brushed their hair pompadour-fashion in the center and cut it short at the sides. Horn shells or hair pipes were tied to the braids.

Suspended round his neck by a thong, each member wore a whistle made from the wing bone of a young "white-head" eagle and wrapped with colored bird quillwork. Several buckskin strips terminating in quillworked loops hung down from the whistle, and gum was put into the upper part of the instrument.

The Little Dogs wore no shirts and used red body paint. Some wore buffalo robes with a two-foot fringe at the bottom. Others wore red blankets decorated with bands of beadwork. One member painted the center of his robe with a yellow circle surrounded by dog tracks. Two types of rattles were employed, a globular type and a loop-shaped type. The latter was edged with red cloth and shortened raven wing feathers. The handle was wrapped with red cloth.

The Crazy Dogs Society

The Crazy Dogs society was derived from the Northern Cheyenne. A Cheyenne named Lean-elk dreamed it and gave it to the Hidatsa.

Two officers wore caps adorned with sections of mountain sheep or buffalo horns and trimmed with weasel skins. The horns were painted white and the tips were wrapped with quillwork and decorated with strips of weasel skin. Owl wing-feathers were attached below the horns. A band of red cloth, about four inches in width, was attached across the cap. It was decorated with white beadwork, and three rows of raven wing-feathers nearly covered the cloth. In the back an eagle wing-feather was fastened to a strip of red cloth so as to hang between the shoulders. Raven feathers were also tied between the horns of the headdress.

Two other officers wore a pair of sashes of red cloth that crossed in front and trailed on the ground behind. Individual war medicines were attached to the sashes. When one of these sash-wearers died, the society met to appoint the bravest among them as his successor. The man selected usually declined the honor for a long time, but it was finally forced upon him. When the others fled, the officers were expected to make a stand. Their song was:

> *This is the way*
> *I sing*
> *when I*
> *want to die* [6]

One or two other men carried quirts. These had a handle of elk horn and a wrist-loop of fox skin.

Some of or all the members had ring-shaped rawhide rattles, to which war honor feathers were attached. Thus while an eagle feather referred to the striking of a coup, a horse-tail dyed yellow symbolized the theft of a horse. During a dance the performers wore eagle bone whistles on a thong round the neck and carried whatever weapons they chose. Some had lances, which were sometimes decorated with raven wing-feathers. Very few of the Crazy Dogs wore war shirts. Bodies were painted red or white. As they danced, the members stooped and walked around. Toward the end of a song, the musicians beat their drums faster and then all the Crazy Dogs straightened up suddenly and yelled. For accompaniment, the members shook their

172

rattles and blew their whistles, making a great noise. Women were invited to join in the singing.

The Raven Society

The Raven order passed out of existence very early. At one time it had a large membership, but most died in wars or from smallpox. The general regalia of the society was a raven skin headband; no shirts were worn and the body was painted black. In 1913, a single survivor of the organization wore a necklace made of the whole of a raven skin, with the head on the left side and the tail on the right; a piece of red cloth was held in the raven's mouth to represent the tongue, and a small piece of rawhide hung from the raven's shoulder. Maximilian says that every Raven carried a long lance wrapped with red cloth and trimmed with hanging raven feathers.

Hidatsa informants limit the number of lances to two. The shaft was of blackened ashwood, about six-and-a-half feet long, with a one-foot-long point originally made of flint but later of tin or steel. To the shaft was attached a flap of black cloth four inches wide and running along the entire length of the stick. The flap strip was perforated at intervals so that it could be secured to the shaft by means of buckskin ties. Sleighbells were attached to the cloth in a vertical line, as were raven tail-feathers through which ran a string of the sort used for snares. In reality, this lance should be referred to as a flag.

Their dance was like that of the Kit-foxes, with the chest thrown out, the back bent and the arms slightly flexed. All sang:

> *Raven I am*
> *me look at*
> *(as) he (the enemy) comes*
> *I will not flee*

If, during a battle, a Raven began to sing this song, all the Ravens stopped and made a stand.

The Buffalo Bulls Society

Some Bulls were old and some were young. Several women helped them in singing and occasionally prepared a feast for them. They called themselves Buffalo Bull Women.

All the members, with the exception of a horseman and two officers, wore the same headdress, consisting of a cap made from the skin of a buffalo's head above the eyes. In the back this cap extended a trifle below the neck, and in front it was tied with chin straps. From the cap there rose two buffalo horns, cut short at the bottom, with their tips approaching each other; they were perforated so that they could be fastened to the skin with buckskin strings. A few members tied a dried buffalo tail to the back of their belt so that it extended out from the belt and was almost erect. These, after dancing forward, would run back again, hold their right horns with their hands and act as if they were going to hook some of the spectators. In war these men were obliged to make a stand against pursuing enemies. Accordingly, they would address the Hidatsa people as follows:

> *You see my tail in the air*
> *because I am brave.*
> *Once the enemy were pursuing us*
> *I got so angry that my tail rose erect*
> *and I turned about to chase the enemy.*

Members wore a broad society belt of red cloth extending just below the knees. At the bottom it was edged with tin cones, and directly above the cones small bells were fastened to the cloth. Shirts were not worn, and the body and arms were painted with blue clay. All carried guns and wore their honor marks. Among the Hidatsa, a man who had killed and scalped an enemy tied the scalp to his gun and painted a white line on it for each man he had slain. If a Bull had been wounded, he would whittle the center of a stick so that the shavings were still attached at one end. He would then tie the stick to the hair on his cap. If wounded on the chest, he would put red paint on the lower half of his face. Fingerprints on both sides of the breast indicated that an enemy had been seized with both hands. Anyone who had ever driven the Sioux from behind their breastworks or had entered a Sioux tipi was permitted to enter the dance lodge before the other members.

Two Bull officers, known as Blind Bulls, wore fantastic masks consisting of the skin of a whole buffalo head with the mane and horns. Blue trade glass was put in place of the buffalo's eyes, and below them were the eye slits for the wearer. The entire lower half of the mask from the nose downward was painted blue. The Blind Bulls carried lances decorated with long feathers, tied at the top, and horse-tails dyed yellow. Pieces of white weasel skin were tied to the shaft, all of which was painted black. The lance head was over a foot in length and was held pointing downward.

During a parade one member wearing no headdress and on horseback preceded the others. The horse had sections of horn with a piece of buffalo skin fastened to its head and a piece of rawhide painted yellow attached to its face. The rider carried a shield and wore the society belt.

In dancing, the Bulls stamped their feet as angry buffalo do. When performing outdoors, they acted as fierce as possible to show what kind of men they were. If one had slain an enemy, he might run toward the spectators and discharge his gun. Anyone wounded in battle had the privilege of kicking his neighbor during the dance. The Blind Bulls acted as if they did not hear the sounds but merely walked and jumped around, apparently to show that the noise of a battle would not frighten or deter them. When the Bulls danced, a container of water was placed in their midst. Those who had helped a wounded comrade in battle were permitted to drink from it and then to tell their story. It is said that there were generally very few of them.[7]

7

THE MANDAN

The Mandans say they migrated from the Great Lakes region to the headwaters of the Mississippi, then overland to the Missouri before the beginning of the historical period, finally establishing themselves at the mouth of Heart River, North Dakota. Like the Arikara, the Mandans evolved a complex ceremonial structure for their lives. Though they numbered 3,600 in 1780, diseases brought by the Whites decimated the Mandans in a series of ghastly blows. In 1880, only thirty-one were still living. It is all the sadder when one considers that in 1832, Catlin found them garbed in magnificent clothing and living in a rich way, a happy people involved in marvelously productive lives.

The warrior society system of the Mandans consisted of seven age-graded orders through which a man passed successively. Curtis lists the groups as follows:

Fox
Foolish Dog
Half-sheared
Make-mouth-black
Dog
Buffalo-bull
Black-tail-deer

Besides these, there were five women's societies:

Enemy-women
White-buffalo-cow-women
Goose
Skunk
Creek (River-women?)[1]

Lowie's Mandan list is as follows:

Men's Societies	Women's Societies
Cheyenne	Skunk women
Kit-fox	Enemy women
Little Dog	Goose
Crazy Dog	Old women
Crow	Gun
Half-shaved	River women
Black mouths	Cheyenne women
Bull	White buffalo cow [2]
Dog	
Old Dog	
Coarse Hair	
Black-tail-deer	
Badger	

According to Curtis, the usual age of entrance into the Fox order was "eighteen or twenty years" and "no one younger than fifty years was permitted to enter the [Buffalo] Bull society." Of course, this was around 1900; it is indicative of the changes that took place over the years that in 1833, Maximilian established the age-span of the Mandan Crazy-dogs as from ten to fifteen years, that of the Crow society as from twenty to twenty-five and that of the Black-tail-deer as over fifty. Note that the Crow society no longer existed by Curtis's time, 1900.[3]

A "Crow or Raven society" is mentioned by Maximilian as being

Opposite: *Cap of fox skin worn by officer of Mandan Kit-fox society (AMNH).*

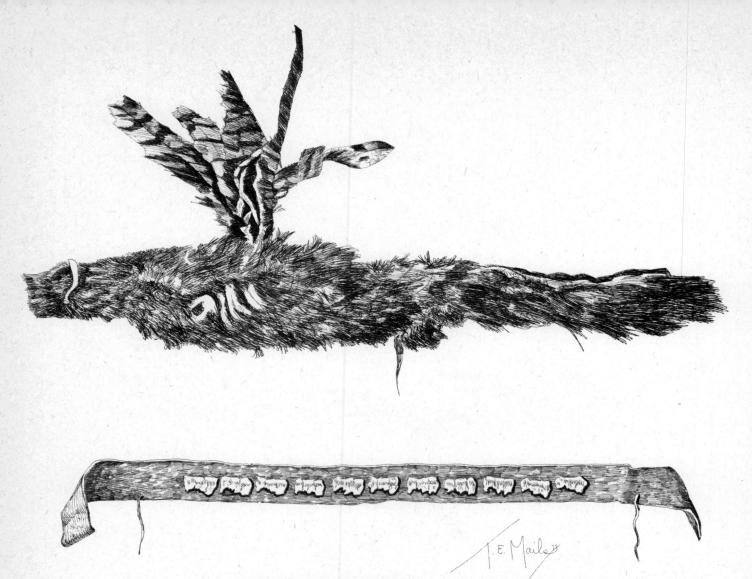

among the Mandans.[4] Lowie includes a Crow society in his list and also a Kit-fox order. Wissler cites a Badger society as being among the Mandans, "which became extinct about twenty years ago." Maximilian states that the Black Mouths were "soldiers" who alone exercised police control among both the Mandans and the Hidatsa.[5]

To become a member of the Mandan age-system, one first had to join with others of his own age-group in purchasing the rights of the lowest order before he could pass successively through the others by the same means. Each society had its own lodge for a meeting place— to which only members and past members were admitted. It also had its own songs, which were considered its most valued possession. Indeed, it was the songs that were purchased by the new members. In the Mandan view they were not buying membership so much as they were purchasing the songs; that is, the right to sing what belonged exclusively to the society. And, once it had sold its songs, the former members of a society were not permitted to sing them again.

A typical illustration of the Mandan custom of acquiring society membership is as follows: The Foolish Dogs purchased the rights and privileges of the Half-sheared, leaving the latter without membership in any society. After a time the Half-sheared assembled, but not as an organization, and decided that the time had arrived for them to buy the privileges of the soldier order. They collected quantities of blankets, shirts, moccasins, pemmican, pipes, tobacco and horses, and when sufficient property had been accumulated, they took it all to the lodge of the Make-mouth-black soldier order and placed the ceremonial pipe inside the door. When the soldiers assembled, if the quantity seemed to

178

Mandan society regalia. Top: *Skunk-skin headband of White Buffalo Cow society;* bottom: *Headband of fox jaws worn by members of Kit-fox society* (AMNH).

be sufficient, they smoked the pipe, thus signifying their acceptance. If, however, the property was considered inadequate, they left the pipe untouched until the Half-sheared members added a sufficient amount. If the Foolish Dogs purchased the songs of the society next above them before their own rights were disposed of, they would possess two memberships but would not exercise the song rights of the lower order. This meant that the society remained dormant until the Foxes were ready to purchase the Foolish Dogs' songs.[6]

Each society had its own dances, in which the members alone might participate; but the performance was not conducted in secret. Each also had its own regalia, which sometimes, as in the case of the Bulls, included masks; and in each were two leaders, who carried the staffs and were committed to deeds of exceptional bravery, as in the military organizations of other Plains tribes.

Once again, the American Museum of Natural History has a number of pieces of Mandan society regalia in its display. It includes a cap of kit-fox skin worn by an officer of the Kit-fox society. It is a small cap, with the skin laid over a hide skullcap and an extension of fur hanging down the back for about twelve inches. Regular members of the Kit-fox wore a narrow headband of hide, to which eleven or so jawbones of the kit-fox were attached. The officers of the Black-mouth order carried a beautiful pointed lance, about seven feet long, wrapped with otter fur and further adorned with three groupings of golden eagle feathers. Some of the feathers were cut to make an interesting arrangement, and several were loosely hung by thongs from the butt of the lance.

Several pieces of women's society regalia are also included in the museum collection. There is a White Buffalo Cow Women's headdress, or cap, topped with a fan of hawk feathers. These are shaped like a Turkish fez, high and round, and made of the prized skin of a white buffalo. This was the highest order among the women's organizations of the Mandans and Hidatsa. Their ceremony, in which the members represented a buffalo herd and imitated buffalo, was believed to attract the buffalo herds close to the villages. According to a Catlin drawing, dancers wore buffalo robes and carried dry branches with tufts of eagle down tied to the ends. The Goose society headbands were made of rolled duck and goose skins. The ceremony of the order was held annually to promote the growth of the corn, and accordingly the members carried ears of corn as they danced.

A rather mysterious women's organization was the River Women, called the Grass-crown society by the Hidatsa. They conducted an annual performance that lasted four nights and took place after a woman had dreamed of holding the ceremony. Participants wore headbands that included a golden eagle tail feather tied horizontally on the forehead.

An Enemy Women's society performed victory dances to celebrate the deaths of enemies and to mourn the fallen warriors of the Mandans. Dancers wore hide headbands with serrated edges, arrangements of dentalium shells at each side together with eagle down feathers and an eagle tail feather extending off to the left side. A pendant of four hair-pipe bones hung from each side of the headband down the cheeks of the wearer.

One of Carl Bodmer's most famous paintings, done during his 1833 trip with Maximilian, was of the Mandan Buffalo Bulls. Their

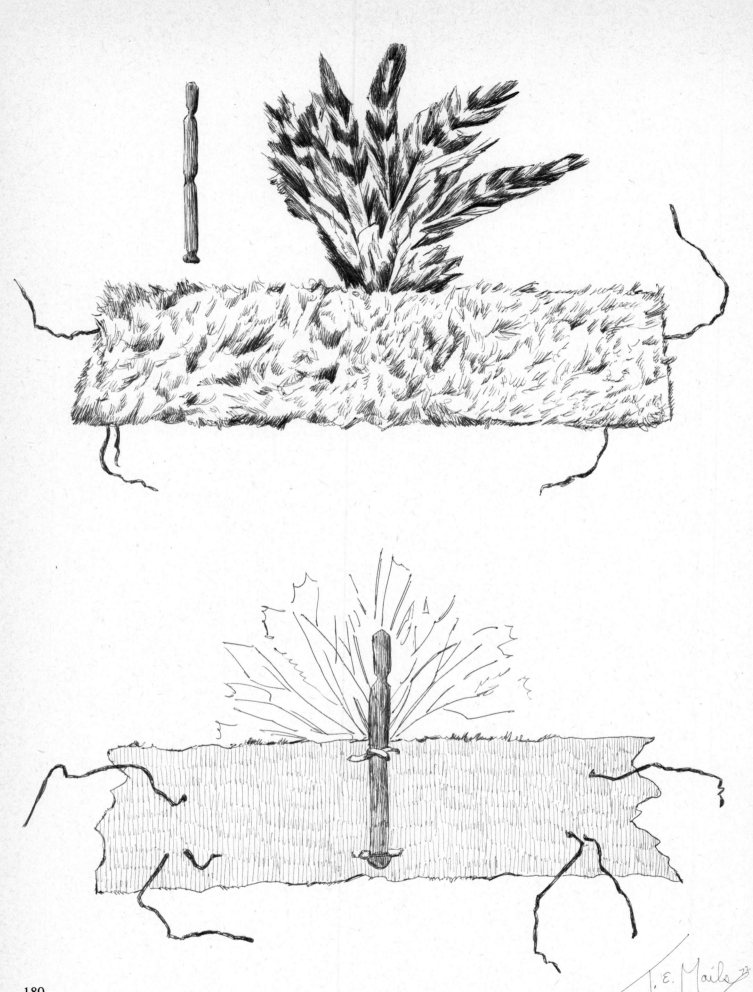

Headband worn by members of Mandan White Buffalo Cow Women's society. Top: *outside;* bottom: *inside (AMNH).* Opposite: *Mandan White Buffalo Cow Women's society member wearing order's headband and carrying branch to which feather plumes are attached.*

bodies were painted with horizontal stripes to indicate their war accomplishments. On their heads the officers wore masks fashioned from the heads of buffalo, with the long winter hair left on and trailing halfway down the dancer's back. Wooden eyeholes and mouth slits were inserted for vision and comfort, adding greatly to the external appearance of the mask. The horns were attached to the masks also. Buffalo tails were tied to the dancer's legs at the calf and to the heel of each moccasin. A stiffened tail, which stuck out behind the dancer in a rounded or cascading form, was also appended to the back of the belt. The officers of the order carried lances with huge iron points and a large eagle feather attached so as to protrude straight out from the butt. Lesser officers wore buffalo horn bonnets and carried less impressive lances. Regular members also wore buffalo horn bonnets and carried a variety of weapons, including guns. Nearly every dancer carried a shield, and it is worth noting that the shields were twice the size of an average Plains shield—some thirty to thirty-six inches in diameter—beautifully painted and hung with trade cloth, hoof rattles and feathers.

Bodmer has also illustrated the Half-shaved Head dance, and the society regalia can be plainly seen. Four officers carried long fur-wrapped hooked staffs, with unusual puffballs of fur appended at intervals of eighteen inches or so. Two eagle tail feathers were tied to each of these. Six officers carried flags—pointed lances with feathers appended horizontally for the full length. Some dancers wore what must have been an impressive painted hide pendant, which hung from the back of the head down the wearer's back. Hair, probably a horse-tail, was added to the end of the pendant, making its full length reach nearly to

183

Above: *Mandan Buffalo Bull wearing buffalo head mask with wooden eyeholes and mouth slit. Details based on paintings by Carl Bodmer.* Opposite: *Headband worn by members of Mandan Enemy Women's society* (AMNH).

Mandan Half-shaved (or sheared) Head society officer with fur-wrapped hooked staff.

the ground. Headdresses themselves varied. Some members had their hair packed with either paint or paint-filled clay, which caused it to separate into broad strands. Several dancers had wolf tails tied to the heels of their moccasins to indicate their war honors.

The Cheyenne society consisted of boys ten or twelve years of age. Every member wore a head ornament consisting of a round piece of rawhide with a bone feather-holder. Two officers wore society belts of red cloth edged with eagle feathers, which hung down. Two other officers had a sacred bow and two arrows, one painted red and the other black. Two officers carried spiked clubs, the spike being made of horn. The sacred bows were for use against the enemy and were said never to miss.

Before the boys could buy the society, a group of older men called them together and said something like the following: "We wish to give you a society." Then property was collected and brought to the sellers. The same night the men sang songs, to which the young boys danced. After the dance, the warriors addressed the boys, saying, "You are growing up now. You must go against the enemy. Try to be brave and conquer the enemy." [7]

The Crazy Dog society was the next youngest age-group, embracing boys from at least twelve to fifteen years and older. The regalia of all members included a whistle made from the wing bone of a wild goose. Everyone carried a rattle of either globular or ring shape, trimmed with raven wing feathers. An ornament of split raven wing feathers was attached to the back of the head. Some members bore lances while dancing. Bodies were daubed with yellow paint, and no shirts or leggings were worn.

185

Opposite: *Mandan Buffalo Dancer painted and dressed for one phase of their Sun Dance ceremony, called* Okipé. *He wears buffalo-hair headdress, with thongs, through which numerous green willow branches are thrust* (SM).

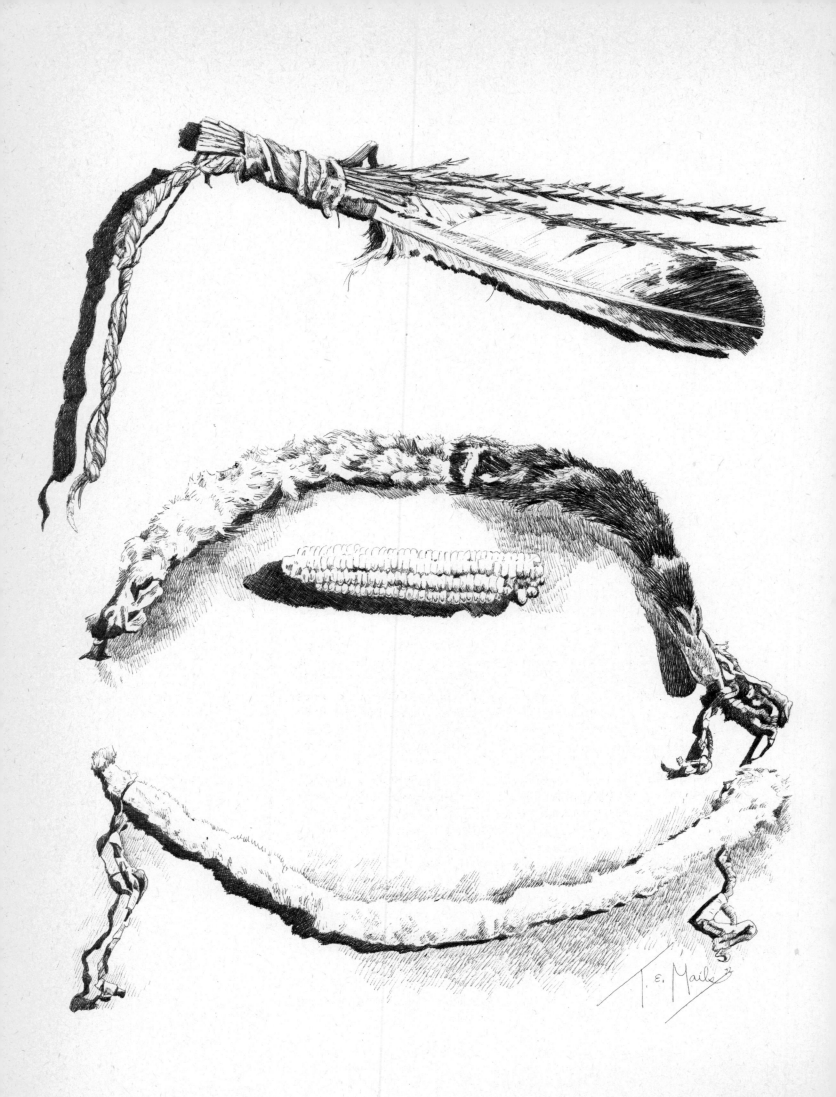

Three sash-wearers wore sashes made from red trade cloth and edged with white cloth. The sashes had a slit and were slipped over the head. At the shoulder, near the white edging, was attached the war medicine given by the seller to the buyer at the time of purchase.

Three other officers wore headdresses of buffalo skin, decorated with split horns and weasel skins. To the back of these were attached strips of rawhide, about three-and-a-half feet in length and decorated with quillwork. Horsehair tufts, dyed yellow, were fastened to the tips of the horns, and occasionally hawk wings were used for additional decoration.

Two additional officers bore lances, which were adorned at the top and center with bunches of short raven wing-feathers. The use of a feathered string with these lances was optional. There were four drummers.

The Crazy Dogs performed the Hot dance, in which the boys danced on hot coals with their bare feet. After this they extracted meat from a kettle of boiling liquid with their bare hands. Those coming last to the pot had the worst of it, for they had to go deeper than the rest.

The Old Dog society painted their bodies white and their hands red and black. They wore a grizzly skin robe and head feathers that hung down the back.

The Coarse Hair society consisted of very holy men. On their heads they attached a small piece of scalp from a buffalo head. This was covered with feathers taken from birds of prey. Hair was attached to the scalp so as to hang over the members' faces in flat braids. Honor marks were placed on their clothing. The left leggings were painted red up to the knee, and black marks were put around the lower legs to show that the wearers had counted coup on many enemies. Those who had killed enemies tied hair locks to the leggings. For each enemy struck in war, a feather was placed on the head. A gun wound was indicated by a stick about nine inches in length and whittled at the lower end so that the shavings remained on the stick. A man wounded by an arrow wore the split feather from an arrow, dyed red, on his head.

It was customary for a young man on a raid or a war party to promise the members he would give them a dance and feast provided that he performed some brave deed. If he did, he also filled a pipe for them on his return and, if possible, presented them with horses. He asked them to continue to pray for him.

One member carried a beautiful fan of white feathers and wore on his head a complete swan's tail, each feather of which was tipped with dyed horsehair. The members wrapped themselves completely with robes and carried bow-lances trimmed with feathers, colored cloth, glass beads and the like. Most of them had fox skins attached to their moccasin heels. In dancing, several men beat a drum while the rest formed a circle and imitated the sounds of buffalo bulls. After a while, the spectators threw a quantity of tobacco down upon them from the tops of the huge earth lodges. At this the members departed from the village, removing their face wigs on the way.

The Black-tail Deer society consisted of men over fifty years of age. The men all wore a wreath of grizzly bear claws on their heads and displayed their war achievements in the form of feathers, hair-locks, scalps and paint marks.

The Badger society did not dance but instead assembled to go

187

Opposite: *Mandan society regalia.* Top: *Headband of River Women's society, grass tied to feather;* bottom: *Duck skin and goose skin headbands of women's Goose society; ear of corn similar to that carried by each woman* (AMNH).

into the sweat-lodge together, on which occasion they imitated badgers. In leaving the lodge, they always proceeded backward. Only those who had sold all the other societies could share in the Badger proceedings.

According to Maximilian, the Mandan women were originally grouped in four age societies: the Gun, the River, the Hay (or Grass), the White Buffalo; the Hidatsa women were grouped in three: the Skunk, the Enemy and the Wild Goose. Later the societies of both tribes merged, in that all seven became common to each through adoption.

The mode of entrance into these groups was by purchase, a method similar to that of the male societies. Three of the women's organizations —the River, the Wild Goose, and the White Buffalo—were rather sharply separated from the others by their clearly sacred character and a cleansing ceremony that concluded their performance. In particular, the Wild Goose and White Buffalo societies were associated with securing food through religious means, while the Skunk, the Gun and the Enemy Women were associated with war activities. If, however, a member of any Hidatsa society was ill and unable to do her planting, the members of all the other societies would do this for her.

8
THE ARAPAHO

The oldest traditions among the Arapaho place their original home somewhere east of the headwaters of the Mississippi River. Here they lived in stationary villages and tilled the soil, raising large crops of corn. They eventually migrated to the headwaters of the Missouri River and from there onto the Plains. At this juncture they ceased to farm and became nomadic buffalo hunters. In their first migrations, the Arapaho moved in company with the Cheyenne. About 1835, both tribes divided, the greater portion of each moving south to the Arkansas River region in what is now eastern Colorado. After that, the Southern Arapaho and Southern Cheyenne remained closely allied, but the Northern Arapaho and Northern Cheyenne became mainly independent nations.

Before 1840, the Arapaho were at war with the Navaho, Utes, Shoshone, Sioux and Pawnees. After that time they were at peace with the Plains tribes but sometimes joined the Comanche and Kiowas in raids into Mexico.

The tribe numbered something like 3,500 in 1775 and had decreased to about half that size by 1900. They were known by all as a friendly, contemplative and religious people who were nevertheless renowned for their accomplishments in war. The Sun Dance was their greatest annual religious ceremony, and much of their personal lives was centered in visions and dreams. They were a trading group between the Pawnees, Osage and others on the north and among the Kiowas, Comanche and others on the south, which caused them to be referred to as "he buys or trades." The Cheyenne called them Cloud Men, and they referred to themselves as People of Our Own Kind.

The Arapaho grouped their tribal ceremonies into three divisions. The first of these was the Sun Dance ceremony.

The second ceremonial division of the Arapaho consisted of the male societies. The men and youths of the entire Arapaho tribe were organized into eight age-graded societies, comprising a system that closely resembled that of the Gros Ventre. These groups were both military and religious in spirit, and the two societies composed of the oldest men were almost totally religious. The regalia of the first six orders included either actual war weapons or symbols of weapons. Following the usual Plains custom, in most of the orders selected individuals were expected to evidence special heroism in defense of the tribe whenever the people were hard pressed in battle. Accordingly, in each society there were certain renowned positions held by especially courageous and capable men, who were distinguished from the rest of the society members by their special regalia and their parts in the conduct of ceremonies.

Curtis names the eight Arapaho societies as follows:

Fox-men
Star-men or Star Falcons
Club-men or Tomahawk
Lance-men or Staffs
Crazy-men—also called the Lime-crazy Men or Moths
Dog-men
Sweat-lodge or the Stoic-lodge
Water-pouring or Water-sprinkling Old Men [1]

According to some authorities, boys under twelve years of age

were permitted to serve in menial capacities for the various societies, and girls under the age of fifteen could dance in restricted roles in the Women's Buffalo dance.[2] However, actual membership in the first and lowest society could not be purchased until the age of fifteen or sixteen had been attained.

Once that age had been reached, a youth was expected to begin his climb up through the eight orders, and he would continue to do so until he was killed in battle or reached the venerable age of seventy or so, at which point he could retire.

The procedure for advancing from one order to the next was a standard one. When for some special reason a man wished to obtain Divine favor, he promised God that in return for the blessing desired, he would perform the ceremony of the society next above the one to which he currently belonged. When the request had been granted and when the traditionally designated time in the summer arrived, he and his "brothers" enacted the rites of the next older order, being provided with their regalia and instructed in the proper procedures by older men who already knew this ceremony. The Arapaho scheme assumed that every male would pass through the entire series of orders, and a higher ritual automatically became the right of the lower group whenever they determined to purchase it through the method just mentioned. As in the case of the other Plains tribes, the mature Arapaho warrior societies performed in regular rotation the annual duties of camp police.

The Fox Men Society

The Fox Men were first and lowest in rank, consisting of young men who might remain as members up to the age of about twenty-five years. They had no special duties or privileges. They did have a dance called the Fox dance but no special ritual.

The Star Men Society

According to Mooney, the Star Men group consisted of young warriors about thirty years of age.[3] However, Trenholm indicates a more logical age bracket of from eighteen to twenty. Their dance was called the Star dance, and they too had no special ritual.[4]

The Club Men Society

The Club Men dance was known as the Club dance. The members played a central role in the warrior society scheme, for they were men in the prime of physical life. The four leaders carried broad wooden clubs called swords, which were painted and adorned with eagle feathers hung in beautiful balance. Some have said they resembled a gun and were notched along the edges, but the actual artifacts do not look like guns. In an attack on the enemy, it was the duty of the four leaders to ride or run ahead and strike the enemy with the clubs. If successful, they returned and took their places in front of the rest of the war party in readiness for a general charge. It was a dangerous responsibility, but the attendant honors paid by the tribe were in proportion to the danger, so there were always candidates for a vacancy. Also, it was an office that the holder never resigned. The rest of the Club Men carried unusual sticks carved at one end to represent a buffalo head and tapering to a dull point at the other. Buffalo hair, quill-wrapped thongs and an eagle feather were tied at the pointed end

Opposite: *Arapaho Tomahawk society regalia.* Top: *Wooden club, called* sword, *carried by officer;* bottom: *Carved stick carried by ordinary members* (AMNH).

for spiritual power. Black horse-hair was attached to the head and white beads were used to represent the buffalo's eyes. In desperate encounters the Club Men were expected to plant their buffalo sticks in the ground in front of themselves and then to fight there to the death or until a retreat might be ordered by the war chief.[5]

The Lance Men Society

The fourth order was called Lance Men, and their ceremonial dance was called the Lance or Staff dance. This order was adopted from the Cheyenne, and it remained active until 1916. They served as police while in camp, when the village moved and when on the hunt. In general, they enforced the orders of the camp chief, making certain they were obeyed by every member of the tribe. Their punishments for violations were typical. If any person violated the unwritten but strict tribal code, by such actions as failing to attend a general ceremony or council, a delegation of Lance Men was sent to kill his dogs, destroy his tipi and in extreme cases to shoot his ponies so as to render him nearly helpless. On large hunting expeditions, it was their duty to restrain the party until the proper religious ceremonies had been performed and the order was given by the civil chief to proceed with the hunt. The police were regarded as the guarantors of law, order and fairness and could not be resisted as they performed their duty or inflicted punishment. In an interdependent social order, this was a must, and the people understood it.

In battle or raiding performances, the Lance Men equaled or even surpassed the ferocious Club Men. Trenholm says there were ten warriors in the order with special regalia to identify them. Two carried crooked lances with a long lance point attached to the straight end. The shafts were wrapped with otter skin. Two others carried straight lances wrapped with otter skin. Four Lance Men carried lances that were painted black. One man carried a large wooden club shaped something like a baseball bat, and one carried a rattle, the hoop of which was covered by the scrotum of a buffalo and the handle of which was ornamented with buffalo hair. This ensured the members of the strength of the buffalo and successful hunting. In battle, if the enemy took shelter behind log or rock defenses, it was the Lance Men's duty to lead the charge, throwing their rattles in among the enemy and then jumping into the midst of them. It is not surprising that the Lance Men held the special respect of the tribe.[6]

Some authorities refer to the Lance Men as the Drum society.[7] Under this title, society artifacts in the American Museum of Natural History include a club—probably the instrument referred to by anthropologists as the "club shaped like a baseball bat"—and a society belt, not referred to elsewhere.

According to museum references, "the Drum Society, whose members were men about thirty years of age, ranked between the Tomahawk and the Crazy societies in the Arapaho hierarchy. Symbolic references to thunder, believed to be a supernatural being, were prominent in the society's regalia and ceremonies. The Drum Society had a hierarchy of five officers, chosen for their bravery."

The club was carried by the highest officer of the society. A representation of the thunderbird, who was a supernatural being, was carved on the thirty-inch-long club. The skin of a kit-fox was attached at the

195

Opposite: *Officers of Arapaho Lance Men (Drum) society in ceremony carrying hooked staffs and wearing society belts. Officer in rear wears society sash (AMNH).*

T·E·Mails

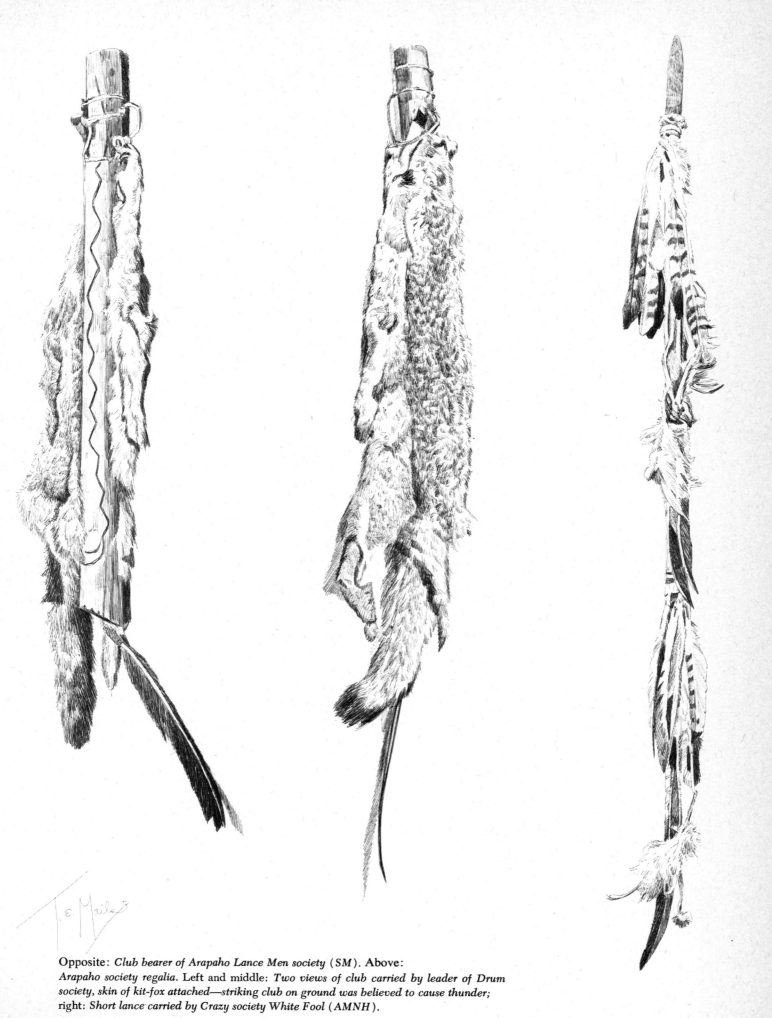

Opposite: *Club bearer of Arapaho Lance Men society (SM).* Above:
Arapaho society regalia. Left and middle: *Two views of club carried by leader of Drum
society, skin of kit-fox attached—striking club on ground was believed to cause thunder;*
right: *Short lance carried by Crazy society White Fool (AMNH).*

end nearest the handle, with the lower part of the skin left hanging loose. Pointing the club upward was believed to cause thunder.

The belt was worn by the ordinary members of the society. Six green-painted crosses along its middle, at which points cut eagle wing (or pinion) feathers were attached in bunches, represented "Our Father, the Morning Star." Four vertical green-painted lines stood for the four days of the ceremony. A narrow strip of green-painted skin sewn along the top of the belt symbolized the straight path to be walked by society members and the good life that would result from doing so. The bottom of the belt had a serrated edge, and the notches represented clouds, hence a prayer for rain. Bunches of cut black feathers were also added to the bottom of the belt at the center and ends. The usual belt was about twelve inches wide and thirty inches long.

The Crazy Men, or Lime-Crazy, Society

The fifth grade, the Crazy Men, consisted of men about forty years of age and older (Mooney says "more than fifty years") who had served their time in the field and were no longer expected to go constantly to war. They must, however, have graduated through all the lower orders. Their duties were mostly religious, hence ceremonial, and their insignia consisted of a bow and a bundle of blunt arrows, an eagle bone whistle hung on a thong round the neck, a buffalo hide cape and a distinctive headband of owl feathers. Their dance was the Crazy dance, which well deserved the name.

Members of the Crazy (Enchanted) society acted as ridiculously as possible and "talked backward," that is, expressed the opposite of their intended meaning and did the opposite of whatever they were asked to do. To get them to perform what one wanted, one had to ask for a reverse action. As peculiar as the custom seems, it portended strength and intelligence, for it required an agile mind and caused the members to do readily the tasks others avoided in the ordinary instance. Clownlike behavior was thought to be connected somehow with the society's headband of owl feathers. The band also had a root attached to it, which was supposed to make the wearer unusually active and to invest him with the power of paralyzing men and animals.

The two leaders of the Crazy society were known as the White Fools. Their office was symbolized by an eagle bone whistle, the neck strap of which was wrapped with quills and hung with breath feathers, and by a short but beautifully decorated lance hung with owl and eagle feathers. During a ceremony, their bodies and cheeks were daubed with white clay and their ears were filled with buffalo hair, which conferred strong religious powers. Their dance was an exhibition of deliberate craziness, in which the performers strove to outdo one another in nonsensical and frenzied actions, particularly in constantly doing the exact opposite of what they had been told to do. It was performed only in obedience to a vow made by someone for the recovery of a sick child, for a successful war party or for another blessing. It continued for four days, the performers dancing without costume for the first three days and in full costume on the fourth.

Men, women and children joined in the ceremony and on the fourth day dressed magnificently in the skin outfits of the foremost animals of the Plains—buffalo, mountain lions, deer, elk and birds. In particular there were always one bear, two foxes, seven regular wolves and two

199

Opposite: *Arapaho Crazy Men society member performing in ceremony (AMNH).*

"holy wolves." Each participant imitated the animal or bird whose skin they wore to the best of their ability. The two foxes ran continually and stumbled over the others in their supposed attempts to escape them. The White Fools were permitted every license because they were "feared" by the others.

Among other things, the Crazy dancers would dance back and forth through a fire until they had extinguished it by their tramping. This was done in imitation of the fire moth, called "crazy" by the Arapaho because it would hover about a fire until it finally flew into it and died. Witnesses were often perplexed as to how the dancers avoided severe burns, yet none were seen. Some suspected that certain herb medicines were applied before the performance. Nevertheless their accomplishments did indicate that God's power to heal was working through them because of their ritual supplications before him. The Crazy Men also handled poisonous snakes, and it is said that sometimes they even surrounded and killed a buffalo by sheer physical strength.[8]

The Crazy ceremony was considered the most picturesque and amusing dance of the Plains tribes. Its song was:

> The buffalo head,
> The half buffalo,
>   the half buffalo, etc.

The words referred to the buffalo hide cape worn by certain of the dancers and to the hide with horns attached worn on the heads of other dancers. The Cheyenne had an animal dance that was similar to the Crazy dance of the Arapaho, and several other Plains tribes duplicated it to some degree.

The Dog Men Society

The Dog Men's dance was called the Dog dance. They had four principal leaders and two lesser leaders, and the four principal leaders always served as generals and directors for major battles.[9]

Authorities say that the median age for Dog Men was fifty, although that seems to exceed the age at which most of the Plains tribes

200

Arapaho Crazy Men society regalia. Left: Bone whistle on quill-wrapped thong; right: Bow, wooden reed and quilled loop attached to corner of cape (AMNH).

warriors ceased to carry on active warfare—at least that of the nature to which at least certain of the Dog Men were called. The four principal leaders wore society sashes of buffalo hide. These were about six inches wide and six or seven feet long. Some had a vertical loop at the top for inserting the head and left arm so that the sash was worn over the right shoulder, and others had a slit for the head so that it could trail down the middle of the back.

Also, according to existing specimens, the Arapaho sashes were not identical in finish. One in the American Museum of Natural History is painted a dull red, with four horizontal bands of yellow quills spaced about eight inches apart on its lower half. One in the Smithsonian has the skin painted or dyed black and has round, painted hide targets placed at intervals along its length. Both of these have a bunch of eagle tail feathers tied at the base of the neck slit and eagle breath-feather fluffs added along the edges for further decoration. Of course, these fluffs were really placed there to gain eagle "power" and as spiritual protection, guaranteeing that arrows would pass as harmlessly through the warrior as wind did through the fluffs.

Yet another sash in the Smithsonian has no fluffs, no quilled bands and no dye color. It does have a bunch of cut feathers at the base of the neck opening, the cut feathers probably indicating that the warrior had slit an enemy's throat in battle. Mooney says he was told that of the four sashes, two were yellow and two were black.[10]

The Dog Men's lance was curved or hooked at the top like a shepherd's crook, and the wood was wrapped for its entire length with otter fur strips. The strips were secured to the shaft with buckskin

201

Arapaho Crazy Men society members dancing to extinguish hot coals of fire.

thongs at four places, and bunches of small eagle feathers and fluffs were tied at these points for power. At the second thong from the top, a piece of hide, cut to represent a dog's foot with claws, was tied. The Dog lance of the White settlement period had a very long and narrow iron point, almost like a spike, eighteen inches or so in length.

The officers of the Dog Men wore identifying ornaments tied on the left side of the head, the highest ranking officer wearing a golden eagle tail feather combined with white breath-feathers and the next highest a hanging of black horsehair held together by buckskin thongs.

The rattle carried by all Dog Men could be easily associated with the sash, for it consisted of an eighteen-inch-long round stick covered with hide; the hide had four quilled bands on it like those on the sash. Dew claws were hung from it to provide the rattle's sound. The rattles have a fine sculptural quality, being evenly balanced by a golden eagle feather pendant placed at the head and by a long, ornamented hide tab at the handle—often the custom for tomahawk designs.

The eagle bone whistle worn by the Dog Men was of an unusual style, for in addition to the quill-wrapped neck strap, there were seven or eight very long quilled thongs attached at each side of the neck strap, which were brought forward to hang loosely on the warrior's chest alongside the whistle, making it in its totality a very handsome piece of artwork.

Whenever the society confronted the enemy, the sash-wearers went in front of the others, shaking their rattles vigorously and chanting the society's war song. They were to do this until other warriors of the society took the rattles out of their hands. Then, as the group began the attack, the sash-wearers dismounted and drove their lances through the bottom of the sash and into the ground, thus anchoring themselves there in the midst of the battle. Here they remained until either the battle was won or they themselves had given the order to retreat. Even then, they could not release themselves but had to wait until some of their own society members freed them by pulling the lances out of the ground and whipping them away from the place with a special kind of quirt carried only by designated members of the organization.

In fact, no Arapaho was supposed to retreat without a sash-wearer's permission, on penalty of total disgrace. And, should their own members panic and neglect to set them free in the confusion of retreat, they were expected to remain and die at their lances, for when they were secured to the ground, their positions represented their home country. Further, if their village was fleeing, the sash-wearers had to give up their own horses to the women and either find other horses or turn and face the enemy alone and on foot. Understandably, they seldom accompanied any but the larger war parties, and, although they usually did little actual fighting, their very presence on those special occasions inspired the warriors of all societies with the utmost courage, for the driving of their lances into the ground was always understood as the resounding signal for an encounter to the death![11]

In recognition of their bravery, the Dog Men were given the annual honor of raising the center pole in the offerings lodge for the Sun Dance. They also had certain food privileges in ceremonies. Trenholm states that whipping was a form of discipline common to Dog Men, and the act of whipping on the battlefield supports the contention.[12] Anthropologists have mentioned the order's practice of the ceremonial surrender of members' wives to one another, which was said to be the supreme test of manhood. If a member could surmount jealousy, he was respected for it. Apparently, though, this was a custom restricted to the society and, even then, one that was seldom abused by members, for the moral code of the tribe frowned on wife-trading.[13]

The Sweat Lodge, or Stoic, Society

The Sweat Lodge society was a secret order of mature men. They had no special dance, and their ceremonies were shared only with each other. They did not fight but sometimes accompanied the war parties, going aside every night along the way to perform secret ceremonies for the success of the party.[14]

203

Opposite: *Arapaho Dog Men warrior, named Powder Face, wearing full-tailed golden eagle warbonnet and carrying hooked lance—typical camp scene with meat-drying racks and hides stretched for tanning in background* (SM).

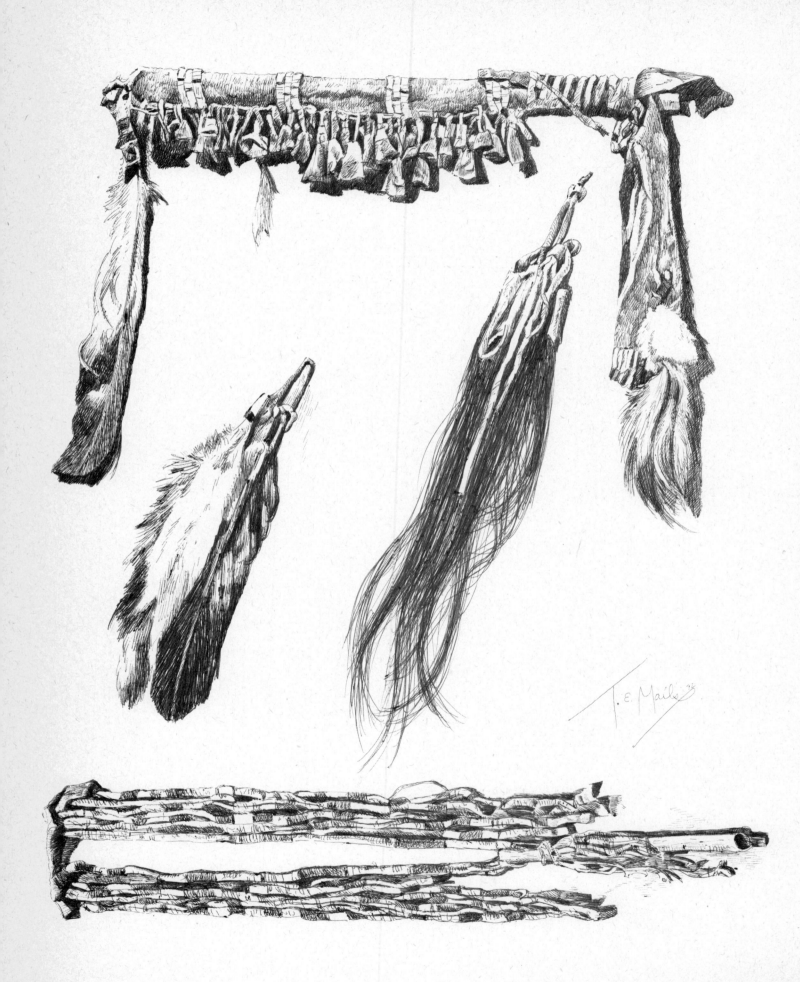

Since they had served in all the orders up to this point, they were living proof that God favored them and would work His powers through them for the good of the nation.

The Water-pouring, or Sprinkling Men, Society

The Water-pouring society members were the "seven venerable priests" who served as instructors for all the other orders, for they were selected from among the oldest and wisest warriors of the tribe. Their name came from their practice of pouring water over the heated stones in the sweat-lodge to produce the steam that carried prayers up to God for the removal of human ignorance. They had no dance and were not expected to go to war, although one of the seven was allowed to accompany a war party if he cared to. Their ceremonies were always performed in a large sweat-lodge. When the entire tribe was encamped at one place, the Water-pouring Men's sweat-lodge occupied the center of the camp circle, just between the main circle entrance and the lodge in which was kept the sacred medicine pipe of the nation. Unlike the standard sweat-lodge, this one had no fire mound or buffalo skull placed in front of the entrance.[15]

Each of the Water-pouring Men was keeper of an important medicine bundle. During a vision, the founder of the order saw himself in a cave in which were the sacred medicine arrows of the Cheyenne. Fearing to take them because of their power, he removed instead seven medicine bags also there and gave them to the seven aged men who were most revered by the Arapaho nation.[16]

The Women's Buffalo Society

The third ceremonial division of Arapaho society, the Women's Buffalo society, included all the women of the tribe. The women danced in a single ceremony, the ritual of which was similar to that of the men's ceremonies. It too had its origin in a national myth. It was commonly called Buffalo Lodge after the character of its dance, but the true meaning of the name could not be given or revealed by the Arapaho.

In the myth, Bluebird married Elk Woman and Buffalo Woman, and the latter, being unhappy, ran away with her son, Calf Stands Up, to the land of the buffalo people. Bluebird followed her and there beheld the holy dance of the buffalo. Before he was permitted to depart with his wife and child, it was decreed that he should be tested in various ways, one of which included identifying his son from among a crowd of calves who looked exactly alike and the second of which was the running of a race with young bulls. His final ordeal was that he had to remain awake during four days and four nights of story-telling by the buffalo people. In all the previous trials, Calf Stands Up had been able to assist his father, but since he was unable to sleep for him, Bluebird at last nodded and fell asleep. Immediately the buffalo people began to dance, circling round and round, coming ever closer and finally trampling upon the body of Bluebird until he was ground into the earth.

Before setting out to find his wife and child, Bluebird had told his brother, Magpie, that if any harm should come to him while he was among the buffalo people, a column of dust would ascend to the sky. When the buffalo danced over his body, the dust indeed rose in a huge cloud. Seeing it from afar, Magpie said to Elk Woman: "What my brother told me has happened. Make a sweat-lodge, and I will search

Opposite: *Arapaho Dog Men society regalia.* Top: *Rattle;* middle: *Horsehair and feather emblems worn on head by officers;* bottom: *Bone whistle (AMNH).*

for a piece of his body." Thereafter he flew toward the cloud of dust. When he arrived there, he heard groaning. Approaching the sound, he discovered a piece of the feather Bluebird had worn on his head, and he flew homeward with it. He placed it inside a sweat-lodge. Then he stood outside the lodge at the southeastern corner and cried, "Oh Father, I have brought back my brother!" At the same moment he shot a black arrow straight into the air and called out as it flew, "Look out, brother, the arrow will strike you!" In the same manner he shot another black arrow at the southwestern corner and a red one from each of the remaining corners. Each time he shouted his warning, the sweat-lodge shook from within; the fourth time he shouted, the wooden frame was violently shaken and Bluebird stepped forth alive! "I have much to tell you," he said, "but first we must prepare, for the buffalo will soon be here, and they will be angry."

Elk Woman proposed a plan. Using the bark of the chokecherry, the red osier, the cottonwood and the alder, she formed four great circles about the camp. Each one immediately became an immovable barrier. No sooner had she finished than the buffalo were seen thundering down the slope and the Arapaho ran for their weapons. The buffalo savagely attacked the outer circle and demolished it, but the horns of some were broken and some animals were slain by the arrows of the warriors. The second barrier and the third were also crushed, but with great losses to the buffalo. At the fourth circle, Buffalo Woman, leader of the herd, snapped off one horn and got the other hopelessly entangled in the bark. Thereupon Elk Woman killed her. It was then that the buffalo first became food for the Arapaho people, and it was only proper that the first buffalo-lodge was built under the direction of Bluebird.

Bluebird's instructions included the regalia to be worn by the participants as they enacted the story, thus continuing to guarantee the seasonal availability of the buffalo to the tribe. According to some researchers, Arapaho informants stated that there was a lodge in which the buffalo people danced. The women wore wide buffalo hide belts and buffalo hide headdresses. They carried small hoops and blew eagle bone whistles, while some old men who sat at the rear of the lodge shook their rattles and sang. When their fourth song was finished, the women turned into buffalo cows and the men into bulls. Then all but one vanished, a white cow. She was a woman who had been painted white and who wore white regalia during the dance.[17]

After the story was first told, a woman with a relative who was ill pledged to put on the ceremony as a prayer for her recovery. From then on, it was done whenever a woman wished to do the same thing.

The participants were any women and girls who wished to join in and who could afford the expenses incurred in obtaining or making the costumes. Each dancer procured the services of an older woman who had already taken part in the ceremony and who was known thereafter as Grandmother. A few women were distinguished from the others by their special costumes. These were the pledger, who was called White Woman; several women who dressed alike and were known as Red Stand; some others whose costumes varied from those of the Red Stand only in being white and who therefore were called White Stand; and two young girls who enacted the part of Calves. All the other dancers wore headdresses that consisted of a piece of beaded buffalo hide, with horns attached, covering the head, neck and

Opposite: *Arapaho flag bearer with war shield.*

shoulders like a hood. They also wore special belts at their waists, similar to that of Red Stand, a description of which follows. White Woman carried a large wooden staff in each hand with which she made pounding noises like the buffalo.

The first two days of preparation for the ceremony were taken up by the making of regalia. Those present in the lodge at this time were the old man who played the part of Bluebird, the Grandmothers and their husbands and the dancers. To make the sumptuous costume of the Red Stands, a piece of deerskin was placed before the old man and each Grandmother of a Red Stand cut a strip for the preparation of the headdress. Then, working under the direction of her husband, she embroidered the skin with yellow and black porcupine quills, arranging them in four separated rectangles so that they divided the length of the skin into four parts. In each of the four open spaces of hide thus created, she embroidered a cross, the symbol of the morning star. Then the edges of the strip were folded and united in such a way "that the effigy of a rattlesnake was produced." In effect, it became a tube.

Tobacco was then crushed and, by means of a stick, was stuffed into the form as a filling, which rounded out the hide. The rattlesnake was then smeared with red paint where the hide was not quilled. In all this the Grandmothers were guided by their husbands, but if additional advice was needed, they consulted the old man in charge and paid for his knowledge. Sixteen sticks, such as those used for arrow shafts, were prepared by peeling and pointing them, and to the shaft of each was bound a large, downy owl feather dyed a dull red. These were then thrust upright, eight on each side, into small holes along the top side of the rattlesnake skin band. In front of these were thrust two black eagle wing feathers, mounted on wooden shafts, the bases of which were quilled or beaded. A red feather from the crest of a golden-winged woodpecker was then attached to the quill end of each plume.

After this, to make a belt for Red Stand, a piece of elk skin about twelve inches wide was serrated along the lower edge and a band of yellow porcupine quills was embroidered along it. Along the upper border was a narrow strip of rawhide that was completely covered with yellow quills, except for a few black ones placed at each of four equidistant points. Three vertical bars of yellow quills, broken by black quills, were then embroidered around the belt at its middle. In the center of each space thus defined, a yellow quilled cross was added. At the rawhide strip and just above each vertical bar, a pendant buffalo tail was attached. The belt was then finished by painting it with sacred red paint.

Two small hoops, made of bent willow wrapped with quill-embroidery, were then prepared. One of them with a cross made by two deerskin thongs was attached to the belt and the other was added to the rattlesnake headdress, although a costumed figure in the American Museum of Natural History has two such hoops attached to the belt with down-feathers appended to them. Next, two quilled armbands and a pair of quilled earrings were made. Finally a willow stick about an inch in diameter and three or four feet in length was peeled, painted yellow and provided with a wrist-thong passing through a hole at the upper end. This would serve as Red Stand's cane. The thong was wrapped with quillwork, and owl feathers were hung from

Opposite: *Regalia of White Woman, officer of the Arapaho women's Buffalo society; typical Arapaho lodge in background* (AMNH).

it. The cane completed the outfit of the Red Stands. In the meantime, the costumes of the other dancers had been fashioned, all with the same ceremonial attention. Then all the costumes were hung in readiness on the lodge poles.

On the third day, all the performers assembled in their lodge and the dancers were painted and dressed by the Grandmothers. In the case of the Red Stands, the robing procedure was as follows: More gifts were presented in a pile to the old man in charge. He then took the headdress and the apron from the lodge pole and laid them on top of the presents. The woman sat before him, and her Grandmother placed the apron about her waist, tying it in front at the top and again at the middle with the hoop. Then, with four preliminary motions, she lifted up the rattlesnake headdress and slowly placed it like a crown upon the woman's head. With her left hand, she put the cane into the woman's right hand and placed a bone whistle to Red Stand's lips, bidding her to blow it. As the woman began to blow, the Grandmother stood behind her, placed her hands under her elbows and lifted her to her feet. The woman began to dance, as did the others, who had been undergoing similar preparation at the same time, each having been instructed in the traditional movements by her Grandmother. They proceeded single file (as buffalo do) out of the lodge and circled four times around the camp, after which they returned to the buffalo lodge. As the spectators crowded about, the women sang and danced around the lodge, still in single file. At first they proceeded slowly, but they gradually increased their speed until at the fourth

Headdress worn by Arapaho women's Buffalo society officer, named Red Stand (AMNH).

song, they were running as fast as they could, all the while imitating the actions of buffalo, first lying down, then standing, walking, going to water and running in terror. When the fourth song was finished, they entered the lodge and sat down. At one point a hunter would pretend to kill one of the cows. As she died, he pretended to butcher her and removed some buffalo fat that she had already hidden beneath her belt. Finally the old man directed the Grandmothers to remove the costumes from the dancers, wrap them up and deliver the bundles to the women. Then the performers raced each other to a nearby river and back again to the lodge, for it was regarded as a good omen to be first to drink or first to return to the lodge after this part of the ceremony.

The Buffalo Women then went about the camp collecting food from each family, which they brought to the lodge and used for a feast. The night was spent in singing, dancing and feasting. The three days following duplicated the first, the constant aim being the imitation of the buffalo people. The mode of painting changed slightly on each day. At the end of the fourth and last night, the women crept quietly from the lodge, shook themselves like buffalo awakening, stood upright and made their way to a sweat-lodge for purification before returning to the daily routine.[18]

The Arapaho had a group of seven old women who corresponded somewhat to the Water-pouring old men. Their power was also derived from an ancient myth, but they were not organized as a lodge. Their seven medicine bags contained holy tools, which they, for a fee, used to teach craftsmanship skills to other women. These were always considered to be the most skilled artists in the tribe, and their position was greatly respected.[19]

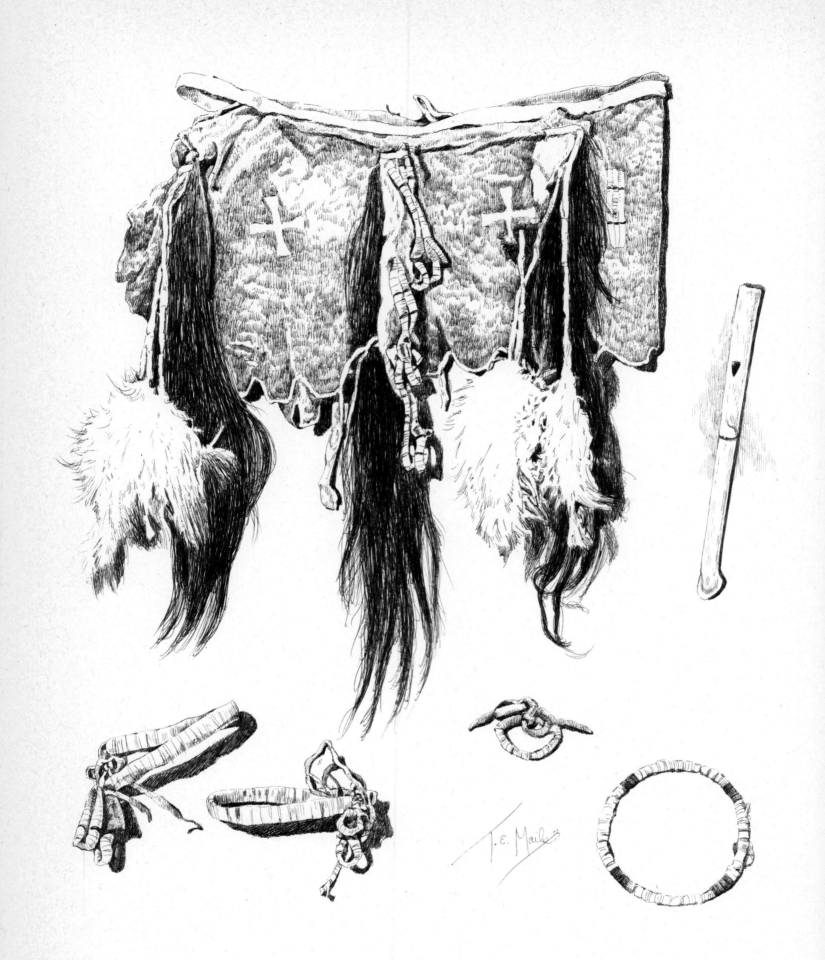

212

Arapaho women's Buffalo society regalia worn by third-highest officer, called Red Stand.
Above: Belt; right: Eagle-bone whistle (also used by all members); bottom: Quilled
hoops and robe ties (AMNH).

9
THE GROS VENTRE

T.E. Mails 71

Anthropologists believe that the Gros Ventre, or *Atsina,* were originally a division of the Arapaho nation when it dwelt on the northeastern part of the Plains. As the Arapaho began to migrate southwest, the Gros Ventre separated from them for reasons unknown and moved northwest instead. Arriving at the Milk River area, they settled down and formed an alliance with the Blackfoots.

In 1780, there were approximately 3,000 Gros Ventre. They called themselves the White Clay People, but the Indian nations who knew them had other, and sometimes unflattering, titles for the tribe, apparently because the Atsina did not particularly distinguish themselves in war. By 1910, their population had been reduced by war and the White man's diseases to about 500 persons.

The ceremonial life of the Gros Ventre found its main expression in its system of age societies. These were similar to the groups of the Mandan, but the Gros Ventre included a feature not found in the case of the other tribe. Among the Mandans, each society consisted of a single group of men who passed step by step as a unit or whole through the various grades of the age-system, and a society ceremony could be performed only by the single group of men owning it. Among the Gros Ventre, however, each age group was subdivided into several units that could perform the next higher ceremony without the others. In other words, different segments moved to the next grade at different times. The Gros Ventre subgroups bore such names as Ugly Dogs, Young Sheep and White Noses, and they always retained these titles as they moved through the various grades of the system. As it passed each age limit, each subgroup acquired at that moment the right to perform the ceremony of the next higher society, even though the other subgroups might not be ready to make the move.[1]

According to some Indian informants, the Fly society was said to have been outside the regular scheme of societies. Curtis believed that this may have meant only that the Flies were in a state of transition from a special ceremonial organization to a place in the series of recognized societies.[2] There was also a Star dance order, whose place was between the Dogs and the Drums. It seems, however, that this— even more than the Fly society—may have been outside the regular order, for some men seem to have performed its ceremony early in their life, others much later and still others not at all. Furthermore, while all the other ceremonial organizations were given a title indicating that they were a society, no such term was applied to the performers of the Star dance. All the Gros Ventre society ceremonies were of a distinctly religious character, and while they differed greatly in their themes, they were much alike in the way they were begun and carried out. The ceremonies of transfer from one order to the next were performed at the request of a member of one of the subgroups who wished to redeem a vow he had made, either in return for the recovery of a relative from illness or for the preservation of his own life in the midst of danger. Once his prayer had been granted, he obtained the services of an elderly man to erect the performance lodge. The man selected also had charge of the ceremony itself. The lodge, which always faced eastward, consisted of two ordinary tipis placed together to make a double lodge. Next, each member of the society secured the aid of an old man versed in the ritual, who was known

Opposite: *Gros Ventre warrior in full regalia, carrying war shield and carved coup stick and wearing beaded hair bows on sides of head* (SM).

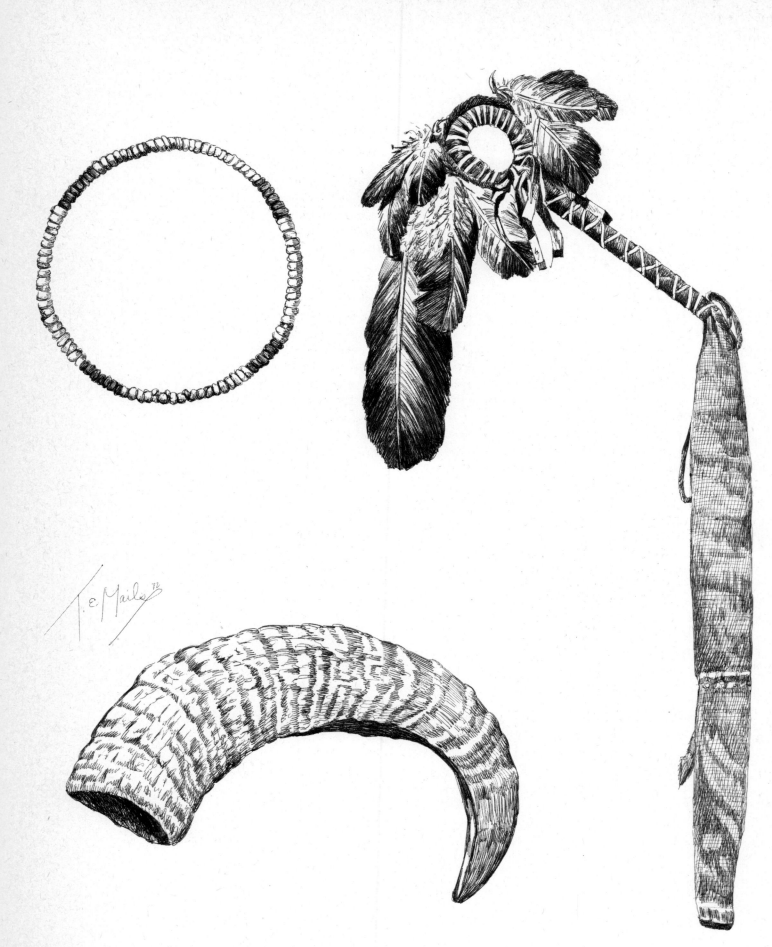

thereafter as his Grandfather. Each morning of the ceremony, the Grandfathers painted the dancers and the dancers' wives, and each night the Grandfathers left the camp with the wives to observe certain rites by which the old men transferred their medicine to the dancers through the medium of their wives.[3]

The Fly Society

The exception to this was the Fly society. Their dance lasted but one day, and the performers were of four grades. First there was a leader, who was not painted but wore a buffalo robe with the hair side out and carried a wand. Second there was the pledger of the ceremony, who was painted yellow. Third there were four "elder brothers," who were members of a group who had already given the Fly dance; these were painted yellow and acted as guides in the dance. Fourth there were the lay members, who were painted with white stripes across cheeks, nose, arms, legs and abdomen, with a band of red around the neck. The Grandfathers chewed an herb, which they rubbed on the dancers to make them brave and strong. Each of the lay members carried a flat stick about three feet long with a cactus thorn inserted at one end.

About noon, the members of the Fly society assembled at their double lodge and then began to walk in a circle about the camp carrying buffalo robes. Four times they halted, formed a circle and then danced up and down without moving from their places. While thus dancing, they held their robes outstretched so that they looked like huge kites and they made a buzzing noise like mosquitoes. To close each segment of the dance, all fell to their knees and touched their heads to the ground. When the fourth dance ended, the Flies scattered to pursue the laughing spectators and attempt to stick them with their thorns. Finally, they gathered in the center of the camp and ran four races, after which they proceeded to their double lodge and feasted on meat that one of their members had cooked.[4]

The Crazy Society

A man who vowed to give the Crazy dance and thus to join the Crazy order took a pipe to an old man familiar with its details. If the pipe were accepted, the old man became the "Maker of the Crazy Dance," and he directed the members of the Crazy society to choose Grandfathers to paint them. Each member of the company was expected to participate; if one were unavoidably absent, a relative took his place. The dancers were painted yellow to the knees and elbows and wore buffalo robes as capes or with a hole cut near the top through which the head passed, poncho-fashion. Two loose strips, with the feathers and claws of an owl fastened to their ends, hung down the sides from the shoulders. Each of the men carried bows and arrows to which crow feathers had been attached and had eagle wing-bone whistles. One side of the head was daubed with white clay, both ears were stuffed with a spongy fungus that looked like a puffball and an owl head was worn either on the forehead or at the right temple. The members also carried straight staffs, about four feet in length, from which were hung as rattles the hooves and claws of various animals.

Two or three lodges were combined to make one large enough for the ceremony. Inside these was erected a very small lodge, in which the man giving the dance remained for the night. The ceremony

Opposite: *Gros Ventre society regalia.* Top left: *Quilled hoop of Fly society, four inches in diameter;* bottom left: *Fly society horn used to scratch spectators, eight inches long;* right: *Rattle carried by members of Star Dance society (AMNH).*

lasted four days and four nights, but the dancing for each day ended when darkness fell and the dancers' wives left with the Grandfathers to go outside the camp to receive "medicine" from them. Each woman, on her return to the lodge in the morning, was kissed by all the members in turn, and her husband completed the greeting by kissing the head Grandfather.

After the performers had been painted each morning, they assembled in the great lodge, with the members' wives taking places behind the Grandfathers. After the members had marched once around the lodge and stopped, the singers began to sing and the dance started. When the dancers sat down to rest, they planted their bows and arrows in the ground in front of them. These remained there except during a certain brief ritual when they were held first to one shoulder and then to the other, at the end of which they were again thrust into the ground. On the fourth day a huge fire was kindled in the center of the lodge and the head Grandfather said, "It is time for the Crazy men to dance in the fire." At this point the relatives of the dancers brought gifts of clothing and robes to the Grandfathers, who took them home and then returned as the members began to dance in a circle around the fire, which was now reduced to glowing coals. They approached closer and closer until suddenly all leaped upon the coals and stamped upon them until they were extinguished. After this, they ran outside and, standing close together, fired war arrows straight up into the air; then they exhibited their bravery by looking at the ground and standing motionless among the falling shafts while the spectators hurriedly drew back to escape them!

218

Gros Ventre Fly society members performing ceremony (SM).

Gros Ventre Crazy society regalia. Left: *Small fur and quilled hoops attached to front corners of cape worn over shoulders; right: Bone-bead necklace with stuffed owl attached (AMNH).*

Below: *Gros Ventre Crazy society members firing arrows straight up into air to demonstrate bravery as they stand in place among falling arrows (SM).*

Three wordless songs followed while the Crazy men danced, after which "they did all the mischief they could until nightfall." At such times they would run in all directions shooting people with blunt arrows; they would also say the opposite of what they meant, do the reverse of what they were told to do and, in everything, act as if they had lost their senses. The only protection one had from them was to seek refuge behind one of the Grandfathers. It was said that if, during these antics, a Crazy dancer became displeased with anyone, he would chew a root and blow it toward the offender, paralyzing him until the dancer touched him and then blew upon him again.[5]

The Fox Society

The ceremony of the Fox society was begun in the same way as were the other dances, with the man who had promised its performance first soliciting the aid of an old man and each man of the society then selecting a Grandfather. The ceremony lasted four days and four nights, with the actual dancing taking place during the daytime.

Four of the Fox members carried hooked staffs about seven feet long, bent at one end like a shepherd's crook, wrapped with otter skin and further decorated with eagle feathers. The bearers of these staffs were men of proven bravery, and once they had planted the staffs in the ground during a battle, they could not retreat. The four staff bearers also wore the full skin and feathers of a crow around their necks. The regular members painted their faces red with four black pipes on each cheek, the stems pointing downward and the bowls toward the eyes. For regalia they wore a society belt of prairie-dog skin and an eagle down feather in the hair.

Each ceremony of this order began when a member fulfilled his vow by choosing a virgin to represent the "Fox Mother," whose children the members were supposed to be. In the center of the camp was a double lodge, in which the members seated themselves in two rows, one around each side of the lodge interior, extending from the door to the center of the rear. A staff bearer sat at each end of each row. The Fox Mother was seated at the rear beside the members who formed the end of the southern row. A small tipi was set up between the lines and near the door, and the man who had vowed the dance slept in this during the four nights of the ritual.

To start the ceremony, the men rose, formed a circle and moved toward the left, while the Fox Mother passed outside the circle in the opposite direction. On the fourth and last night, the relatives of the members brought gifts for the Grandfathers. Early the next morning, the camp began to move, halting about halfway to the next campsite. The dancers then went a short distance ahead and placed the gifts that had been received in a pile on the ground. The members then charged the gifts, and each man seized an article that was similar to something he had captured in battle.[6]

The Dog Society

The dance of the Dog society resembled in its principal features the ceremonies of the other societies. For regalia, the two leaders wore war shirts, one painted yellow, the other red, and each trimmed with black crow feathers. They also wore stunning headdresses made from a profusion of owl feathers. All the other members wore short society sashes made of hide and worn passed over the right shoulder and under the

221

Opposite: *Gros Ventre Dog society member wearing society war shirt and headdress of owl feathers (AMNH).*

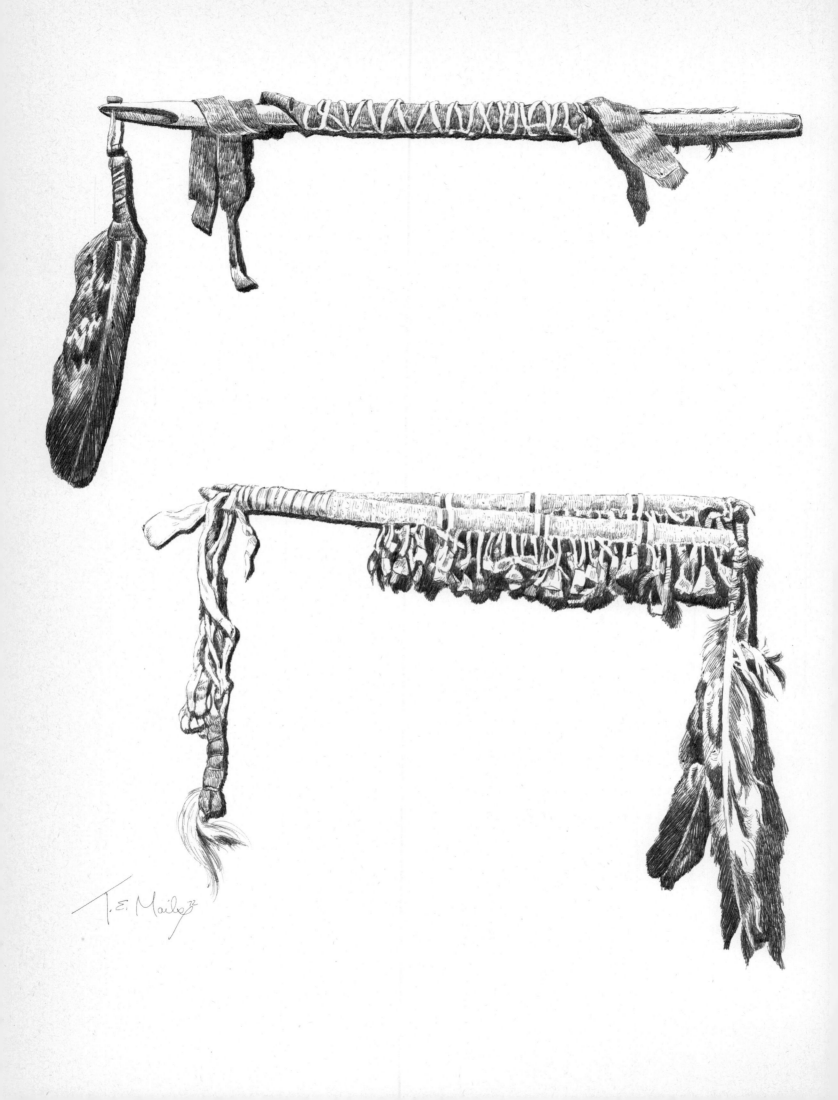

left. In later days these were made of red trade cloth. As was generally the case with sash-wearers on the Plains, the ends of these were secured to the ground with lances when the tide of battle turned against the Gros Ventre. The warrior was not permitted to retreat until someone other than a member of the Dog society had driven him away by speaking to him as one would to a dog. The Dog members wore eagle bone whistles hung on thongs around their necks and, for dances, carried short, small deer-hoof rattles. The officers carried a longer rattle made of a forked stick, with dew-claw rattles and feathers at each end. All members were battle veterans and were entitled to wear eagle feather headdresses in war. Their ceremony went on for the usual four days in the typical double lodge that was placed in the center of the camp.

The Drum Society

The Drum society was made up of the bravest and most experienced warriors in the Gros Ventre tribe. They possessed as part of their medicine bundle a special drum, which, if their ceremony had been performed only a short time before, they could throw toward the enemy during a battle. The members would then run to it and stand beside it, fighting until either the enemy gave way or they themselves were killed. Their ceremony lasted four days and four nights. The four leaders carried staffs hooked at one end and wrapped with the especially prized white buffalo skin. All the members painted themselves red from head to toe, then covered the red with white dots representing hail and white zigzag lines for lightning. For clothing they wore only a breechclout, and their only ornament was an eagle down-feather attached to the side of the head.[7]

The Buffalo Cow Society

The Buffalo Cow order was a women's society. Its ceremony was performed when a woman either dreamed of the dance or pledged it on condition that her child or other relative recover from illness. When the prayer was answered, the pledger went to an old man who knew the ritual and asked him to take charge of the rite. He then arranged for the erection of a double lodge and selected two old men as singers. There were four women leaders, four younger women assistants and two girls who represented buffalo calves. Each woman wore a buffalo skin cape to which two feathers were attached in an upright position to symbolize horns. The ceremony continued for four days, with the leaders giving the signal to begin each dance by standing up and commencing to sing. In dancing, the women did not lift their feet from the ground but simply swayed from side to side like buffalo. A pool of water was placed in the center of the lodge, from which at one point during the ceremony a warrior was called upon to drink like a buffalo. On the fourth day the women, imitating a herd of buffalo as they walked, went to the river and drank. At the water's edge, a man lay in wait for them with a gun. They pretended to scent him and acted afraid, pawing the ground and sniffing the air to determine his position. But the hunter always managed to shoot and kill one of the buffalo, and as the woman fell to the ground, the tribe was assured of good hunting for the season.[8]

The Soldier, or Police, Society

The Soldier society was reorganized each spring when the bands as-

Opposite: *Gros Ventre Dog society regalia.* Top: *Rattle borne by ordinary members;* bottom: *Rattle carried by highest officer (AMNH).*

sembled for the great tribal encampment after the usual winter's separation. Those who had been members during the previous year and who wished to join again met together with new volunteers, and elected four leaders. The group served the civil chiefs and had the usual power to punish offenses against the public welfare. Their meeting place was, once again, the double lodge pitched in the center of the camp. It served as the meeting place of the members and was in truth the very center of community activities. The two youngest members of the society acted as servants, whose main duty was to recruit the women of the tribe to provide and cook the meat for the Soldiers' meals. The most influential members of the Soldiers frequently pitched their own painted tipis near the double lodge at the center of the camp to emphasize their position of authority.[9]

10

THE NON-GRADED SOCIETIES

THE SIOUX AS EXAMPLE

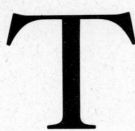he Sioux, or *Dakota,* were the largest of the Plains nations, numbering some 25,000 in 1780. The word *Dakota* means "allies." In the Teton dialect, it is *Lakota,* but it signifies the same thing. There were seven main divisions, called Seven Council Fires. Several of the main divisions were further divided into bands. The authority John R. Swanton sets them forth as:

1. Mdewkanton
2. Wahpeton
3. Wahpekute
4. Sisseton
5. Yankton
6. Yanktoni
   a) Upper Yanktoni
   b) Lower Yanktoni or Hunkpatina
7. Teton
   a) Brule—upper and lower
   b) Hunkpapa
   c) Miniconjou
   d) Oglala
   e) Oahenonpa or Two Kettle
   f) Sans Arcs
   g) Sihasapa or Blackfoot [1]

The earliest known home of the Sioux was in what is now known as southern Minnesota, northeastern Iowa and northwestern Wisconsin. Archaeologists think there is even evidence to suggest that they began on the Atlantic coast and then moved slowly west before the pressures of other tribes. The exact date of their first move onto the Plains is not known, but several authorities feel certain they were latecomers to the area, making an astonishingly swift transformation in the space of fifty years or so from a farming and woodlands hunting people to a thoroughgoing nomadic buffalo culture.

Once they had arrived, the Sioux quickly dominated an enormous territory, reaching from Canada to the Platte River and from Minnesota to the Yellowstone River, including the Black Hills and the Powder River country.

The seven divisions grew even stronger on the Plains, meeting in regular council together, sharing festivals and religious ceremonies and acting in concert against the other Indian nations. Those who have researched Plains history are unanimous in praising the Sioux for their courage, resourcefulness and accomplishments in war and raids. In the fashioning of their apparel and regalia, in their social, society, cult and religious rites, they were unsurpassed.

Because of their comprehensive society and cult structures, the Sioux provide excellent examples of the non-graded orders of the Plains nations. As was the case with the Blackfoots, many photographs were taken of the Sioux in the late nineteenth and early twentieth centuries. Sadly enough for our purposes, though, the pictures included but little of the precious society regalia. Most of it has to be reconstructed from oral descriptions and old pictographic drawings.

Two classes of non-graded societies existed among the Sioux—dream societies and military societies. Both classes are mentioned by

Hayden, one of the earliest writers on the Indians of the upper Plains.

He lists the dream societies as the "Buffalo Head, Elk and Bear," and the military societies as the "Scalp, Strong Heart, Fox, Big Owl and Soldier." In every instance the Sioux language equivalent is given, identifying the societies with organizations of comparatively recent times.[2]

The dream societies (or cults) were composed of men who, in their dreams or fasting visions, had seen the same animal. The animal that appeared to a man in a vision during his religious fasting always determined the group to which he must belong.

Among the Teton Sioux, some societies having a cultic origin in dreams of a name-animal evolved over the years into military groups. Thus while the Elk, Buffalo, Horse, Wolf and Bear remained distinctly dream societies or cults, the Strong Heart, Tall Ones, Owl and White-horse Riders cults developed into orders that were mainly military in character.

Since the dream cults did not hold regular meetings and since new members did not emerge during the late nineteenth century, anthropologists say it has been more difficult to secure reliable information about the cults than about the societies among the Sioux.

Lewis and Clark made what was probably the first recorded mention of societies among the men of the Sioux tribe. Under the date of August 30, 1804, their journal contains the following section written by Clark:

> I will here remark a SOCIETY which I had never before this day heard was in any nation of Indians, four of which is at this time present and all who remain of this Band. Those who become Members of this Society must be brave active young men who take a Vow never to give back let the danger be what it may, in War Parties they always go forward with screening themselves behind trees or anything else to this Vow they Strictly adhier dureing their Lives. an instance which happened not long sence, on a party in Crossing the R Missourie on the ice, a whole was in the ice imediately in their Course which might easily have been avoided by going around, the foremost man went on and was lost the others wer draged around by the party. in a battle with the Crow (Kite) Indians who inhabit the Cout Noir or Black Mountain out of 22 this Society 18 was killed, the remaining four was draged off by their Party. Those men are likely fellows the[y] Set together Camp & Dance together. This Society is an imitation of the Societies of the de Curbo or Crow [De Corbeau Kite] Indians, whom they imitate.[3]

Clark's reference is apparently to one of the military societies of the tribe, for the action described is that of the police groups.

Dr. Wissler divides the Oglala Sioux societies for men into Police societies, Headmen's, or Civil, societies and War societies.[4] The Civil societies were the Big Bellies, the White-horse Owners, the Tall Ones and the Owl Feather Headdresses. At the time of his observation, among the Oglala on the Pine Ridge and Rosebud reservations in South Dakota, there were six Police societies, these being the Kit-fox, the Crow Owner, the Strong Heart, the Badger, the Bare-lance Owners and the White-marked. Only the first four of these societies were found by Densmore among the Teton Sioux on the Standing Rock reservation. Fr. Hennepin mentions finding Police societies among the Sioux in 1680.[5]

Another society mentioned by Densmore was known by two

names, the Silent Eaters and the Strong Heart at Night. It was a secret society, entirely distinct from the Strong Heart society described later in this section, and no songs or further information concerning it were obtained.

The police or guard societies were those whose members acted as guards in the village when the tribe was moving and, most importantly, on the buffalo hunt, during which time they saw to it that no one disregarded the laws of the chase. They also played central roles in large war parties.

Lewis and Clark refer to these men as follows:

> Those people have Some brave men which they make use of as Soldiers those men attend to the police of the Village Correct all errors I saw one of them today whip 2 squars, who appeared to have fallen out, when he approach. all about appeared to flee with great terror. at night they keep two, 3, 4, 5, men at different distances walking around Camp Singing the accurrunces of the night.[6]

Wissler states that the manner of selecting the camp police was as follows: The camp or civil chiefs chose the four leaders from one society, who in turn engaged the rest of the members of their society. The selection was usually made at the beginning of the summer hunt, and service continued to the close of the season. It seems to have been customary, but not obligatory, for the chiefs to choose from the societies in rotation.[7]

The organization of the Sioux societies was surprisingly uniform in its details. All had from four to six lance bearers, who were the most important personages in the society. They were usually grouped in pairs, as were nearly all the other officers. After the two leaders was another pair: Among the Strong Hearts and the White-horse Riders they were known as bonnet bearers and among the others as pipe bearers, but their functions were much the same. The two ranking pairs were sometimes spoken of as the four chiefs in charge of the organization. There were two whip bearers in all the societies except the Crow Owners. As to food passers, drummers and singers, there was general uniformity throughout. Evidently, then, whatever the origin of these societies, they all came eventually to be of one type.

Perhaps half the young men of the nation were organized into the Police societies. When the chiefs of a village met, the Police

228

Sioux warriors mounted on war ponies: warrior in front wears split-horn buffalo bonnet with full tail and carries coup stick with scalp-lock attached; second warrior carries coup stick with feather attached; third man wears eagle feather bonnet with single tail and carries Winchester rifle (SM). Opposite: Sioux, named One Feather, wearing wolf hide headdress of type used by scouts on war parties and raids (Smithsonian).

gathered at the council place and took their position in front of the tipi. Before doing so, however, they first went about the village gathering food for the council members. If a man were asked to give a dog for the feast and refused, the Police would simply kill the dog and take it away, and if any resentment were shown, they were permitted to punish the offender by either destroying some of his property or beating him. Understandably, they were seldom refused. The discipline seems stringent, but it was all part of the obedience-testing assuring the tribal leaders that the people would act as one body on command. If the chiefs decided to move the camp on the following day, the Police were so informed, and when morning came, they would ride about the camp and see that all made ready to take the trail. Here again, if one should refuse (without acceptable reason) to obey the command, the Police would cut his tipi to pieces and might kill a horse or two. If the man being punished gave vent to anger, his life might even be forfeited on the spot. Even the desire to move the camp to a new site sometimes originated in a Police lodge, but this was only made as a suggestion and the camp chiefs agreed or disagreed as they saw fit.[8]

According to Curtis, the Police of each village had two leaders, called Soldier Chiefs, through whom all commands of the camp or civil chiefs were transmitted to the other members of whichever societies were on police duty.[9] Wissler says there were four leaders, whose commands were as follows: If scouts were sent out to look for buffalo, the Police saw that only those so authorized left the village. When the scouts returned to report where the buffalo were, the Police assumed charge of the preparations for the hunt and saw that all hunters and their families left the camp together. A few of the Police remained at home on such occasions, guarding the village both against unauthorized departures and enemy attacks, while the rest accompanied the huntsmen and kept them together until they came to the herd. Any man who began to hunt before the proper ceremonies were completed or before the signal was given to begin was severely beaten by the Police, sometimes to insensibility. His horse might be killed, his clothing cut to pieces and his weapons broken, as well. After all, any premature action on the part of a hunter showed selfishness and might well stampede the herd. Thus if someone evidenced even the slightest resentment when he was disciplined, he was likely to be killed. The same treatment was accorded a man who stole away from a band while it was on the march and killed a lone buffalo, even if he hadn't alarmed the herd.

Each autumn, several of the Sioux bands united to form a single large buffalo hunting party. On such occasions the two Soldiers were charged with keeping the entire party together, and once they had joined together, no band was permitted to leave the others until the hunting grounds were reached. Then scouts were sent out, and when the buffalo were located, the bands hunted together until everyone present had been supplied with enough meat to last the winter.

The Police headquarters was always a large lodge pitched near the tipi of the head chief, and it was the general rendezvous and lounging place for the society members. If there were a shortage of food in the lodge, a member was sent to distribute a hundred red sticks throughout the camp. Each of these emblems was a plain sign that the recipient must quickly furnish meat to the Police lodge. If

230

Opposite: *Sioux Shirt Wearer, wearing a shirt fringed with hair-locks, an otter skin society collar and a double-tailed eagle feather headdress revealing stupendous war accomplishments, and carrying a fur-wrapped straight lance of type used by Crow Owners society or carried on war parties (SM).*

one Police member kept the others waiting after a meeting had been called, he was treated somewhat roughly on his arrival, but the injuries inflicted were not serious, consisting principally of the cutting up of his robe and other clothing.[10]

Curtis states that new Police candidates were appointed by the Police chiefs, "who donned their war-bonnets and rode from tipi to tipi, shaking the hand of each man chosen."[11] To be selected a Soldier was a distinct honor, open only to men who had had a successful vision quest and counted at least one undisputed coup.

Sioux Civil Societies
Big Belly
White-horse Owner
Tall One
Owl Feather Headdress

The Big Belly Society

The Big Belly society was the chiefs' society and the source from which all tribal leadership came for the Sioux nations. These were older men of proven worth, such as the holy men, doctors, renowned warriors, wise men and village chiefs. It was the council of the tribe, and all important decisions and appointments to office were made by its members.[12]

Sometimes the Big Bellies, whose name came about as people observed their healthy and aging stomachs, appointed a younger group of ten men to act as an executive or subcouncil in interpreting and implementing the decisions of the chiefs among the people. These in turn appointed a number of "shirt wearers," who became the direct voice of the executive council. As they were selected, each man was presented with a traditionally painted war shirt fringed with hair-locks. Some shirts had a blue upper half and a yellow lower half. Others were red and green. A few shirts were solid yellow, and some had vertical black stripes. The colors in each instance represented the hues of God's providential creation and served as a constant reminder to the wearers of their first responsibility to Him and under Him. The hair-locks always symbolized the people of the Sioux, for whom the shirt-wearers were responsible. Lowie says the shirt wearers wore buffalo horn bonnets during dances and on war parties. They also carried lances and shields. When on the march, they hung their shield on the rear horn of the saddle and the headdress on the front horn. The lance was carried in the hand.

Howard's Teton informants mentioned two chiefs' society "dances," which seemed to him to be of the warrior society type. The first of these was the "Big-belly" dance, in which buffalo bulls were imitated. Only older men, perhaps chiefs, participated in it. Members painted their bodies and lances white, One informant referred to the order itself as the "Bulls" warrior society.[13]

The White-horse Owners, or Riders, Society

The White-horse Owners was not considered a tribal society as such but was an ancient organization that in the opinion of some informants, remained local in character, being confined only to those band divisions deserving it. The term *white-horse owner* is not an exact translation of the two-word Sioux designation, in which the first word

Sioux warrior wearing war shirt with hair-lock fringes and quilled armbands and shoulder bands and carrying staff similar to that of the White-horse Owners society. He has an eagle wing fan in his left hand (DPL).

Depiction, taken from pictographic drawings by Sioux artists, of Sioux White-horse Owners society illustrating typical horse markings.

meant "white horse" and the second was a compound word indicating age and experience.

The members were mostly mature warriors who had earned the right to paint their horses for parades or the warpath, thus portraying their brave deeds in billboard fashion. White horses were chosen for two reasons: White was regarded as a genuinely spiritual color depicting purity through cleansing and a white horse was the only one on which the symbols and coup marks would show well. The usual marks employed were horses' hoofprints to symbolize successful horse raids and handprints to represent the warrior's having touched an enemy with his hand during a battle.

The parade of the White-horse Riders always made a great impression upon a camp. It was said that if the White-horse Riders came to the tent of a man who had been wounded in war, they would fire their guns into the air, whereupon the women of the family would cook a quantity of food and place it in the middle of the camp-circle. The custom was that "those who had no one to cook for them went and ate this food." [14]

The Tall Ones and/or the Owl Feather Headdress Society

The Tall Ones and/or the Owl Feather Headdress order was a most important civil-military society among the Teton Sioux, the members of which were exempt from Police duty. Originated in ancient times by a man who dreamed of an owl, the society was sometimes erroneously called the Owl society. The word *miwa'tani* is not fully explainable, as it is not found in the common speech of the Sioux. Two informants said that it was not a Sioux word and that they thought it meant "owl feathers." Wissler states that according to one of his informants, the society was so named because an owl-being in conferring the ritual said, "My name is Miwi'tani." Informants in general agreed that the term was associated with no concept other than that of a particular society. The word miwa'tani was also the Sioux name for Mandan, the tradition being that the latter were so named because of some resemblance to the Miwa'tani society. [15]

Some other tribes show evidence of having had a similar organization or of having borrowed parts of such an organization. The Omaha tribe had a society known by a slight variant of the same name (*Ma-wa-da-ni*), whose dance was called the Mandan dance. J. O. Dorsey believes the Omahas borrowed this society from the Poncas, who in turn had taken it from the Dakotas. Alice C. Fletcher feels that the Omahas probably borrowed the institution directly from the Sioux. [16]

The Tall Ones society, besides being one of the most difficult to enter, was one of the most exacting in its requirements. Each member pledged himself to sacrifice his own life in war in defense of a wounded member. When anything was needed by the society, the head officer appointed members to collect what was required and the demand was never refused. The collecting was usually done at a public meeting of the society and formed one of the tests the civil leaders of the tribe used to determine which men were qualified to be especially useful to the tribe. If an officer of this society saw a supply of provisions he felt should have been donated to the society, he could take it. He had the traditional right to do this, and it was expected that he would do so forcibly if donations were willfully withheld. [17]

The purpose of this society was to promote friendliness and help-

234

Opposite: *Sioux society regalia.* Left: *Lance of Crow Owners society;* middle: *Supporting stake and sash of Tall Ones society;* right: *Lance of Fox society (AMNH).*

T. E. Mails

fulness among its members, to serve the people and to present an example of generosity and valor. The more important of its meetings were for the initiation of new members. Any member of the tribe could apply for membership, and if his application were accepted, he was notified by the camp crier. On the day of an initiation ceremony, the officers of the society, wearing headdresses of owl feathers with four eagle feathers in the center and made like warbonnets, took their position in the place of honor, opposite the entrance of the lodge. In their hands they held the owl feather headdresses the new members were to receive. It was required that the newly elected men should show the assembled society that they were qualified for the honor being conferred on them by passing a traditional test. Behind the fire was an earth altar. Each candidate rose from his seat, took live coals in the palm of his hand, which had buffalo grease rubbed into it, and turning to the left, walked slowly around the lodge four times, pausing at the altar space each time and pretending that he would place the coals upon it. After the fourth round, he slowly lowered his hand and gently rolled the coals to the earth. If he could do this without flinching, he was considered qualified to be a member of the society.

After all the men had placed their coals in a heap, sweetgrass was placed on the coals and the headdresses were held in the fragrant smoke, after which they were placed on the heads of the new members as the following ceremonial song was sung:

this one who is holy
has made this for me [18]

There was a similar feature in the initiation of the four sash bearers of the society. When they assembled to take their oath of office, they were painted entirely red and then stood side by side as buffalo grease was rubbed into the palm of the right hand of each one. Immediately thereafter, the "servant" of the society placed a live coal in the treated palms and the men walked slowly to the consecrated altar at the back center of the lodge and placed their coals upon it.

The wearers of the society sashes were obligated to stake themselves down in battle by driving a wooden stake pin through a small hole in the end of the sash, remaining there unless or until a fellow member could drive off the enemy, pull up the stake and so release his comrade. The Tall Ones are generally conceded to have been the first to institute this no-flight regulation.[19]

Once a man was a member, he donated his best horse to the society. He also hired a member to make his regalia, usually giving a horse as compensation for this service also. There was a whistle made of the wing bone of an eagle and wrapped end to end with beads, which hung on a thong around his neck. There was also a rattle he carried during the dances of the society. It had a beaded shaft and tab, with rattles made by boiling the hoof of a deer and cutting the hard, outer part into small curved pieces of the desired shape and size.[20] All the feathers used by members of this society were owl feathers, tipped with red down, and owl feathers were used to fletch their arrows.[21]

The society lodge was painted with red and green designs given in a vision, but informants of later times were not able to explain the symbolism.

A feature of the dance peculiar to this society was the regulation that no member could be seated after the drumming and singing had stopped until he had been touched by the whip bearer nor could he resume his dancing when the music started again until he had been touched by that officer.

Two of the dancing songs of this society went as follows:

friends
whenever you pursue anything
friend
may I be there [22]

the Crow Indians
rushing to fight
I a Miwa'tani
took courage [23]

Wissler states that the organization of the Tall Ones consisted of:

Leaders (2)	Lay members (x)
Sash bearers, or bonnet men (2)	Drum bearer (1)
Whip bearers (2)	Singers (8)
Food passer (1)	Herald (1)[24]

But Blish lists the following regalia:

1. Four feathered headdresses and four stake sashes with the small stakes attached by a thong near the end of each sash; ("The headdress is made of crow feathers centered with eagle feathers." [25])

2. Two whips similar to those of the Strong Hearts. These had broad, flat handles with sawlike edges, lashes of rawhide and wrist-loops of otter skin.

3. A drum with eagle feathers appended.

4. Two rattles made of antelope dew claws, which were symbols of office for two other officers. A wooden frame about sixteen inches long, made in the general shape of a long-handled gourd, was first decorated with beadwork and porcupine quillwork, and then the frame head was thickly hung with the dew claws.

Including these two officers, there were nine in all in the society.

The peace-time or reservation-period dance costume consisted of only a bunch of spotted owl feathers worn in the hair, the whistle and a breechclout.

Sioux Military Societies
Kit-fox
Crow Owner
Strong Heart
Badger
Bare- or Plain-lance Owner
White-marked

The Kit-fox Society

In ancient times the Kit-fox society was the most prominent of all the warrior societies. Its members were noted for their concern for the Sioux people in times of peace as well as in times of war. Fox men were heroic in the face of danger and were ready to meet any emergency. Their song expressed their attitude:

I am the kit fox,
I live in uncertainty,
If there is anything difficult
If there is anything dangerous to do
that is mine

Sioux Kit-fox headdress of wolf hide and items carried on war parties—wooden bowl, buckskin paint pouch and eagle bone whistle with medicine bag attached (Smithsonian).

The rules of conduct for the members called for bravery, generosity, chivalry, morality and fraternity. Men who joined the society were required to live up to these teachings, and the whip bearers of the group had lashes of a peculiar kind with which they punished those who disregarded their vows.[26]

Fox societies were vital units among many of the Plains tribes in the early days. Maximilian discovered a society of "the foxes" among the Arikara about the year 1833. In his list of the Hidatsa and Mandan societies, Dr. Lowie includes the "Kit-fox society," and states further that among the Crows, "the Foxes and Lumpwoods had become the most important military societies in the decades immediately preceding the breakdown of the old tribal life." [27] Miss Fletcher states that the Omaha Toka'lo (Toka'la) was one of two "social societies that were borrowed or introduced from the Dakota." [28]

Denmore learned that among the Tetons and on the Standing Rock reservation, it was said that "fox songs and coyote songs are the same." [29] It was also decided that certain songs called wolf songs, or "Wolf society songs," should be included in the same category. Dr. Lowie found that the Kit-fox dance was called the Coyote dance by the Santee at Fort Totten, North Dakota, and the Crows of Montana told him that "all the societies were originated by the mythical Old Man Coyote." Mooney found that the "fox" and "coyote" were names of the societies of the Cheyenne, and George A. Dorsey mentions the Coyote as being one of the original Cheyenne societies.

239

Opposite: Member of Sioux Kit-fox society, wearing kit-fox skin around neck in typical society style and an unusual type of war bonnet with a single row of feathers running over crown and down tail. Style is similar to that of Blackfoot Horn society bonnet (DPL).

The following song of the Sioux Kit-fox society was sung by one
of its members:

> the Fox
> whenever you propose to do anything
> I consider myself foremost
> but
> a hard time
> I am having [30]

Two other songs of the Kit-fox society show first their determination and second the type of song that was composed in honor of a
member of the group who had been killed in battle.

> the fox
> I am
> something
> difficult
> I seek [31]

> that Fox leader
> now
> did not return
> you said
> White Butterfly
> is whom you mean
> but then
> he went looking for this
> and it has come to pass [32]

The Kit-fox society received its name because its members sought
to be as active and clever on the warpath as this little animal was in
his native state. For regalia, the members wore like a poncho a kit-
fox skin with the head in front and the tail in back. Small bags of
medicine were attached to the animal's nose, and the edges, feet and
ears were embroidered with porcupine quills and hung with bells
according to the tastes of the individual owners. The jawbones of
several foxes were painted red or blue, fastened at intervals on a broad
strip of otter skin or some similar material and worn as a headband
with the jaws on the forehead. For a typical example see the drawings
in the Mandan chapter. A bunch of crow tail feathers was fastened
sideways to the back of the head, and two eagle feathers were inserted
upright in the scalp-lock knot. When participating in a dance, the
officers painted their bodies yellow.

Part of the regalia of the Kit-fox society officers consisted of two
pipes and four bow-lances. The bow-lances were the truly distinguishing features of the organization. Unlike the lances of any of the other
societies, these were made in the form of bows that strongly resembled
the Sacred Bow of the tribe but were unstrung. The shaft was wrapped
at intervals with beadwork, and the grip was wrapped with colored
sinew and trade cloth. At one end was a large lance head. From this
same end, attached to the bow wing a few inches below the point,
hung a long, spectacular pendant of rawhide with a profusion of feathers ingeniously attached to it, and from the very tip dangled two
golden eagle tail-feathers on beaded or quilled thongs. To be invested
with the bow-lance was a signal but challenging honor, for its four
carriers were men who were expected to take their places unflinch-
ingly in the front line of every battle and to seek to count coup with the
bow. [33]

There were also two flat, broad whips similar to those of other societies, with serrated edges, painted stripes and an otter skin wrist-loop
and hangings. The two headdresses of the whip bearers consisted of
two eagle feathers each, worn in the hair. Pictographic drawings show
what appears to be small attachments to the base of the feathers. This
could have been eagle down but was more likely sweetgrass or juniper,
which appealed to the good powers, and sage, which was repugnant
to evil forces. One of the officers was also custodian of the drum.

The reservation dance costume of the Fox consisted of shirt and
leggings and, if possible, a bone breastplate. A hair-plate strap of
spaced silver disks was a common and prominent feature. This was
attached to the scalp-lock and often hung almost to the ground.[34]

The medicine rattle carrier for Kit-fox society dances had an unusually large black rattle. The rawhide head of it was shaped while
it was still wet into the form of a man's face and head. The carrier
was painted entirely black, and he danced by himself more vigorously
than the others. He was commonly spoken of as "the black man." The
rest of the dancers arranged themselves at either side of him to form
a circle. A little space was left at both his right and his left, and then
the circle was almost completed by two balanced segments of dancers
standing in close formation. Directly opposite "the black man," a
small break was left in the ring, but informants could not explain its
significance.[35] According to Howard, the dance was phasing out and
"seldom seen among the Yanktonai and Teton Dakota" by 1915.[36]

The Crow Owners Society
The Crow Owners society was also widespread among the tribes of

241

*Sioux warrior named Pretty Voice Eagle wearing wolf hide with lateral slit through which
head is inserted—as was done by the members of the Kit-fox society (SM).*

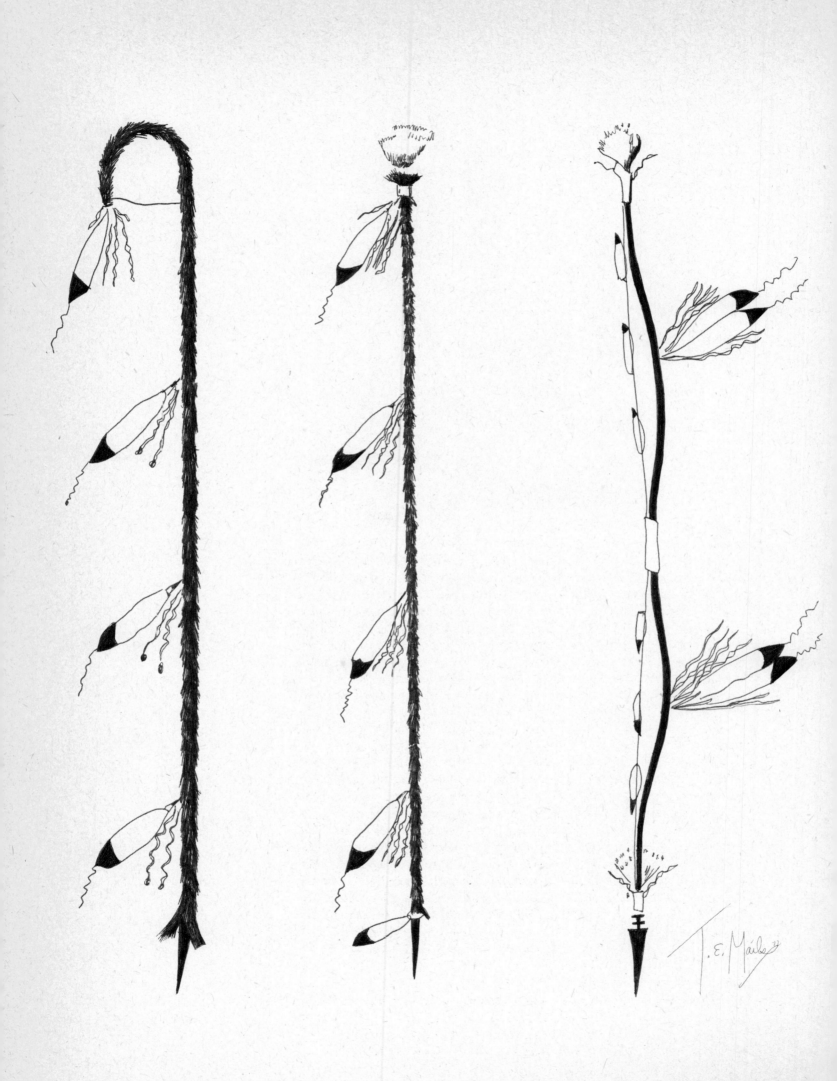

the Plains. Miss Fletcher reports that among the Omaha, "the wolf and the crow were not only connected with carnage but they had a mythical relation to the office of 'soldiers,' the designation given to certain men on the annual tribal hunt who acted as marshals." [37] Maximilian found a "Crow or Raven society" among the Mandans. In fact, it was common for all the northern tribes to associate the crow and the raven with success in war, for the birds were always seen at battlefields. The stuffed skin of the bird was bent and worn around the neck, or it was attached near the head of the lance that was carried on raids. Densmore discovered that the Crow Owners society of the Teton Sioux and the Raven Bearers society of the Mandan were similar in essential features. [38] Lowie notes a Crow Owners society among the Crow Indians, and Wissler specifies the Raven Bearers as being among the Blackfoot Indians.

Over the years of its history, the Crow Owners society of the Sioux became a large organization to which only proven and successful warriors could belong. Admission was accomplished by petitioning the society leader and giving a feast for the members.

A special painted lodge in every village was used as its meeting place. During peaceful times, when the village was full of noise with children shouting at their games and women singing and dancing, the members of the Crow Owners liked to spend the evenings in their lodge, singing and enjoying themselves. Over the door of this lodge was hung one of the Crow lances in its case or wrappings. According to informants, before a fight the carriers of the lances unwrapped them and passed them over the smoke of burning sweetgrass to increase their power. Once the lance had been stuck in the ground during a fight, it marked a place from which the members of the society could not retreat unless they withdrew the lance and took it with them. As has been shown in discussions regarding other warriors societies, the lances were not to be withdrawn without adequate reason, such as evidence that the battle was going well for the Sioux. Otherwise the Crow Owner was expected to remain at his bow-lance and to fight to the death. [39]

When going forth on a horse raid or to war, each Crow Owner painted his body black and carried his crow skin "necklace" in a painted, round rawhide case like the typical warbonnet container. Before putting it around his neck as a fight was about to take place, he passed it over the smoke of burning sweetgrass. [40] Golden eagle coup-feathers to be worn on the head were also carried in this case, as well as special red-painted sticks, which were notched for each wound received. Before a battle the Crow Owner warriors always put on their finest regalia so that, if they were killed, they would die in a manner worthy of their position and thus be prepared for their trip to the "other-side" world. The underside of the sleeves of the society war shirts were not sewn but were instead tied together with thongs at several points along the underside of the length of the arm. Before an engagement, the warrior untied the fastenings and threw back the sleeves to permit the free use of his arms. [41]

When asked why the crow was honored by the society, a Sioux named Eagle Shield said:

> We want our arrows to fly as swift and straight as the crow. The crow is always the first to arrive at the gathering of the animals in the Black Hills. The reason why the Black Hills were so long unknown to the white

Opposite: *Sioux society regalia. Left: Hooked lance of type carried on regular war party; middle: Straight lance of type carried on regular war party; right: Bow-lance of Kit-fox society (AMNH).*

man was that God created them as a meeting place for the animals. The Indians had always known this and regarded the law of God concerning it. By this law they were forbidden to kill any of the animals during their great gatherings. In the Black Hills there is a ridge of land around which is a smooth, grassy place called the "race course." This is where the animals have the races, during their gatherings. Even small animals like the turtle are there. The Crow is always first to arrive, and the other birds come before the animals, while insects and creatures like the frog travel slowly and arrive last. Sometimes it takes 10 years for all the animals to arrive, as they come from long distances and camp wherever winter overtakes them.[42]

The members of this society also served their turn as camp police. They were among those who protected the people, who watched for buffalo when the camp was moving and who assisted in the selection of suitable places for the winter camps.

A typical "praise song" of the society follows and, after that, one of the dancing songs given in connection with a narrative of a personal experience on the warpath:

friends
Sitting Crow
friends
returned not [43]

soldiers
you fled
even the eagle dies [44]

The full organization of the Crow Owners society is given by Wissler as follows:

Leaders (2)	Lance bearers (4)
Rattle bearers (2)	Lay members (x)
Pipe-keepers (2)	Drum bearers and singers, two of whom carry
Short-lance bearers (2)	rattles and sit about the drum (4)
Crow-skin bearers (2)	Herald (1)[45]

The regalia of the officers of the Crow Owners society included two pipes and two short lances. One of the latter was made of ash and was painted blue and black; the other was made of cherry and was painted red. There were also two straight crow-skin or crow-feather lances. A lance point was attached to one end of each lance. One shaft was painted blue and the other red, then each was wrapped with otter skin. An upright eagle feather and a few owl feathers were hung from the upper end of the shaft, tied to it a little below the top, and the stuffed skin of a crow with its black feathers still intact was bound to each lance just above the lance head. Mention is also made of four other rattles similar in design to the Kit-fox medicine rattle, but smaller.[46] Two bows and two arrows with blunt tips were part of the regalia, as were two whips like those of other societies and two crow feather bustles, which were worn by two officers called "servants." Yet they were important men, for they directed the singing and gave the signals for the dancing at the ceremonies. They were also responsible for securing food for the whole group. In connection with these duties, they carried, respectively, a rattle, bows and blunt-tipped arrows. When the village was moving to a new site, they shot their

245

Opposite: *Sioux society regalia. Left: Bead-wrapped eagle bone whistle of Tall Ones society; top right: Crow-skin necklace and painted rawhide case of Crow Owners society; bottom right: Crow Owners member, named Eagle Shield, wearing crow skin on neck (Smithsonian).*

blunt arrows at parflèche food cases, which they knew were well filled, thus obligating the owners to donate buffalo meat for the society at its next dance and feast. If they hit men in the legs, the men were required to donate even choicer food, such as dog flesh or special cuts of jerked buffalo meat. If they hit a dog, its master was obligated to kill it and cook it for the society's feast. When a society dance was held, the bowmen kept the members dancing by shooting any who slowed down or tried to stop before the leader felt it was proper to do so.

The peace-time dance regalia of the members consisted of breech-clout, rattle and feathers in the hair.

The society lodge had a crow painted on the door flap.

Wissler declares that no large drum was owned by the society, but that small hand drums were borrowed on ceremonial occasions. Indian informants bore out this finding.

The Strong, or Brave, Heart Society

It was said that the Strong Heart society among the Teton Sioux was organized by Sitting Bull, Gall and Crow King, prominent chiefs who were, practically, in command of all the warriors. It was their desire to have a body of fearless warriors to meet any emergency, and the society was organized to accomplish this. If a man had proven himself to be fully qualified for membership, it was not necessary for him to undergo any tests. Indian strength, patience and philosophy came only by long training, and all a warrior had to do when initiated was promise to be brave in the defense of the tribe, to take care of the poor and needy and to maintain a good moral character.[47]

Densmore says the distinctive headdress of the society was an eagle feather warbonnet made of the tail feathers of the golden eagle, with a pair of horns attached to the sides of the cap. Lowie indicates a buffalo hair bonnet, with quilled bands on the back. The headdresses were always taken along when society members went on a raid and were put on for actual battle. If a member had been successful in war and had never shown cowardice, the society code permitted him to be buried with this bonnet on his head, but if he had shown cowardice on the warpath, he was punished on his return by being severely reprimanded in the presence of all the members, his headdress was taken away and he was expelled from the society.[48]

All members of this society were allowed to carry a banner or flag made by fastening feathers horizontally to a long strip of red flannel, which was tied to a staff sharpened at one end. This was called "a waving banner," and women whose relatives had been killed in war were allowed to carry it at ceremonies and parades.

One of the precepts of the society was to increase the self-control of its members. A Sioux informant reported that in the old days there were four lodges of the Strong Hearts in the center of the village. Every morning the Strong Heart men met in one of these lodges and sang their songs. Then two young men with rattles and two with bows and arrows went around the village and killed dogs, which were later eaten in the Strong Heart lodges. It was noted, however, that some Indians were short-tempered, and the Strong Hearts were careful not to kill their dogs. But they did kill dogs belonging to prominent families, and once a dog was shot, they shouted and shook their rattles. The profession or excuse was that it strengthened a man's heart to have his dog killed and not show anger. The women cooked the dead dogs and took them to one of the Strong Heart lodges. There they all sang and danced, and the dogs were eaten as a part of the feast, while songs such as the following were sung:

My friend, whoever flees
will not become a member,
therefore I hardly live.[49]

For the Strong Heart society dances, all members dressed in war shirts and leggings and all shook their medicine rattles as they danced. The society regalia consisted of:

1. Two shirts fringed with hair-locks. These were worn by the leaders. Wissler does not mention the shirts in his discussion of Oglala societies, but such differences can usually be accounted for by the fact that the various bands were likely to differ somewhat in the matter of paraphernalia.

2. Two whips. These had broad, flat wooden handles with painted diagonal stripes and serrated edges, lashes of rawhide and wrist-loops of a full otter skin. The owners of these wore two eagle feathers at the back of the head. The shirts, whips and eagle feathers were all symbols of the same office.

3. Six lances. There were four straight lances. Two were wrapped with otter skin and had four eagle feathers evenly spaced along their length as well as a feather at the top. Two others were made with a lance head on one end, and the full length of the shaft was wrapped with a piece of red flannel about four inches wide. To this was appended a horizontal row of black feathers alternating with a row of white feathers at repeated intervals. There were two curved lances whose design is not known but which were probably wrapped and adorned like the straight lances.

4. Two headdresses. These were made with a skull cap of buckskin as the base. Blish refers to these as "feathered" headdresses, but the Indian drawings show no feathers, revealing instead what appears to be a covering of buffalo hair. A split buffalo horn was fastened to each side of the cap, and the front of the cap was decorated with a headband of beadwork. The tail of the bonnet was made of a four-foot-long strip of red flannel to which four rows of eagle feathers were fastened horizontally, five feathers to a row.[50]

5. Two White man's swords with black otter skin wrist-loops and hangings. The drawings seem to show a late-date hanging of red or blue cloth instead of otter skin.

6. Medicine rattles. The rattles, made in the shape of a ring on a handle, were carried by all regular members of the society. A common method of making these was to cover the ring part with the skin of the buffalo phallus. Dew claws were attached at intervals to the ring to provide noise, and two eagle feathers were also appended to the ring.

The distinctive rattle of the Strong Heart society officers consisted of a rawhide receptacle on which were incised the lines of a turtle shell. A strip of buffalo fur was wrapped around this, and the handle was covered with hide or red flannel. The head contained a few small stones or shot to provide the noise. For dancing, the rattle was held vertically in the hand and shaken in a short, jerky fashion without bending the arm.[51]

The Badger Society
Wissler discovered that the Badger society had existed among the

Oglala Sioux, and Dr. Lowie found information about it among both the eastern Dakota and the Mandans.[52] It is said to have become extinct about 1895, and very little could be learned about the group by investigators.

The badger was the society's helper animal, having come as such to the founder in a vision. At each side of the door flap,[53] the society lodge bore a painting of a badger standing upright. The peace-time dance costume of the group was composed of a war shirt and leggings. A fan was carried and feathers were inserted in the hair. An otter skin collar was also worn; later it was decorated with rows of round trade mirrors.

Sioux informants stated that when the society members went to war, they carried wolf skin banners. Actually the lances were more properly staffs or ensigns, for they were made while in the field. The lances were carried by men on horseback especially deputized as lance bearers when it was discovered that more officers than usual would be needed. The lances had to be made in great haste and from green wood. The top of the shaft was bent over in the traditional crook form, but since the timber was green, the crook stayed in place only when it was tied.[54] After being bent, the entire shaft was wrapped with strips of wolf skin, which members carried for the purpose. Some strips were left to hang free as pendants, and small medicine objects were tied to the hook end.

In a unique society custom, a boy who hoped to join the society was made the water carrier of the organization. In order to test his courage and to develop it, when the group went on a horse raid or to war, the boy was often sent, after dark and in dangerous circumstances, to obtain water for the warriors.[55]

The water bag was of a very special type. The water sack itself was called a "heart bag" and was fashioned from the large sac-covering of a buffalo heart. It was hung from the large end of a stick about five feet long, which forked at the opposite end. Decorations of feathers and other small objects were appended to the forked ends, and wolf skin strips were hung at the V of the fork. By tradition, the bag itself was hung from the stick with four thongs, and feathers were attached at the places where the thongs were tied to the bag.

The insignia of the officers of the Badger society was made up of the following:

1. Two pipes.
2. Six lances. Two of these were crooked and wrapped with otter skin. Two were straight and fur-wrapped. Two were straight with black-and red-dyed buckskin stripes made by wrapping the shaft with the two colors. Single eagle tail feathers were added to the fur-wrapped lances, and pairs of tail feathers were tied to the striped staffs. Lances like these varied in length from seven to nine feet.
3. One drum.
4. One sword with a full black otter skin hanging from the handle. Eagle tail feathers were tied to the skin in pairs.
5. Two painted buckskin shirts fringed with buckskin, with quilled or beaded shoulder bands and armbands.
6. Two whips. These had serrated edges, were painted and had otter skin wrist-loops and hangings.
7. Two head decorations consisting of two eagle tail feathers each. These were worn by the whip bearers.[56]

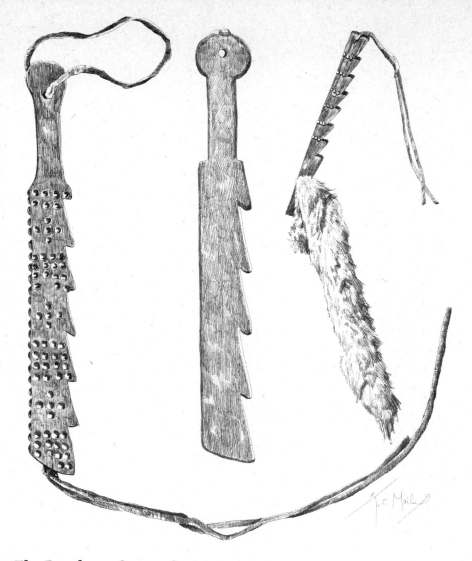

The Bare-lance Owners Society

The Bare-lance Owners society was said to be a very old society, coming between the Tall Ones and the Strong Hearts in age. It had an absolute membership limit of twenty-four warriors. Like many others, it ceased to exist before anthropologists could learn much about it. Wissler feels that it was difficult to secure a good translation for the name of the society: "It is said to imply a smooth, unadorned stick; hence they that have empty lances, referring to the custom of investing certain members with plain lances to which they may tie feathers as coups are counted." [57]

The society regalia shown in pictographic drawings consisted of the following:

1. Two pipes.
2. Six lances. Two of these were crooked and four were straight. The crooked pair were fur-wrapped and closely resembled those of the White-marked society. The third pair resembled the straight fur-wrapped lances shown for the Strong Hearts and White-marked. The other two were wrapped with a strip of black flannel and a strip of red flannel so that the black and red showed like stripes in succession. Blue and black were frequently used interchangeably, however. Lance members also carried shields.
3. Two buckskin shirts fringed with either hair-locks or buckskin thongs. The shirts were painted and had quilled or beaded armbands and shoulder bands.
4. Two whips. These were painted and had a serrated edge. An eagle feather was attached to the lash, and there was an otter skin wrist-loop. A Sioux warrior pointed out that the shirts and whips belonged to the same officer.

249

Sioux society whips. Right: Flat club type carried by members of several societies with kit-fox skin pendant and wrist-loop—otter skin pendants and loops were also used; middle: Quirt or "whip" without loop; left: Quirt or "whip" with rawhide lashes and brass tack decorations. Note serrated edge on all whips (DPL).

5. A sword with a pair of full black otter skins tied to the guard. Eagle feathers were attached to the skins in pairs for added power.

6. A flat drum. Eagle tail feathers were attached to this for decoration.

7. Two head decorations consisting of two eagle feathers each.

The peace-time dance costume included a long scalp-lock strap decorated with silver hair-plates and hanging to the ground. Shirts and leggings were worn, and a fan was carried.

The society lodge was painted with vertical stripes extending from top to bottom. These covered all sides of the tipi and even crossed the door flap.[58]

The White-marked Society

A pictographic drawing of the lodge of Chief Red Cloud depicts in a beautiful way the deeply spiritual nature of the White-marked society members. The huge rainbow painted on each side of the lodge cover was Red Cloud's personal emblem. The red disk on the rear of the tipi represented the sun, and the encircling yellow ring its halo. The top of the tipi was painted black to represent the heavens at night. The dark green color at the bottom represented the earth. The buffalo symbol on the rear of the lodge was painted yellow on the hump to indicate old hair not yet shed, for the hump sheds last. By these colors and images, Red Cloud appealed to the Great Spirit through several of the mightiest spirit powers.[59]

In dancing, the White-marked members wore war shirts and leggings and carried on their arm a robe or blanket with a quilled or beaded blanket strip attached.

The symbols of office of the ten leaders of the society were as follows:

1. Two pipes.

2. Two eagle feather bonnets of the traditional type. These had the head bonnet with a full, single tail reaching to the ground. Split buffalo horns were attached to the sides of the cap and a beaded band was sewn to the cap front. Blish describes the order as the "society of those who carry something white," and states that the "white" refers to the feathered bonnets. Wissler again indicates a buffalo-hair headdress, with eagle down on top and a red flannel tail with eagle feathers appended.

3. Four lances. Two were crooked, wrapped with otter fur and decorated with eagle feathers, and two were straight and fur-wrapped with two single eagle feathers attached to the staff and a single feather placed upright at the top. The latter were wrapped with spiraling strips of red and blue flannel, held in place with sinew ties.

4. Two White man's swords with a pair of black otter skins attached to the guards. Eagle tail feathers were tied to the otter skins.[60]

(Wissler does not refer to swords as regalia for this society. He does, however, speak of two whips, which the Sioux informants did not mention. These had nicks and brass nails on the handle, plus otter skin and eagle feathers. They also had fox skin wrist-loops and pendants.[61])

The Omaha Society

The Omaha society is not mentioned in the lists of Hayden or Wissler, although Wissler records it as being a dance association. It is clearly an importation, probably coming from the Pawnees through the Omahas.[62]

Among the Oglalas, it was originally a warrior society similar in general outline to the others described. A remnant of it still exists in the popular, and now social, dance called "the Omaha" or "the Grass

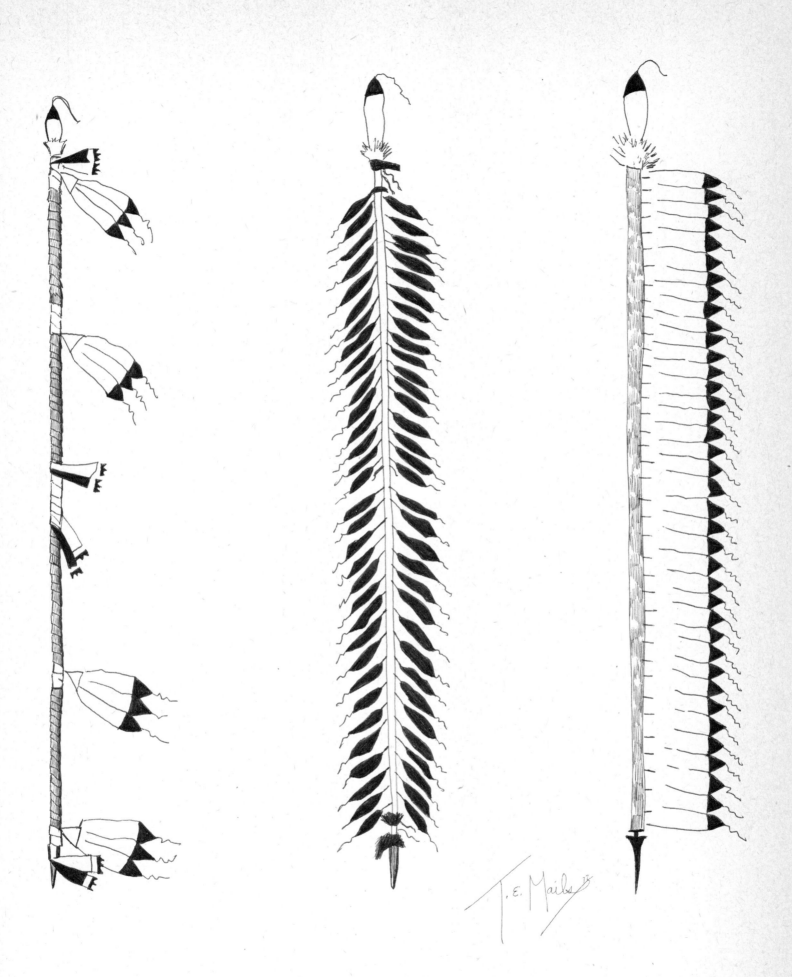

Sioux society regalia. Left: *Lance of White-marked society;* middle: *Lance of Crow Owners society;* right: *Lance of Strong Hearts society* (AMNH).

Dance." The most significant part of the original dance ceremony was the more or less ritualistic Grass dance.

Blish reports that "as a significant incidental phase, a healing ceremony developed in the Omaha Society, in which the Grass Dance played a significant part. In fact, this healing ceremony came to be considered one of the most important social elements of the organization and was looked upon as one of the chief methods of securing supernatural aid for bringing about the recovery of someone who was ill." [63]

The customary way of dressing for the Omaha dance was to wear a breechclout, a chest covering such as a bone vest and a roach headdress. Bodies were painted according to individuals' personal wishes.

The regalia for the leaders of the Omaha dance consisted of the following:

1. Two short lances or staffs wrapped with otter skin with an eagle tail feather standing straight up at the upper end.

2. One large flat drum, for which there were several drummers.

3. Four feathered dance bustles with split tails of red or blue trade cloth with rows of eagle feathers appended horizontally.

4. Two whistles with an eagle tail feather dangling from each.

5. Two ornamented forked spears.

6. Two rattles, each with a ring at one end and an eagle feather attached to the handle.

7. Two whips. These were made like all the others, with a serrated edge, an otter wrist-loop and hanging and an eagle feather attached at the lash end.

8. Two horse-tails, each decorated with an eagle feather. Only men who had had their horses shot from under them had the right to carry these.[64] In some tribes the tails were worn at the back of the belt, but the Sioux apparently carried them, instead, because their dance bustles would interfere with the belt custom.

9. Old drawings always show one or more dancers wearing an eagle feather warbonnet of the traditional style. Some dancers carried weapons of war, ranging from war-clubs to bows and guns.

A typical Omaha song went as follows:

He was their friend,
They were his friends,
Everyone failed him,
Even his own people.

It was sung in commemoration of a famous fight on Powder River, March 17, 1876, when a part of Crook's command under Col. J. J. Reynolds attacked and burned a Sioux-Cheyenne village. The composition and the singing of songs of this nature on special occasions was customary with the Omaha society.

The public and social portion of the Grass dance took place within a circle of pine shade boughs, which were placed around the dance area. The typical posture for dancing was a slight crouch. At one side, opposite the entrance, sat the drummers and singers, and those who would serve as the mounted officials for the day stood at each side of the entrance to the circle.

The Omaha ceremony included a dance of two forked-spear bearers, who in traditional fashion charged a pot of stewed dog with the forked instruments held above their heads. This is said to have

Sioux dance rattles. Left: *Hide rattle with buffalo tail pendant of type used by Omaha society;* middle: *Dance rattle with beaded handle and tab for unidentified society;* right: *Tall Ones society dance rattle with beaded tab—last two rattles have cut dew claws (MAI).*

been the most spectacular and exciting dance act of the ceremony, and artists portrayed it more often than any other part. In the opening portion of the Grass dance, the chosen dancers also "charged the dog" in single file, with each man placing his right hand on the shoulder of the dancer in front of him.

Wissler describes the dog ceremony as follows:

Of the more fundamental concepts and procedures of the ceremony may be mentioned the serving of dog flesh. In this there are several distinct performances:

1. The scouting of the food kettle after it has been carried into the dance house and the counting of coup upon it as if it were an enemy.

2. The serving of small bits of dog flesh to a few distinguished men by the bearers of the pointed stick the [dog fork] or ceremonial spoon.

3. Presenting the dog heads to the most distinguished men present and the counting of coups by them over the skulls at the end of the feast.

4. Gathering all the other bones and passing them around to be prayed over; finally secreting them in some secure place.[65]

The Omaha dance ceremony was more or less social before the dog ceremony. With that and the Grass dance, however, it became ritualistic, taking upon itself the aspect of a healing ceremony. At the ritual's end, the crowd, including spectators, was fed, and there was a ceremony of dismissal.

Sioux Dream Cults
Buffalo
Horse
Elk
Bear
Sacred Bow Racing

Regarding dreams and their obligations upon the dreamer, Frances Densmore has made the following excellent summary statement:

> The obligation of a dream was as binding as the necessity of fulfilling a vow, and disregard of either was said to be punished by the forces of nature, usually by a stroke of lightning. Dreams were sought by the Sioux, but it was recognized that the dream would correspond to the character of the man. Thus it was said that "a young man would not be great in mind so his dream would not be like that of a chief; it would be ordinary in kind, yet he would have to do whatever the dream directed him to do." The first obligation of a dream was usually its announcement to the tribe. This was by means of a performance which indicated the nature of the dream and allied the man to others who had similar dreams. If the dream were connected with sacred stones, or with herbs or animals concerned in the treatment of the sick, it was considered obligatory that the man avail himself of the supernatural aid vouchsafed to him in the dream, and arrange his life in accordance with it.[66]

The ways in which dreams came to people have been considered in earlier chapters, but it should be repeated here that the recipients of the dreams sometimes banded together in loose organizations, now and then referred to as "societies" by anthropologists but more properly called "cults" to distinguish the one from the other. Societies often originated in dreams too, but the nature of the groups evolving thereafter differed considerably. Societies had traditional rules, set numbers of officers and specific duties in the tribe. None of these things was so with the cults. Despite the common bond of the cultic people, they remained as individuals in their practices, with most activities being of a personal and secretive nature.

Nevertheless, the people believed fervently in the efficacy of dreams, and the cult members were held in great respect. It was, indeed, this very respect that made their work so productive, for the practitioner and patient were of one mind, hence open to God mentally and physically in such a way so as to receive His blessings without the hindrances that doubt and enlightened intellect so often place as barriers in the way. Despite the persistent attempts of the Whites to put down the Indians as "savages," attitudes like this challenge the position considerably. Furthermore, one who investigates the personal narratives of the Indian peoples discovers a sense of reverence that was, and still is among those who live according to the ancient ways, monumental, as is shown by this prayer from a Sioux warrior named Lone Man: "A man from the earth I am, I have sung concerning an event, for which have compassion on me, whoever from above, you the supreme ruler."

As to his medicine or doctor's work, he declared that his instructor had told him:

> All herbs and roots were made for the benefit of animals or men. . . . all are carefully tested, and if one is found to be a cure for a certain disease,

Sioux Omaha society dancer wearing otter skin society collar adorned with trade mirrors, crow bustle and roach headdress (SM).

Sioux Omaha Grass dance participants cooking dog in buffalo paunch filled with heated stones. The men will perform as the two forked-spear bearers in the ceremony to follow.

it should be regarded as a gift from God, and intended especially as a remedy for that disease. It should be reverenced, and this reverence should be closely observed, as without it the herb will have no effect. Because of the reverence due to these medical herbs certain songs are used expressing this feeling.[67]

The Buffalo Cult
Concerning the Buffalo cult Dr. Lowie writes:

> Among the Santee the men performing the Buffalo dance had had visions of the buffalo, though apparently the sons of such men were also entitled to join. One man might dream that he . . . had been shot by an arrow so that he could barely get home. . . . Such a man painted himself vermilion to represent the trickling down of the blood. Another man dreamed of being shot with a gun. Such a one would act out his dream during a Buffalo dance.[68]

The following songs were said to have been sung by Buffalo cult members. Some of them had been received, or composed, in a dream of buffalo, but the story of the dream had been forgotten and only the songs remained as a tradition in the tribe.

> *northward*
> *they are walking*
> *a sacred stone*
> *they touch*
> *they are walking* [69]
>
> *Brave Buffalo [a man's name]*
> *I am*
> *I come* [70]

Catlin witnessed the Buffalo dance at Fort Snelling, Minnesota, and Densmore saw one in South Dakota in 1913. The dancers wore buffalo headdresses with the horns attached and carried shields with buffalo symbols painted on either the shield or its cover. In dancing, the performers sought to imitate the buffalo. Music was supplied by a drum. Buffalo cults were always connected with the calling of the herds closer to the village, with healing and with the gaining of buffalo "power," or the strength and durability of the animal.

There was a traditional dream-cult ceremony which featured the buffalo dreamer. Coyote, Wolf and Thunder dreamers also took part in the dance, but the buffalo was the center of attention and significance.

Wissler describes the main points of the performance as follows:

> There was a group of men and occasionally a few women, known as the buffalo dreamers. When they had their dance, a shaman (holy man) would appear in the head and skin of a buffalo. As he ran about the camp a nude young man (the Thunder dreamer) stalked him, while the cult followed singing. At the proper time the hunter discharged an arrow deeply into a spot marked on the buffalo hide. The holy man would then stagger, vomit blood and spit upon the arrow point. The Wolf cult would then pursue him. Later, another shaman would use medicine, pull the arrow out and at once the wound was healed.[71]

By tradition the Wolf and the Thunder dreamers were linked together. Whenever the Wolf dreamers gave a dance, their herald pro-

257

Opposite: *Sioux Omaha society member, wearing beautiful crow bustle, performing Grass dance (SM).*

claimed the invitation to the camp and also notified the Thunder dreamers to get ready, as soon there would be a wolf coming over the hill.

Blish states that the Wolf dreamers wore wolf skins over their backs, arms and legs, but drawings indicate that as was the usual fashion, an entire wolf skin was worn hanging down the back. The cultic performers also wore head masks made of rawhide with holes for the eyes and the mouth. These were probably made like the painted clown masks of the Assiniboine Fool society, about the construction of which more detail is available. However, the Sioux masks were also topped with animal horns or with long feathers bent to resemble horns, which led Blish to feel that the masks bore a striking resemblance to some of the masks of the Indians of the Southwest, such as the Navaho, the Hopi and the Zuni. The horns or feathers of the Sioux masks formed almost a circle. A cross-tie of buckskin held them in place, and sometimes a round trade mirror was attached to the crosspoint of the ties.[72]

Blish adds that "the symbols of the owner's dream may be painted on the mask. The legs and arms are painted red, the bodies white. Some carry an imitation snake from which they shoot wakan (holy) influence. Some also carry the pipe."[73]

The Thunder dreamers, said to have been the most important dreamers in the minds of the Sioux, were the clowns of the cultic organizations. In this regard they were much like the inverted or crazy societies so common to the Plains tribes, since they often spoke and performed backward or in reverse fashion. "The main fact regarding their actions is that they are consistently anti-natural."[74] It was said

258

Sioux cult member wearing headdress covered in its entirety with golden eagle body feathers (DPL).

that those people were Thunder beings because they had dreamed of Thunder. Blish defines them as "clowns," but Densmore is probably more correct when she uses the former term. In any event, after dreaming, the recipient was required to go through a public performance lest he be killed by lightning. Some Indian informants reported that Thunder dreamers bore some relation to the weather; and on special days of feasts and ceremonies if the skies appeared threatening the dreamers were called upon to perform in order to pacify the sky spirits.[75]

In the Buffalo dance, the snakes and pipes were usually carried by men who had been successful in horse raids. As such, the snake represented a rope, either that carried by the raider or the picket rope he cut at an enemy's tipi, and the pipe indicated leadership of one or more raids.

One Sioux pictographic drawing is either different from or enlarging upon the costume of the Buffalo dreamer previously described, for it shows the performer wearing only a buffalo head mask rather than the entire skin. The dancer also wears a long shirt and carries a staff approximately six feet in length.[76] The mask in this case was probably made after the manner of those fashioned by the Mandans and the Assiniboines.

The Horse Cult

No dream of a horse was related to Helen Blish, but there was among the Teton Sioux an organization called the Horse society.[77] It was said that some of the songs in the following group were used in this society and also on the warpath to make a horse swift and sure. The

259

Sioux warrior, named Buffalo Boy, who received his name in a dream in which he saw buffalo. He wears a hawk and owl feather headdress and a war shirt with quilled honor bands on shoulders and sleeves (Smithsonian).

estimation in which a capable horse was held by the Sioux was shown by a speech by a warrior named Brave Buffalo, which went as follows:

> Of all the animals the horse is the best friend of the Indian, for without it he could not go on long journeys. A horse is the Indian's most valuable piece of property. If an Indian wishes to gain something, he promises his horse that if the horse will help him he will paint it with native dye, that all may see that help has come to him through the aid of his horse.[78]

A renowned Sioux warrior named Teal Duck said that on one occasion when he was hard pressed on the warpath, he dismounted and, standing in front of his horse, spoke to him, saying: "We are in danger. Obey me promptly that we may conquer. If you have to run for your life and mine, do your best, and if we reach home I will give you the best eagle feather I can get and the finest sina' lu'ta, and you shall be painted with the best paint." The eagle feather spoken of was tied to the horse's tail and sina' lu'ta was a strip of red cloth that was fastened around the horse's neck.[79]

Teal Duck's song went as follows:

> *a root of herb*
> *sacred*
> *it is*
> *(that which) I have used*
> *the tribe of men*
> *therefore*
> *toward them*
> *it is*
> *I have used it* [80]

Other Horse songs included by Densmore were:

> *friend*
> *my horse*
> *flies like a bird*
> *as it runs*
>
> *daybreak*
> *appears*
> *when*
> *a horse*
> *neighs* [81]

The Elk Cult

The Elk cult was comprised of men who had dreamed of the elk and then banded together, calling themselves the Elk society. Two Shields, one of the singers and drummers for this society, stated that the last official meeting of the group was held about 1885. The following song was used by this society, and Two Shields said it had been handed down for many generations. He stated further that the song is still sung by an Elk dreamer at dances and must always be paid for by the man who asks that it be sung.

> *Whoever considers themselves beautiful*
> *after seeing me*
> *has no heart* [82]

An Elk dreamer always carried a conspicuous hoop, which was

described in songs as "a rainbow." In explanation of the description, Two Shields said, "Part of the rainbow is visible in the clouds, and part disappears in the ground. What we see is in the shape of a hoop. This word is employed by medicine-men and especially by dreamers of the elements of the air and earth." The hoop of an Elk dreamer was considered sacred, and the dreamer took great pride in his right to carry it. In performing, he sometimes put it around his neck or thrust one arm through it and carried it on his shoulder, although drawings more often show it as being held in the hand.[83]

In his dream of the elk, a man named Brave Buffalo received explicit directions as to how he should conduct his ceremonies, make his regalia and paint his tipi. A downy white eagle feather was to be worn tied to the right side of his headdress during regular times and to the right horn of his mask during ceremonies. The mask was to be made of the headskin of an elk hide, with the horns attached. He was to paint himself yellow and to hold in each hand a hoop wrapped with elk hide, with the hair left on and decorated with an herb the elk liked. This was later identified as wild bergamot, an herb much used by young men because of its fragrance. His tipi was to be painted yellow on the outside with drawings of a crane and a crow on its inner walls. The crane held a pipe with the stem pointed upward, and the crow held a pipe with its stem pointed downward. He was to devise his own performance, but it had to plainly show the people who his patron animal was.[84]

It is said that on occasions, after an Elk dreamer had passed over a damp spot, people saw only the footprints of an elk rather than those of a man. When an Elk dreamer was performing, no woman was allowed to stand or pass by on his windward side and no one was allowed to come too near him.

After performances, dreamers believed they would be given special powers to find medicinal herbs. When in doubt about what herb to use for a specific illness, an appeal was made to the elks, and "they told him what to use and where to find it." [85]

When he was not performing, the Elk dreamer wore a hair-hoop consisting of a small hoop wrapped with porcupine quills with a downy white eagle feather suspended from its center by a thong. The hoop was fastened to the left side of the man's head by its center so that the feather hung over the ear.

Wissler states that the elk was closely associated with the Indian idea of love and sexual passion. "Supernatural power lay behind manifestations of sex desire; consequently, numerous mythical creatures were thought to control such power, and of these, the bull elk was the most important." [86]

Cult dreamer performances were usually given in response to someone's dream or vision in which he was told first to test his medicine and then to exhibit the continuing guardianship of the particular animal seen in vision. The day set apart for such a performance was known as a Medicine Day.

Two "holy women" were characteristically a part of the ceremony, and they were regarded with a certain superstitious fear by the people because of the magic powers they were supposed to possess. They carried the sacred medicine pipes during the ceremony and were understood to be making an offering to the Great Spirit. A robed holy man served as priest of the ceremony. Another medicine man played

262

the role of the "magic shooter," who tested the medicine power of the dancers. These attempted to dodge whatever he shot at them, and if their medicine was strong, no injury resulted even though they were struck. The "magic shooter" was really the evil-spirit element in the performance, and he was often put to flight by the onslaughts of dancers, whose faith in their medicine, shown by their courage in attacking him, added strength and power to themselves.

The Elk cult included dreamers of the long-tailed deer, who painted themselves red, and the black-tailed deer, who were painted blue and black. Like the Elks, these had their own headgear; they carried an eagle feather in the right hand and a hoop in the left hand. There were slight variations in the headgear and hoops, each individual fashioning his as a matter of his personal dream and tastes. The black figure in one pictograph carries a small hoop and wears another larger one upon his head. Both the head hoop, formed by the horns, and the hand hoop often contained small mirrors tied in the center on crossed laces. The mirrors were believed to possess the power to detect and track ill feeling, so they were of great value when an evil spirit was present to harass one and thus test his strength and power. The hoop itself was the embodiment of the circle, which represented the universe in Sioux lore. It was the emblem of the fork-horned animals and was always prominent in their ceremonies.

The so-called ammunition the dreamer used to combat evil was attached to the hoop. This consisted of such items as bear claws, eagle claws, grasshoppers, deer hooves, etc., as these were parts of animals or insects whose protective powers were especially valued. A circle was also painted on the body of each dancer. When they performed elk and deer imitations, it was known that the circle had to be worn "to make things complete." So powerful was the application of one that a dancer could be struck on that spot by any kind of weapon or missile, and if his medicine were really strong, he would not be killed. Instead it was believed that death would come to the one who tried to kill him.

During cult performances, small leafy branches were stuck into the ground, and offerings to the Great Spirit in the form of purple or red banners were hung from them. Some Elk dancers also carried leafy branches in their hands as they performed. These were described as long canes with leaves at the top.[87]

The Bear Cult

The bear was another of the animals dreamed of by many of the Plains tribes. In most instances the dream imparted information concerning the use of herbs for treating illness and also offered the strength of the bear through the dreamer to warriors about to go on a horse raid or war party.[88]

In doctoring a sick child, a Bear cult member was seen to hold a rawhide rattle in one hand and sagebrush in the other. Later he placed the sagebrush in his mouth and blew out a substance that looked like yellow paint.[89] Sage was believed to repel evil. The significance is not known, but it was used by Blackfoot doctors and by the Apaches, who employed yellow pollen in their most sacred ceremonies. It was common for several Bear cult members to assemble at any curing rite. At such times they carried the traditional bear knives, made with handles fashioned of bear jawbone.

263

Opposite: *Sioux Elk dreamer regalia: hoop made of sacred herbs and elk fur; quilled hoop and breath-feather worn as hair ornament (Smithsonian).*

The Sioux performed a ceremonial bear hunt as a prelude to the departure of a war party. In this, the Bear was chased by the members of the party in proper ceremonial fashion, and it was believed that the first warrior to touch the Bear would kill an enemy. In one such performance the Bear member carried hoops in his hands to lengthen his arms so that he could walk on all fours like a bear. A pictographic drawing shows a Bear dreamer carrying a bird in his hand. Blish explains that "the emblem was of the duck family, known as huntka by the Indians." The bird was skinned, then ground up, bones and all, with a special medicine, and then eaten by the dreamer. The stuffed skin was thereafter carried in the public ceremony as a medicine charm.[90]

Bear feasts were given from time to time by cult members, to which all Bear dreamers and those who had been cured by them were invited. The cult members in these feasts wore bear skins, painted their bodies red and, in dancing, imitated the actions of a bear in his daily habits. It was not, however, the custom to eat bear meat at these feasts.

The Sacred Bow Cult

The cult of the Sacred Bow, although a military one, was another of those groups that came into existence as the result of a dream, said to have been the dream of a powerful Dakota holy man named Black Road. There were four bow carriers, four men who carried long slender staffs with an eagle feather at the upper end and two club bearers. The staffs were known as hangers, and they were used to support the bows when they were not in use. In time, the sacred bow came to be

264

Sioux Elk dreamer wearing mask with elk horns and carrying hoop—Sioux pictographs of Elk dreamer drawings in the background (adapted from pictographic drawings in the book A Pictographic History of the Oglala Sioux *by Blish).*

looked upon with reverent fear by the Sioux, for both the bow and the bow ceremony proved to be strong medicine in accomplishing important ends in peace and in war. The bow itself was made like a regular bow with a double curve, except that it was longer and heavier, with a lance point added to one end.[91]

For the public ceremony, the order's sacred lodge and sweat-lodge were set up at the center of the camp-circle. Then four posts symbolizing the four cardinal points were set up at the inner edge of the camp-circle to represent enemies. After the traditional rites of purification by a holy man in the sweat-lodge and sacred tipi, the runners of the race left the sacred lodge and stood facing the west with their right hands raised in an appeal to God. After this they ran to the west, struck and circled the post, ran back and circled the lodge, and then continued to run in the same manner till all four directions had been compassed. At the end of the race, the dancers entered the sweat-lodge and there participated in a final rite of purification.

The race was really an endurance test for the performers, for the camp-circle was sometimes a mile or more in circumference. There were no rules concerning the order in which the performers had to run after the start; indeed, each one attempted to pass others because the first man to finish the course won the race.

The main spiritual and supernatural forces invoked symbolically in the Sacred Bow rite were all capable of killing men: the lightning, the wind and the hail. The snake and the bear were also invoked, but they were considered intermediaries rather than powers from Above. The swift-winged creatures of the air were also called upon by the aid of two feathers worn in the hair in an unusual fashion, the quill base protruding forward over the forehead. Their use was in reality a prayer that the warrior might, like them, be swift in flight and hard to hit.

Dancers wore only breechclouts for clothing. The paint used on the racer's body also made its mystic appeal to unseen powers and transmitted this message to the spectators. The entire body was painted red to represent the earth in a buffalo wallow. The face painting consisted of a black or blue line drawn in a curve from temple to temple across the bridge of the nose. The line was forked at each end and represented lightning. A crescent in a quarter-moon shape was drawn upon the chest. The wrist, ankle, elbow and knee of each dancer was ringed with a blue line, known as the "blue stone mark," symbolizing the wind god. Two other methods were used to mark the arms and legs. In one, wavy lines, forked at both ends, extended down the arms and legs from the shoulders and the thighs. The other method differed only a little in that the line on one leg was straight "to signify the desire for the ability to think straight or to possess presence of mind, in contrast to the state of mind supposed to be produced by the power of the whirlwind." [92]

The Sacred Bows were entrusted only to carefully chosen and qualified men, and a number of strict rules governed both the bestowal and the consideration of such an honor. The selection of the hanger carriers was only slightly less important. The club bearers were chosen last. The ten men held their office as long as they were able, but the duration of the term was usually short, for the demands made upon them were exceedingly heavy. Nevertheless, the posts could be vacated only by death or resignation. Since the group was primarily a military

Sioux warrior wearing unusual headdress fashioned from coyote skin with beaded ear-flaps added (DPL). Opposite: Omaha Horse society performers wearing stiffened horsetails and hair-falls and necklaces made of horses' manes. Opposite above: Omaha Bear society member performing Bear dance.

one, success in war was its chief concern.[93] Therefore, each officer had to lead in battle, show great bravery and manage to strike at least one or two enemies with the bow or hanger in every battle. This of course was an especially serious undertaking, since approaching close enough to do that with a clumsy instrument like the bow or hanger multiplied the possibility of personal injury or death. The constant challenge was, to say the least, strenuous and wearing, and after an officer had proved himself beyond reproach, he sometimes returned his bow or hanger to the holy man of the organization, thereby resigning.

Another ceremony was usually performed then that combined marking the resignation and an initiation ritual for a newly appointed officer. The race was also run, however, when new members who were not officers were received; in such cases it was considered to be a pledge of faith and fidelity. In the same way, the race might also be run as the fulfillment of a vow to a spirit power for the recovery of someone who was ill or as a prayer for power to fulfill vows or as a prayer for protection in time of great danger, such as a revenge raid. Helen Blish feels that this last was the chief purpose of the ceremony.[94]

11
THE
OMAHA

According to tradition the Omaha lived at one time in northern Kentucky and southern Indiana. About A.D. 1500, they began to migrate westward with the Ponca, the Osage, the Kansa and the Quapaw. When they had reached the Red Pipestone Quarry in Minnesota, the Omaha and Ponca settled down there together for a hundred years or so. They built stationary earth-lodge villages and raised agricultural crops, but they also ventured onto the Plains in quest of buffalo and other game.

When, by 1650, the pressure from the Sioux proved too much to take, they moved westward. In South Dakota the tribes separated, the Omaha settling with the Iowa on Bow Creek, Nebraska, and the Ponca continuing westward to the Little Missouri and the Black Hills. Soon thereafter, however, the Ponca returned and the three tribes were united. Eventually, the Iowa moved to what is now known as the state of Iowa, but the Omaha and Ponca continued to live together until the Whites separated them on reservations.

The Omaha population was about 3,000 in 1780. Their name means "Those Going Against the Current." In 1905, Alice Fletcher found that the Omaha had a most profound life-way, with detailed costuming, involved methods of self-painting and complex symbols and rituals. Their society structures were very dramatic, with religion and tradition playing the central roles in the people's activities.

There were two classes of societies among the Omaha: social and secret (or mystery).[1]

Membership in the social class was open to those who had earned the right and were able to perform the acts required for eligibility. To this class belonged both the warrior societies and the purely social groups.

The secret societies dealt with supernatural mysteries, and membership was generally attained by a dream or vision related to the nature of the society. Some of the secret societies had knowledge of the medicines, roots and plants used in healing. Others were noted for their prophetic and magic abilities; according to Fletcher, they furnished the only examples of such practices in the tribe.[2]

There were no societies composed exclusively of women.

THE SOCIAL SOCIETIES

The Thunder Society

The Thunder society was one of the largest and most important social societies. Omaha tradition indicates that it was known at the time when the Omaha, the Ponca and other related tribes were still living together as one nation. The "Wind people" were the hereditary custodians and bearers of the two pipes sacred to the special rites of the opening ceremonies, when the members first assembled. As the society members moved in a procession around the tribal circle, they followed the pipe-keepers. The Thunder society was established to encourage a heroic spirit among the people and keep alive the memory of historical and valorous acts, and thunder was its patron god. Songs and ceremonies focused on the destructive power of the lightning, with its accompanying thunder and clouds that terrified man and beast alike. Among the Osage the same society was spoken of as "those who partake of the nature of the thunder." The society was a part of the Iowa and Oto tribes as well.

In the eighteenth century, the Thunder society spread to other branches of the Siouan family. Among these were the Pawnee, who, according to tradition, were at one time close allies of the Omaha. They and other tribes took great pleasure in dancing to the rhythmic cadence of the Thunder songs, but they had words of their own composition. Any tribe familiar with the Thunder dance still recognizes one of its songs no matter in what tribe the song was composed. However, it is important to note that although the Thunder society had so wide a popularity, the Omaha remained the only tribe wherein the religious rites and songs of the opening ceremonies were observed. The others omitted these observances and used only the dramatic dance, the songs and the feast that concluded the gathering.

The membership of the Omaha Thunder society was restricted to proven warriors. As such it included both chiefs and lay members. The one requirement for eligibility was that the man had to have received public war honors before the "Packs Sacred to War." To join, a desirable candidate was recommended by a member and invited to a meeting. If no one objected to his joining the society, he was accepted as a member from that time forward.

The officers of the society were the leader, a herald and the keepers of the pipes. The leader held his office until he chose to resign. At that time another renowned warrior would make his candidacy known by inviting the members to a feast. His candidacy would be discussed, and if no objections were raised, he was accepted as the new leader. The herald had to be a proven warrior with a strong, clear voice so that his reports could be heard. At each meeting, the leader appointed two or more aspiring young men to act as servants in attending the fire and assisting in the ceremonies.

Thunder meetings were held at irregular intervals, usually about once a month, in the lodge of a member who was respected by the tribe. Another member volunteered to be the host, or feast-giver, and it was his duty to furnish the food for the feast and the tobacco for the pipes. He could not fill the pipes or prepare them for smoking, however, as that could be done only by a pipe-keeper. The host also prepared the sacred black paint, made of charred box-elder wood mixed with water, and put it into a special wooden bowl that the society kept for this purpose.

Each member had his appointed place within the lodge. The leader sat in the middle at the back part of the lodge, directly opposite the door. The men who were his equals in war honors sat next to him on either side; then came those of the next lower rank in accomplishments; and so on, by grades, around to the door. The honors by which the places of the members were determined were those that had been publicly given the warriors at the last tribal ceremony for this purpose. On each side of the entrance sat one of the young servants appointed by the leader. Regardless of his rank, the host or feast-giver of the meeting always sat near the door on the right. The drum was placed just to the left of the leader's seat. The men singers, two or sometimes four of whom used drumsticks, were grouped around it. Immediately behind the men sat a few women who possessed fine voices. This choir led in the singing of the songs, in which all the members usually joined when not dancing.

The Thunder members each wore only a breechclout with a long bunch of braided grass, representing scalps the wearer had taken in battle, fastened to his belt at the back. Originally the members wore the scalps themselves, but in time substituted the braided grass. Eventually, this decoration was worn by all the members without regard to personal achievement. By the time the dance became known to the Dakota tribes and the Winnebago, the significance of the bunch of long grass had already been forgotten, and they gave it the name "Grass Dance," or "Omaha Dance." Each Thunder member painted himself in accordance with the directions given him at the tribal honors ceremony, and he also wore the coup marks conferred on him at that ceremony. The leader himself had to be of sufficient rank to be able to wear the "Crow" bustle, which was a decoration of the highest order. Sometimes dance bells were strung on straps and tied about the legs and ankles.

The rules and influence of the society tended to promote peace and harmony in the tribe. If a member became a disturber of domestic or tribal affairs, the herald was sent to proclaim him to the people. He would give the man's name and say: "My friend, the door of the society is closed against you, that you may remain among the common people where such acts [naming his offense] are committed." This was considered a great public disgrace, and members did their best to avoid it.

When a meeting was held, all the belongings of the family were removed from the lodge being used and it was left vacant for the society. The two young servants brought wood for the fire and the host sent the food to be cooked. As the hour for assembling approached, the host put the bowl of paint and the two pipes, which had been prepared for smoking by the keepers, before the place belonging to the leader. When all the members were in their assigned places, the leader took up the bowl of black paint and the following song was sung by all present:

Before me stands, awaiting my touch, coal-black paint,
Heavy black clouds filling all the sky o'er our head.
Upon our faces now we put the black, coal-black cloud.
Honoring war, wearying for the fight, warriors' fight,
Waiting to go where the Thunder leads warriors on.

The words conveyed the idea that the desire for action was so strong within the warrior's breast that he was weary of the lack of opportunity that withheld him from heroic deeds of war. The music itself expressed both the warrior's eagerness and the portentous stir that filled the air as the birds swarmed when the black storm clouds came up. In effect the song suggested both the psychical and the natural influence of the thunderstorm, the visible, symbolic sign of the warrior god. As the song was sung, the leader dipped the fingers of his right hand into the paint and touched his forehead, cheeks, chin and both sides of his chest as the sign of the Thunder god. Then the bowl was passed about the lodge by the servants, and as the song was repeated, each member did the same. When all had been painted, the leader took the pipes, dropped some tobacco on the earth, lifted the stems upward, paused a moment, then turned and pointed them to the north, east, south and west; he then lighted the pipes and handed them to the servants while this prayer was sung:

Wako'da, we offer this smoke,
Wako'da, accept now our prayer,
Let the smoke rise upward to thee,
It bears our prayer, Wako'da, to thee.

The words and music are in marked contrast to the description and impatience expressed in the opening song, shifting in this one to stately measures that turned the thoughts of the members from the Thunder god's display of power toward the invisible life force that permeates all creation. As the pipes were passed, one to the right and one to the left, among the members, the ascending smoke carried with it each warrior's prayer to the invisible life force. This concluded the opening ceremonies of the Thunder society.

Shortly afterward, the choir began a song in fast time, and whoever wished, arose, dropped his robe and stepped forth. Then, with great intensity, in a traditional pantomime dance he acted out one of his experiences from which he had gained a public war honor. The emotional character of the dance made it impossible to sustain for any considerable time; therefore the dance and song were always short. Rest songs, slower in time, followed a dance, and during these songs the dancers sat wrapped in their robes, often dripping with perspiration and panting to recover their breath. When the food was ready, two men who had each broken an enemy's neck were selected by the leader to act as servers. Then the choir began the song that was the ceremonial call to the feast, to which the two men danced.

The feast awaits you—come, eat,
The feast is awaiting you,
Members, comrades, come and eat.
The feast awaiting stands before you, come,
Members, comrades, come and eat! He tho.

Two sticks were used in serving the food, and the choicest pieces were given to the bravest man present. When all had been served except the host, who according to tribal custom did not partake of the food he had provided for his guests, the society leader arose and made an address in which he thanked the feast-giver and discoursed on the need of food for the preservation of life. He told of the trials, dangers and hardships encountered in securing food, of how the hunt represented both a man's valor and his industry, and of how since no one could live without it, food was to be considered a gift of the greatest value. Therefore no one should eat without thanking the giver, nor should he forget to include the giver's wife and children, who relinquished to outsiders their share in this great necessity of the family. At the close of this speech, everyone ate the food provided. After dinner, the member who had received the choicest part of the meat held up the picked bone and acted out in a dramatic dance the story of his exploit. Shortly after this dance, the choir began the song of dismissal. During the singing of the first part the members rose in their places, and at the beginning of the second part the member who sat with the door to his right circled around the lodge perimeter and was the first to leave. Each member then followed in his turn, all singing as they did so. When they had gone, the choir rose and left the lodge in silence. The dismissal song was choral in character, yet had the rhythm of a march:

We say, Friend, arise!
Arise, Friend, we say.
Arise, Friend, and stand.
We say, Now arise and stand.

We say, Friend, now walk,
Now walk, Friend, we say.
We say, Friend, now walk.
We say, Friend, now walk we away.[3]

The Chiefs' Society

The Chiefs' society was a society whose membership was open only to chiefs, and outsiders were seldom permitted to listen to its secret songs. Although it ceased to exist about 1860, the few past members who were living in 1890 still clung to their exclusiveness and were hesitant to speak about the society's songs. The final dissolution of the society came because of a certain unlucky officer in the organization, known as the keeper of the songs, whose duty was to train his successor in the knowledge and stories of the songs. Through a series of tragic coincidences a superstition grew up that whenever the keeper sang one of the old songs, death would visit his family. Members became reluctant, therefore, to take on the responsibility of asking that they be performed. Whenever a request was made, it was accompanied by expensive gifts offered the keeper to atone for any ill fortune that might come to his family as a result.

The songs of the Chiefs' society that survive are warlike in character in both words and music, as might be expected of a society composed exclusively of men who had won special distinction.[4] Also, as all the songs referred to the deeds of chiefs, each was of historical importance to the tribe. At meetings of this society, the chiefs wore their full regalia and awesome head masks made from the head of the buffalo.

The Gatherers

The Omaha name of the Gatherer society meant "to gather together" or "to build a fire," indicating its social purpose—to gather about a fire. It was made up of the leading warriors of the tribe, though there was no formal membership. A single officer was chosen to preside over the gatherings, which were for social pleasure and discussion on subjects of interest. During meetings, the place in the middle at the back part of the lodge was always kept vacant as if for an honored guest. A bowl or platter with a horn spoon was placed before it, and it was explained that the place was kept in recognition of God, the provider and ruler of mankind, who was thus present with the men as they met together and talked. This society was given up about 1870, when contact with the White settlers began to seriously affect the tribe.[5]

The Death Society

The Omaha name for the Death society group meant "to simulate death." It was an ancient social society that disappeared before 1850. The Death society had songs that were sung at its gatherings but they are now lost, together with all the customs once observed.[6]

The Mandan Society

The social Mandan society was borrowed from the Sioux, and it too ceased to exist about 1850. Its meetings were public, and membership was open to any man of good repute. The members sometimes paraded on horseback around the camp, moving to the rhythm of the songs of the society. Their dances were said to be dignified rather than dramatic, a statement borne out by the surviving songs. Whether the music was composed by the Omaha or came from the Dakotas is not known. There are no words to them, a fact making it probable that the music was adopted from another tribe and the foreign words dropped.[7] Dorsey reports that it was a custom to cook a dog for each of the Mandan feasts.[8]

SECRET SOCIETIES

The Bear Society

Entrance into the Bear society was restricted to "those to whom the bear has shown compassion" by appearing to them in a dream or vision and giving them his power. The society practiced magic, such as the thrusting of wands down the throat. These abilities were said to have been given to them by the animals. There was also a Bear clan among the Omaha that took part in the ceremonies held in the sacred lodge when the thunder was first heard in the spring, but the two were distinct and unrelated. The Bear society became extinct about 1860. The following song belonged to this order:

> Here, at this place; I came; I stood; badger;
> I was; as I appeared.
> [*The word* badger *was sometimes used to designate animals with claws
> —in this instance the grizzly bear was really meant.*]

The words recall the time when the man referred to in the song went out to fast. When he came to a particular place, the grizzly bear appeared as he stood there and the man felt that he was mysteriously related to the bear. The song established the man's right to become a member of the secret Bear society.[9]

The Bear Dance was performed any time the members wished to do so, and all the people of a village could witness it. During the day it was held outdoors, but at night it was held in a lodge. There were several singers and one drummer, and the rest of the performers imitated grizzly bears.

Their appearance was spectacular. One man wore the entire skin of a grizzly bear, pushing his fingers through the holes where the claws had been removed from the front paws. Some members wore grizzly-bear claw necklaces. The dancers other than the bear wore no clothing other than a breechclout. Yellow clay was used by many to coat the torso, hands and legs, although sometimes the legs were painted red. Some dancers painted themselves with large white or red spots as well. Some wore white eagle plumes in their hair, and others red plumes.[10]

The Black Bear Pawnee Society

The Black Bear Pawnee society was a medicine society whose dance was one of the ancient tribal dances. During the day the women danced with the men, but at night the men danced alone. Its members would not eat green corn or fruit until they had been consecrated by their dance.

Music for the dance was provided by four singers, each of whom had a gourd rattle, a white-painted bow and an arrow. The bow was

held in the left hand and the rattle and arrow were held in the right; the arrow was struck against the bowstring as the rattle was shaken.

The only clothing for male members was a breechclout. They painted themselves in different ways, some whitening bodies and legs, others drawing white lines like deer tracks over themselves, and yet others adorning themselves to look like bald eagles with white faces. Costume regalia varied too; some wore gray fox caps or fox necklaces, and others had on necklaces made of a combination of black-tailed deer and ordinary deer hair. Some dancers carried a gray fox skin on their arm while others carried a red fox pelt. Some carried great owl feather fans or wore owl feather waistbands. "A [small] red medicine with the skin adhering to it" was tied up in a bundle and worn like a coiled lariat, with one end over the left shoulder and the other end under the right arm. All members carried and blew either whistles or flutes that varied in length from twelve to eighteen inches.

The members of this society had a red herb medicine that they employed in three ways: they rubbed it on their bodies before going into battle; they applied it to bullets to make them kill the enemy; they administered it to horses, making them smell it when they were about to surround a buffalo herd. If the horses appeared to lack strength, they also had them eat some of the medicine.

A candidate for membership invited the society members to a feast that he hosted. It took three days to prepare it according to traditional practices, and on the fourth day there was a public ceremony in the earth lodge wherein the candidate was admitted by being sprayed with the red medicine.[11]

The Buffalo Society
The members of the renowned Buffalo society were also the possessors of stunning costumes. A dark, green-gray earth was rubbed on their bodies and arm joints. Some also rubbed it on the lower half of the face. A few members wore only leggings and breechclouts; others added buffalo robes with the hair outside. Some wore buffalo tails fastened in their belts, while others carried staffs of red willow branches with the leaves left on. Four of the dancers wore the entire skin of a buffalo's head over their own heads, parting the skin and hair to expose the dancer's face from the eyes down but leaving it hanging on each side of his chest, and down his back. In addition they wore necklaces made from the hair of the throat of a buffalo. Naturally they imitated the buffalo in dancing, thereby gaining his "power" for the tribe. Music was supplied by one or two drums and as many as five drummers.[14]

These were men to whom the buffalo had shown compassion, by coming to them in a vision and giving power. The society was dedicated to the knowledge and application of medicines for the curing of wounds. They were doctors, and membership was granted to persons of both sexes to whom the buffalo had appeared in dreams, although few women belonged. The roots of the wild anise, the hop and *Physalis viscora* were used for healing. Bits of these roots were ground between the teeth, then water was taken into the mouth and the medicated liquid was blown with force into the wound.[15] After the recovery of a patient, a dance was held to which only the members of the Horse society could be invited.

277

Opposite: *Omaha(?) warrior wearing southeastern Plains style of turban headdress with cloth, ribbonwork and bead-covered triangular rawhide extension out to right. He also wears a southeastern style bear claw necklace on an otter skin base* (SM).

The Horse Society

The Horse society was made up of men who had supernatural communication with horses. None were doctors, and they never danced except in connection with the Buffalo society members. When invited to a feast of the latter, they imitated the various gaits and actions of horses. In painting, they first whitened themselves with clay and then rubbed earth on their shoulders and Indian red on other parts of their bodies. They wore necklaces made from horses' manes with feathers appended and a horse's tail attached to a belt at the back. The tail was filled with clay and dried stiff so that it would stand out from the belt and the body, and feathers were suspended from it at intervals.[12]

The Wolf Society

Wolf society men had had supernatural communication with wolves. They too could dance only in connection with the Buffalo society, and then when the recovery of a Buffalo patient was not involved. At such times, however, the Buffalo, the Horse and the Wolf societies might celebrate together.

None of these were doctors, and they did not practice the shooting (or spraying) of medicine paint on patients. The dancers did act mysteriously, however. For regalia they wore wolf skins over their heads and shoulders and painted the tips of the wolves' noses red. Bodies were painted in imitation of the blue wolves. Those who had held enemies with their hands, or who had cut them up, painted their hands and wrists red to symbolize blood. The rest used white clay on their hands, wrists and feet. All whitened their faces on the lower half from ear to ear. Some danced barefoot. All danced in imitation of wolves.[13]

The Ghost Society

Both men and women to whom ghosts had appeared in dreams or visions were eligible for membership in the Ghost society and were known as "those to whom ghosts have shown compassion." Members were believed to have the power to predict events, particularly those associated with death. If a death were foretold, the relatives of the doomed person might ask the Ghost member to prevent it. To accomplish this, he would heat water as he sang his songs and then cast the water on the ground to the right or left of the entrance to the threatened person's lodge, though never in a straight line from the door. By this act, the spirit was believed to be halted in its progress toward the spirit world and was forced to return so that the person would continue to live. The members of this society could also stop a rainstorm, but it was a power exercised only by request. To do this, the Ghost member filled a small, unornamented pipe to show his modesty in addressing the cosmic forces, elevated the stem and smoked, singing his songs as the smoke was wafted upward. Whenever the storm ceased, he would take credit for it.

One of the songs of this society went as follows:

Night; moving; yonder moving; come; moving; here.
"Night is moving toward us here."
[Night refers to death, by which one enters the realm of ghosts.] [16]

278

The Storm Society

The Storm society was open to men or women who had heard the Thunder beings in dreams or visions. It was believed that through this medium, powers were imparted whereby rain could be summoned or a storm driven away. Future events could also be foretold. Sometimes the Storm members pitted their powers against one another or against those of other tribes, and some of their songs commemorated these contests. For example, on one occasion a number of Omahas went to visit the Ponca. Among the visiting party was a member of the Thunder society noted for his occult powers. He met a Ponca Thunder society man, and while they feasted each other, they secretly sought each other's death by means of their magic. The Ponca drew on the ground a picture of the Omaha and struck it with his club (the club being the weapon of the Thunder beings), at the same time calling on the Thunder beings to strike the picture. In witnessing this, the Omaha suspected a magic attempt on his life, so he sang his songs, relying on them for his protection. After the Omaha party returned home, the Ponca man was himself struck by lightning. The incident was speedily reported to the Omaha magician and a song was composed to commemorate the event. The name of the Ponca was mentioned in the song, where he was represented as weeping because his request to the Thunder beings to strike the Omaha had been turned upon himself.[17]

The Honorary Chiefs' Society

The Honorary Chiefs' society was composed of men who had accomplished one hundred or more noteworthy acts and gifts, and membership in it was considered one of the highest honors a man could secure. To gain membership a man had to have earned the right to tattoo on a maiden certain cosmic symbols of night and day. The woman thus tattooed was called a woman chief. The requirements for admission were so stringent that the successful candidate was said to have been "pitied by Night," who was the mother of Day—otherwise he could not have accomplished the tasks required. The symbols tattooed on the girl signified a mark of honor or of distinction. Permission to place the marks of honor on a girl had to be given by the Seven Chiefs, as well as by the members of the society.

In the ceremonies of the Honorary Chiefs' society the songs and symbols referred to the creative cosmic forces typified by night and day, the earth and the sky. These were forces upon which the tribal organization itself was founded.[18]

The Hundred Gifts Society

Among the classes of acts and gifts that "counted" for membership and ranked high in the Hundred Gifts society were those benefiting the tribe and those made on behalf of a very poor man or woman. Contributing to the establishment of peace both within and without the tribe was an act of public merit and could be "counted"; so also could gifts made in order to put an end to a period of prolonged mourning for a respected tribal member. Another form of giving was to place a robe on the arm of a child and send him to the lodge of a leading man, who, on receiving the gift, would emerge from his lodge and call aloud the name of the giver. Gifts of horses on special occasions were accounted among the most valuable. The Peace-Making feasts offered another occasion for men to make gifts that could be counted. This feast occurred when there had been a difference between two tribes and the chiefs wished to make peace. The Seven Chiefs called the various chiefs and young warriors together and told them of the proposed feast, to which the tribe with whom there had been trouble had been invited. All gifts made on such an occasion could be counted. The last such feast took place shortly before the middle of the nineteenth century. Another act that could be counted and ranked among the highest was saving the life of a comrade in battle or preventing his capture, as such an act could be done only by risking one's own life.

A man could seldom count his hundred honors before he was forty, even if he wasted no opportunity. During all the years of his preparation, he had to work silently and not disclose his purpose to anyone. Nor would he reveal which maiden he had chosen to receive the mark of honor. There was a general belief that if a man made his choice known before he was ready to have the tattooing done, either the girl would die or some other terrible misfortune would befall him.

Success in passing the long test was regarded as proof that the members were favored by God and that they possessed willpower capable of producing amazing results. It was said that a disturber of the peace or one whose acts were offensive to the chiefs was sometimes punished by the concerted action of the society members, who merely concentrated their minds on the offender, thus heaping upon him the fullest consequences of his actions so that "he was kept from all helpful relations with men and animals." Misfortune and death were believed to follow inevitably as the result of this awesome treatment.[19]

The Shell Society

The Shell society seems to have been organized for the express purpose of preserving the story upon which it was founded, and its dramatic presentation formed the basis of the ceremonies observed at regular meetings. The membership was composed of five groups, each having a "leader" or "master." Each group had its place in the dwelling set apart for the meetings of the society. This was originally a large tipi, later an earth lodge, and in more recent years a circular wooden building arranged like the latter.

The position of each group had a cosmic significance, and the manner in which the leaders were painted with the colors of nature bore out this significance.

All the offices of the society were obtained by purchase. When a person holding an office felt that age or ill health made it difficult to fulfill the duties required, the office was sold, generally to a relative. The five principal officers had to be present at all meetings. No substitutes were allowed, so the absence or sickness of any one of them prevented a meeting from being held. Besides these officers there were several minor positions, the holders of which had certain duties connected with the dramatic rites. The right to wear certain regalia also had to be purchased, so the man who bought the office generally purchased the right to wear the regalia worn by his predecessor.

A candidate for membership had to "be able to keep a secret and not be of quarrelsome disposition." The unanimous consent of all the members was necessary for admission to membership. In ancient times four years had to elapse between the presentation of a name and the acceptance of a person as a member, but later the time was shortened considerably. When a man was initiated, he was required to bring the skin of an otter, a mink or a beaver to represent the water, the skin of a squirrel or a badger to represent the earth and that of a crow or an owl to represent the air. So, too, whenever a member shot a bear, an elk, a deer or a buffalo, he saved a portion of the meat for use at a meeting of the society, since all these animals were closely connected with the society rites.

Each group possessed a large medicine bundle in which articles belonging to the association were kept. It contained the purchased regalia of the members, medicine for curing diseases and poisons for punishing offenders.

The dress of the members depended upon their wealth, although no one was expected to wear more than breechclout and moccasins. Most of the men wore war shirts or leggings, and a zigzag line of paint, which ran down each arm to the base of the thumb, was drawn on the sleeve of the shirt. The face was painted with a line from the mouth to the ears to represent a ray of sun, and the zigzag lines down the arms indicated lightning. Down feathers from under the left wing of a swan were tied to the hair.

Among the special purchased regalia was an otter skin cap, a beaded cap with a feather in front that slanted to the left, a black squirrel skin bag, a red squirrel skin bag, a pair of black skin moccasins with a bear embroidered on the left foot in black beads against a background of white beads, the head toward the toe, and a buffalo similarly embroidered on the right foot. The right to wear these descended to "the eldest son." The right to carry a silver fox skin bag was purchased by a woman. Each member had his own otter skin mystery bag and a left wing that represented the wing of the "holy bird," the swan. The mystery bags were not buried with the dead but were generally passed on to new members. Two shells were used: a white one regarded as female and a dark one considered male. Besides a sacred wooden bowl, there was a special board used for the preparation of the tobacco for smoking. There was also a drum, two gourd rattles and two pillows on which to strike the rattles. All these articles were the property of the society, and each had its special keeper.

The regular meetings of the society were held in the months of May, June, August and September, these being the mating seasons respectively of the black bear, the buffalo, the elk and the deer. Irregular meetings had to be held at night and were informal in character. (The details of these gatherings are marvelous but much too lengthy to include. Those interested can find them in the Fletcher BAE report, 1911, pages 509 to 565.)

Society ceremonies included special rites performed upon the death of a member and rites for punishing offenders. When a man committed an offense that deserved punishment, the society met at night to consider the matter, at which time both the act and the man's character were discussed. If the society decided to punish the man, an ancient hide figure with incredible powers was brought out. It appears to have stood as a symbol of the united purpose of the society, for on such occasions the members were required to act as a unit. Action began early in the morning at a secret place, where lengthy ceremonies were conducted to punish the offender.[20]

The Pebble Society

The Pebble society was known as "They Who Have the Translucent Pebble." Membership was gained by virtue of a dream or vision, received while fasting, of water or its representative, the pebble, or of the water monster. The water monster was said to be a huge creature in animal form that lashed the water with its mighty tail. It was generally spoken of as living in a huge lake in a far-off place.

The members of the Pebble society wore only the breechclout, but the body was painted with designs indicating the animals or monsters that members had seen in their dreams. Plumes were worn in the hair and eagle wing fans were carried. In this respect, the Pebble society differed considerably from the Shell society.

The meetings of the Pebble society were held only during the summer season. The opening part of every session was secret; only members could be present. (Once again the enthralling account of their ceremonies is too lengthy to be detailed here but can be found in the 1911 BAE report, pages 565 to 581.)

The exact organization of the society could not be definitely learned, except that it was divided into four groups or lodges. The members of this society treated sickness by physical means, bleeding or sucking out the disturbing object and practicing a kind of massage, which consisted of kneading and pulling on the region below the ribs, a rather severe and painful process. The rituals of this society were not fully obtainable either, but each group seemed to have had its particular ritual that, when joined together, made up an entire ceremony. Fletcher doubts that the complete set of rituals was even known to any living Omaha by 1911. The opening ritual itself dealt with Creation and the cosmic forces. The sweat-lodge was used as a preparatory rite and whenever a member was about to minister to the sick. The sweat-lodge rituals were complicated and carried out with great care. According to ancient custom, one of the articles to be served at the feast given as part of the ceremony for the initiation of a new member was a white dog; this was cooked as the stones were heated for the sweat-lodge ritual. All the leaders of the society had to be present during the preparation and cooking of the dog. The dog was painted and then strangled; a band of red paint was drawn across the nose and the feet, and the tip of the tail was painted with the same color. Songs preceded the sacrifice of the dog, the dressing of it and also the feast. Any mistake made while singing these songs or reciting the ritual itself was believed to result in the early death of the offender.[21]

12
THE
CROW

B efore early historical times the Crow lived together with the Hidatsa on the upper Missouri River. An argument caused them to separate, and the Crows moved westward until they arrived at the Rocky Mountains. In 1780, they numbered about 4,000 and dominated a fairly large territory of beautiful country rich with game animals. In fact it was so desirable that other nations, mainly the Blackfoots and the Sioux, invaded it regularly to raid and hunt. Considering the superior numbers they faced, the Crows acquitted themselves nobly, proving themselves to be excellent warriors in both defense and attack. This last factor as much as anything else led to the establishment of a detailed Crow warrior society structure of the non-graded type. The Crows proved to be a deeply religious people whose faith in God led them into a ceremonial attitude concerning all things. In conjunction with this, the Crows developed enviable gentleness and intelligence in child training and an admirable respect for the authority of elders. Their craftsmanship abilities in all fields were extraordinary, and many feel that their costumes were the best on the Plains.

In accordance with their religious nature, tobacco was looked upon as having a sacred character. Therefore a Tobacco society came into being through a vision, and the planting and harvesting of crops was intensely ritualistic in nature.

The Crow called themselves *Absaroke*, which means "Bird People." It was one of the few tribes that, in following guidance received from a prophet, refused to fight against the Whites. In consequence, the Crows were allowed to remain in their beloved mountain country when the reservation period ultimately arrived.

Typical Crow war-medicine helpers. Above left: *Rawhide figure attached to hoop from Long Otter's war-medicine bundle;* above right: *Water-monster effigy from Iron Fork's war-medicine bundle;* bottom: *Hide-wrapped hoop medicine with hair-lock and beaded tab pendants* (MAI).

In the old days virtually every Crow man belonged to a warrior society. Since these were not age-graded, each society took its own initiative in securing new members. When a member died, an attempt to fill the vacancy was immediately made by offering gifts to one of his kinsmen. They were also likely to entice any man of renown whose affiliation would enhance the order. In short, each society welcomed whomever it could attract by its status, ceremonies or regalia, and it is not surprising that formal invitation and entrance fees were forgone.

No special lodge was set aside for society use; Crow society meetings were held in the tipis of different members, the cover being rolled up at the bottom in good weather so that those who could not find room inside might sit in the open. At times, for special meetings, two or three lodges were placed together.

The society activities were social and military. Each spring the camp chief appointed one group to serve as police, but rotation was not fixed and the same organization might act in this capacity year after year. Each society had its own regalia, decoration, dance and peculiarities of behavior, but the scheme of officers was essentially the same. These men were not the directors of their society, for this was a duty imparted to the older men. The officers were simply members who promised to be exceptionally brave in war and received special regalia in recognition of this.

In 1833, Maximilian discovered eight Crow societies: the Bulls, the Prairie-foxes, the Ravens, the Half-shaved Heads, the Lumpwoods, the Stone Hammers, the Little Dogs and the Big Dogs. Beckwourth states that between 1825 and 1855, keen competition divided some of these, such as the Foxes and the Dogs. There was once a group called the Muddy Hands, but these joined with the Foxes about 1865. About 1875, the Hidatsa introduced a Hot Dance, which spread to the Crows and led to the establishment of four societies that took the place of the older clubs and were still in full swing in 1910. Lowie lists the Crow societies as the Lumpwood, the Fox, the Big Dogs, the Muddy Hands, the Raven, the Little Dogs, the Hammer Owners, the Bulls, the Hot Dancers and the Crazy Dog.

Originally a man belonged to a single club. Except for some special occurrence, a man would remain loyal to his first club, and one of the first questions he was asked when he joined was whether he intended to stay. On occasion a particular young man might be summoned first to succeed a kinsman in one club, and later a friend in another society. Occasionally a man left his original club in a huff and then joined another. In the later transitional period, some belonged simultaneously to one of the old and one of the new orders.

The most comprehensive and perceptive account of the Crow societies is that of Robert H. Lowie. In 1907, Dr. Clark Wissler, of the American Museum of Natural History, commissioned him to make a survey of the Crow Indians. Several expeditions were devoted to this, and the society material which evolved was published in 1913, Anthropological Papers, American Museum of Natural History, *Military Societies of the Crow Indians*, volume 11, pages 145 to 217. Most of the following information concerning the Crows is derived from this indispensable source. A composite of Lowie's writings about the Crow culture was published in 1935 and then reissued in 1956 by Holt, Rinehart and Winston. It is now available in paperback form, entitled *The Crow Indians*. Since it is currently available, I have footnoted some

statements in my text with page numbers from the book. This will enable readers to compare the comprehensive source material with my condensation, for the original anthropological report is virtually unobtainable.

The Lumpwood Society

The ancient name for the Lumpwood society was "Knobbed Sticks." Tradition tells of a member striking a first coup with such a club, whereupon his entire society, before that known as the Half-shaved Heads, changed its name in honor of his weapon. An Indian informant had heard his father speak of a former symbol of the organization consisting of a club carved at one end in the shape of a horse's head. In the Hidatsa equivalent society, there was certainly such a stick that was conspicuously associated with the capture of buffalo. By 1870, the officers' emblems were the same for the Lumpwoods and the Foxes, and only their dances remained distinct. The Lumpwood performers simply stood in their places, alternately raising the right arm as far backward as possible and then bringing it back to its normal position, while a whipper lashed reluctant members to make them stand up and dance.

The society was subdivided, partly on the basis of age: There were the Lumpwoods without Sweethearts; the Tall Lumpwoods; the Old Lumpwoods. Nevertheless the long winters were spent in the warmest kind of social fellowship, with an emphasis upon brotherhood and sharing. As the cold season passed, the orders began to stir. During the spring and summer, when the tribe still camped together, there were frequent, even daily, meetings of the societies. Usually, one member invited the others, all of whom were expected to come and enjoy his hospitality. Such meetings were, for the most part, purely fun and fellowship.

The Lumpwoods reorganized early each spring, the officers being chosen for one year only. To do this, all the Lumpwoods were called to meet in a large tipi. Four of the elders in charge offered a filled and lighted pipe to each man chosen for the eight positions, of which two were leaders, two were bearers of straight staff, two were bearers of hooked staffs and two were rear men. A man could refuse by declining to smoke, but the elders might frustrate this by pulling his head down by the hair until his lips touched the pipestem. This automatically broke his resistance and made him an officer. At the time of the assembly, the four staff bearers received only dummies, which consisted of peeled willow sticks with bark wrapped and tied on to represent the genuine otter skin wrapping yet to come. When all the officers had been selected, the entire group paraded through the camp. Then they split into four groups and feasted while the true emblems were being prepared. These were made by predecessors who had gained war honors in the same offices. They wrapped the sticks with otter skins and prayed on behalf of the young men. When they were finished, they handed the staffs to the novices, a service for which they were paid with four kinds of property.[1]

The men were free to choose either the straight or the hooked staff. One elector carried the willow dummies, another the pipe. When a candidate had smoked, they would simply ask: "Which stick will you have?" Then they would give him the kind he asked for.

One of the unusual promises made to members was that of ample mourning in case of an honorable death. In these instances the elder

Opposite: *Crow warrior with face painted for war and full eagle skin mounted on head—figure in background is same man carrying coup stick and mounted on war horse* (SM).

Typical attire for Crow scouts serving in that capacity for war or raid parties—figure at left has full wolf skin on back, figure in front shows how wolf skin was tied over shoulder. Note how war-club and knife are carried in belt (SM). Opposite: Crow Fox society members carrying regalia of that order. Figure at left holds straight staff and war shield, figure at right holds rattle (SM).

Lumpwoods supplied each of their brothers with a knife and an arrow or two. Everyone knelt about the corpse and cried, and then the dead man's closest friends cut off the last joint of one of their fingers while the others pushed arrows through their flesh and left them sticking there for a while as they wailed. Afterwards the Lumpwoods would dance toward the corpse. When at last they stopped and sat down, the slain man's parents distributed presents in gratitude for the club's mourning.

The Fox Society

As mentioned, the Foxes and the Lumpwoods were similar in most respects. However, the Foxes danced differently, forming a circle that moved to the left, with each participant making a low jump with both feet. In fact, the two clubs were so closely allied in native thought that one informant gave a single origin account for both. A Crow, he said, returning from a buffalo hunt had a vision in which were revealed two hooked and two straight pine sticks wrapped with otter skin, the latter two tipped with eagle feathers. On getting back to camp, he cut his hair short, leaving a central roach, and plastered the shorn part of his head with white clay. He also made a headdress of bear guts painted with red stripes. Then he organized the Foxes and the Lumpwoods, but the latter cut their hair short only in front.[2]

The Foxes wore belts of kit-fox skin or fox-skin ponchos. These were made by bisecting the skin and uniting the halves so as to leave a slit for the man's head, with the head of the fox in front and the tail hanging down the wearer's back. One informant declared that the Foxes painted one side of their face red and the other yellow; they used black and yellow body paint, while the Lumpwoods substituted pink.

After lengthy investigation Lowie concluded that although the two societies had different insignia before 1870, they were strikingly alike in organization during the last half of the century. Thus there were Fox subdivisions that corresponded to those of the Lumpwoods, though the Foxes were perhaps more definitely divided into age groups.

As to dress, emblems and eligibility for office, there were no differences between the subdivisions, although some had special functions.

As among the Lumpwoods, the officers were regarded as men "made to die." Their attitude is reflected in the following song, which embodied the ideals of all the members:

> *You dear foxes*
> *I want to die*
> *thus I say*

The tenure of officers was limited to one short season. They were chosen in the spring and completed their office at the first snowfall. Any man could, however, be reelected to his former office the following spring. The Foxes had two leaders, two hooked-staff bearers, two straight-staff bearers and two rear men. In addition one or two special men were selected as the bravest of all. These could choose whatever food they wished at a feast and eat it before the rest had begun their meal.

Those who carried the staffs of the society were expected to drive them into the ground when the enemy came into view, and they had to remain there until a fellow member withdrew them.[3] The carrier of a hooked staff was permitted to run a short distance before making a stand, while a man with a straight staff was not supposed to retreat at all. The function of the rear man in battle was to face about and attempt to put the enemy to flight. Any officer who ran from the foe was held in contempt and compared to a woman. It was said that the staffs symbolized trees too heavy to be lifted.

No special value was set on preserving the wooden staffs, which were usually discarded. On the other hand, the otter skin wrapping was highly prized and preserved for future use. The shafts of the society officers were made of pine wood stripped of the bark. Instead of having a stone or an iron lance head attached to the end, they were merely sharpened. The shafts were wrapped with otter skin and a pair of narrow strips of otter skin was appended to dangle at intervals. The straight staff was topped by an erect eagle feather, and the hooked staff was formed by lashing an arched stick of red willow to the pine staff with a buckskin cross-tie holding the tip of the bent end in position. The loop was also wrapped with otter skin, and long narrow strips of it were hung from the tip of the hooked part.

The election of Fox officers paralleled exactly that of the Lumpwoods. As in the other society, peeled willow sticks wrapped with bark to simulate otter skins served as dummies until the otter skin wrapping was applied. Curtis states that a small lodge pole was shaved to make the final staff and that red birch was bent and spliced to it to make the hook.[4]

When completed, the staff was thrust through the tipi cover where it was pinned together, and the war leader, who had counted grand coup with a similar staff, began to dance and sing, holding it with the end projecting between the edges of the covering. Then he spoke:

> It was this society that gave me the staff. In a great battle I took it and counted a grand coup on the enemy, having this stick in my hand. It was clear and good. He That Sees All Things looked down and saw me, saw that it was good. May this young man do the same. When a great battle takes place may arrows and bullets pass by him and do no harm.[5]

The war leader then presented the staff and a robe to the new bearers, who danced while all the other members gave the war cry and sang. When all the officers had been selected, the members arranged themselves in pairs, the leaders standing beside each other; behind them were the pairs of standard-bearers and then the rank and file, including the musicians, who held single-headed skin drums and drumsticks. Then came the second pair of staff bearers and the two special men in the rear. In this order they marched through camp, singing their songs. By the time the march was completed, enough otter skins to wrap a staff had been obtained for each new staff bearer. Then the club broke into four parties, each one helping the officers to cut up the otter skin and wrap the strips around the shafts. Predecessors of the newly chosen men recounted their war feats performed while in office and concluded with such words as: "I should like you to do the same and to strike the enemy. We know you are brave, we wish you to fight for your people." The knife used by the man who cut the skin was painted black to symbolize a coup. The trimmer of the skin kept the knife and the awl used in stitching the strips. After singing for a time, the members all went home.[6]

Informants declared that each of the clubs danced four times during the active season. On such an occasion the Foxes formed an

unclosed ring, with the staff bearers turning their backs on the rest of the members, the only ones privileged to act in this way.

From 1860 to 1880, the grouping of most men into either the Lumpwood or the Fox club provided a natural line of cleavage, and in certain games the married men and their wives of one society were pitted against the men of the other society and their wives. This revolved essentially about two activities: mutual wife-kidnapping and competition for the honor of striking the first coup of the season.

The period of licensed kidnapping was brief, lasting usually not longer than a fortnight. When all wives amenable to capture had temporarily swapped husbands, the two groups went on the warpath together, each striving to score a coup before the rival organization. Whichever did this first did not matter really, for it was known that the competition served to make men fearless. Ordinarily, a Fox was not allowed to sing a Lumpwood song and vice versa; to do so would be an affront. Yet the society that struck the first coup was said to take away the other's songs. Then it could use the loser's tunes and adapt to them words composed for the occasion. This meant, of course, mockery at the expense of the vanquished, who did not recover the songs until they had struck the first coup in a subsequent encounter. When the first snowfall came, the spirit of competition disappeared as if by magic and the two clubs lived together in perfect harmony until the next spring. It was said, however, that whenever one of these societies had a member whose feats in battle or raids could not be equaled by any member of the other group, it became for the time being the dominant organization of the tribe.

292

Crow Big Dog society members beginning a ceremonial dance.
Opposite: *Crow society regalia.* Left: *Crazy Dog society rattle;* right: *Big Dog society rattle* (AMNH).

The Big Dogs Society

The Big Dogs society ceased to be active so long ago that in 1910 Lowie found only a single man, Fire-weasel, reputed to be over ninety years old, who had been a member and one of the sash-wearing officers.

The Big Dogs originated with the Hidatsa, and the society did not subdivide among the Crows as did the Lumpwood and Fox societies. The members were mostly mature warriors, although a few young men were chosen from time to time to succeed relatives who had fallen in battle. The organization took turns with the rest in policing the camp for a season. It was reported that if anyone were to move prematurely in a tribal hunt so that he might frighten off the game, the Big Dogs, led by their officers, would advance menacingly upon him and address him as if he were a dog, saying, "Stop, go back!" When he halted, they would ask, "Why are you moving away?" If he replied gently and showed his willingness to obey orders, that was the end of it; otherwise they might whip him so vigorously that he was hardly able to move.

The mourning customs of the Big Dogs closely resembled the Lumpwood ritual, and their reorganization method in the spring was also the same.[7] The elders offered a pipe to various young men, and those who smoked it were forthwith pledged to special bravery. The customary parade followed the election: There was a division into four groups, each accompanying one of the sash-wearers. When the staffs had been completed and picked up by their owners, all the members reunited outdoors and performed a dance. This was begun by a belt-wearer, who seized one of the sashes and pulled its wearer forward. The dance itself consisted in a forward jump, with the performers leaping

293

individually instead of lining up in a row or circle. They also leaned their bodies as far forward as possible. Finally, as the last song was sung, they jumped more vigorously than before.

There were no initiation fees, and vacancies were filled in the manner described for Crow societies. It is said that even an infant might be chosen to succeed a slain kinsman, though naturally he would not be received as a member until he was old enough to fulfill his duties. The scheme of officers consisted in their being paired off and pledged to bravery. They served from early in the spring until the first snowfall, and they could be reelected.

In contrast to other clubs, the Big Dog members had a common badge owned by each member. This was a stick about eighteen inches long and covered with buckskin, to which pendant deer hooves or dew claws were attached for rattles. Later, tin cones and bells replaced the dew claws. A graceful pendant consisting of a rolled white ermine skin and a down-feather was attached to each end of the stick. The rattle took the place of the single-headed drum used by the other societies. The novice either made this for himself or received it as a gift from a former member. Most members also wore an owl feather headdress whose feathers fanned out in a most dramatic style. All members had an eagle bone whistle, which was hung from a thong round the neck, to be blown at will during a dance.

The officers consisted of two leaders, two rear men and four sash owners, two of whom wore a single sash, and the others two sashes that crossed each other in front; and two men wore belts of bear skin with the legs and claws still attached. The belt-wearers daubed their bodies with mud and bunched up their hair in two balls to resemble a bear's ears. One Indian authority tells of a single-belt wearer being paired off with a whipper; the line of parading Big Dogs, according to him, was comprised of the two leaders, two sash-wearers, the rank and file, the single-belt wearer with the whipper beside him, two sash owners and two rear officers. An officer with a single sash walked abreast of one wearing two sashes.

Men who were offered the bear skin belt were seldom eager to take it, for the wearer was required to walk straight up to the enemy regardless of danger, under no condition retreat and rescue imperiled tribesmen. Understandably, certain honors were extended to the wearers, such as eating first at a society feast. Another authority says that in a parade the belt-wearers were followed by the leaders, the sash-wearers, the rear officers and finally by the rank and file. At a Big Dog assembly the belt-wearer also led the dance, for, as mentioned, he would seize one of the sashes and draw its owner behind him, followed by the other members. At the close of the singing, everyone would stand still and some would blow whistles while the rest clapped their hands over their mouths in mock astonishment. Finally the belt-wearer would touch each member with a quirt, thereby allowing him to be seated. However, if anyone continued dancing, it was a sign of daring and the belt-wearer would lash him more vigorously than he did the others. During a public parade a belt-wearer remained among the singers. After a dance was begun, he could sit down wherever he pleased and, in general, act as he wished. At society meetings a special seat was reserved for him near the door.

Society meetings might take place at any time, but they were always held when a Tobacco meeting or Sun Dance was in progress,

294

since most of the Crow people were gathered together then. On such occasions the Big Dog who owned the finest lodge offered it for the use of the order. Sometimes the Big Dogs met at night, and, joined by women, proceeded through camp singing. They always sang at a chief's lodge, and the chief usually had food cooked for their entertainment. The drum for such marches was a huge piece of rawhide with a rope passed through perforations along its edge. The members would stand in a circle around it and beat on it with their dew claw rattles, going from lodge to lodge and expecting food or tobacco from everyone.

Whenever the Big Dogs were involved in a battle, the officers were to take the initiative in any emergency. If enemies were entrenched, it was their duty to charge straight at them. However, contrary to the situation in other tribes, they were not pledged to make a stand if the Crows were routed. They did so voluntarily on occasion but not as a matter of obligation. The sash-wearers could also retreat, but if a fellow warrior called out for help, they were expected to go to his rescue. The rear officer's job was to mount a delaying action against the enemy in any instance of retreat. The belt-wearer had no special duties as long as all was going well; but if the Crow began to break and run, he was to stand his ground. If he failed to do this, he was treated thereafter as a coward and an outcast.

Traditionally, the belt-wearer remained seated at a dance to indicate that he would not run away in a fight. Informants say that his whipper would whip him into dancing, and in a battle, if the belt-wearer were standing before the enemy, the whipper could also

295

Crow Muddy Hands society member mounted on war horse, carrying buffalo hide war shield and wearing sash measuring twelve feet or more in length (as reported by Robert H. Lowie, The Crow Indians. *Drawing is adapted from photograph in* The Boy with the U.S. Indians, *by Wheeler).*

whip him and release him. The sash-wearers were expected to fight to the death in any battle of consequence; to return alive when the group had been defeated was to become a laughing-stock. Witnesses reported that while a number of officers had been slain in battle, not one was ever known to act the coward.

The Muddy Hands Society

The Muddy Hands group also conformed to the general Crow pattern for societies. It had three subdivisions, composed of boys, middle-aged men and old men, respectively. Their names were Those-who-put-on-guts-for-headgear; the Muddy Hands proper; and the Bags-for-necklaces. Anyone entering from another society joined the group suitable for his age bracket. There were two leaders, two or four sash-wearers, two rear officers and two belt-wearers. The leaders were expected to perform feats of bravery at the beginning of an encounter, while the rear men were to be the last to retreat. The belt-wearers were also to remain and to help any tribesmen who were on foot to escape; hence these had the customary right to eat before their fellows. The sash-wearers practiced no distinctive form of bravery. Each of them wore two red trade cloth sashes that trailed on the ground when the bearer was afoot and hung clear to the ground when he was mounted, since they measured twelve feet or more in length. At dances, these officers were led around by their sashes. The sash-wearer's regalia included a cap of dried bear guts, painted red. The guts of bears were used because of the animals' strength and ferocity.

Like all the other societies, the order reorganized itself each spring. On this occasion four elders discussed the candidates outside the lodge, then entered to offer the pipe to those assembled. Willow bark was used to make temporary sashes, which were slipped over the heads of the officers-elect. Following the election, the Muddy Hands paraded, sang and danced through camp, finally dividing into the customary four groups, each going to the tipi of one of the newly elected officers. There a former officeholder cut the cloth into strips about five inches wide and four feet long, sewing them together to make a sash of the proper length. A slit was cut at the top through which the elected man inserted his head. Then all went outdoors to show the people who had been chosen. A dance followed, although the group did not dance very often, since their main ceremonies were held at the time of the great Tobacco ceremony.

At Muddy Hand performances, the two leaders dressed themselves in their finest war outfits and carried weapons in their hands. A pole representing the enemy was stuck into the ground, and a buffalo robe, hair side out, was tied to it. The two men rode up to the pole, struck it with coup sticks and acted out exploits they had performed in battle. A curious custom peculiar to this society was that members almost never put out a fire, which to them symbolized the enemy; instead outsiders were asked to do it for them. An exception was made when a man of proven bravery dismounted from his horse to extinguish a fire, since by doing so he was understood to pledge himself never to retreat from the enemy.

Lowie states that about 1870, the Foxes came to the Muddy Hands with a pipe and asked them to join their ranks. The Muddy Hands, possibly fifty in number at the time, accepted the proposal, and in consequence their wives became fair prey in the wife-kidnapping game already shared by the Foxes and the Lumpwoods.

Opposite: *Crow Raven society member wearing war shirt and leggings and carrying society staff (DPL).*

The Raven and the Little Dog Societies

Maximilian found a Little Dog and a Raven society among the Crows, but by 1907, Lowie could not locate a single survivor of either order. An informant who had witnessed a dance of the Ravens, or rather Raven Owners, was able to tell him that the performers, who were all elderly men, had their bodies painted red and wore stuffed raven skins for necklaces, with the tail feathers spread out on their shoulders. Another informant, speaking only from hearsay, stated that one Raven carried a long staff topped with a single eagle feather. A cluster of raven feathers, perforated at the butt end for stringing and trimmed at the upper end, was fastened to the center of the staff. Other members bore staffs or flags that were feathered from top to bottom, and some had raven feather fans decorated with quillwork. There was also a herald, four sash-wearers "made to die" and functionaries who were charged with preparing the food for feasts.

The Little Dogs had either two or four wearers of red flannel sashes and two officers who carried three-foot-long wooden quirts, serrated along one edge and trimmed with raven feathers. The society was said to have come to the Crows from the Hidatsa, who had such an organization. The Hidatsa Black Mouth society visited the River Crow and taught their dance to the Little Dogs of that band, who thereupon assumed the name of the Black Mouths. Maximilian described these as "Soldiers" among both the Mandans and the Hidatsas: middle-aged men who alone exercised police control in the villages. In the Crow scheme, this club, like the other societies, took turns at police duties. However, it evidently imitated its Hidatsa model in restricting membership to middle-aged and distinguished men.

The Muddy Mouth dance was similar to the Hot dance. To conclude the dance an officer wearing a bear skin belt touched performers with a quirt; until then they had to remain standing. The rank and file wore no distinctive costume, but daubed black mud or a mixture of pounded charcoal and ashes over their mouths or across their eyes. Members who had struck enemies with tomahawks carried them, and others bore war-clubs with skunk skins wrapped around the handles.

In dancing, the membership divided itself into two lines facing each other, with two officers, called "rattlers," standing between them. As they began to sing and dance, they crossed each other's paths, as the members shouted and joined in.

When at last the Crow Muddy Mouths dwindled in number, they joined the Crazy Dogs.

The Hammer Owners Society

The Hammer Owners included practically all the Crow boys who were about sixteen years old. A pair of older youths instructed them and made four wands for the officers; then as the Hammers matured, each entered one of the regular societies. They too held an outdoor assembly in the spring, feasted and held an election the following day. Four willow sticks were laid outside against the tipi. The two instructors went outdoors to discuss potential officers, reentered with a pipe and chose successively the leaders, the rear officers, the four staff bearers, and the four belt-wearers. The society broke up into the usual four companies, the sticks were finished and bestowed and each group feasted, sang and danced. Finally, everyone joined together outdoors for a dance that continued until dark.

The staff bearers were expected to be especially brave in training fights, and the belt-wearers were to show the same bravery when they faced wild animals, such as wolves or buffalo, counting coup on these as though they were enemies. The special emblem of the order was a hammer made of wood, shaped like a railroad-spike hammer, with a hole in it so that a tall staff could be inserted through it. The hammers were painted yellow and red or yellow and blue, with the colors corresponding to the members' body paint. The shaft itself was over eight feet in length. It was painted with white clay and topped with an erect eagle feather. Two long feathers and a bunch of shorter ones were attached at three points along the shaft (see Chapter 3 for illustrations).

While the primary purpose of the group was training for the future, the boys were not by any means restricted to mock fighting. When the situation demanded, they took part in real battles, counted coup and were often more reckless than their elders.

If a Hammer member failed to attend a club meeting, the rest of the group went to his lodge and stood there until his father came out and pacified them with a pipe or a gift of food.

The Bulls Society

There was a difference of opinion among the Crow informants as to the age of the Bulls, setting it at anywhere from fifty to sixty-five years. Lowie prefers the lower age for several reasons: The Bulls acted as police and also took part in warfare until a certain fight in which they were driven down a cliff, and they were dubbed thereafter "Bulls-chased-over-the-cliff." This was about 1875, and the shame of it terminated the society.

The two members whose foolhardiness ranked them with those "made to die" in the other societies wore buffalo head masks. In all, there were two leaders, two rear officers, two mask wearers impersonating blind bulls and two men wearing bear skin belts who whipped tardy members into rising to dance and also touched performers with their whips to conclude the dance. Some witnesses said that all rank-and-file members wore skin caps topped with horns, but others said they wore only red-flannel aprons hung with bells and blackened their bodies with charcoal.

To conduct a society ceremony, a herald summoned the Bulls to an evening gathering in a member's lodge, beating a drum to hurry them along. Arriving there, the members all pretended to be bulls, painting their faces and bodies with mud in imitation of wallowing buffalo. Their legs were adorned with anklets of buffalo skin and other hangings. The mask wearers plastered their hair and the horns of their headgear with white clay. Those who had dismounted in battle to fight were allowed to wear buffalo tails on their belts at the back. These were stiffened with mud or clay and made to stand erect. As the musicians beat their drums, the parade started, with the leaders in front, followed by the rank and file and as many as ten drummers bringing up the rear. One man carried water in a large container and held it out for the members, who simulated shyness, sticking out their tails and running away prancing and snorting. The mask wearers imitated wild bulls, snorting and charging the crowd so as to frighten women and children, and excited boy spectators daringly prodded the Bulls with sharpened sticks to make them jump and snort like real bulls. Those members who wished to show their willingness to die

Crow Hot Dancers performing society dance wearing roach headdresses, feather bustles and trade bells strung on leg straps (SM).

approached the water, bellowed like bulls and lapped up the water, for drinking symbolized a pledge not to flee. The Bulls carried shields, lances and guns on such occasions, and those who had earned them wore warbonnets. Brave warriors told about their feats and reenacted them; a coup-striker would count coup on some spectator, while those wounded in battle pretended they had been shot. Informants reported that the displays were most dramatic and stimulating.

The Hot Dancers Society

According to Lowie, about 1875, the Crow adopted two features from the Hidatsa, the Hot Dance and the Crazy Dog society, also called Long Crazy Dogs to distinguish it from another institution of the same name.[8] While one can hardly quarrel with the date and idea of adoption from the Hidatsa, it is probable that the Crow groups doing the adopting were already in existence and simply changed their nature somewhat. In support of this contention, it should be noted that the Crazy Dogs at least were military or war societies and that by 1875 the Indian wars were already grinding toward the halt that came with Custer's defeat in 1876. As such, new war societies were hardly called for in 1875.

The Crow Hot dance corresponded to the Omaha or Grass dance of the other Plains tribes, and in 1910 practically all the men belonged to one of the four orders associated with the performance.

The dance lodge resembled the earth lodge and the village tribes. At meetings, the four groups sat quartered off according to their affiliations. The Big Ear-holes and the Night Hot Dancers had straight

300

and hooked staffs wrapped with otter skin, while the Last Hot Dancers and the Dakota had nothing distinctive in the way of regalia.

The Crow Hot Dancers combined the Hidatsa idea of purchase with their own concept of free admission. An officer adopted his successor by giving him his insignia in return for certain expensive gifts, while admission as a lay member did not involve formal adoption or payment.

One Crow informant listed the following officers:

> Two leaders; two drummers; four crane-stick bearers pledged to strike enemies with them; eight officers wearing the feather bustles called "crow belts"; two heralds; two pipe-fillers; one man privileged to sing the closing song; four women singers; two whippers; two war-bonnet wearers; two men with long sticks feathered from top to bottom; one man carrying a stick representing a fork wrapped with beads and with a scalp at one end; one officer with an American flag, which was hoisted on a pole; and one man wearing a red-fox skin necklace.

The American flag was carried because the Crows served as U.S. Army scouts and never fought the Whites. The warbonnets were actually two buffalo horn headdresses with weasel skins attached to the front.

The officer with the forked stick always danced before food was distributed, dipping his emblem into the bucket containing the dog meat and then offering it to four brave men, who licked off the stick. After this the officer ordered all the others to eat. In concluding the dance, a Crow-belt officer who had been wounded in battle left the lodge before the rest.

The warbonnet wearers decided when to hold a dance and began the preparations by giving away a horse each. During a parade through camp, any member might give away his mount. After this they would enter the dance lodge, where everyone was expected to eat dog meat. To obtain food for the feasts, a procession of members went from lodge to lodge and planted a crane-stick in front of each one who was expected to contribute.

The Hot Dancers were noted for their lavish generosity, for members gave away property of all kinds to aged and destitute tribesmen and even to alien visitors. Women were seen literally staggering away under loads of blankets presented to them and their husbands. Some men rode horses directly into the dance lodge and gave them away. Once a man stripped himself to his breechclout before a large crowd and gave away all his clothing. Sometimes the giveaway even included wives.

The evening before a dance, one member beat a drum while the rest sang. Then the drummer announced the dance, and the two head men ordered the herald to select two others who were to kill and cook two dogs for the ceremony. Ten officers were also summoned to cook food for all the people, while ten others were to provide cloth goods for the occasion. The sacred drum used for dances had a deer or horse-hide head, and only two special officers were allowed to touch it. One of them was the keeper of a drumstick decorated with feathers and ribbons. When the officers had beaten the drum four times, the singers gathered around the drum and began to beat it. At this moment the dancers entered and suspended their regalia from the lodge poles. As successive songs were sung by the musicians, the officers took their insignia in order of rank and gave presents to anyone they pleased.

Four women took part in the singing; however, they did not dance, merely giving away presents. Next the rank and file danced. After this the dog-killers placed a kettle containing the dog meat near the entrance, and the Crow bustle wearers went through an elaborate ceremony around it. The food-distributors then served the selected men and officers first and finally the other people, though all refrained from eating until another ceremony with the dog flesh was completed. To conclude the feast, the dogs' skull bones were laid on the ground and eight of the officers danced toward them, enacting the same parts they had played in battle. Then they all stood in a row, and each in turn recounted his coups. The head men ended the dance by thanking the crowd. The people responded in kind, and the ceremony came to a close with one of the bustle wearers leading the way out of the dance lodge.

The Hot Dance leaders held their office for a year or so. To reorganize, a meeting of all the officers was called to see whether they would give up their regalia. If so, at the next dance two Crow belt wearers were appointed to choose new leaders.

According to Lowie, the eating of dog flesh was an essential part of the Hot dance among the people who passed the ceremony on to the Crow and Hidatsa. Thus the Crows sometimes came to eat dog, even though they had a general aversion to its flesh. Even then, Hot Dancers sometimes substituted other flesh, such as chicken. Lowie also reported that the ceremony was still being observed as late as the summer of 1931, when it was celebrated in the town of Hardin, Montana, in honor of a White attorney who had assisted the Crows.[9]

The Crazy Dog Society

The Crazy Dog society originated about the same time as the Hot Dance order. The Crazy Dogs were young men who often served as camp police and are credited with displaying special strictness while acting in that capacity. The officers were elected each spring according to the usual Crow custom. Their number varied according to the camp. One informant listed the rank and file at about twenty-five men, with only a single leader and a single rear officer. The former, he said, wore a buckskin cap attached with deer horns and trimmed with weasel skins in the back. This warrior was required to advance against the enemy and never retreat. The rear officer wore a red-flannel society sash decorated with beadwork. He had to dismount and stand in place against the enemy if the rest of the Crows were retreating. Another informant stated that all the members carried ring-shaped skin rattles, and he listed as officers a dance director, four sash-wearers and four officers with horned bonnets. A third man said there were either two or four sash-wearers, a fourth listed a pair of leaders and two rear men in addition to four sash-wearers and a fifth reported two whippers and two belt-wearers in addition to the others.

The rank and file painted themselves with dark and light shades of red, as well as with white clay. Distinguished warriors were permitted to wear white weasel skins on their shirts, while the rest dressed alike in regular war shirts and leggings.

Lowie noted that "The modification of the Crazy Dog club by the Main Body is well brought out in Gray-bull's lively report:

All the men of the Main Body who had not joined the Hot Dancers went to Plenty Coups' lodge and formed the Crazy Dog society. I also

Crow Tobacco society adoption lodge (SM).

joined. The Foxes and Lumpwoods had given up wife-stealing. We met in the spring and made long sashes with slits, one for each two officers. Punching holes in baking-powder cans and putting beads inside, we made rattles. The dance was similar to the Hot Dance. At the end of a song all members raised and shook their rattles, the eagle feathers on them producing a fine effect. Those who in battle wished to aid the two officers "made to die" seized the trains of their sashes. After the dance we all assembled in the evening and went around the camp, where we were sometimes invited to partake of a feast indoors.[10]

The Tobacco Society

Among the Crows, the Tobacco society held a high position, for it promoted the welfare of the entire nation. The tobacco plant was believed to have a sacred character, and its planting and harvesting were rituals that had been performed for as far back in time as Crow lore went. Both men and women belonged to the order, which had a number of chapters, each of which originated in a supplementary vision in which instructions were received regarding the founding of a new branch.[11] Each group was small. It had its own leaders, its distinctive songs and regalia. Lowie secured the names of about thirty subdivisions.

Two kinds of tobacco were raised, one for ordinary smoking and the other, called "medicine tobacco," for smoking only on special occasions and during religious rites. Each chapter planted its own garden after holding a ceremony in which the seeds were mixed with traditional ingredients such as dung, flowers, roots, berries and bones. The observances in the planting of the medicine tobacco included the painting of the members; the holding of a "solemn march," in which outsiders were kept away from the marchers by the police societies; the running of a footrace among the young men; the planting of the seed; the building of a hedge of green branches around the seed bed; a visit to the sweat-lodge followed by a bath and a solemn smoke; and finally the ending of it all with a feast.

The medicine tobacco was nurtured with great care, the garden was inspected ceremonially at four intervals and the patches were closely guarded. When it had ripened, it was harvested with its own ceremony, including songs and dances. The leaves were stored in specially constructed shelters, and the seeds were put into deerskin pouches to be kept for the next planting season. As a gesture of thankfulness to the patron spirit of the tobacco plant, some of the stems and leaves were cut and crushed into fine bits, mixed with meat and ordinary tobacco and then thrown into a creek. Informants did not know the reasons for this but suggested it was a sensible thing to do since the tobacco had been mixed with water before planting.[12]

Candidates for admission to one of these chapters paid a staggering price in material goods for the privilege. After this, they were instructed during the winter and formally initiated in the spring at a public ceremony. To "adopt" a member or members, there was a gathering of the adopting chapter in a preparatory tipi, the formal march to an adoption lodge, a sweat-lodge ritual and the selection of medicines by the leaders. An adoption lodge consisted of ten large pine-tree trunks, tied together at the top and spread out in the shape of a huge tipi. The coverings were rolled up at the sides and put on so as to leave openings in places where sunlight could stream through. Candidates met in a preparatory tipi and were painted with designs conforming to their visions. As drummers began to beat their drums and others shook rattles, the candidates exited, doing a traditional dance step, from the preparatory tipi. They were followed by the society members, and all went to the adoption lodge. Ceremonies involving warriors who attributed their success to the tobacco came next, then songs, smoking, dancing and property giveaways.

Of special note were the large Tobacco society bags, made of either rawhide or tanned skins, which had shoulder straps on them so that they could be carried on the back in processions. These were often decorated with stripes, circles, dots and round trade mirrors. The designs represented either the seeds or the garden.

A medicine bearer, whom some think was the highest officer of a chapter, always led the procession to the garden. The bearer carried an especially powerful medicine, such as a weasel or an otter skin. Several others came immediately behind bearing other medicines, such as different birds or skins.

Each planter used a special digging stick made of cherry wood. These varied in shape and served as markers after the planting to identify an owner's row. Some had crooked handles, some were painted

Crow Tobacco society garden showing ownership sticks placed to identify owners' rows (SM).

304

one color, some were striped and some had items tied to them for further identification. In such cases these appendages were also thought to promote the growth of the tobacco.

After the planting, it was customary to lie for hours by the garden in order to receive a vision, and Tobacco songs were often received in this way. Some people received assurances of a good crop. Between the planting and harvesting, members followed strict rules of conduct—which went even further to ensure a good crop.

The Bear-Song Dance

The Crows had an annual ceremony in which those who danced had dreamed of certain animals or birds and afterwards were "inhabited by some part of them." The ceremony was held in the fall when the berries were ripe and "the bears danced in the mountains." A cottonwood post was set up and a tanned bear skin was fastened to it. A great quantity of pemmican was brought to the site, and the spectators formed a large circle around the post. The dancers assembled in a tipi to dress up and, led by an old woman, marched toward the skin in single file, the men in the rear. They danced up to the skin, then backwards away from it. Musicians sang the Bear song; then all the dreamers were "irresistibly" drawn toward the pole, performing gestures when they reached it that illustrated the nature of their animal or bird power. All in all, the ceremony seems to have been directed more toward the personal welfare of the dreamers than it was toward the tribe. No mention is made in informants' accounts of healing having been practiced by the members, although it seems reasonable to conclude it was.[13]

The Sacred Pipe Dance

This Sacred Pipe dance ritual was somewhat similar to the Blackfoots' Medicine pipe order. It centered in a medicine bundle that included two pipestems, decorated with, among other things, a fan of eagle feathers. The Sacred Pipe was said to belong to the Sun, and people were "afraid" of it. Its principal use was a peace pipe. For example, if a Sioux carrying such a pipe approached the Crows during a battle, no Crow would dare strike him. Within the tribe it was used by the police to pacify a murdered man's kin.

In any Sacred Pipe dance, there were never more than one or two spectacularly costumed performers. In a dance seen in 1931, there were two. Both of these were clad in tight-fitting cloth outfits (like long underwear), one dyed yellow and the other black. Both wore crow bustles on their backs and roach headdresses made of deer-tail hair, and each held a rattle in one hand and a pipestem in the other, crossing the two objects at certain points in the performance. A cord of braided sweetgrass passed over the shoulder carried a buffalo skull, which was slung on the back of one performer during the ceremony for the initiation of a candidate. In dancing, one dancer knelt down a few times, and a low swoop was characteristic of the movements.

Besides the parallel to the Blackfoot order, the Mandan and the Hidatsa had pipe dances conforming in many respects to that of the Sioux and the Crow.[14]

Crow Tobacco society regalia. Clockwise from top: *Society buffalo hide rattle; tobacco offering stick with packet of tobacco attached;* ownership stick (AMNH); *weasel carried by procession leader.*

Crow Sacred Arrow ceremony—a demonstration of bravery, thus fitness to lead in battle, as the warriors shot the pointed arrows straight up and then stood among the falling shafts without trying to dodge (SM).

Crow clown—actually a member of Crazy cult—in disreputable costume worn for fun performances (AMNH).

13
THE PONCA

The Ponca were an exceedingly small tribe of 800 or so persons who during an ancient migration drew apart from the Omaha, the Osage, the Kansa and the Quapaw. When the group reached the Mississippi, the Ponca went downstream to the Arkansas River. For a long period after that, the Ponca were separated from the Omaha and were at war with the Sioux. During this time they had moved again and settled in several permanent villages in earth-lodges in the Dakotas. Sometime after this, the Ponca and the Omaha rejoined for a period, then separated again.

The Ponca were primarily farmers but engaged in seasonal buffalo hunts. Whites who contacted them described them as being a superior tribe mentally and morally and as a kind, generous people who loved their children.

In this light it is an especially sad experience to read the story of their tragic removal to Indian territory in Oklahoma after 1876. They are part of the Siouan linguistic family, and their name has been interpreted by some authorities as "That Which Is Sacred."

The Ghost, or War Dancing, Society

The Ghost, or War Dancing, society was originally a warriors' dancing society. Its officers included a drum keeper, eight dance leaders and two whip men who started each dance episode and who also whipped reluctant dancers across the legs to make them get up and perform. The characteristic regalia of the society included the porcupine and deer-hair roach headdress and the "crow belt" or feather dance-bustle. The latter symbolized a battlefield, and its use was restricted to certain officers of the society who were distinguished warriors. Both of these ornaments were ritually purified during a ceremony by holding them over a cedar-needle smudge. Dancers painted their bodies gray and called themselves "ghosts," or "those invisible in war."

With the decline of intertribal warfare about 1880, the society's emphasis became religious. Prayers replaced the war speeches and coup-countings of the earlier dances, and gift-giving, rather than war honors, became the basis of admission to membership. Also, women were not admitted as dancers.

Later still the society entered a purely social phase. Even the religious elements were left behind, and the ceremonial dance was no longer performed. All dancers were welcome, including visitors from other tribes, and gift-giving, except for one afternoon performance, was eliminated. Costumes were considerably modernized, and the once-profound symbolism of the roach and the crow belt was virtually forgotten.

The preferred dance of the society of early times was the war dance, and it was said that anyone who was ill or in mourning would be made happy by the sound of the drum.[1]

This dance, while common to several tribes, was a part of Ponca culture for so long that they considered it their own and they even had an origin legend to explain its introduction.

The War society dance consisted of individual dancers performing any steps they chose while circling the drum. The traditional progression around the drum was clockwise, but the Southern Poncas attributed this change to the influence of southeastern tribes such as the Creek and the Cherokee, whose dances progressed in a counterclockwise direction. Many of the Ponca songs described the exploits of Ponca heroes in their wars with the Sioux. Beginning in 1958, there was an attempt to revive the old War, or Ghost, organization among the Ponca, and several performances of the war dance in its oldest form have since been held.

In a variant style of the War dance, the performers shaved their foreheads and the sides of their heads and let the rest of their hair hang loose. Authorities suspect that some of the present "fancy dancing" style comes from this source. The Ponca War society also performed a dance known to the Sioux and certain other Plains tribes as "the kettle dance." Dancers circled a pot of cooked dog meat four times; then, on a certain musical cue, the leader dipped his bare hand and arm into the pot and seized a piece of meat. Usually this was the dog's head. Poncas said it was originally a part of the full War society performance but later evolved into a separate dance similar to one that is still performed by the Sioux. Yet another dance that was once a part of the War society ceremony was "the Going-to-war dance."

The Poncas had a number of warriors' societies besides the War Dancing society. Each had its characteristic costume, songs, customs and roster of officers. The society dances were introduced, enjoyed a period of great popularity and then were abandoned. Perhaps only two or three would be active at one time. There was apparently a rough sort of age-grading among them, but it was not as clearly defined as in other Prairie-Plains groups.

The Kit Fox Society

The Kit fox group seems to have been made up of the youngest warriors. Its dance was, along with the Sun Dance, the War dance and the Not-afraid-to-die, one of the tribe's oldest. Authorities state that apparently it was borrowed from the Sioux, since the name *kit-fox* is meaningless in the Ponca language.[2] This group had a traditional rivalry with the Mandan Warriors society, which sometimes resulted in wife-stealing of the type so well known among the Crow. In later years the society disappeared, and its dance became only a "silly dance" performed to work up enthusiasm for the War dance. Its original dance was much like the Round dance, and no animal imitations were involved. Two members carried long sticks in their hands, to which eight eagle feathers were attached.[3]

The Make-no-flight Society

In dancing, the Make-no-flight society members held gourd rattles, and each one carried many arrows, both in a quiver on his back and nestled in his arms. Members vowed not to retreat from a foe. To symbolize this willingness to die, they blackened themselves all over with charcoal. Skinner gives the society name as Not-afraid-to-die, and in his description of the society's dance, "all [the dancers] stood in a row and danced up and down, remaining 'stationary.'"[4]

Society members wore warbonnets with split horns at the sides, suggestive that the group was a Ponca parallel of the Dakota No-flight and Strong-heart warriors' dancing societies, which were virtually identical with one another. In any event, the members of the Ponca Make-no-flight society, together with the members of the War society group, seem to have been the military elite of the tribe, the "shock troops" in every battle.

The Veteran, or Mandan, Warriors Society

The Veteran, or Mandan, Warriors society was a society made up of "none but aged men and those in the prime of life. . . ." [5] It performed a bravery dance, which functioned as a sort of military funeral over the bodies of warriors who had been slain by the enemy. Each body was placed in a sitting posture in the dance lodge as if alive, with a deer hoof rattle fastened to one arm. The dance was apparently identical with the War dance. It was performed in 1853 but became obsolete shortly thereafter.

The Retired Men Society

The Ponca name the Retired Men society means the same as *White-owners,* or "those who own white things," in Sioux and indicates the origin of the group. This society was noted for the richness of its costumes, which were adorned with a number of silver hair-plates. The White-horse dance was a lively dance much like the War dance, and many gifts were given away at its performance. Among the Dakotas, in the early reservation period, the members of this society rode nothing but white horses, hence the name of the group. A second Ponca name for the dance referred to the noise made by the clashing metal ornaments and mescal-bean bandoliers and bracelets worn by the dancers. The group was made up of chiefs and older, respected warriors. [6]

The Big Belly, or Bulls, Society

The Big Belly, or Bulls, society performed the Big Belly dance, in which buffalo bulls were imitated. Only older men, perhaps chiefs, participated.

Buffalo horn headdresses were worn, and shields were carried on the dancers' backs. Earth was rubbed on the body. Anyone who had stabbed a foe with a lance carried the lance, and there were deers' dew-claw rattles with sharp iron points which were used as knives in battle. The dancers marked time in place during the first part of the song, then, on a musical cue, one man—a different person each time—would charge to the center of the lodge and pretend to hook something with his horns. He would then give a present to someone in the audience, and the dance would continue.

In the Teton Sioux parallel, dancers also wore a buffalo headdress. This society was found in many Plains tribes and was always composed of chiefs and old men. The name "Big Belly" attached to this society referred to the corpulence common to Plains Indian men of this age group. [7]

The Not Ashamed Society

The name Not Ashamed society refers to the fact that the participants were not ashamed to be seen taking part in an Indian dance. Only young men danced. They wore fancy broadcloth blankets as their distinguishing costume. As the song began, they would arise from their seats around the lodge and dance to the center of the floor, proceeding in the War dance style but with shorter steps and subdued head and body movements. [8]

The Chiefs' Society

The Chiefs' society ceremonial dance was described as slow and dignified in character, in keeping with the high rank of the participants.

On a certain musical cue the dancers would all take four steps forward. Then they would dance in place for a short time until, also on cue, they took another four steps forward. The dance would proceed in this manner for the duration of the song.[9]

The Night-Dance Society

The Night-Dance society was a prestige society. Men donated large sums of money and gave away large amounts of goods for the privilege of joining the group. This entitled them to have their daughters tattooed with the sacred insignia of the society. The Night dance lasted until the 1930s among the Southern Ponca, and in 1954, several Southern Ponca women who bore the characteristic blue spot of the society on their foreheads were seen by Howard,[10] whose BAE report on the Ponca was published in 1965. The accompanying design tattooed on the head of a Ponca girl strikingly set forth the meaning of the society. Between the emblems of day and night stood the forms of children. By the union of Day, the above, and Night, the below, came the human race and by them the race was maintained. The tattooing of this figure was said to be "an appeal for the perpetuation of all life and of human life in particular." [11]

PONCA WOMEN'S SOCIETIES

The Women's War Society

This Women's War society's name was taken from the warpath songs, composed by the braves, with which the women accompanied their dances. Its choreography was not known to Howard, although he suspected it was "like the Soldier and Round dances." [12]

The Medal Society or Those-who-wore-silver-necklaces

The Medal society, or Those-who-wore-silver-necklaces, was a women's dancing society called the Medal dance. The members of the society wore chiefs' medals around their necks.[13]

The Scalp Society

The Scalp dance was a dance for women among both the Ponca and the Omaha. The dance was performed the day after the return of a war party. The women who danced bore the scalps, tied to short sticks. In dancing, the women formed a big circle facing the center and moved around the drum to the left.[14]

The War Mother Society

George Dorsey, who wrote a number of accounts about Plains societies from 1881 to 1905, mentions two other women's dancing societies whose members were mothers of war victims.[15] Neither was known to Howard's informants. As with the men's societies, new groups were continually being formed and older ones passing out of existence. In a slightly modified form, this process has continued up to the present day. Following World War II, several such women's groups were formed among the Ponca, each distinguished by its characteristic blanket or shawl with the group's name appliqued upon it. Usually the function of these groups is to honor the returning veterans of the tribe. At powwows, the members of such a group, attired in identical blankets, often lead off in the Soldier or Round dance.[16]

The Bear Cult

Among the Ponca, as in most Plains tribes, holy men were organized into groups on the basis of spirit helpers held in common. For example, the Bear Doctor cult was composed entirely of medicine men who claimed to derive their powers from the bear. They did this either directly, by means of visions, or indirectly, by means of purchase from other members of the group. For the most part they used herbal remedies and were the physicians of the tribe.

The Bear dance was one of the so-called mystery dances. It had four leaders, two servants and a herald. A cedar tree was pulled up by the roots and set up in the center of the lodge. During the dance one of the participants would approach the tree, break off a branch and scrape off the bark. Then he would circle the lodge four times, show it to the members and announce that he would run the branch down his throat. He would then thrust it into his mouth until only the tip showed. After a moment he would pull it out, and blood would gush forth. One Bear had the power of thrusting the cedar branch through his flesh into his stomach. After he pulled it out, he would merely rub the wound and it would be healed. Still another would swallow a pipe, cause it to pass through his body and then bring it out and lick it. One cult member performing in the Bear dance was seen to take a muzzle-loading rifle and load it in everyone's presence. Another man circled the tent, singing. On his fourth round he was shot by the Ponca with the gun. Everyone was certain he had been killed, but he soon sprang up unhurt. Another performer took a buffalo robe, had a third man reload the magic gun, then fired it at the robe. There was no hole visible, yet the bullet was found in the center of the robe.[17]

Though the Ponca Bear cult no longer exists as an organized group, in the 1950s there were still a few Southern Ponca who claimed Bear power and practiced it individually. One such who abandoned the practice when he "turned Christian" (that is, joined the Peyote religion), stated that when he practiced as a Bear doctor, he painted his hands black with yellow between the fingers in imitation of a bear's paws.[18]

The Buffalo Doctor Cult

The members of the Buffalo Doctor cult were devoted to the healing of wounds by "surgery." The officers were four leaders, two servants and a herald. This once-powerful society became obsolete when there was no further need for the practice of surgery because there was no more war among the Indians. When a man was wounded in battle, the Buffalo Doctors, who were always present, assembled around him and squirted water on the wound. If conditions permitted further treatment on the field or at home, they would dance in imitation of the buffalo, wearing robes, buffalo horn bonnets and buffalo tails on their belts. They painted themselves only with gray clay, which was the buffalo's color after wallowing. Only the upper or lower halves of the faces were painted. A Ponca informant, however, who wore a buffalo headdress similar to that of the Buffalo Doctors' cult when he danced the War dance, has stated that "only red, yellow, and black face paint should be worn with this headdress," and he criticized a Sioux buffalo dancer who used white paint for not respecting the "old buffalo ways."[19]

Opposite: *Ponca warrior in dance costume wearing otter skin society collar and carrying eagle skin fan over right arm; detail of fan at left, showing how entire body of eagle was used for fan by members of Southeastern tribes (GI).*

The Medicine Lodge Cult

The Medicine Lodge cult was the largest and most important of the Ponca medicine societies. Originally it was entirely a magicians' group, but in later years it became a sort of "service club" as well. Though the leaders were still magicians, and practically all the members of the Bear and Buffalo cults were members as well, there were many Medicine Lodge members who were not magicians at all. Even women and children, in fact, could and did belong. The professed goals of the society were the mutual benefit and prolongation of the lives of the membership. The men who had dreamed of buffalo sat on one side of the lodge and those who had had other dreams sat on the opposite side; the songs were sung first by a man on one side and then by one on the other.

The Ponca name for the group may be translated "White-shell owners." It refers to the medicine projectiles used during a part of the ceremony known as the "medicine shoot." In historical times, these were usually cowrie shells. Other items such as small, round stones were also used as medicine arrows, however. For this reason the group was sometimes called the Pebble society, and other projectiles, such as rooster spurs, fish bones or mescal beans, were now and then used as well. The Ponca believed that sorcerers could magically "shoot" or project these objects into the bodies of their enemies with their medicine bows. One of the badges of membership in the society, the bows were actually slings made from the decorated skins of small animals, such as mink, otter, weasel or raccoon. Occasionally, however, an eagle's wing was used, and one account mentions the use of a black silk handkerchief.

At meetings of the society, members were lectured on morality, taught the legendary history of the order and instructed in the use of various herbal medicines. There was also singing, dancing and magical performances by the Buffalo and Bear cult contingents of the organization. The rhythmic singing for the dancing that accompanied the ceremony was provided by a group of singers seated around a large drum. However, the highlight of each meeting was the medicine shoot, which always followed the initiation of new members. These were contests in which the various magicians, often called shamans, tested one another's "power." One member, gasping the magic cry, "Hex! Hex! Hex!" would point the nose of his animal skin bag at another, thus "shooting" his "medicine arrow" into that person's body. The person "shot" in this manner would stagger and fall, apparently unconscious. Other shamans would then "doctor" the person, who would shortly recover and then "shoot" the man who had wounded him, and the process would continue until all members had participated. If a person "shot" in this manner were not immediately treated by other members of the society or if they failed to retrieve the "medicine arrow" of his assailant, it was believed that he would soon sicken and die.

Admission to the important Medicine Lodge cult was by purchase, and the price was high. However, if a candidate had relatives who were already members, the price was slightly lower. Persons who had been "doctored" by the society were also eligible for admission at lower rates.

Apparently the Medicine Lodge ceremony, unlike most of the old Ponca rites, persisted the longest among the Northern Ponca, the last ceremony taking place about 1910. When Alanson Skinner inquired about the ceremony among the Southern Ponca in 1914, he found that it had been "so long extinct . . . that practically nothing was remembered about it." [20]

The Mescal Bean Cult

The rites of the significant Mescal Bean medicine group centered around the mescal bean, the fruit of the leguminous shrub native to northern Texas, Mexico and Arizona. The cult was secret, and even the form of the ritual was learned by hearsay. Meetings were quite similar to present-day Peyote meetings. They were customarily held in a tipi, the entrance to which faced east. The leader of the rite sat opposite the door in the place of honor and held a staff as his emblem of authority. Another important officer, the fireman, sat across from him, just to the right of the entrance.

Each member of the order owned an individual sacred bundle, but the principal bundle was kept by the leader. These bundles were opened during the ceremony, first by the leader, then the members, and their contents displayed. Following this, the members drank tea brewed from mescal beans. Sometimes the participants had visions after drinking this infusion; one sip was said to be enough. Songs were sung to the accompaniment of a rawhide rattle that was struck upon a buckskin pillow filled with bison wool. Sometimes there was dancing as well.

Yellow flicker feathers were worn by cult members, for the flicker was the "main bird" of the Mescal Bean group—just as the "waterbird" is now the "main bird" of the Peyote religion—and as such was believed to carry prayers of the members from earth up to heaven. The Ponca respected the flicker because the bird was always able to find bugs and other creatures under the bark of trees, so the Poncas associated him with doctoring, for he could seek out hidden impurities.

In the old days of tribal warfare, the mescal bean was used as a war medicine. Just as the red bean was very hard to crack, a man who carried it as his medicine would be hard to pierce with arrows or bullets. When employed as medicine, the beans were wrapped in a small circle of buckskin, which was tied at the top with a buckskin thong. This wrapper was always perforated, since the bean "would die if it was not able to breathe." Warriors going into battle were often said to put a mescal bean in either ear. So long as these did not fall out during the action, the wearer would be almost impervious to arrows and bullets.

According to Howard, the "use of the mescal bean as a war medicine has not completely disappeared. When Parrish Williams, the son of James Williams (now deceased) went into the service in World War II, his father gave him a mescal bean to carry with him. Parrish still keeps this as a good luck charm, carrying it in an old-fashioned leather coin purse." [21]

The mescal bean was also strongly identified with horses and mules, and these animals were given mescal-bean tea to make them swift and to cure their infirmities.

The mescal bean was sacred to many of the Prairie and Plains tribes. Several, including the Wichita, the Pawnee, the Tonkawa, the Osage, the Iowa, the Oto, the Kiowa and the Arikara, also possessed cults centered about it in which mescal-bean tea was drunk by the members. In view of the fact that the Mescal Bean cults are much older in the Plains area than is the Peyote religion and in view of the fact that some forms of the ceremony were very similar to the later Peyote rites, particularly those of the Ponca and the Tonkawa, Howard feels it is interesting to speculate that perhaps the Mescal Bean cult smoothed the way for the Peyote religion and contributed much to the ritual form of the Prairie-Plains Peyote ceremony as well.[22]

The Thunder Cult

The Thunder cult was made up of "those to whom the thunder has shown compassion." The society was open only to men who had been visited by thunder beings in dreams or visions. Members were believed to be able to control the elements, to bring rain or drive storms away. Future events could also be foretold, and sometimes members pitted their power against one another.[23]

The Crazy Cult

The Crazy cult men danced in companies in the spring. They used backward speech and extracted food from boiling liquid with their bare hands. Some even poured boiling water over themselves. The similarity to the Contraries caused Skinner to suspect that the cult was of Sioux origin.[24]

The Those-who-imitate-mad-men Cult

The Those-who-imitate-mad-men cult was entirely distinct from the Crazy cult and originated with the Ponca. They did ridiculous and foolhardy things, such as crawling up and prodding a woman in broad daylight; or coming to a stream, they would strip off one legging and moccasin and cross it by hopping on the clad leg while carefully keeping the bare one from getting wet. They were looked upon as clowns and fun-makers and their antics are said not to have been significant.[25]

316

14

THE

CHEYENNE

The Cheyenne, who were first encountered by **Whites in Minnesota**, moved west into what is now known as **North Dakota** sometime after 1680. In some ways at least they were still an agricultural people at this point. The Sioux pushed them southwest to the Black Hills, then west to the upper branches of the Platte River. Along the way the Cheyenne became allied with the Arapaho and enemies of the Kiowas. After a treaty with the United States in 1825, the Cheyennes divided. The northern division settled above the headwaters of the Platte and Yellowstone rivers, and the southern division located on the Arkansas River in what is now southern Colorado. Both groups became confirmed nomadic buffalo hunters.

By 1840, the Cheyennes had made peace with the Sioux. The years of warfare between the Southern Cheyenne and the Kiowa ended with a bloody battle in 1840. Two years later, that peace too was made, and thereafter the Arapaho, the Kiowa, the Kiowa-Apache, the Comanche and the Sioux all remained reasonably good friends of the Cheyenne.

Cheyenne religious history preserved an ancient tribal protective ceremony that revolved around four sacred medicine arrows. Their Sun Dance was an annual event of great magnitude, and they adopted a buffalo-head medicine ceremony from the Sutaio, a small tribe with whom the Cheyennes allied during their early migrations. In costumes and ceremonies, they became one of the most colorful nations on the Plains and were noted for their abilities in wars and raids. They fought the Whites bitterly; in return they were treated brutally by the armies of the United States, who among other things slaughtered hundreds of Indian men, women and children at Sand Creek in what has been called the foulest and most unjustifiable crime in the annals of America.

In 1780, the Cheyenne numbered about 3,500 persons; in 1900, there were still 3,000—which meant that they fared better than most other tribes against the White man's armies and diseases. They called themselves by a name meaning "Our People" or "People Who Are Alike." In the sign language of the Plains Indians, the Cheyenne were indicated by drawing the right index finger across the left several times. This meant "striped arrows" and depicted their penchant for using striped turkey feathers to fletch their arrows.

It is said that before the time of the original Great Prophet, the Cheyenne were governed with absolute power by one chief and a magician who assisted him. But when Sweet Medicine brought the four great medicine arrows, each of a different color, to the Cheyenne, he separated the tribe into individual bands, instituted the office of civil or camp chief and gave the rank of warrior to all males of fifteen years and older.[1]

In the Cheyenne form of government after that time, the duties of the chiefs were much the same as they were among other tribes of the Plains. The Cheyenne do seem to have been more closely organized than some others. Two factors contributed to this. In the first place, theirs was a small-enough and compact-enough tribe to maintain unity of action. In the second place, their head men formed a self-perpetuating council of forty-four men representing all the band.[2]

Of these forty-four, five were priests, or "holy-men." It was they who elected one of their own number as head chief of the entire tribe.

The council possessed two sacred bundles to denote its position of leadership: the sacred arrows and a bundle of forty-four "invitation sticks."

Whenever they made a major attack upon the enemy, the warriors of all the societies assembled in a long row. In front was a line of holy men, chiefs and the head chief, who performed a traditional ceremony to the Great Medicine. He would point the sacred arrows at the enemy as he had been taught by Sweet Medicine, thus guaranteeing victory to his tribesmen. The head chief, keeper of the medicine arrows, always charged in front of everyone else—no one was ever permitted to attack in front of him. Cheyenne authorities say that in ancient times, the great medicine arrows were very effective. When directed toward a foe, they rendered him helpless, and they believed their success with these arrows against their enemies accounted for the numerous captives found among the Cheyenne.

The holy men conducted all the great tribal ceremonies. The head chief, who was called the "Prophet" and stood for the Great Prophet in the eyes of the people, presided at the council meetings and served as keeper of the two sacred bundles. Whenever one of the holy men retired, he chose a holy man to succeed him from among the council members. If he died unexpectedly, the other holy men selected his successor. Once a holy man had retired, he simply became a regular council member; regular council members who retired left the council and were replaced by new warriors of proven ability, whom the remaining council members selected.

The lodge of each camp chief was a center for dispensing charity to needy tribesmen and for providing hospitality to visitors. But before any decision was announced on such questions as making peace, moving camp or planning a general hunt, the chiefs first had to secure the ratification of the chiefs of the five warrior societies, who played a central role in each band. Each of them would have already discussed the pending questions with his principal followers and informed the chiefs of the other societies of the stand he proposed to take. By this means the society chiefs always reached substantial agreement on any proposal and could react in concert to whatever ideas were submitted to them. It was the head men of the powerful warrior societies, therefore, who were the real governing power, while the council of forty-four constituted little more than an advisory body. In addition, the warrior societies also took regular turns serving as camp police to maintain order and regulate buffalo hunts.[3]

Curtis states that the warrior societies were originally four in number—Dog Men, Kit-fox Men, Lances and Red Shields—and adds that at a later period the Bow-strings were organized, while among the Northern Cheyenne appeared a sixth order, the Crazy Dogs.[4]

However, Dorsey [5] and Densmore [6] list the society names as being the Red-Shield, the Hoof-Rattle, the Coyote, the Dog-Men and the Inverted or Bow String.

According to Dorsey, each society was originally formed by certain holy men who had been instructed by the original Great Prophet and each society was controlled by a relatively young warrior chief and his seven assistants, who were elected by the lay warriors of the society according to their proven courage and leadership in war and horse raids. Each warrior chief was required to know and understand all the songs of his society, while the assistants served mainly as counselors

319

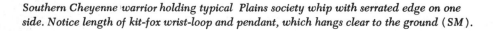

Southern Cheyenne warrior holding typical Plains society whip with serrated edge on one side. Notice length of kit-fox wrist-loop and pendant, which hangs clear to the ground (SM).

among the lay warriors in ceremonial, personal and military matters. When the warrior chiefs attained the age of about thirty-five years, the time that their active participation in field warfare usually ceased, they often became camp chiefs and one of the assistants would move up to become war chief.

Hoebel and Llewellyn, in their engrossing book *The Cheyenne Way*, take pointed issue with Dorsey on two counts. They first of all insist that there were six military societies among the Cheyenne: the Fox Soldiers, the Elk Soldiers, the Shield Soldiers, the Bowstring Soldiers, the Dog Men and "the Northern Crazy Dogs." [7]

They consider it an error to list the Inverted Soldiers as Dorsey does, explaining that Grinnell had properly written, "There was no band or guild of these; they were merely brave individuals bound by certain beliefs." What Grinnell actually says is that there was "a Contrary Society which appeared to have no connection with the Contrary warriors who carried the thunder-bow lance." In other words, it appears that there were two Contrary groups among the Cheyenne. [8]

Hoebel and Llewellyn explain helpfully that the Bowstring society was limited to the Southern Cheyennes; it is sometimes called Owl Man's Bowstring, but more commonly the second name for the society is Wolf Soldiers. They add that the Northern Crazy Dogs were limited to the Northern Cheyennes and are sometimes called simply Crazy Dogs or Foolish Dogs. "The Crazy Dogs and the Bowstring Soldiers were two societies of recent origin which were formed by fission of an older Wolf Society after the separation of the Southern Cheyennes from the Northern." [9]

Second, they state that their informants unanimously contradict Dorsey by denying that there was one chief and seven assistants, claiming instead that there were two head men and two servants in each organization. The head men sat at the back of the society lodge and the servants, ranking next in order, flanked the doorway. [10]

The situation becomes quite confusing when one discovers that Grinnell reports there were generally four servants in number per society and speaks of "the chief," as if to indicate that there was only one for each order. [11] Then in speaking of the Dog Soldiers, he mentions "eight principal men." [12]

Grinnell's list of societies is as follows:

Kit-fox men (Fox Soldiers) or Coyote
Elk Soldiers or Elk Horn Scrapers or Hoof Rattles
Dog Men
Red Shields or Bull Soldiers
Crazy Dogs or Foolish Dogs
Bowstrings or Owl Man's Bowstrings or Wolf Soldiers
Chief Soldiers [13]

He agrees that there were originally four soldier bands, to which the Crazy Dogs and Bowstrings were late additions.

The Chief Soldiers were in reality the Cheyenne council of forty-four chiefs, which served as the governing force for the nation. Therefore, they were not a warrior society per se and perhaps should not be included in their listings. [14]

Cheyenne societies of the historical period were primarily war-based in their spirit, purpose, regalia and ritual. Even those religious features that appeared had their origin in the passionate desire to persuade the supernatural powers to lend their providential aid in battle. As to general function, the societies were virtually independent of one another. They were not age-graded. A young man from thirteen to sixteen years of age joined a society at the invitation of its members. If he accepted, he was conducted from his tipi to the lodge in which the society members were assembled in preparation, arrayed in their most distinguished regalia. There the initiate danced, sang and feasted with them, and thus became a member. If he wished, he could change his affiliation later on. After the election of new war chiefs each spring, anyone had the privilege of providing a substitute and joining another society. Sometimes the transfers were so numerous that a complete reorganization of all the societies was required, which again involved the selection of new warrior chiefs. The high regard in which virtue and ethics were held by members of the Cheyenne societies is indicated by the fact that the transgressions of the family were always visited upon the innocent head of a warrior member, and he was summarily expelled from the organization. In 1858, White Bull, of the Northern Cheyenne, after having served nearly four years as a member of the Crazy Dogs and two years as an officer, was expelled from the society simply because an uncle had fired at a man who had shot his favorite dog. Yet that same day, members of the Lances came for the talented White Bull, and he at once joined them. Cheyenne men guilty of killing a tribesman, whether intentionally or accidentally, were forever barred from membership in any society.

Whenever a member of any of the warrior societies distinguished himself in battle by the performance of some heroic act on behalf of his tribe, he was permitted to wear thereafter a buckskin shirt adorned with captured enemy hair-locks. In late years he might also wear a warbonnet, with a tail of golden eagle feathers trailing down his back to the ground. If he had earned sufficient coups, he could also tip the eagle feathers with locks of human hair, and if he had done the Sun Dance, a Sun Dance plume could be added to his warbonnet.[15]

The paint, the dress, the songs and the dances of the members were traditional and individual for each of the warrior societies. Each had its four sacred songs sung to different tunes, some with words and some without words. In addition, there were four sacred songs for each society that were sung to the Great Medicine and four battle songs to be sung by individual warriors while on the battlefield or in concert at a council of warriors. The members of each society addressed each other as "friend" or "brother" and entered into a covenant of mutual protection.[16]

The Red Shield, the Coyote and the Hoof Rattle or Dew Claw societies included four Cheyenne maidens in their lodge ceremonies. These were usually selected from among the daughters of the forty-four leading chiefs, and the warriors called them either "female soldiers" or "sisters." The warriors were not allowed to marry any of the four maidens of their own society, though they might marry the maidens of other societies. The maidens were given prominent places in all dances, and they were seated in front of the war chiefs at all of the council meetings.

Dorsey says that the Inverted and Dog Men societies did not admit women into their society lodges. Their reason for this was that when the Great Prophet directed the holy men to establish the warrior societies, he gave them the option of admitting to their lodge four chaste and neat women, who were to come from the best families. However, he added that misfortune would surely befall the society who violated the condition. Fearing that through deceit, unchaste women might come into their societies, the Dog Men and the Inverted or Bowstring warriors refused to admit them at all. Whenever each of the great societies gathered in their lodges, they continually burned incense to the Great Medicine so that the prayer-carrying smoke might ascend to remind him they were continuing to carry out his sacramental instructions he had so mercifully given their ancestors through the Great Prophet.[17]

The Red Shield Society

The Red Shield society usually numbered from one to two hundred warriors, plus the four women. When the society gave a public dance, the sisters occupied a place in the center of the council circle and danced continuously in front of all the warriors, beating upon drums they carried. As the Red Shields themselves danced, they followed a traditional style; first the men trotted, then halted, then with bodies bent forward danced up and down, moving around, then hopped and skipped heavily along. All this time each warrior uttered a sort of guttural sound like that made by buffalo bulls during the hunting chase.[18]

The emblem of the Red Shield society was a unique buffalo hide shield, which was round "like the sun" and painted red. Contrary to the usual Plains practice of taking the shield hide from the buffalo hump, this shield was made from the buffalo's hips with the tail left attached. In war days certain medicines dictated by visions were appended to it, and whenever the warrior swung it in a circle before the enemy, it was believed that the enemy's arrows would hit neither man nor shield. Indeed, all Cheyenne shields had their origin in this society, for the shield was given first to them by the Great Prophet. Every warrior of the Red Shield society carried a red shield and lance. The order also had two special straight lances, which were ornamented with raven feathers. When the society served as police, the lances were set in the ground at an angle pointing in the direction the camp was to move.

Whenever the warriors of this society assembled for a dance or council of war, they were dressed alike. Their headdresses were buffalo horn bonnets with the horns attached and the hair taken generally from a two-year-old bull. If a member had counted coups, the horns were always painted bright red, and the bodies of the members were painted either red striped with white or white all over.[19] The Red Shield lance was about eight feet long, straight, originally with a stone point, later on a trade steel point; the entire lance was also painted red. The wearing of the buffalo headdress with the attached horns and the carrying of the shield with the tail often caused people to call them by the popular name, "buffalo warriors." About their waists, Red Shield dancers wore a broad skin belt or skirt like those worn by other Plains society members. It was adorned with porcupine quill bands and had buffalo dew claws attached to it in such a way so as to produce a rattling sound during the dancing. Along the lower edge of the belt were long buckskin fringes, some of which hung below the knees. Like everything else the belt was painted red. The experience of seeing a

Opposite: *Cheyenne society members and regalia.* Left: *Hoof Rattle member holding dew-claw rattle and fur-wrapped hooked staff (shirt and leggings from MAI, emblems from FCM);* right: *Red Shield member wearing buffalo horn headdress and carrying war lance and buffalo tail shield (FCM).*

hundred or more of these so adorned at one time must have been like gazing at an immense blazing fire! [20]

The Hoof Rattle Society

The Hoof Rattle society was comprised of more than a hundred warriors and four Cheyenne sisters. There was a keeper of the drums and a keeper of the sacred elk antler emblem, which was fashioned like a rattlesnake. Two of the bravest Hoof Rattle men carried lances with crooks at one end and wrapped with otter skin. The shaft was further ornamented with two bands of otter skin placed about two feet apart and four golden eagle feathers attached to each band. The lances were about eight feet long. [21] All the other warriors carried straight lances with war points. These were wrapped with otter skins that had been dressed on the outside. Every Hoof Rattle warrior carried a special rattle. It was made of a stick about a foot long and covered with buckskin. To this stick were sewn or tied several dew claws of elk, deer or antelope.

The keeper of the elk horn was the leader of all the dancing and singing. The elk antler was straight, about eighteen inches long and about two inches in diameter. It was shaped like a snake, with both a head and a tail. Grooves were cut about half an inch apart on the top of the snake's back. To employ it for ceremonies, they placed one end on top of a piece of rawhide, suspended just above the ground, which served as a resonator. Holding the snake's tail in the left hand, they rubbed the shin bone of an antelope rapidly back and forth over the grooves in the snake's back, producing a loud, shrill sound. The Hoof Rattle had four sacred songs, four war songs and about two hundred dance songs, and when a hundred or more warriors sang in unison to the accompaniment of the rubbing of the elk antler, they made themselves heard for a considerable distance.

According to the teachings of the Great Prophet, the snake-shaped antler was given to the Cheyenne to charm or call the herds of buffalo, elk or deer to come near their camp. To make it even more effective, the warriors would come together, chew the herb medicine used in all the sacred arrow ceremonies and then blow it upon the elk antler. The keeper would then hold the snake effigy by the tail and draw the shin bone toward himself so that the motion was made from the head to the tail. After he had made this motion four times, the buffalo and the deer would inevitably be charmed and come close to them. All the antelope and deer thus affected were then killed, the meat and hides taken and their dew claws kept for making ceremonial rattles for the warriors.

Aside from the rattles, spears and bows and arrows, Hoof Rattle members satisfied their own desires as to dress. When dancing, they held their lances in one hand and kept their bodies erect, jumping up and down and keeping time with the singing and the rattle. [22]

The Coyote, or Fox Soldiers, Society

The Coyote society received its name from the fact that its founder instructed its members to imitate the coyote in endurance, cunning and activity. By diligent practice, they often bested their fellow-tribesmen in running long distances, playing games, etc. There were approximately one hundred fifty warriors at any given time in this society. The warrior chief carried for an emblem a kit-fox skin or a coyote hide with the hair left on, and the society regarded this hide as sacred, for the Great Prophet had brought the sacred arrows wrapped in just such a hide. Once they had rubbed or hung their medicine on the coyote hide and on themselves, the Coyote warriors felt as light as a feather and could run amazing distances without stopping. This society also had a rattle-keeper, who always carried a red-painted gourd filled with stones. Historians have said that in ancient times the rattle was made of buffalo hide but that with the passage of time the gourd had taken its place. The rattle was used to mark time for the dancing and singing, and its keeper was the leader in the ceremonial activities, for he knew all the songs. The society had four sacred songs that related to the coyote, four war songs and about three hundred dance songs.

To celebrate a four-day dance, the Coyotes erected their lodge either in the center or in front of the camp-circle, then placed the coyote hide just within the interior of the lodge so that its head was facing the entrance. The warrior chief, together with his assistants, sat immediately behind the hide. Whenever it was unwrapped, the sacred coyote hide was placed in front of the Coyote chief and his assistants in the council circle. Once again, the four sisters sat by the hide in front of the chiefs. Four of the Coyote warriors carried black-painted lances the shafts of which were an inch and a half in diameter. Between the ends was stretched a string, which when pulled taut gave each lance the form of a huge bow. Several kinds of feathers were hung at intervals from the bow-lance, and a lance head was fastened to one end to make it a more versatile weapon. The other members all carried straight lances and regular bows and arrows. Each warrior wore two eagle feathers stuck vertically in his scalp-lock. All the lay members of the society were painted alike. Their bodies and the upper parts of their arms and legs were painted yellow, while the lower halves of the arms and the legs from the knee down were painted black. On the chest of each warrior, suspended by means of a string about the neck, was a quarter-moon symbol. This was a crescent-shaped, black-painted piece of rawhide. When dancing, the Coyotes jumped up and down rapidly, keeping time to an ever-increasing tempo of the music. For ceremonies the four sisters always decorated their dresses with expensive elk teeth. Their faces were painted yellow, and they too wore a pair of eagle feathers upright in their hair.

The ancient tales of the Cheyenne declare that the warriors of this society once roached their hair to represent a long scalp-lock, the sides of the head being entirely shorn of hair. The members of the other societies all wore their hair loose and as long as possible.[23]

The Dog Men Society
The Dog Men society, termed by the White men the "Dog Soldier" society, was by far and away the largest society among the Cheyenne. It was made up of males fifteen years old and older and usually contained at least half the men of the entire Cheyenne tribe. In fact, this society once controlled the nation by sheer numbers alone. At an early date, which some informants loosely give as two generations before 1900, the Dog Men were joined by all the men of one of the tribal divisions. The reason for this unusual occurrence was not known, but they suspected that it was because of the popularity stemming from the war successes of the war chiefs and assistants of that society. This distinguished position was perpetuated over the years; in time the tribal

band and the Dog Men became practically one so that even the name of the band was changed to that of the society. Thus the important Dog Men became the famous Dog Soldiers so frequently mentioned by early observers and writers and later by army officers and Indian Bureau officials, constituting at the same time both a powerful military organization and a distinct tribal group. Its members were persistent raiders, roaming almost at will over the Plains between the Missouri and Arkansas rivers and using the upper Platte in Nebraska as their headquarters.

The four bravest Dog Men were chosen to defend the society and the tribe from the raids of the enemy in a particular way for year-long terms. Each of them wore a sash of tanned skin eight to ten feet long and five or six inches wide, with a lengthwise slit cut at the head end. These were called "dog-strings" or "dog-ropes." They were worn over the right shoulder and under the left and trailed behind on the ground.[24] The sashes of the two bravest men of the society were elaborately decorated with horizontal bands of yellow and red porcupine quills and eagle feathers. The other two wore a less conspicuous pair. A red-painted wooden picket-pin was attached to the bottom end by a braided buckskin thong. Whenever a battle was going badly for the Cheyennes, those who had been selected to wear the dog-ropes for that year drove the stakes into the ground and, remaining attached there, fought desperately to cover the retreat of the others. It was expected that they would die rather than pull up the pin themselves and retreat. However, the Indian nations always provided a way of escape from such stringent requirements. Among the Cheyenne, as with some tribes

326

Cheyenne Coyote society members carrying bow-lance and straight lance (FCM).

described earlier, the provision was made that if a comrade sharply ordered them away as if he were speaking to a dog, they were free to retreat with the others.

Dorsey states that at the end of a year's term, the sash-wearers still surviving gladly relinquished the emblems to four other members newly chosen for the position, and if one had been killed and the dog-string lost, his widow prepared a new one for his successor. Again Grinnell differs, declaring that when a Dog Soldier had carried a sash as long as he wished, he let it be known and the eight principal men of the society chose a brave young man to succeed him, the sash-wearer-elect purchasing the sash for a very high price.[25] The two foremost Dog Men were also allowed to fringe their leggings with human hair-locks, but the lesser two sash-wearers were not permitted to do so, for they had not proven themselves to be as brave as the former two.

All the warriors of the Dog society dressed alike. Their usual style of headdress consisted of a cap with a narrow beaded band along the front edge. The crown was entirely covered with the gorgeous tail feathers of the golden eagle (Grinnell says raven feathers),[26] and the sides were covered with the feathers of the hawk and the crow. The unusual thing was that the feathers were fastened in such a way so as to make them stand erect all over the headdress. Suspended by a string from the neck of each warrior was a whistle made from the wing bone of an eagle. Both the whistle and the string were wrapped with porcupine quills.

According to Dorsey, each warrior carried a rattle fashioned in the form of a snake. To make the rattle, the Dog Men used a round stick about a foot long and one and a half inches in diameter. It was covered on one side with a narrow strip of rawhide about three-quarters of an inch wide, the ends of which extended beyond the stick. The headpiece and the tailpiece were attached to the extensions, the headpiece extending beyond the end of the shaft or body about two inches and the tail over two feet. The rawhide was then bound to the stick with sinew, and the whole, except for the head, was covered with buckskin. The head was painted red, eyes were drawn on it and an eagle feather was attached to it. After this, rows of the dew claws of a deer or antelope were tied to the entire body. Those parts of the body still exposed were decorated with quillwork. The finished length of the rattle was about two and a half feet.[27] In contrast, Grinnell describes the Dog rattle as "a small, short rattle—a hollow ring of rawhide with a short handle. The outer border of the ring was ornamented with fur or with deerskin fringe or with red cloth." [28]

To use the rattles the Dog Men grasped them by the head with their right hand and shook them to measure time for their dancing and singing. The society belt worn for dancing was made from four skunk skins with the heads left on. Two heads met in front and two at the back. The fur was left on the skins and faced outward. Fringes were attached, and dew claws were tied to these for rattles.[29]

Dog Men always carried a bow and arrows. When they danced, they let their hair hang loose and blew their whistles constantly, moving forward rapidly in a stooping position, bending each leg forward alternately. Leggings with painted stripes were worn, but the upper parts of the body and face were exposed and painted red. This society had between five and six hundred songs, exclusive of their four sacred songs and four war songs. The society emblem was the dog, which they re-

garded as sacred and which they associated with the origin of the society. Understandably, the Dog Men society regarded itself as distinguished and special, and the whole tribe as well as neighboring tribes were made aware of its importance. In the early days, this society above all was noted for the great number of captives it held. In fact, the old-time warriors claimed that at one time three-fourths of the entire Cheyenne tribe were captives.[30] In all probability this was an exaggeration, but it did emphasize their accomplishments in that regard.

The Dog Men society was organized late in Cheyenne history, after all the other societies had been formed. It was begun by a young man of limited influence, who was "chosen" for the great honor by the Great Prophet.[31]

Whenever the Dog Men society erected its four days' lodge for a ceremony, they restored their unique headdresses, reconsidered the assignments of all the warriors and, if one of the four sash-wearing members had died or been killed in battle, elected another to take his place. Whenever the other warrior societies set up their lodges, they were allowed to locate them in the center of the camp-circle, but the Dog Men warriors could place their lodge either in the center of the camp-circle or wherever they chose. An essential feature of the site chosen had to be a tree leaning toward the north, to which they could lash the three sacred saplings vital to the erection of their society lodge. The stationary tree was located at the back on the inside facing the entrance. The three movable saplings were always trimmed except for the upper branches. Buffalo hides were then used to cover the lodge. These poles of the Dog Men's society were always different from those of the other societies' lodges.

Also, the other societies burned incense to the Great Medicine, who had sent the Great Prophet to establish them and the ceremonies by which they would honor him; the Dog Men, however, placed an earthen pot about half full of water in the center of their lodge and dropped a piece of beef weighing about two pounds into it. The beef remained there during the four days' dance. On the fourth day, just before the dance was ended, the members took the meat from the pot and passed it around. Each person bit off a large piece, chewed it and swallowed it, in memory of their society's founder and in remembrance of the original dogs who followed the founder out from the camp-circle and encouraged the warriors to organize the Dog Men society. From that day forward, all the Dog Men preferred cooked to fresh meat.[32]

The Inverted, or Bowstring, Society

The Inverted Warrior society was founded by the Great Prophet when he last appeared in the spectacular dress of that society. In his hand was his celebrated bow-lance. A stuffed owl was tied over his forehead with a buckskin band, and a bone whistle hung from his neck by a string. The Great Prophet founded the society when he returned from a four-year trip to a holy mountain, but he organized the society without a chief. Each warrior was independent of the others, though all the warriors dressed alike and were always prepared to unite as one in war.[33]

Inverted Warriors were required to be strong and brave. Another requirement of the society was that the men be solemn and calm. Their bodies, clothing and buffalo robes were painted red. For regalia, each warrior carried a bow-lance about eight feet long, fashioned from

Opposite: *Cheyenne Dog Men society member holding snake-effigy rattle and wearing society sash and headdress (FCM).*

a sound, straight, well-seasoned stick shaped like a bow. It was flat on the front side and round on the back, except for the handle, which was completely round. The bow was two inches wide at the grip and one and a half inches at the wing tips. Its twisted buffalo sinew string was huge—one-third of an inch in diameter. A bunch of sage grass was bound around the grip. Originally a sharp flint lance head about six inches long was fitted to one end, later trade steel points were substituted. A few owl feathers were attached to the other end of the bow. Four bunches of magpie feathers were lashed to the bow wings to add medicine power. The bow was painted red, and the lance head was painted blue. The bow-lance was never unstrung; it was encased in buckskin when not in ceremonial use, and it was usually carried by the warrior at all times. It was never placed on the ground but hung in a tree or hidden elsewhere where it could not be found by anyone other than the owner. Only society members were allowed to handle the bow-lance, and no woman was ever allowed to touch it.

The warriors of the society remained single, and the sisters kept their beds apart from those of the warriors. Each man's food was cooked separately at home and was served individually. If any were in council with other society warriors, their food was still served separately. The close observance of this regulation in particular gave the Inverted men a character distinct from that of the members of other societies—they were regarded as being especially pure. In accordance with this attitude, they rejoiced in the beauty of nature as the prime work of the Great Medicine, who created the rivers, the hills, the mountains, the heavenly bodies and the clouds. They were the accepted philosophers among their people.[34]

The term "Inverted Warriors" came from a secret medicine by means of which their actions and speech were reversed. For example, while the members of the other societies might ask, "Father, will you come here?" the members of the Inverted society asked, "Father, you will not come here?" The characteristic reached to every dimension. When the warriors of other societies had given up and fled from the enemy, the Inverted Warriors blew their whistles and charged straight at the foe, fighting furiously until they either were killed or defeated the opponent. They usually stripped to their breechclouts for battle. Their faces and bodies were painted red. On their heads was the stuffed screech-owl to remind them to conduct themselves wisely. They carried their bow-lances in hand, and no one was allowed to pass in front of them. Should they wish to transfer their bow-lance from one hand to the other, they passed it behind their backs. When attacking an enemy's camp or when defending their own camps, the Inverted Warriors charged as a group independent of the main body, thus performing a flank movement.[35]

The Owl-Man's Bowstring, or Wolf Warriors, Society
The Owl-Man's Bowstring society was the sixth and latest warrior society in the Cheyenne tribe, being founded by a Cheyenne warrior named Owl-Man during the period of White settlement, not by the Great Prophet. Like the other societies, if Dorsey is correct, it had one head chief and seven assistants or subchiefs, under whom there were usually from one to two hundred warriors. The members of the society were known for their constant parties, their noisy songs, their effusive dances and the sparkling and varied colors of their outfits. Each mem-

Cheyenne Inverted Warrior society member carrying bow-lance and wearing stuffed owl skin on head (FCM).

Cheyenne Inverted, or Bow String, society warrior wearing buffalo robe with hair side turned in and carrying bow-lance (FCM).

ber dressed as he chose, and there was no standard society costume, although there was standard regalia, such as a wolf hide worn in poncho fashion. The Bowstrings were open to any warrior of fifteen years of age or more. The society did not invite members to join it, but the warriors came of their own volition to request admission.[36]

The way in which Owl-Man received the guidance for founding his society is typical of many Plains societies. He was traveling alone, toward the north. As he rode along, he was caught in a driving rainstorm that soon turned into a heavy snowstorm. Searching for shelter, he discovered a deep canyon and went into it to spend the night. The canyon was of little help, however, for the snow fell steadily and the bitter cold increased until Owl-Man's clothing was first wet and then frozen stiff. His pony froze to death. Then Owl-Man stripped the bark from trees, built a little fire and made a small shelter for himself. This together with his buffalo robe kept him from freezing, but when morning came, he was so hungry and cold that he was ready to lie down and die. Suddenly a mysterious voice spoke from behind him and told him to travel west until he found a creek, where there would be a lodge. No Indian ever questioned the validity of such mysterious events, and he immediately started west through the deep snow. Shortly he saw the creek, and as he drew near it, he heard a drum beating, just as if there were a dance going on; then he saw the very lodge which the voice had mentioned. As he approached it, the drumming ceased. By this time he could barely move, for his clothing was frozen and his feet and hands were frostbitten. Apprehensively entering the lodge, he saw a fire in the center and noticed that the ground inside was perfectly smooth. At the back of the lodge was a flat drum, nothing else. At this point Owl-Man collapsed on the ground and remained unconscious until early evening, when he revived and sat up.

As he sat there pondering his situation, he heard people outside the lodge talking animatedly and telling each other to go in and see the stranger in the lodge. At this Owl-Man arose and peeked through the entrance. To his astonishment, from as far away as he could see, there were dozens of wolves approaching the lodge and they even spoke his own language! One by one the wolves entered the lodge, and as they entered, they were instantly transformed into human beings! Soon the lodge was filled, and still there were hundreds more remaining outside the lodge. After as many Wolf men as possible had taken their seats inside, forming a circle around the lodge, an old Wolf-man came in and took his seat in front of the circle, directly opposite the entrance. He began immediately to speak to Owl-Man as follows:

> We have powers of cunning such as no other animals have, and we have the whole earth for our home. We this day have come here to bless you and your people, so that you may live and go back to your people and show them what we are, and we will instruct you for the next four days. Our people possess the whole earth, and our braves do the fighting in companies. We do not allow women to mingle with our braves. If you allow maidens to do your work, take four maidens, who are to wear belts made of rattlesnake skin.[37]

When he finished talking, the old Wolf man burned incense, and in an instant every Wolf warrior in the lodge was gorgeously arrayed. The old Wolf man himself was covered with a bear's hide, dressed with the hair on. All the other Wolf warriors were cloaked with wolf skins,

tanned with the hair on. These had a hole cut at the center of the pelt, big enough to permit the insertion of the head, so that the skins were worn as capes, with the wolf heads hanging on their chests and the tails hanging down the middle of their backs. The lower half of their faces, necks, arms from the elbows down and ankles were painted red, and the rest of their faces and bodies were painted yellow.

Each Wolf warrior carried a lance about eight feet long, with a flint lance head at one end. These lances were not all alike, for they were trimmed in different ways with the feathers of every kind of bird to be found. Two of the lances had eagle tail feathers attached from one end to the other—like Plains war flags. These were planted in the ground at each side of the entrance of the lodge, while two other lances, wrapped with otter skin, stood upright directly in front of the Wolf chief, who now held in his hand the flat drum Owl-Man had first seen at the back of the lodge. Several other Wolf men held smaller drums and a special hoop rattle with an eagle tail feather appended to it.

The Wolf men paid close attention to their chief as he continued to burn incense to the Great Medicine. After a while he held his flat drum over the incense, passing it back and forth, first to the east, then to the south, the west and the north. Then he took his drumstick and struck the drum four times. At this, the old Wolf men stood up and began beating their drums and yelling with all their might. Then they sang and danced for four days, and before they were finished, Owl-Man had learned about three hundred sacred songs. Four of these were especially sacred songs and four in particular were war songs. While dancing, each warrior held his lance. When the dancing ended for a

333

Cheyenne Owl Man's Bowstring society member wearing fox skin and carrying ring-shaped rattle (DPL).

time, they planted the lances upright in front of themselves. Then they danced again.

Each night during the ceremony, Owl-Man would fall asleep. When he awoke in the morning, all the Wolf men would be gone, but they would shortly return and change into human form, ready to dance again. On the afternoon of the fourth day, four old men came to the lodge and made speeches about their exploits to the assembled Wolf men. When the speeches were completed, the Wolf men were ordered to go outside the lodge and stand in a row, ready to run a race. As one of the old men called out the name of the Wolf society, they all ran a long race at full speed. When they returned from the race, they entered the lodge and the old men said to Owl-Man:

> Arise and go on your way. In one and a half days you will reach your people. We have blessed you, and now in addition to what we have shown you, go and teach your people to be brave. Take this wolf-medicine; it is to be worn by the warriors of what will now be your society whenever they go on the warpath or dance. And when they dance they are not to stop dancing until a renowned old warrior comes before them and tells his exploits, the same as we have done. Then you are at liberty to dismiss the dancers.[38]

Then the four old men departed, and once they were outside the lodge, it disappeared instantly, leaving Owl-Man sitting there on the prairie in the midst of the four patriarchs. In a moment more, there were only four real wolves running swiftly away from him. The weather was clear, the snow was gone and a greatly moved Owl-Man arose and began to search for his Cheyenne village.

When he arrived, all the people ran to see him, asking in amazement how he had survived the incredible snowstorm. He told them what had happened, and they simply shook their heads in awe over the never-ending wonders of God. On the first good day thereafter, they camped in the form of a circle and Owl-Man erected his lodge in the very center of the camp. He had the ground inside made as smooth as possible and then called for eager young men to come and join his exciting new society. When enough had done so, he performed the marvelous ceremony exactly as he had been instructed by the Wolf men.[39]

After that time, any warrior in the tribe who was not already a member of one of the five sacred warrior societies was free to join the Wolf society. Whenever they went on raids or to war or whenever a ceremonial dance was held, they wore the medicine and paint given to them by the original Wolf men through Owl-Man. It brought them great power and success, and it was still being used in the society in the early 1900s. Observers who saw them dancing said that the warriors held their lances in one hand and stood erect. They jumped up and down very heavily and moved slowly. These society members alone danced with guns and shot noisy blank cartridges. The guns were used to indicate that the society was organized after the advent of the White man with his powder and gun.[40]

A COMPARISON OF THE CHEYENNE AND ARAPAHO SOCIETIES

The regalia and organization of the Cheyenne societies were similar in a general way to those of the Arapaho, except that the Arapaho

Opposite: *Cheyenne Owl Man's Bowstring, or Wolf Warriors society member carrying rattle and flag* (FCM).

groups were age-graded. The belt of the Red Shield society was much like that of the Arapaho Lance or Club-board society, although the Red Shield lance was suggestive of that employed by the Arapaho Tomahawk society. More particularly, the Arapaho Tomahawk and the Cheyenne Hoof Rattles had much in common. The Coyote society of the Cheyenne was similar in most respects to the Star or Kit-fox of the Arapaho, and the Cheyenne Dog Men shared the customs of the Arapaho Dog Soldiers. The characteristic features of the Inverted society were similar to those of the Lime-Crazy society of the Arapaho, whose speech and actions also reversed the usual order. The two wore virtually the same headdress.

When Frances Densmore was studying among the Sioux of the Teton and the Standing Rock reservations before 1918, she was told that "fox songs and coyote songs are the same" and that certain songs called wolf songs or "Wolf society songs" should be included with them.[41] Dr. Lowie found that the Kit-fox dance was called the Coyote dance by the Santee at Fort Totten, North Dakota, and that the Crows of Montana believed "all the societies were originated by the mythical Old Man Coyote." [42] A similar correspondence between the terms "fox" and "coyote" was discovered in the names of the Cheyenne societies by Mooney, who reports one of them as being the "foxmen" (specifically, the kit, or swift, fox), while George Dorsey lists the Coyote as being one of the original Cheyenne societies.[43]

The Cheyenne Women's Guilds
George Grinnell reports that "some Cheyennes declare that women who have been to war constitute a society, but what ceremony there may be connected with it, I do not know. It may be that instead of constituting a society, they constituted a class." [44]

The most important women's association consisted of those who were devoted to the ceremonial decoration of hide objects with porcupine quills. Its complex ceremony and ritual dated from the legendary times of the people. Any piece of work being done in fulfillment of a vow must be adorned in a prescribed ceremonial way, and a woman outside the society wishing to do a robe or anything else made of hide had to be taught to perform it properly by a member of the Quilling society who had done the same thing. "The making and offering of such a robe in the prescribed way secured the maker admission to the society of women who had done similar things. Thereafter she might attend the feasts, and, having herself been taught, might teach others." [45]

While the Quilling order of the Southern Cheyenne was a single unit, among the Northern Cheyenne it was divided into several grades, each of which specialized in certain work. These were the makers of the following: moccasins, baby cradles, stars for ornamenting lodges, buffalo robes, lodge linings, back rests and possibly sacks.

Besides the Quilling society, there were guilds of women who specialized in the use of feathers, fine roots, cornstalks, beadwork and painting. All these had very sacred and involved rituals for the beginning and conduct of their work.

The guild members

had strict rules in their designs and they kept secret the meaning and arrangement of the colors, as well as the relation of the designs to each other. The designs were always symbolic and talismanic, representing

concrete organic objects, whereas the colors were more emblematic of the abstract in creatures and creation, e.g., white for active life; very light blue for quietness, peace, serenity (from the cloudless sky); green for growing life; red for warmth, food, blood, home; amber, yellow, ripeness, perfection, beauty (from the sunsets); black for cessation of enmity or hostilities (from a dead glow being no more hot). The meaning of the colors ramifies as they are combined, or, according as they are lighter or darker shade.[46]

The Mescal Bean Cult

Informants tell also of a Cheyenne Mescal Bean cult with its own sacred bundle. This group became effective enough to influence its spread to the Ponca in 1902 and thereafter to several other tribes.[47] The Ponca in turn are credited with having introduced the Stomp dance among the Cheyenne and several other southern nations.

The Contrary Society (or Cult)

Grinnell reports at length about a Contrary society with many members who appeared to have had no connection with the Contrary (Inverted) warriors who carried the thunder bow-lance.[48] Yet it bore the same name, its members acted backwards and it had some relation to thunder. Most of the society members were old men and women who feared lightning and thunder. In this society the members attempted by word and action to reverse things, that is, to do the opposite of what they were supposed to do; they backed into and out of tipis and sat with their backs on the ground and their legs in the air. "They are funmakers, and their absurd actions are enjoyed and applauded by the people."[49]

It was believed that Contraries could aid the sick. If one touched a sick person or jumped over him, it "is a great help to him." Sometimes during a Contrary ceremony, they lifted up the sick and put them down again. At other times, they lifted them up and held them head downward. Obviously their treatment dealt with the attitude of the patient, seeking to bring some laughter into the midst of his misery.

The Contrary ceremony centered around a considerable amount of public misbehavior, with the participants being painted as wildly as possible and dressed to match. Even the preparations lodge was consistent with this, having the covering inside out, the lodge poles on the outside and the smoke-hole turned the wrong way.

In the so-called Grazy or Animal dance, *Massaum*, members of the Contrary society took the part of hunters who carried four arrows and pretended to kill the "animal people" of the dance. The *Massaum* was an ancient Cheyenne rite of legendary origin; next to the Sun Dance, it was their most colorful event. It was sometimes spoken of

337

Cheyenne Contrary society member wearing "Yellow Wolf" robe during Animal dance, or Massaum, *ceremony (SM).*

as the ceremony during which people acted as if they were crazy or foolish, or perhaps one should say enchanted. According to some Cheyenne informants, the ceremony began when the first great herds of buffalo came to the Cheyenne. After this, the herds gathered from all directions, and from then on the people always had plenty of buffalo. All kinds of animals also came to the first meeting place, and in commemoration of this assembly, the people instituted the *Massaum* ceremony. In ancient times, they said, the buffalo would always appear to them two or three days after the conclusion of the ceremony.

The Animal ritual was often vowed during a war journey in return for success. It lasted for five days. A center pole was cut with great ceremony and set up, around which a large principal lodge was erected. The first day was occupied with the building of the preparation lodge. The second day began at daylight when certain sacred objects, including a buffalo skull, were brought into the lodge. Then two wolf hides were brought in, which played a most important part in the ceremony thereafter. The first step was to soften and prepare the wolf hides for use and also to build a special trench bed for the buffalo skull, which had already been painted.

On the third day, several preliminary ceremonies, which included the painting of the participants, preceded the painting of the wolf hides. One was painted yellow, and the other white. During the night, the wolf skins were formed into the rounded shapes of real wolf heads and then placed on beds of red calico near the fire and the buffalo skull.

On the fourth day, the participants were painted again and a messenger was sent out to call those who were to take part in the ceremony. The buffalo skull was painted red on the face area and black on the crown. Then two black lines were drawn down the face, and certain symbols were placed on prescribed spots. Grass was then bound in a traditional fashion into three balls, which were inserted into the eye and nose holes of the skull. All these actions were performed with complicated and numerous ceremonial gestures and accompanied by constant prayers. Special attention was then given to the finishing of the altar on which the skull was placed.

Long bundles of grass were used to stuff the head of a wolf skin (informants say that originally a kit-fox skin was used), after which the fur side of the hide was painted with yellow paint. The wolf's mouth and throat were sewn closed. That night there was singing and the offering of sacrifices.

On the fifth day the hide was painted in a traditional way with many colors and important symbols. At this point the pledger who was to wear the wolf-skin was ceremoniously painted. He wore only a breech clout and moccasins. Then a crier announced to the camp that the wolf was coming out. It was brought out with attendant ceremonies and placed on a travois, the head facing east. Now everyone came to see the wolf, regarding it in silence or praying in low tones. After an hour, the hide was returned to the lodge and preparations were continued. The exciting climax came when cultic people from different lodges about the camp came in animal costumes to join with the wolf skin wearers in a complex drama that told again the old story of the appearance of the animals for the benefit of the Cheyenne. From beginning to end, it was a stupendous rite—one whose details have barely been touched on here. It took Grinnell fifty-one pages just to relate that part of the ceremony his informants could remember.[50]

338

Cheyenne Contrary cult members participating in the Animal ceremony, wearing masks with eagle wing feathers tied to them and carrying bows and arrows. Bodies are daubed with white paint (SM).

15
THE ASSINIBOINE

The Assiniboine were the equal of the Blackfoots and the Sioux as leaders in all respects on the northern Plains, being noted for their cunning, courage and capabilities as warriors and for their intelligence and enterprise as producers and traders.

When Catlin visited these nations in 1832, he described them as undoubtedly the finest-looking, best-equipped, and most beautifully costumed of any on the continent . . . and they are the most independent and the happiest races of Indians I have met with; they are all in a state of primitive rudeness and wildness, and consequently are picturesque and handsome almost beyond description. Nothing in the world, of its kind, can possibly surpass in beauty and grace, some of their games and amusements—their gambols and parades.[1]

The Assiniboines migrated to the Plains from the Ohio River region in late prehistoric times. They were a Siouan people, thought to have once been a part of the Yanktoni Sioux. The two separated at the upper Mississippi River, when the Assiniboines allied with the Crees and moved northward. Early traders estimated their number at more than 10,000 and found them spread over an enormous territory in the north middle Plains and an area of Canada just above that. They remained constantly at war with the Sioux and Blackfoots and invaded the territories of other tribes as well. In the end, they left a name as renowned military strategists and outstanding warriors. More than anything else, the diseases of the White man brought them down. In one siege alone, more than 4,000 lives were taken. The killing of the buffalo finished the job, and in 1900, less than 3,000 Assiniboines were left.

There was no system of age societies among the Assiniboine. However, there was a specific fraternity of young warriors or soldiers that stood apart from the other societies and cults. This group consisted of young men who had proven their courage and recklessness on the battlefield and in raids, and their lodge stood in the center of each tribal camp. They had to be unmarried, and they spent practically all their indoor hours in the society lodge. They were the camp police, and it was their duty to maintain order. It was said that if anyone resisted their efforts to do so, they had the right to kill him and cut him to pieces. It was also said that each soldier would eat a small piece of the victim's flesh, but a broader understanding of Indian attitudes suggests that the society probably did nothing more than cultivate fear, hence obedience, by occasionally pretending to kill and then eat a victim. (Another reputed way of showing their fearlessness was to mix human and dog excrement and devour it, though more probably again they only pretended to do so.)

Each soldier member was told by his spirit helper in a vision the age at which he should marry. If he were to do so before that time, it was generally believed he would not live long and would immediately lose the power of his vision helper. In any event, after marrying, the solder power left him, and he could no longer be a member of the fraternity. Whenever the enemy was engaged, the soldiers, wearing their medicine power, led the fighting. They were expected to be absolutely fearless and reckless at all times.

The Assiniboine term for fearlessness is said to refer to the following unusual custom of the soldiers: One of the society would suddenly appear entirely naked in the center of the camp. Then when he had everyone's attention, he would dance as he shook his rattle, singing and looking down intently at himself. This signified that he was truly unashamed and reckless. Such men fearless enough to do this were chosen for the leadership of the society. Sometimes two rival members would do this at the same time, each sincerely believing that his "medicine" was stronger than that of the other and hoping he would be chosen as head of the society. If so, a traditional contest took place between the two. Both would be offered a mixture of dung and admonished to prove their courage by eating it. If either failed to eat, he was automatically disqualified.[2] One man actually died from attempting to eat what was put before him. When, in ordinary circumstances, the leader of the society was ready to retire because of advancing age or a desire to marry, he selected a soldier member to take his place and gave him his medicine fetish helper as a loan. The new chief, once he had the full approval of his fellows, selected an aspiring young warrior to take his place in the soldier group, and the two of them danced in the public and "unashamed" manner just mentioned. Should the retiring leader feel a need for his "medicine" later on, he could always borrow it back, but at his death the fetish became the permanent property of the man who had replaced him.

Ordinary membership in the Soldier society was gained only by the unanimous agreement of the members, and it is not surprising that the group, to all intents and purposes, ceased to function about the year 1860.

The Grass dance was regarded as the dance of the Soldier organization.[3] The drums used in this performance were made from hollow logs and decorated with war, raid and celestial symbols. Of the drumsticks used, four were of a ceremonial character. They were forked and wrapped with beadwork for about half their length. White eagle feathers and hair from a horse's tail, dyed different colors corresponding to the color of horses stolen by each of the owners of the drums, were tied to the forks. To begin the dance, these sticks were handed to four distinguished men who served as honorary drummers. The first man hit the drum once and publicly gave away some of his property. The others then followed suit. When the four had again hit the drum one after another, they were relieved by six Soldier members with ordinary drumsticks.

All society lay members wore roach headdresses made of porcupine- and deer-tail hairs; otherwise the costume consisted of whatever the members wished to wear. Most wore leggings fringed with weasel skins or human hair-locks. A few carried war shields painted with pictographic representations of their war honors. It was customary for a grass-dancer to indicate his battle and raid achievements in a traditional way. If he had slain an enemy, he wore golden eagle feathers in his hair. If the victim was a Sioux, a skunk skin was sewn to the heel of the dancer's moccasin. An X painted on the dancer's body or an acute angle pointing upward with a small circle resting on the apex represented a wound. Some men put these designs on their shirts and leggings. A horseshoe- or U-shaped design indicated a horse raid. This might be repeated indefinitely in a vertical column according to the number of successful raids. Each pipe drawn on a member's shirt showed that he had been leader of a successful raid or war expedition. The four society officers or head dancers were distinguished by their crow bustles, the leader's being dyed red. These four were assisted by two "whippers." At a tribal buffalo hunt, two leaders and four heralds were employed to control the actions of the hunting party.

Society dances could be held at any time. Whenever the leader decided to have a dance, he ordered the herald to invite the people to prepare a feast. Along with the other food, it was absolutely necessary to cook a dog for the society feast, otherwise no dance could be held. Next the crier called the members of the society four times, and everyone was expected to be present after the fourth proclamation. The last man to appear had a large bucket of food placed before him, and he was obliged to eat it all on the spot or pay a forfeit, such as a blanket, to some old man or woman; then the rest of the food was served to the other spectators. The four officers sat behind their feather bustles, and the bucket containing the dog meat was placed outside the lodge, near a large bowl. At this point the singers began, and at the fourth song the officers put on their bustles and danced in a circle. This was repeated three times. The fourth time the leader, standing near the bucket, showed everyone how he dodged the weapons of the enemy. Finally he touched the bucket, went around in a circle and sat down. The other officers then went through the same motions. After this, one of the leaders arose and performed a traditional ceremony with the dog meat and bones.

At the conclusion of the ceremony, the dog's skull bones were kept and the other bones were thrown away. The remaining contents of the other buckets were served to the spectators, and a dance began in which all could join. It was customary on these occasions for the officers to "give away" their insignia. Each one looked about for a conspicuously brave man, sat him in his own place, untied his crow bustle and surrendered it to the prospective officer; the other leaders then followed suit. In return for the belt, each recipient gave someone a horse. A new man became the keeper of the pipe smoked at the ceremony, and the ceremonial drum and drumsticks also changed hands. The heralds, however, did not change.

Another dance then took place, followed by a smoking song during which everyone seized his pipe and began to smoke. Then followed an intermission, during which the people were free to dance or not dance, as they pleased. A herald approached the dog's skull, pointed it toward each of the four directions and put it down with the nose pointing east. Then eight distinguished warriors danced four times around the bones. After the fourth dance, the first one picked up the skull and pointed it in the direction of the country where he had accomplished a certain deed. He then recited the story and put it down. The remaining seven men followed the same procedure; the last man was permitted to throw away the skull. If at any time during the ceremony a feather or any other part of the ceremonial regalia fell to the ground, a man who had killed an enemy picked it up and, before handing it to its owner, recited a war story.[4]

ASSINIBOINE CEREMONIAL ORGANIZATION

A most important piece of Assiniboine soldier regalia not mentioned in their literature but illustrated by Carl Bodmer was the bow-lance, a weapon similar to that carried by several of the Plains societies.

The bow-lance was a heavy and apparently awkward weapon over eight feet in length. It was really a huge bow, with a thick grip and wings and a large lance head inserted and bound to one end. In the Bodmer illustration, it has two hangings of hide or cloth strips on the long upper wing. The curved wings of the bow differ considerably, with the wing at the opposite end from the lance head being about the same length and curvature as that of a regular short Plains bow. In all probability the lance was used in the conventional way during a battle. Judging by the design of the bow, when the sash-wearers dismounted to take a stand, planting the lance head in the ground through the sash would just about bring the bow grip to the right height to enable the warrior to use it for launching arrows—even with the lance head still imbedded.

Bodmer's drawing also shows the Soldier carrying a heavy, bone-handled quirt with a fur wrist-loop and an eagle feather pendant hanging from the loop.

Besides the Soldiers, there were twelve societies or cults:

Prairie-chicken
Horse Dance
Fool
No-flight
Fox
Crazy
Dirty Dance
Brown Crane
Buffalo
Whelp
Duck
Bear

The Prairie-chicken Society or Cult
The Prairie-chicken society or cult was an order that Lowie believes was adopted from the Cree. The name was descriptive of their curious dance position, in which the men's feet were bent inward to form an acute angle. In dancing, one foot alternately crossed the other. From time to time, each dancer bent down low, his hands resting on his thighs. The rattle used was supposed to imitate the sounds made by prairie-chickens. In the society war dance, the dancers carried red-painted scalps and knives to symbolize the blood of slain foes. Some members painted half of their club handles red and the other half black. One dance was for men only, the costume for which consisted of breech-clouts and eagle tail feather warbonnets. Half of the face was painted red, and the other half black. In later times, a squaw dance was added. In this ceremony, men and women danced in a circle toward the left. A society skunk dance was also mentioned by informants. In all the dances, both large drums and hand drums were employed. The only regalia seen by Whites was a roach headdress and two feathered lances or flags with bone points on one end.

The Horse Dance Society or Cult
The Horse Dance society or cult differed from other societies in that it was primarily religious and its ceremony was commonly regarded as being as important as the Sun Dance. The Assiniboine obtained it from the Canadian Blackfoots in ancient times.[5] An Assiniboine visitor was

told by the Northern Blackfoots that if he performed the ceremony, he would obtain horses. They also instructed him to offer the pipe to Life-Giver and to the sun, the thunderbird and the earth. The price of membership was high. One member paid a bay horse, a black horse, two white horses and a lodge with all its contents as an initiation fee. This was surrendered to his sponsor, who divided the property among the members.

There were four head men, or officers. A candidate was taught the order's ritualistic songs and was told that through his membership he would get many horses, enjoy prosperity and live to be an old man. Two lodges were united to form a huge dance lodge. Wild berries and choke-cherries, stored in buffalo skin bags, were prepared for a feast to which all spectators were welcome. The weeds and grass in the back of the lodge were cleared to make room for an oblong altar about three feet by one and a half feet in area. Here sweetgrass and juniper needles were burnt for incense. All present smoked the order's sacred black pipe. It was laid on the altar, then offered to Life-Giver, the sun, the thunderbird and the earth.

A dance followed, with the wives joining their husbands in it. The performers did not change their positions in the circle while dancing. For music, two drummers sang, a third man sounded a clapper rattle and eagle bone whistles were blown. No special costume was worn. On joining the society, each candidate received a war-medicine consisting of something like an "unidentified" bird skin, a weasel skin, a weasel skin headdress and a large square piece of buffalo skin. When going to war, he used the square piece of buffalo skin for a saddle blanket. He might also paint his horse's legs with a long, zigzag red line representing lightning and a yellow circle around its eyes and above its tail, although each man always painted his horse a little differently from the others.

The Fool Society

The Fool society originated in the dream of a young man who "awakened" and found himself in a strange lodge. From time to time, a man came to the door and beckoned to him, but whenever he went to the door, the man vanished as soon as he was outside. This dream came to him many times. Once as the youth slept outdoors by a *tanzūk* bush, he dreamed that a man came, saying, "Let us go to my camp." He arose immediately and began to walk, but the man disappeared again. After this dream, the same man returned in another dream and said, "They want you over there, let us go." The youth followed him to a little hill, where he saw a jet-black rock, a white rock, a *tanzūk* bush and an old woman. The woman said, "Grandchild, sit on this black rock." He sat down. The rock began to move, and a crow emerged and flew off. Then he was asked to sit on the white rock. He sat down. It moved, and when he arose, he saw a white owl emerge and fly away. "Sit on the bush," she said. The youth leaned against the bush. Then the old woman said, "You are going to manage the fool dance, good will come to you therefrom." As she gave him the instructions concerning it, he saw a man standing nearby in dirty clothes, wearing a strange head mask with eye slits. The woman said, "That is you, you will dress in this way. Whenever there is a camp, you can make the fool dance. It looks dirty, but all the people enjoy it. If you fail to conduct it, you will not enjoy life long. Perform it at least once a year." He promised to obey. There was

Opposite: *Assiniboine warriors in ceremonial and war costumes. Man at left carries typical war-club and has war honor, or "coup," marks painted on leggings. Man at right carries gun in beaded case and leads horse with beaded horse gear on head* (AMNH).

a large lodge nearby, and he went to it. In the center of it was a stick standing upright decorated with red flannel and with deer hooves tied to it. As he looked at it, the woman said, "Some Fools are going to come in; watch their performance." Then fourteen or fifteen Fools with different kinds of head masks approached in single file, each packing some meat. The youth noted all their actions, and in obedience to his story and instructions, the Assiniboines conducted the Fool ceremony thereafter.

To hold the ceremony, a dance lodge was erected and an experienced old man was invited to assist in the ritual, being paid for his services after the dance. The latter first made masks for himself and his employer, since these masks differed from those of the other dancers. Then the old man toured the camp, asking for canvas and used clothing, after which he returned to the lodge and made masks for prospective dancers. As a rule, no one knew exactly who would be asked to join in the dance, although the relatives of people who had recovered from serious sicknesses were often the first to be chosen. Upon completion of the masks and the head performer's body garment, which consisted of a woman's dress fringed at the bottom, either the leader or the old man helper put on the leader's dress and mask, placed a whistle in his mouth, took a bow and two arrows in his left hand and the deer-hoof rattle in his right and began to walk around the camp. Dancers were summoned by pointing the rattle-staff at them; sometimes the selector entered a lodge; at other times he merely raised the door flap. Some men joined willingly, while others wished to run away, yet no one dared to refuse outright after being pointed out, for a misfortune would certainly befall him or his family. If anyone declined to go but hoped to avoid evil consequences, he would take a material offering to the leader, explaining that he did not want to join in the performance. The leader then excused him and sought an additional participant. Fourteen or fifteen dancers were usually called. This was no age limit, but older men predominated, and in the early days distinction in war played an important part in a man's selection.

On invitation from the leader, the Fools assembled at the dance lodge to obtain their masks. The costumes varied but were supposed to be as odd assemblages as possible. The men often made one legging of one material and the other legging of another. When all were ready, they stood in a circle in the lodge, the leader at the rear, and danced up and down. After four performances, the leader went outdoors, followed by the other Fools in single file. After walking some distance, he halted and his followers surrounded him to perform their dance. This too was repeated four times. After the fourth dance, they proceeded to a spot where a buffalo had been killed and was lying with its face to the south. Sneaking stealthily up to the buffalo, the leader drew his bow as if to shoot and blew his whistle. Then all the Fools fell back, some rolling over as if caught by a strange force and knocked to the ground. After a while they arose slowly and again approached the animal on tiptoe. The odd proceedings were repeated until the fourth approach, when the master of ceremonies finally shot his arrow. At this, all ran up and surrounded the buffalo, dancing four times as they had done in their dance lodge. The head performer then took his deer-hoof rattle and pretended to throw it on the buffalo. He repeated the motion four times and at the fourth gesture actually threw the rattle. It was said that it always fell in the proper position on the buffalo's back and that it never rolled off. The master then sang songs, two of which were:

Buffalo horn gray [i.e., gray-horned buffalo] just now
I have killed, I went and stood there, I shot it

Buffalo this like the sun goes around,
it has been knocked over.
Around four times they danced, making a dancing noise.
Buffalo this around four times they are stamping around.
Bone-whistles blow! Yell!

When he had finished, the Fools seated themselves in a circle around the buffalo. The leader filled his pipe, prayed to the six cardinal directions, smoked and passed the pipe. When everyone had smoked, the bison was butchered in the customary way and there was another dance around the animal. Then each one bundled up a part of the meat. Buffalo paunches were filled with the bull's blood and suspended from the neck or attached to the belt of each member, one more dance was conducted around the remains of the carcass and then they started back toward the dance lodge followed by a laughing crowd. Whenever the spectators pressed too close, the performers doused them with blood taken from the paunches, whereupon the people immediately fell back. After making a circuit of the camp, the procession approached the Fools' lodge. On reaching the door, the members turned to the left, walked around the tipi once, halted and loosened the fastenings above the entrance. The leader blew his bone whistle and three times pretended to throw his meat through the smoke hole into the lodge while his companions whistled. The fourth time he actually threw the meat, entered and sat down. If he missed the smoke hole, neither he nor any of the other members were allowed to pick up the meat, and it could be appropriated by any spectator. The members repeated the throwing performance one by one and successively joined their leader in the lodge. Once all had assembled, they removed their costumes and went home. In actuality, the entire ceremony took only from two to four hours. From then on the performers were required to "talk backwards," that is, to express exactly the reverse of whatever meaning they wished to convey, whether speaking among themselves or to others. Thus, if a man was thirsty, he had to say, "I am not thirsty, I don't wish to drink."

In dancing the masked Fool dancers assumed characteristically grotesque positions. Lowie obtained three of their masks made about 1905. One of them was made of two rectangles of canvas (originally this would have been buckskin) sewn together and fringed at the top and sides. At the middle of each side was attached a tin disk about three inches in diameter, apparently representing an earring. The front of the mask was decorated with vertical lines of white clay and at either edge with a pair of irregular, approximately parallel curves. A ludicrously crooked nose was formed of cloth, sewn to the face and stuffed with grass. There were small eye slits and also an opening for the mouth. The back of the mask lacked both the nose and the vertical clay decoration, but the eyes were surrounded with symmetrical daubings of clay extending down the cheeks. Below the mouth slit an elongated curve of clay extended from side to side, and below the top seam was an inverted crescent-shaped figure. A second mask differed in several particulars. The nose was neither sewn on nor indicated in any way, the parallel stripes were lacking on both sides and red, blue, black and yellow paint took the place of the white clay. In the front, a series of isosceles triangles, differentiated by color and with bases touching the line of the top seam, were flanked by two blue rectangular crosses.[6]

347

The No-flight Society

The No-flight order is said to have originated with the Sioux, but three origin accounts exist. According to one, an Assiniboine captured by the Sioux returned after a long time and introduced the No-flight dance. In another account, the dance was derived from an unidentified Plains tribe. A woman was also credited with having dreamed the dance. After giving the ceremony to the people, she told her son that her husband was going to be killed by the Sioux in the young man's presence. While the dance was being performed, she sang a song about it.

The regalia of the order consisted of rawhide rattles decorated with feathers and flannel, two lances wrapped with otter skin and buffalo horn headdresses. There were sometimes as many as thirty lay members. In battle they were never to flee; if they attempted to do so, their leaders had the right to kill them. Instead, the two lance bearers were to plant their lances in the ground and the entire group was to stand and fight by them. However, a warrior of another society could remove the lances for them, freeing the officers and other men to retreat.[7]

The Fox Society

The Fox dance originated in a dream, and it was performed several times every summer. There were four leaders, two whippers and an indefinite number of ordinary members. The leaders wore a red-fox skin around their necks and a cloth headband hung with a strip of fox tail at each side and the upper jaw and nose of a fox sewn to it. The whippers bore whips with fox skin hangings and used them to touch the legs of the performers to keep them dancing. In dancing, the performers moved smoothly around in a circle to the accompaniment of drums. After a first dance in the society lodge, the four head men walked once around the lodge and then passed outside in single file followed by the others. They circled around the camp, halting four times, and at each stop went through the same performance. Then they separated.

The officers of the society always met before a dance. At such times, some might give away their regalia to one of the rank and file. If so, each donor announced to the other officers the name of the member to whom he wished to present his insignia, but it was kept secret from the recipient himself. The next day the officers invited the entire membership and a dance was performed in the usual way. After a certain length of time, the whippers instructed the drummers to sing a song indicating what was going to happen. The whippers stood at the entrance and declared that no one could leave the lodge. All the leaders danced. Each of the donors then announced his successor and presented him with the insignia of the higher degree. The recipients were expected to offer tanned robes, horses, saddles, etc., to their electors. By giving away their regalia, the officers merely gave up their degree of responsibility but did not forfeit their membership in the society. No initiation fee was required of men joining as ordinary members, but usually men of wealth were solicited more often than others.[8]

The Crazy Society

The Crazy society was said to have originated among the Crow Indians, having come to the Assiniboines in their early history. The name suggests inverted actions such as those characteristic of the Fool society. The members wore a breechclout and belt, brass armbands and bracelets and a bead or bone necklace. Each carried a quiver on his

Above: *Assiniboine Fool society members in ceremonial costumes including face masks. Clown at left bears staff hung with dew-claw rattles (after Lowie,* The Assiniboine). *Left:* Assiniboine Fool society masks described in text. Fronts and backs of two masks shown (AMNH).

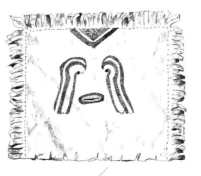

349

back and held a strung bow in his left hand and an arrow pointed downward in his right. Whenever the members desired to have a dance, they notified the leader. If he and two whippers consented, the dance was held. The men danced around in a circle to the beat of hand drums. While dancing, one of them would suddenly shoot his arrow so that it fell among the crowd, but he aimed so carefully that no one was ever hit.

Other than proven war and raid experience, there was no qualification for admission to the society. At one of the meetings, the members discussed the desirability of candidates—for instance, men who were known as misers were never chosen. If a man were elected, he was summoned to the lodge, where he gave away robes and horses. The society dance was occasionally performed in the daytime, but more usually at night. Late at night, after the conclusion of the performance, any dancer could visit a fellow member's lodge and sleep with his wife, but such license among the Assiniboine never extended beyond the limits of the brotherhood. According to one Indian authority, the society exercised police functions together with the Soldier society. Whenever a man had prematurely frightened the game in a tribal hunt, the members would take their guns, go out together and shoot into the air to indicate their intentions. Then they surrounded the culprit's lodge, tore it up and killed his horses and dogs.[9]

The Dirty Dance Society

The Dirty Dance society also originated with a dream. The leader and the singers were men, but the dancers were women. In the late spring of each year, the leader would summon the members to a large lodge, where they were entertained and told to dance. At this they returned home, and each put on his best clothes. Sometimes the ceremony was performed on behalf of a sick person, and for any ceremony a sacrifice of expensive material to the Great Spirit was said to have been essential. The dance lodge was made by uniting two ordinary lodges. The leader, who had a rattle, appointed between two and four helpers to drum and sing. The women stood up and merely moved up and down in their places, without changing their positions in the circle. After dancing, they left the lodge and arranged themselves in a straight row, in the center of which stood the men. Then they walked a certain distance and performed their ceremony, repeating this four times altogether. After the fourth time, they separated and went home. The women dancers wore necklaces and braided their hair like men. The master of ceremonies wore a sleeveless shirt and painted his arms and legs with white clay.[10]

The Brown Crane Society

The Brown Crane society had a large dance lodge that occupied a permanent place within the camp-circle. There were four officers, two men bearing war-clubs and two carrying long, flat pipes. After dancing within the lodge, the performers, grouped in the shape of a horseshoe, proceeded around the camp, halting four times and repeating their performance each time. Then they returned to their lodge and disbanded. The pipes were presented only to brave and kind men.[11]

The Buffalo Society

The Buffalo dance was said to have been derived from an unknown tribe. To start a ceremony, one man was appointed to gather up the members' headdresses. These consisted of the skin of a buffalo head, the horns and nose left on, with a stuffing of grass to fill it out. Two tipis were joined to form the dance lodge, outside of which all the headdresses were tied to a big pole. First a feast was held and then the members put on their costumes, which consisted of flannel clouts decorated with beaded buffalo hoof designs and the horned headgear. Four leaders of proven bravery were chosen. One of these men painted one of the horns of his buffalo mask red and tied an eagle feather to it. If a member had carried a shield in battle, he displayed it now; if anyone had killed an enemy with a lance, he held it in his hand during the ceremony. Four singers without headdresses beat hand drums while the performers danced in the lodge. After a while, one of the four leaders would rush out of the lodge, followed at intervals by the rest of the dancers and then by the four singers. The last one to emerge was a boy called Buffalo Boy, who wore a buffalo-calf headdress. Everyone trotted to a first halting place and performed his dance publicly there. A recital of war and raid deeds also took place. In recognition of special bravery, one of the horns of a man's headdress might then be painted white. Each man carried a muzzle-loader, loaded only with powder, and while dancing they would shoot at one another. It is assumed that the performance was repeated four times, after which the group disbanded.[12]

The Whelp Society
In the Whelp group there were four leaders, chosen for their bravery, and a crier. When these agreed to have a dance, the members were called together. All painted their bodies red. The badge of the society was a coyote or wolf skin worn around the neck. For decoration, porcupine quillwork was placed around the wolf's eyes, the paws were wrapped with flannel and a buckskin fringe was attached to the jaw. Four drummers sat with hand-drums in the center, and the performers danced around them.[13]

The Duck Society
The Duck society had four leaders, each bearing a flattened stick or club about three feet long, painted yellow and fringed with feathers. The handle was carved into a round knob. A similar club was borne by the herald. The herald's main duty was to announce to the members that a dance would be held on a certain afternoon or evening. A dance lodge was erected; the performers dressed up within it, then filed out of the lodge and performed their dance outdoors in public. In marching out, the leaders preceded the rank and file and the drummers came last. The group marched around the camp-circle, halted four times, returned to their starting point and then disbanded. New members were selected by the leaders, but instead of exacting initiation payments, the old members presented gifts to the novices.

Lowie reports that an informant was able to recollect the names of a considerable number of additional societies, though he was unable to give further information concerning them. The names of these were Little-dog, One-foot dance, Crow-owner, Crow-dance, Striped-dance, Blackening-dance, Circle-dance, Big-horse dance, Dance without blankets, Night-dance and Big dogs.[14]

The Bear Cult

John Ewers makes extensive reference to the Assiniboine Bear cult, having received his information from Henry Black Tail, a full-blooded member of the tribe although not a cult member.[15]

The group was composed of a small number of men who had obtained supernatural bear power through dreams. This power was not transferred to others, ceasing when a cult member died. As bears were feared, so too the cult members were held in awe. The members were also ill-tempered, for they were usually unlucky—as were bears—and that constant knowledge or curse had its inevitable effect.

The adornment of cult members was striking to say the least. Except for the hair that was rolled into two balls and tied on top to represent bears' ears, the top of the head was shaved. The face was painted red, and vertical scratches were made in the wet paint by drawing the fingers through it to represent claw marks. A black circle was painted around each eye and the mouth. The shirt was most unusual. It was made in typical fashion but painted yellow and then perforated all over with round or diamond-shaped holes. Fringe was added to the shirt hem and sleeve ends. In the middle of the chest of the shirt, a hole was cut on three sides to make a small rectangular flap that hung down.

Cult members wore a bear claw necklace over the shirt. When going on a raid or war party or during cult ceremonies, they carried in a large sheath a beautifully sculptured flat knife of the stabber type with a broad double-edged blade. The handle was made of either wood or a bear's jawbone. Members also carried shields with bear symbols painted on the front.

Bear men painted bears on their tipis, usually over a yellow ochre background, with a broad band of black paint at the top or smoke-flap area.

At cult ceremonies, Bear members sang Bear songs but did not eat bear meat. Ceremonial bear hunts would be enacted at various times by individual members for the benefit of the spectators in a camp. In battle, the cult member wore his entire bear outfit and sacred paint. Like the bear, his attacks were ferocious and were accompanied by the "noises of an angry bear."

Cult members doctored sick people with the same herbs used by the bears to cure their ills. They learned about these by following sick bears to herb sources. Since the members did not wear their outfits during a curing ceremony and since the rites were always performed in secret, nothing is known of them.

16
THE OTHER NATIONS

Assiniboine Bear cult member wearing perforated hide shirt and bear claw necklace. His hair is rolled into two balls and tied to represent bears' ears.

Ojibway Windigokan cult members in costume for public performance. Detail of face masks at top of illustration (AMNH).

Since a number of the Plains tribes either did not have society or cult complexes comparable to those just treated or else had orders about which relatively little is known, we can group these in a single chapter, giving a brief treatment to the dances or organizations of these tribes most pertinent to this volume.

THE OJIBWAY

The Plains Ojibway was a small Algonkian tribe that had formerly resided in the woodlands. It eventually moved out onto the northernmost plains in pursuit of the buffalo.

Its general council was composed of proven warriors, who in turn selected a single chief. The proven warriors, called Strong-hearted men, also maintained order in the camp and policed the buffalo hunts. Age was not a factor of membership. These also constituted the main warrior force of the tribe.

A group commanding special interest among the Ojibway was the Windigokan or Cannibal cult. These acted much like the Thunder dreamers of the Sioux in that they acted backwards, healed the sick and exorcised the demons of disease. When a sick person was to be healed, the entire troop was called to the patient's lodge. Here they pounded their rattles on the ground while singing, whistling and dancing. They approached, looked at the sufferer, ran away and approached again, using all manner of grotesque and fantastic actions, until at last the demons of ill health were frightened away.

Windigokans made for themselves a costume of rags with an ominous mask, usually having an enormous hooked, beaklike nose, the whole of which was daubed with red paint. They also carried whistles and branched staffs adorned with leaves, feathers, cloth and deer hoof rattles.

In public performances this group acted as clowns, bringing a great deal of pleasure to their delighted audiences.[1]

THE PAWNEE

The Pawnee had a complex scheme of religiously oriented societies, but their nature was such that they need not be extensively treated here; they deserve separate coverage. Each had its own regalia and war duties similar in a general way to those of the other Plains nations. James R. Murie sets forth the following list of societies, and some of the society regalia is illustrated:[2]

The Bundle Societies	*The Private Organizations*
Two Lance	Crazy Horse
Skidi Red Lance	Children of the Iruska
Red Lance	Wonderful Ravens
Thunderbird Lance	Big Horse
Crow Lance	Society of Crows
Brave Raven	Roached Heads
Fighting Lance	Young Dog
Wolf Lance	Mischievous
Black Heads	Organized War Party
Knife Lance	Women's

Medicine-men's Societies

The Twenty-Day Ceremony	Blood Doctors
The Bear Society	The Iruska
Buffalo Doctors	The One Horn Dance
The Deer Society	

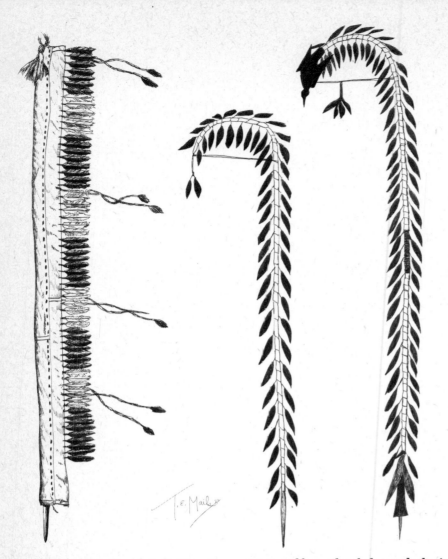

Pawnee society lances. Left: *Two Lance society emblem—the cloth is red, the feathers are white goose and black crow, the pendant feathers are crow and the tuft at the top is owl;* middle: *Crow society emblem—shaft is wrapped with buffalo skin, to which crow feathers are fastened;* right: *Brave Raven emblem—a crow skin is mounted at the hooked end, the staff feathers are crow* (AMNH).

Pawnee society emblems. Above left: *Pipe of Two Lance society—bowl is of red stone marked with black bands;* above right: *Rattle of Red Lance society with rawhide head and eagle feather pendants;* bottom: *Raven Braves society bustle—upright sticks are wrapped with porcupine quills and tufted with horse-hair, pendants are wolf tails and strings of crow feathers* (AMNH).

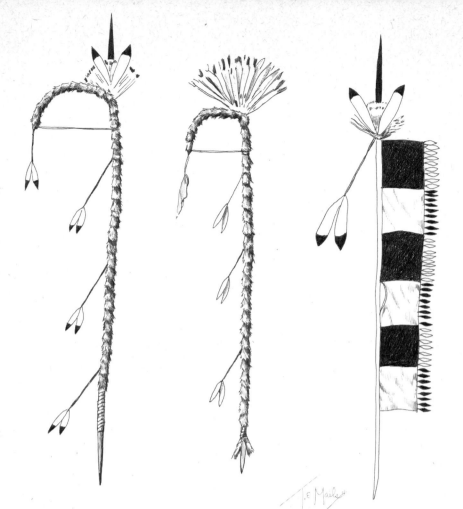

Pawnee society emblems. Left: *Fighting society lance—shaft is wrapped with swan skin, pendants are eagle feathers, iron point is nested in owl and eagle feathers;* middle: *Black Head lance—shaft is wrapped with swan skin, crown is of raven feathers, pendant feathers are crow, buffalo tail hangs from the end of hook;* right: *Knife Lance lance—shaft is trimmed with strouding with alternating bands of red and black, top and pendant are eagle feathers* (AMNH).

Pawnee society emblems. Left: *Red society lance—shaft wrapped with otter skin, grip wrapped with bear gut, all trim feathers are golden eagle;* middle: *Red Lance society lance—shaft wrapped with swan skin, all pendants are buffalo tail;* right: *Wolf Lance society lance—shaft wrapped with wolf skin, two wolf tail pendants at point end, crown of owl feathers, eagle tail feather pendants* (AMNH).

Shoshone Wolf Dancers performing (SM).

Shoshone Deer Dance headdress (MAI).

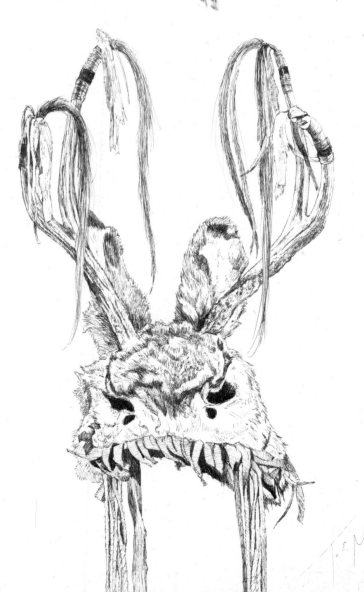

358

THE SHOSHONE

The Wind River Shoshone did not have a society complex as such. They did have a dance that the Whites called the Wolf dance, or sometimes the War dance. The Shoshone, however, did not connect it with the wolf. One informant thought the name might have been derived from the fact that the leader's quirt was decorated with a coyote tail. The dance as practiced toward the turn of the century was identical with the Grass dance of the other tribes, although the Shoshone did not eat dog meat at its conclusion. Some performers wore war-bonnets and feather dance bustles.[3]

THE UTE

The Ute Dog company was the only institution comparable to the Plains societies. It consisted of a number of men and one woman. Members wore a distinctive necklace made from a slit wolf skin. Like dogs, they were to give the alarm to the people whenever enemies approached. They scouted and patrolled at night. When the camp moved, the Dogs brought up the rear. They were always on foot on such occasions.

Dogs attempted to imitate the animal from which they derived their name. They usually ate raw meat, and when they bled from a wound, they tried to lick up the blood, dog-fashion.[4]

THE SARSI

Along with other phases of Plains culture, the Sarsi acquired certain societies, the functions of which were partly social, partly religious and partly military. The following groups are named by Earl P. Goddard:

Mosquitoes
Tawó [a small yellow bird found in sloughs]
Dogs
Preventers
Black-painted-ones
Dogs Reckless

Each society had one, two or four leaders who wore distinctive regalia. Membership was obtained by purchase. Having sold his membership, a man proceeded to join another society. Sarsi societies are not properly described as age societies, but for most men the Mosquitoes were the first step. Each spring or summer the societies pitched their lodges inside the camp-circle and engaged in dancing, a notable feature of which consisted of rushing forth to harass the spectators in a manner suggestive of the name of the society.

All societies except the Mosquitoes and Tawó had camp and military duties. They preserved order in large encampments, especially during the Sun Dance, and had the right to destroy the tipis and clothing of those who resisted or disobeyed them. The Reckless Dogs were pledged never to retreat from an enemy while a companion was in danger.[5]

THE CREE

Large Cree camps were policed by a fraternity corresponding to the Soldiers of the Plains Indians. To test a potential member, they

would cut his clothing to pieces. If he took the chastisement in good spirit, laughing and joking, they would show their appreciation by calling him to their lodge where, after a dance, each of them would give him a garment, so that he departed with more than he had lost. The Soldiers had, in the center of the summer camp, a lodge so long that it required two or three fires. There they spent most of their time singing and dancing.

Men who had performed any one of certain valorous deeds were called Strong-hearted men. These were greatly esteemed and occupied positions of honor at all ceremonies and public gatherings. On such occasions they recited their warlike accomplishments, after having frequently given away valuable possessions in order to demonstrate their greatness and their superiority to ordinary men.[6]

THE WICHITA

The Wichita had fourteen known dance societies, but much information regarding them was lost in the transition of the tribe from their early state, so that while some of their ceremonies survived, of others little or nothing is now known.

The first was the Deer dance, in which all societies were welcome to dance and show their "powers."

Similarly, in the Doctor dance, which was borrowed from the Pawnee, all societies might dance if they wished. As the name implied, the medicine doctors and their pupils appeared in the dance.

Anyone could join in the war dance, but only members of the

360

Shoshone Wolf Dancer wearing crow bustle and roach headdress (SM).

group could sing their war songs. The members did not act as camp police.

When the Gift dance was held, the participants visited every house, telling in song what they desired. The families then rewarded them with gifts.

The men had five other dance societies, but only four of the names are known. These were the Horn dance, the Buffalo Bear, the Big Dog or the Many Dogs and the Mythic Animal of the Mountains.

There were three dance societies for the women. The ritual of the first, the Fancy Woman dance, is lost. In the Turkey dance, the women circled about a pole decorated with a scalp, while a man sang for them. The Flat dance was similar, but the women sang themselves. At the end the leader would sing four songs and then all would run to the river to bathe, the leader going last.[7]

THE OTO

The Oto had several societies for both men and women. Of these two were of first importance: the Buffalo and the Otter. These were even a part of the political organization and indeed the power behind the council. Each clan chief belonged to one society or the other. Prospective members of either had to be men of high moral standing, and they were usually under observation for some time by the members of the societies before being invited to join. A man might himself ask to become a member and to be voted upon, in which case also he was closely watched. An applicant might fail to be elected at one time but

Ute warrior holding wooden musical instrument, called rasp, a bone stick, detail at right shows two items more clearly. One end of stick was placed on a gourd or piece of rawhide set on the ground. This served as a resonator when the stick was rubbed back and forth over the notches (SM).

later become eligible for membership upon proving his worth in battle.

Each society had initiation rites, accompanied by feasting and dancing, and four degrees of membership, each characterized by its own particular clothing, painting and songs, which grew in depth and meaning as the rites progressed. The members who had passed into the final degree selected the head of the society. Complete secrecy was demanded, and the death penalty was inflicted on anyone who violated this stricture. Each society had its own sacred bundle, which was in the custody of the head members, as other hands were believed to lessen its power. This was especially likely if the bundle were to be touched by a woman. The main object of each society was to foster men of worth, hence it was said that all members were persons of special standing in the tribe. A particular function of the Buffalo society was that of counseling or offering economic aid to people in need, illness or other distress and to teach moral living, whereas the Otter society was mainly concerned with the doctoring of the sick. Therefore, the Otter society always included more medicine men than the Buffalo society.

Besides the various dance societies, there was one that was purely social in nature, called the Red Bean. The women had a Drinking Water society, which was charitable in nature, especially toward old and recently widowed women.[8]

THE COMANCHE

362

The Comanche did not develop soldier societies. Most of their

Ute warriors retreating after an engagement. Warrior at left has the demanding obligation to stand and face the enemy while the rest flee. Certain of the officers of many Plains societies were faced with this perilous duty as a requirement of their office (DPL).

Comanche war leader wearing renowned feather bonnet signifying his office (SM).

warrior groups appear to have been informal organizations resulting from mutual friendships and interests, and they were not continuous or permanent. Although not formally organized into an association, the wearers of full-feathered warbonnets formed a special class called war leaders.

According to Wallace, the buffalo-scalp bonnet wearers were of a lower order. This headdress was decorated with a row of eagle feathers, with breast feathers tied about the bottom of the quills and reaching to the waist of the wearer. A bunch of magpie feathers was set at the rear center of the cap. The bonnet could be worn by any warrior who felt worthy of it and desired to accept the responsibility it imposed. There was no ceremonial bestowal. Usually it was made by friends of the warrior and presented to him as a token of esteem. This meant that the acceptance of a buffalo bonnet was a serious matter, for the bearer was expected to prove himself worthy of the givers' confidence. Failure meant ridicule and disgrace. After the surrender of the Comanche at Fort Sill, Gets-to-Be-a-Middle-aged-Man hung his buffalo-scalp bonnet in a tree, never to wear it again. "A man who is beaten has no right to wear such a thing," he said.[9]

A Comanche war leader could retreat only under certain conditions and then only when the other warriors were safe. The feathered warbonnet was to be protected at all costs, and the war leader became a rallying point for all other fighters. Should a war chief fail to measure up to his responsibilities, any other war chief who observed his disloyalty could publicly denounce him, causing him to lose his position and right to wear the warbonnet if he were judged guilty. If a war-

Top right: *Kiowa buffalo hide, horned headdress from Harvey collection;* bottom: *Comanche eagle feather headdress with beaded headband and ermine side fringes. Both styles typical of the headdresses of the tribes.*

bonnet wearer lost or cast off his bonnet and fled from the field, he forfeited his right to wear it, and all other men would address him thereafter as "elder sister." This was an opportunity for any warrior who wished to become the war leader, for he could do so by simply dashing in and recovering the bonnet. He then hung it by custom on a bush and defended it there all day if necessary in the face of the enemy. If after this he charged the enemy four times at sundown, the bonnet and all its honors and obligations became his. A lower-rank bonnet could also be picked up by any one who saw it and was willing to assume its obligations.

Those warriors in the northern Comanche bands who had not reached the high rank of warbonnet wearers sometimes banded together into semimilitary orders or dance groups. Among these were the Crow, the Shield, the Big Horse, the Little Pony, the Fox, the Buffalo, the Gourd and the Drum. A young man usually joined the group of his brother or father, but he could join any order he chose. If the group were willing to accept him, he was admitted. There was keen rivalry among the organizations to secure men with the greatest potential. Sometimes the ritual pipe was even forced into the mouth of a prospective member. Members became like brothers, going on raids and war parties together and sharing in the burial and mourning of a dead fellow member. Each group had its own regalia, songs and dances, and these could not be used by anyone else. Their dances were private, and no one could attend except by invitation. Most dances were held immediately before the departure of a war group or following its return. Some were performed at the time of the communal buffalo hunt. When a member decided to lead a revenge raid, he could usually count on his own group to support him, although other warriors were welcome to join the affair. And when a leader had the support of the majority of the members of his dance order, the War dance preceding the departure was referred to by the name of his group.

In general, the Comanche orders were much alike. The members of the Shield group carried identical shields, which had been inspired by a vision. The shields were sacred, and among the many requirements for handling them was that they not touch the ground. The Crow Tassel wearers wore a special type of warbonnet made of fine feathers clipped short, except for one large feather trimmed to scalloped edges. They also placed a tassel on the left shoulder and one in the hair, reciting as they did so the Crow Tassel pledge to dedicate themselves to the unceasing defense of their people. A man who had no surviving family or who had a family tradition of a fighting reputation to uphold were logical candidates for membership. Such men recognized that they had left all family ties behind and that loyalty to the group was their only obligation. They fought and raided together with such singleness of mind and purpose that they stood apart from the rest. Yet they were free to dissolve the band whenever they wished. If they had been successful in raids and war, they soon became the leading men in their communities.

Among the Comanche were a few "crazy" warriors who did everything backwards. Any man brave enough could become a Crazy simply by deciding to do so. He carried a buffalo scrotum rattle in his hand and would go about the camp singing, no matter what else might be going on. Everything he did was performed backwards, but no one ever corrected him, for he was clearly a very brave man. Every Crazy wore a long war sash over his shoulder and held its free end rolled up under his arm. In a battle whose outcome was in doubt, he rolled out his sash and secured the free end to the ground with an arrow, taking his stand there. With a bow in one hand and his rattle in the other, he sang his songs until victory was won or death took him. Only a member friend could free him, for if he gave way in battle or even released himself after the fight was over, "the other warriors would taunt him in an attempt to egg him into an overt act against them so they could kill him." [10] Obviously there were never many such men among the Comanche at any one time.

THE KIOWA AND KIOWA APACHE

According to Mooney, the warrior organization of the Kiowa was called Soldiers and consisted of six orders, each of which had its own dance, songs and ceremonial dress.[11]

These organizations were as follows:

Rabbits. These were boys and young men from eight to fifteen years of age. Their dance, in which they were drilled by certain old men, had a peculiar step, in imitation of the jumping movement of a rabbit. They leaped up and down without lateral change of position and held their hands to their ears, moving them and imitating rabbit sounds. A strip of elk hide and an erect feather were worn in the hair.

Young Mountain Sheep, literally "Herders or Corralers."
Horse Headdress (?) people.
(?) Black-leg people.
Skunkberry (?) people.

Principal Dogs or Real Dogs. These last were the highest warrior order and also served as the camp police, combining the functions of the Lance Men and the Dog Men of the Arapaho organization. "Their two leaders carried an arrow-shaped lance, with which they anchored themselves at the very front of a battle by means of buckskin straps brought over the shoulders. The Black-leg people captains carried in a similar way a crook-shaped lance, called pabo'n, similar to that of the Spear men of the Arapaho." [12]

Lowie lists six men's societies "of recent times": the Rabbits, the Shepherds, the Rulers of Horses, the Berries, the Black Feet and the Horses. He also mentions two women's orders: the Old Women society and a Bear society. In addition, he found evidence of an ancient men's society called Kiowa's Bone. The leader represented a buffalo cow and each of the members a buffalo bull. If in a battle the leader stood his ground, all the others were obliged to do the same, even at the risk of death. "Thus all of them were killed, and the people were afraid so that they no longer kept up the organization." [13]

The Rabbits were comprised of all the boys of the tribe, while the Real Dogs or Horses were superior to the others, being composed exclusively of eminent warriors. The four middle groups were of equal rank, varying only according to the merit or reputation of the officers at any particular time. Thus the societies of the Kiowa were not graded, and a young man could join any one of these. Some men never advanced beyond the status of Rabbit, for if they were not considered the right sort, they were not asked to join the other groups; except for the Rabbits, however, age had nothing to do with membership. Mem-

bership in the societies was not purchased, and the orders did not offer gifts to individuals sought as members.

The Kiowa societies met only during the period between a Sun Dance announcement and the Sun Dance itself. Lowie points out that this interval varied greatly in length, the announcement sometimes being made very soon after the consummation of the preceding Sun ceremony and at other times only immediately before the performance was to take place. During the period so defined, the societies met frequently, one member inviting the others one day for a feast and the rest following suit on other days. The Real Dogs met less frequently than the rest. There was no rivalry among the groups, although at the time of the Sun Dance any two orders might engage in a kicking contest, the object of which was to teach young boys to stand and fight during a battle. At the time of the Sun Dance itself, a holy man would appoint one of the societies to cut and bring in the sacred tree, and a holy man would also choose one of them to police a tribal hunt.

Each society had two leaders and two whip bearers; these four controlled the behavior of their groups.

Not much is known about the individual orders, but a few notes about each will help those researching old photographs to identify to which order a man might have belonged.

The two Shepherd leaders carried long flat sticks about the length of a man's arm, carved with figures and bearing a pendant skin and a wrist-loop. Lowie says these emblems were shared by the leaders of all the coordinate groups. If one of the leaders arose and put the loop of his stick round his wrist, all the members had to do likewise and dance.[14]

366

Kiowa society members bearing war shields, lances and other weapons (DPL).

The Rulers of Horses leaders carried the two sticks and also used rattles and drums.

The Black Feet had a hooked lance that belonged to one officer. It was wrapped with beaver skin, painted with different colors and tied with pairs of eagle feathers along the shaft and at the tip of the crooked part. In a battle, this lance was to be planted in the ground.

The Berries members had rattles, originally made of rawhide and either spherical or square in shape but later made of baking-powder cans. Two leaders carried the sticks. There was one arrow as long as a lance. If the man carrying it were killed, the arrow was buried with him and a new one was made for the next owner. The arrow was decorated with eagle feathers, and both they and the entire shaft were painted red.

Membership in the highest military order, the Real Dogs or Horses, was restricted to the bravest warriors in the tribe. In age they ranged from twenty-five years old upward. The number seems to have varied from about ten to forty members. It was their duty to lead the most dangerous charges, and they were not allowed to retreat in battle. Around their necks the members wore a rawhide sash, later of red trade cloth, which was long enough to drag along the ground at the man's right side. Mooney distinguishes three types of sash: the leader's, which was of elk skin, colored black; three of red cloth; six of elk skin dyed red. An owner might lend his sash to another man, but on the more important raids he was required to wear it himself. In battle it was the leader's duty to dismount in front of his comrades, thrust his lance (Newcomb calls it a ceremonial arrow) through a hole in the elk skin into the ground and then to remain in this spot throughout the battle.[15] The other Real Dogs then had to do the same. If they were defeated and forced to retreat, members of the Real Dogs could pull the leader's lance from the ground. Otherwise he might not be freed and was often lost. After this another warrior from the Real Dogs was chosen to take his place. All the Real Dogs carried lances, which were very long, some being ten feet or more, with long, narrow steel points. The shafts were wrapped with spirals of rawhide strips in alternating colors.

The leader's sacred sash and lance were used, however, only when an embroiled group of Dogs was prepared to fight to the bitter end. He could join war parties as an ordinary warrior by not wearing the sash, and he might even lend the black sash to another warrior when he was not going along. However, he had to take part in important war parties lest he be called a coward and be removed from his high position. When any Real Dog became too old to go to war, he resigned and passed his sash on to a worthy young warrior.

The ceremonial paint of the Dogs was red, and face, clothes and regalia were covered with it. The leaders did not carry the flat sticks but had red-painted dew claw rattles, the wooden handles being attached to the surface of a rawhide sphere. They also carried eagle bone whistles painted red.

The Kiowa Apaches' ceremonial organization was a reflection of the Kiowas' and was probably borrowed wholesale from them. The Kiowa Apaches had four ceremonial groups—a children's society known as the Rabbits, two adult warrior or military societies and a society for old women. All male children belonged to the Rabbit society, but on growing up they frequently did not join the adult societies because membership carried with it heavy and unwanted responsibilities.

For women there were but two societies. Membership in the Old Women was by invitation, and only mature women were members. They met for feasts—a woman became a member by giving four feasts—and they danced at one point in the Sun Dance. Warriors prayed to them before battle, promising to give a feast if they were successful. Women members selected their daughters or other close kinswomen for successors. The Old Women danced in a circle and had a drum. Even less is known about the Bear Women, the second society. This may have been primarily a religious society, since it was a secret or semisecret group, and people were "afraid" of them. In dancing, they imitated the motions of bears with their hands. No outsiders were allowed to watch when they held a dance.

In addition to the dancing or warrior societies, there were a number of little-known religious societies. These included the Crazy Dogs, a society of great warriors; the Buffalo Doctors, who treated wounds and diseases associated with blood; the Eagle Shields, a doctors' society that treated diseases by sleight-of-hand and other magical measures; and the Sun Dance Shields, who guarded both the sacred Sun Dance doll and its keeper.

Kiowa society members enjoying a social meeting; note shields, headdresses and staff wrapped with white swan skin (DPL).

17

DISSOLUTION AND RENEWAL

Since nearly everything about the important societies and cults has been set forth in the previous chapters, it is necessary only to pull together a few thoughts in conclusion.

According to White authorities and Indian informants, a substantial number of the Plains organizations had their legendary origins in the earliest history of the people and thus were a regular part of their life-way as it evolved over the centuries. These were undoubtedly religious or hunting orders, since war as a way of life came very late to the tribes. Other units were added along the way as founders had their visions and dreams, the majority coming into being during the years of White settlement. In other words, the climate for dreams and visions intensified considerably under the ever-increasing pressures resulting from the need for defense, relocation and barest survival, and it led quite naturally to the founding of numerous societies and cults.

It is clear that the societies and cults came to be an indispensable factor of life during the years from 1750 to 1850.

Authorities have sifted at length through the available information on the age-graded and the non-graded orders of all the tribes in what has proved to be a vain attempt to explain how and why the differences between them came into being. In my view there is definite reason to favor the explanation of a religious foundation's accounting for the difference in structure, suggesting simply that each type was put forward by God in visions as the more productive approach for those who received such visions. In further favor of the age-graded scheme, it evidently served the different age groups more effectively than the non-graded structure could. Each lower-grade order in particular was able to function within its own peer group and had just enough older advisers to provide both curbs when necessary and experienced guides. The regular steps from one society to the next appear also to have led to a greater variety and distinction in regalia for identification purposes—although since a man in the non-graded complex could join any of the available societies, the overall competition did lead to numerous innovations to tempt the candidates.

It might be worthwhile now, after considering the Plains organizations in detail, to review their involved list of functions as set forth in Chapter 2, "The Nature of the Warrior Societies." They:

- preserved order in the camp
- preserved order during camp moves
- preserved order during hunts
- punished offenders against the public welfare
- guarded the camp against possible attacks by an enemy, both at the camp and while moving
- kept the camp informed at all times as to the movements of the buffalo herds
- fostered intersociety rivalry to cultivate bravery and a military spirit among themselves, and among the boys who needed a living example of their future responsibilities
- took the commanding and most dangerous places in battle
- ministered to the desires of members for recreation through feasts and dances
- served as keepers and reminders of the tribe's heritage and traditions
- played a unique intermediary role in government by serving as the active but temporary dispensers of authority
- served as creative display centers where recognition was given for honors earned by warriors and women's guild workers for tasks well done on behalf of the tribe

The cults, for their part, acted as more specialized units of grace—mediums through which God dispensed His supernatural power to the people in circumscribed areas for instruction, healing, prophecy, ensurance and hope.

In examining their exciting details, one surely sees how creative and profound the Plains orders were. Clearly, they were not so battle-oriented as many authorities have made them out to be, since their activities reached deeply into every aspect of Indian life. Thus it is impossible to avoid admitting they engendered virtues that would do credit to any people wishing to live a responsible life. The high quality of purity demanded of the Cheyenne Inverted Warriors and the primary aim of the Arikara Straight-head society to aid the poor are but typical characteristics of the groups of all the Plains nations. And it gives them an elevated stature that has seldom received the honor due it.

One is deeply impressed too with the creativeness shown in costume, regalia, paint and ceremonies. The immense variety leads one almost to forget that they worked with an incredibly limited supply of primary materials—mainly the buffalo but also other animals, birds, grass, wood, nature's pigments and a few trade items—which they turned into enthralling products of unlimited function.

Ute warriors who are "brothers" by virtue of the special ceremony for that purpose, a common rite in many tribes.

Just as clearly evident is a rich sense of Indian balance and humor, in that many societies and cults included moments in their performances that encouraged the utmost fun and happiness for everyone present. One need only remove these instances from the accounts to imagine what life on the demanding Plains would have been like without the organizations.

It is apparent in retrospect that while the societies were not war-based in the beginning, they quickly became so when driven to it during the historical period. Just as they became fully developed, the future of the nations came into sharp question, and the warrior societies rose to challenge in a measure that cannot help but command respect when one knows the insurmountable odds that confonted them. Then the orders became the cohesive forces of each nation. They were the rallying points, the centers of hope, and they led the charges and stands against the foe. It was the very tenacity of the sash- and belt-wearers that became the symbol of a people who likewise decided they would rather die than be broken.

Die they did. Men, women and children together. But we know now that they did not die out.

It is not difficult to understand why the White politicians and military leaders wanted first to suppress the societies and then to eliminate them whenever possible. Hence these were the first to feel the cruel bit as the reservations were established and military supervision was increasingly tightened. By 1840, many societies were already phasing out under the relentless menace of starvation, army guns and severe restrictions. Then with total subjugation came the loss of purpose. What that didn't crush the White man's diseases did. By 1890, the more important groups of many Plains nations had been gone so long that it was difficult to find either a living member or a reliable secondhand informant. From 1875 on, there was, within most of the organizations that did survive, a general shift from a religious and war focus to a merely social purpose, although several Cheyenne societies continued to play vital roles in the principal tribal ceremonies. In the same measure, the cults were disappearing, too, and the craft guilds were gradually losing their force and skills.

Some groups struggled on in the midst of terrible hardships; the Cheyenne Wolf Men were still going through the motions in the early 1900s and a few Crow orders continued to perform ceremonies in the 1930s, as did some of the Blackfoots societies that attempted to survive.

Since the importance of the societies and cults has not been forgotten by those Indians whose roots are buried deep in the rich heritage of their people, there have been frequent attempts to revive some of the defunct organizations. The attempt of the Ponca, beginning in 1958, to bring the old War or Ghost order to life is but an example of this. Dancing itself has remained as a continuing source of cultural identity. When Indian men became United States soldiers during World War II and in Korea and Vietnam, Omaha and Scalp dances were commonly held in their honor. The Sioux maintain a Round dance that is still performed and featured a Rabbit dance from 1925 to 1960.

In the southeastern Plains area in particular, the annual events of the numerous tribes living there center around revivals of the ancient societies. It is also well known among the Indians that many orders and ceremonies are being resurrected and conducted in secret all over America, as indeed they should be in the face of what has happened

Opposite: *Ute chief greeting unseen White explorers with typical warm friendship.*

Ute warriors reminiscing at famous battlefields of yesterday where they had fought so hard to preserve their life-way and homeland—and lost both!

to them in the past. Sacred and awesome Sioux Yuwipi shaking spirit ceremonies are practiced even today in remote and hidden places on the Pine Ridge reservation in South Dakota. In short, as the Indian nations seek their renaissance, the leaders are aware that the old societies and cults might still hold the key to future success. God worked in a marvelous way through them before, and they believe He will again—once they have listened closely enough to Him to learn precisely how He wishes them to do so.

How profoundly their religion was expressed in thought, word and deed! After a close look at them, one wonders whether any people have ever been nearer to the true, living God. And if they are His and if others have done badly by them, what then on the Day of accounting? When the renowned White authority John G. Neihardt, who recorded the fascinating life story of the Sioux holy man Black Elk, was interviewed on television a short time ago, he made an observation vital to a comprehension of the Indian life-way. As he spoke about the brilliant Chief Crazy Horse, he pointed out that the White man's translations of Indian names were more often than not exceedingly poor. The Sioux word that had been interpreted as meaning "crazy" really meant "enchanted," so that his name was really "Enchanted Horse." One immediately sees the enormous and portentous difference! When that truth is applied to the "crazy" societies and cults of the various tribes, one quickly sees why, though they seemed so odd on the surface, the Indian people accorded them the greatest respect. Indeed, the society and cult members were, in their totality, the enchanted people of God.

NOTES

Notes to Chapter 1

1. Edward S. Curtis, *The North American Indian*, 6: 23–24.
2. Ibid., 6: 192–93.
3. E. Adamson Hoebel and Karl N. Llewellyn, *The Cheyenne Way*, pp. 39–44.
4. James Epes Brown, *The Spiritual Legacy of the American Indian*, pp. 8, 16–21.
5. Ibid., p. 83.
6. Margot Liberty and John Stands In Timber, *Cheyenne Memories*, pp. 11–26.
7. Curtis, *The North American Indian*, 3: 60.
8. Frank B. Linderman, *Plenty Coups*, pp. 78–79, 228, 242.
9. Black Elk, *The Sacred Pipe*, ed. Joseph Epes Brown, pp. 13–14.
10. Althea Bass, *The Arapaho Way*, p. 73.
11. James Howard, *The Ponca Tribe*, p. 19.
12. Curtis, *The North American Indian*, 18: 196.
13. Walter McClintock, *The Old North Trail*, p. 89.
14. Brown, *Spiritual Legacy*, pp. 5–6.
15. Clark Wissler, *Red Man Reservations*, pp. 296–297, and John C. Ewers, *The Horse In Blackfoot Indian Culture*, pp. 337–39.
16. Brown, *Spiritual Legacy*, pp. 5–6.
17. Ibid., p. 17.
18. Black Elk, *The Sacred Pipe*, p. xx.
19. Frances Densmore, *Teton Sioux Music*, p. 172.
20. Margot Liberty and John Stands In Timber, *Cheyenne Memories*, pp. 184–85.
21. Linderman, *Plenty Coups*, p. 275.
22. Brown, *Spiritual Legacy*, p. 21.
23. Helen H. Blish, *A Pictographic History of the Oglala Sioux*, p. 40.
24. Densmore, *Teton Sioux Music*, p. 157.
25. Ibid., pp. 157–58.
26. Blish, *A Pictographic History*, p. 433.
27. Densmore, *Teton Sioux Music*, pp. 166–68.
28. Ibid., pp. 204–44.
29. Ibid., p. 175.
30. George Bird Grinnell, *The Cheyenne Indians*, 1: 159.

Notes to Chapter 2

1. Robert H. Lowie, *The Crow Indians*, p. 330
2. Frank B. Linderman, *Plenty Coups*, pp. 20–25, 52–53.
3. Frances Densmore, *Teton Sioux Music*, pp. 68–77.
4. Linderman, *Plenty Coups*, p. 53.

Notes to Chapter 3

1. Thomas E. Mails, *The Mystic Warriors of the Plains*, pp. 244–45.
2. Ibid., pp. 56–67.
3. Ibid., pp. 277–282.
4. Black Elk, *The Sacred Pipe*, pp. 36–43.
5. Robert H. Lowie, *The Crow Indians*, p. 198.
6. Alice C. Fletcher and Francis La Flesche, *The Omaha Tribe*, p. 350.
7. Ibid., pp. 352–53.
8. Robert H. Lowie, *The Northern Shoshone*, p. 223.
9. Ernest Royce, *Burbank among the Indians*, p. 154.
10. John C. Ewers, *Plains Indian Painting*, pp. 3–4.
11. Royce, *Burbank among the Indians*, p. 179.

Notes to Chapter 4

1. Robert H. Lowie, *The Assiniboine*, pp. 75–98.
2. Clark Wissler, *Societies and Dance Associations of the Blackfoot Indians*, 11: 359–460.
3. Edward S. Curtis, *The North American Indian*, 6: 17.
4. Ibid., 18: 183.
5. Ibid.
6. Walter McClintock, *Blackfoot Warrior Societies*, 8: 11.
7. Curtis, *The North American Indian*, 6: 17.
8. Ibid., 6: 16–17.
9. Ibid., 6: 18.
10. Ibid., 6: 19.
11. Ibid., 3: 189.
12. McClintock, *Blackfoot Warrior Societies*, p. 16.
13. Curtis, *The North American Indian*, 6: 20.
14. McClintock, *Blackfoot Warrior Societies*, pp 14–15.
15. Ibid., pp. 15–16.
16. Wissler, *Societies and Dance Associations*, pp. 376–77.
17. McClintock, *Blackfoot Warrior Societies*, p. 16.
18. Wissler, *Societies and Dance Associations*, p. 377.
19. McClintock, *Blackfoot Warrior Societies*, p. 12.
20. Ibid.

21. Curtis, *The North American Indian*, 6: 21.
22. McClintock, *Blackfoot Warrior Societies*, p. 13.
23. Curtis, *The North American Indian*, 6: 21.
24. McClintock, *Blackfoot Warrior Societies*, p. 19.
25. Ibid.
26. Ibid., pp. 21–22.
27. Ibid., p. 22.
28. Ibid., p. 23.
29. Ibid.
30. Ibid., p. 28.
31. Ibid., pp. 29–30.
32. Curtis, *The North American Indian*, 6: 22.
33. Wissler, *Societies and Dance Associations*, p. 392.
34. Curtis, *The North American Indian*, 18: 189.
35. Wissler, *Societies and Dance Associations*, p. 393.
36. Curtis, *The North American Indian*, 6: 25.
37. Wissler, *Societies and Dance Associations*, p. 395.
38. Curtis, *The North American Indian*, 6: 26.
39. Ibid.
40. Wissler, *Societies and Dance Associations*, p. 399.
41. Curtis, *The North American Indian*, 6: 27.
42. Ibid., 6: 26.
43. Ibid., 6: 26–27.
44. Ibid., 6: 26.
45. McClintock, *Blackfoot Warrior Societies*, p. 18.
46. Curtis, The North American Indian, 18: 189.
47. Ibid.
48. Ibid., 18: 190.
49. Ibid.
50. Ibid.
51. Ibid.
52. Ibid.
53. Ibid.
54. Ibid., 6: 28.
55. Ibid.
56. Ibid., 6: 28–29.
57. Ibid., 6: 29.
58. Wissler, *Societies and Dance Associations*, p. 395.
59. Curtis, *The North American Indian*, 6: 22–24.
60. Ibid., 6:22–23.
61. Wissler, *Societies and Dance Associations*, p. 327.
62. Curtis, *The North American Indian*, 6: 24.
63. Ibid., 18: 190.
64. Wissler, *Societies and Dance Associations*, p. 402.
65. Curtis, *The North American Indian*, 6: 27.
66. Wissler, *Societies and Dance Associations*, p. 404.
67. Curtis, *The North American Indian*, 6: 27.
68. Ibid., 18: 191.
69. Ibid.
70. Wissler, *Societies and Dance Associations*, pp. 412–17.
71. Curtis, *The North American Indian*, 18: 192.
72. Ibid.
73. Ibid.
74. Ibid., 18: 190–91.
75. Ibid., 18: 191.
76. John C. Ewers, *Indian Life on the Upper Missouri*, pp. 139–41.
77. Wissler, *Mythology of the Blackfoot Indians*, pp. 95–98.
78. Curtis, *The North American Indian*, 18: 195.
79. Ibid.
80. Ibid.
81. Ibid., 18: 196.
82. McClintock, *The Old North Trail*, p. 253.
83. Ibid., pp. 253–54.
84. Ibid., pp. 252–53.
85. Ibid., p. 254.
86. Ibid., pp. 257–60.
87. Ibid., p. 200.
88. Wissler, *Societies and Dance Associations*, pp. 451–60.

Notes to Chapter 5

1. Edward S. Curtis, *The North American Indian*, 5: 70–76.
2. Robert H. Lowie, *Societies of the Arikara Indians*, pp. 645–78.
3. Ibid., p. 678.
4. Frances Densmore, *Teton Sioux Music*, p. 315.
5. Curtis, *The North American Indian*, 5: 64–65.
6. Ibid., 5: 67.
7. Ibid., 5: 70–76.
8. Ibid., 5: 68–69.
9. Ibid., 5: 69.
10. Ibid., 5: 69–70.

Notes to Chapter 6
1. Edward S. Curtis, *The North American Indian*, 4: 182.
2. Robert H. Lowie, *Indians of the Plains*, p. 98.
3. Lowie, *Societies of the Hidatsa and Mandan*, p. 223.
4. Ibid., p. 239.
5. Ibid., p. 276.
6. Ibid., p. 281.
7. Ibid., p. 293.

Notes to Chapter 7
1. Edward S. Curtis, *The North American Indian*, 5: 144.
2. Robert H. Lowie, *Societies of the Hidatsa and Mandan*, p. 223.
3. Frances Densmore, *Teton Sioux Music*, pp. 311–18.
4. Ibid.
5. Lowie, *Societies of the Hidatsa and Mandan*, p. 295.
6. Curtis, *The North American Indian*, 5: 14.
7. Lowie, *Societies of the Hidatsa and Mandan*, pp. 295–96.

Notes to Chapter 8
1. Edward S. Curtis, *The North American Indian*, 6: 159.
2. Virginia Cole Trenholm, *The Arapahoes, Our People*, p. 77.
3. James Mooney, *The Ghost Dance Religion*, pp. 986–87.
4. Trenholm, *The Arapahoes*, p. 77.
5. Mooney, *The Ghost Dance Religion*, pp. 987–88.
6. Ibid., p. 988.
7. Ibid., pp. 986–87.
8. Ibid., p. 1033.
9. Ibid., p. 988.
10. Ibid., p. 989.
11. Ibid.
12. Trenholm, *The Arapahoes*, p. 79.
13. Truman Michelson, *Narrative of an Arapaho Woman*, p. 596.
14. Trenholm, *The Arapahoes*, p. 80.
15. Mooney, *Ghost Dance Religion*, p. 989.
16. Trenholm, *The Arapahoes*, p. 80.
17. George A. Dorsey and Alfred L. Kroeber, *Traditions of the Arapaho*, pp. 20–21, 49.
18. Ibid., pp. 49–51.
19. Trenholm, *The Arapahoes*, p. 81.

Notes to Chapter 9
1. Edward S. Curtis, *The North American Indian*, 5: 113.
2. Ibid.
3. Ibid., 5: 113–14.
4. Ibid., 5: 114.
5. Ibid., 5: 116–17.
6. Ibid., 5: 116.
7. Ibid., 5: 117–18.
8. Ibid., 5: 118.
9. Ibid.

Notes to Chapter 10
1. John R. Swanton, *The Indian Tribes of North America*, p. 145.
2. Frances Densmore, *Teton Sioux Music*, p. 284.
3. Ibid., p. 313.
4. Clark Wissler, *Societies and Ceremonial Organizations in the Oglala Division of the Teton-Dakota*, pp. 1–100.
5. Densmore, *Teton Sioux Music*, p. 313.
6. Ibid., p. 314.
7. Ibid., p. 313.
8. Edward S. Curtis, *The North American Indian*, 3: 12–13.
9. Ibid.
10. Ibid., 3: 14.
11. Ibid.
12. Royal B. Hassrick, *The Sioux*, pp. 25–27.
13. James Howard, *The Ponca Tribe*, pp. 112, 137.
14. Densmore, *Teton Sioux Music*, p. 330.
15. Ibid., p. 326.
16. Helen H. Blish, *A Pictographic History of the Oglala Sioux*, p. 107.
17. Densmore, *Teton Sioux Music*, p. 327.
18. Ibid., p. 328.
19. Blish, *A Pictographic History*, p. 329.
20. Densmore, *Teton Sioux Music*, p. 329.
21. Blish, *A Pictographic History*, p. 107.
22. Densmore, *Teton Sioux Music*, p. 382.
23. Ibid., p. 395.
24. Ibid., p. 327.
25. Blish, *A Pictographic History*, p. 106.

26. Densmore, *Teton Sioux Music*, p. 315.
27. Ibid., p. 30.
28. Ibid.
29. Ibid.
30. Ibid., p. 317.
31. Ibid., p. 385.
32. Ibid., p. 365.
33. Blish, *A Pictographic History*, p. 114.
34. Ibid.
35. Ibid., p. 115.
36. Howard, *The Ponca Tribe*, p. 783.
37. Densmore, *Teton Sioux Music*, p. 318.
38. Ibid.
39. Ibid., p. 319.
40. Wissler, *Oglala Societies*, p. 25.
41. Densmore, *Teton Sioux Music*, p. 320.
42. Ibid., p. 319.
43. Ibid., p. 384.
44. Ibid., p. 394.
45. Ibid., p. 318.
46. Blish, *A Pictographic History*, pp. 112–13.
47. Densmore, *Teton Sioux Music*, p. 321.
48. Ibid.
49. Ibid., p. 322.
50. Blish, *A Pictographic History*, p. 104.
51. Densmore, *Teton Sioux Music*, p. 322.
52. Wissler, *Oglala Societies*, pp. 13, 31–32, 67.
53. Blish, *A Pictographic History*, p. 109.
54. Ibid., p. 110.
55. Ibid., p. 111.
56. Ibid., p. 109.
57. Wissler, *Oglala Societies*, pp. 33–34.
58. Ibid., p. 108.
59. Ibid., p. 105.
60. Ibid.
61. Wissler, *Oglala Societies*, pp. 34–38.
62. Wissler, *Societies and Dance Associations of the Blackfoot Indians*, pp. 451–56.
63. Blish, *A Pictographic History*, p. 116.
64. Ibid.
65. Wissler, *A General Discussion of Shamanistic Dancing Societies*, p. 864.
66. Densmore, *Teton Sioux Music*, p. 157.
67. Ibid., p. 216.
68. Ibid., p. 285.
69. Densmore, *Teton Sioux Music*, p. 285.
70. Ibid., p. 291.
71. Wissler, *Societies and Dance Associations*, p. 91.
72. Blish, *A Pictographic History*, p. 277.
73. Ibid., p. 277–78.
74. Ibid., p. 278.
75. Wissler, *Societies and Dance Associations*, pp. 82–85.
76. Blish, *A Pictographic History*, p. 273.
77. Ibid., pp. 415–16.
78. Densmore, *Teton Sioux Music*, p. 298.
79. Ibid.
80. Ibid., p. 304.
81. Ibid., pp. 299–300.
82. Ibid., p. 294.
83. Ibid., p. 295.
84. Densmore, *Teton Sioux Music*, pp. 176–77.
85. Ibid., pp. 178–79.
86. Blish, *A Pictographic History*, p. 199.
87. Ibid., pp. 200–201.
88. Densmore, *Teton Sioux Music*, p. 195.
89. John C. Ewers, *Indian Life on the Upper Missouri*, p. 136.
90. Blish, *A Pictographic History*, p. 273.
91. Ibid., p. 184.
92. Wissler, *Some Protective Designs of the Dakota*, pp. 51–52. See also Blish, *A Pictographic History*, pp. 65–66.
93. Blish, *A Pictographic History*, p. 38.
94. Ibid., p. 65.

Notes to Chapter 11
1. Alice C. Fletcher and Francis La Flesche, *The Omaha Tribe*, p. 459.
2. Ibid.
3. Ibid., pp. 459–80.
4. Ibid., pp. 481–85.
5. Ibid., pp. 485–86.
6. Ibid., p. 486.
7. Ibid.
8. James Owen Dorsey, *Omaha Sociology*, 3: 273.
9. Fletcher and La Flesche, *The Omaha Tribe*, p. 486.
10. Dorsey, *Omaha Sociology*, 3: 349–350.
11. Ibid., 3: 350.
12. Ibid., 3: 348.
13. Ibid., 3: 349.
14. Ibid., 3: 348.
15. James Howard, *The Ponca Tribe*, pp. 117–19. See also Fletcher and La Flesche, *The Omaha Tribe*, p. 487.

16. Fletcher and La Flesche, *The Omaha Tribe*, p. 486.
17. Ibid., pp. 490–93.
18. Ibid., pp. 493–95.
19. Ibid., pp. 495–97.
20. Ibid., pp. 509–65.
21. Ibid., pp. 565–81.

Notes to Chapter 12
1. Edward S. Curtis, *The North American Indian*, 4: 15–16.
2. Robert H. Lowie, *The Crow Indians*, p. 181.
3. Curtis, *The North American Indian*, 4: 15.
4. Ibid., 4: 16.
5. Ibid.
6. Lowie, *The Crow Indians*, p. 185.
7. Curtis, *The North American Indian*, 4: 17.
8. Lowie, *The Crow Indians*, p. 207.
9. Ibid., p. 213.
10. Ibid., p. 214.
11. Ibid., pp. 274–96.
12. Ibid., p. 295.
13. Ibid., pp. 264–68.
14. Ibid., pp. 269–73.

Notes to Chapter 13
1. Alanson Skinner, *Societies of the Iowa, Kansa, and Ponca Indians*, pp. 184–85.
2. James Owen Dorsey, *Omaha Sociology*, p. 354.
3. Ibid., p. 352.
4. Skinner, *Iowa, Kansa, and Ponca Indians*, pp. 785–86.
5. Dorsey, *Omaha Sociology*, pp. 354–55.
6. James Howard, *The Ponca Tribe*, pp. 111–12.
7. Ibid., p. 112.
8. Ibid.
9. Ibid., p. 113.
10. Ibid.
11. Alice C. Fletcher and Francis La Flesche, *The Omaha Tribe*, pp. 280, 352.
12. Howard, *The Ponca Tribe*, p. 113.
13. Skinner, *Iowa, Kansa, and Ponca Indians*, pp. 790–91.
14. Howard, *The Ponca Tribe*, p. 113.
15. Dorsey, *Omaha Sociology*, p. 355.
16. Howard, *The Ponca Tribe*, pp. 113–14.
17. Skinner, *Iowa, Kansa, and Ponca Indians*, p. 792.
18. Howard, *Omaha Sociology*, p. 118.
19. Ibid., p. 119.
20. Skinner, *Iowa, Kansa, and Ponca Indians*, p. 306.
21. Howard, *Omaha Sociology*, p. 123.
22. Ibid., p. 124.
23. Fletcher and La Flesche, *The Omaha Tribe*, pp. 490–93.
24. Skinner, *Iowa, Kansa, and Ponca Indians*, p. 789.
25. Ibid.

Notes to Chapter 14
1. James Owen Dorsey, *The Cheyenne*, p. 15.
2. George Bird Grinnell, *The Cheyenne Indians*, 1: 336–48.
3. Ibid., pp. 337–38.
4. Edward S. Curtis, *The North American Indian*, 6: 105.
5. Dorsey, *The Cheyenne*, p. 15.
6. Frances Densmore, *Teton Sioux Music*, p. 312.
7. E. Adamson Hoebel and Karl N. Llewellyn, *The Cheyenne Way*, pp. 99–100.
8. Grinnell, *The Cheyenne Indians*, 2: 79–86.
9. Hoebel and Llewellyn, *The Cheyenne Way*, p. 100.
10. Grinnell, *The Cheyenne Indians*, p. 101.
11. Hoebel and Llewellyn, *The Cheyenne Way*, 101.
12. Ibid., p. 70.
13. Ibid., p. 48.
14. Ibid., p. 99.
15. Dorsey, *The Cheyenne*, p. 15.
16. Ibid., p. 16.
17. Ibid.
18. Grinnell, *The Cheyenne Indians*, p. 62.
19. Ibid., p. 63.
20. Dorsey, *The Cheyenne*, pp. 16–18.
21. Grinnell, *The Cheyenne Indians*, p. 58.
22. Dorsey, *The Cheyenne*, pp. 18–19.
23. Ibid., pp. 19–20.
24. Grinnel, *The Cheyenne Indians*, p. 69.
25. Hoebel and Llewellyn, *The Cheyenne Way*, pp. 70–71.
26. Grinnell, *The Cheyenne Indians*, p. 68.
27. Dorsey, *The Cheyenne*, p. 21.
28. Hoebel and Llewellyn, *The Cheyenne Way*, p. 68.
29. Dorsey, *The Cheyenne*, p. 21.
30. Ibid., pp. 21–22.
31. Ibid., p. 22.
32. Ibid., pp. 23–24.
33. Ibid., p. 24.
34. Ibid., pp. 24–25.
35. Ibid., p. 25.
36. Ibid., p. 26.
37. Ibid., p. 28.
38. Ibid., p. 29.
39. Ibid., pp. 26–29. See also variant story in Grinnell, *The Cheyenne Indians*, 2: 72–78.
40. Ibid., p. 29.
41. Densmore, *Teton Sioux Music*, pp. 314–15.
42. Robert H. Lowie, *Dance Associations of the Eastern Dakota*, p. 105.
43. James Mooney, *The Cheyenne Indians*, p. 412.
44. Grinnell, *The Cheyenne Indians*, p. 159.
45. Ibid., p. 160.
46. Ibid., pp. 168–69.
47. James Howard, *The Ponca Tribe*, pp. 121–24.
48. Grinnell, *The Cheyenne Indians*, pp. 204–10.
49. Ibid., pp. 204–05.
50. Ibid., pp. 285–336.

Notes to Chapter 15
1. George Catlin, *The North American Indians*, 1: 26.
2. Edward S. Curtis, *The North American Indian*, 3: 168.
3. Robert H. Lowie, *The Assiniboine*, p. 67.
4. Ibid., pp. 66–69.
5. Ibid., p. 58.
6. Ibid., p. 66.
7. Ibid., p. 70.
8. Ibid., pp. 70–71.
9. Ibid., pp. 71–72.
10. Ibid., pp. 72–73.
11. Ibid., p. 73.
12. Ibid., pp. 73–74.
13. Ibid., p. 74.
14. Ibid.
15. John C. Ewers, *Indian Life on the Upper Missouri*, pp. 131–45.

Notes to Chapter 16
1. Alanson Skinner, *The Plains Ojibway and Plains Cree Indians*, vol. 11, pt. 6: 475–542.
2. James R. Murie, *Pawnee Indian Societies*, vol. 11, pt. 7: 543–644.
3. Robert H. Lowie, *The Northern Shoshone*, p. 216.
4. Robert H. Lowie, *Dances and Societies of the Plains Shoshone*, vol. 11, pt. 10: 803–35.
5. Edward S. Curtis, *The North American Indian*, 18: 122.
6. Ibid., p. 70.
7. Ibid., 19: 43–44.
8. Ibid., pp. 153–54, 227.
9. E. Wallace and E. Adamson Hoebel, *The Comanches: Lords of the South Plains*, pp. 272–73.
10. Ibid., p. 276.
11. James Mooney, *The Ghost Dance Religion*, Bureau of Ethnology Fourteenth Annual Report, 2: 989–90.
12. Ibid., p. 990.
13. Lowie, *Societies of the Kiowa*, pp. 837–51.
14. Ibid., p. 845.
15. W. W. Newcomb, Jr., *The Indians of Texas*, pp. 203–05.

BIBLIOGRAPHY

Boss, Althea. *The Arapaho Way.* New York: Clarkson N. Potter, 1966.

Beckwourth, James P. *Life and Adventures of James P. Beckwourth.* Edited by T. D. Bonner. New York: Macmillan, 1892.

Black Elk. *The Sacred Pipe.* Edited by Joseph Epes Brown. Norman: University of Oklahoma Press, 1953.

Blish, Helen H. *A Pictographic History of the Oglala Sioux.* Lincoln: University of Nebraska Press, 1967.

Bowers, Alfred W. *Mandan Social and Ceremonial Organization.* Chicago: University of Chicago Press, 1950.

Brown, James Epes. *The Spiritual Legacy of the American Indian.* Pendle Hill Pamphlet 135. Lebanon, Pa.: Sowers Printing Company, 1964.

Catlin, George. *The North American Indians.* 2 vols. Edinburgh: John Grant, 1926.

Curtis, Edward S. *The North American Indian.* 20 vols. Cambridge: The University Press, 1907–30.

Densmore, Frances. *Teton Sioux Music.* BAF Bulletin 61 (1918).

Dorsey, George A., and Kroeber, Alfred L. *Traditions of the Arapaho.* Field Columbian Museum Anthropological Series 81 (1903).

Dorsey, James Owen. *The Cheyenne.* Field Columbian Museum Anthropological Papers 99, vol. 9, no. 1 (1905).

———. *Omaha Sociology.* BAE Third Annual Report (1881–82).

———. *Siouan Sociology.* BAE Fifteenth Annual Report (1897).

Ewers, John C. *The Horse In Blackfoot Indian Culture.* BAE Bullletin 159 (1955).

———. *Indian Life on the Upper Missouri.* Norman: University of Oklahoma Press, 1968.

———. *Plains Indian Painting.* Palo Alto: Stanford University, 1939.

Fletcher, Alice C., and La Flesche, Francis. *The Omaha Tribe.* BAE Twenty-Seventh Annual Report (1911).

Goddard, Pliny Earle. *Dancing Societies of the Sarsi Indians.* AMNH, vol. 11, pt 5 (1914).

Grinnell, George Bird. *The Cheyenne Indians.* 2 vols. New Haven: Yale University Press, 1923.

Hassrick, Royal B. *The Sioux.* Norman: University of Oklahoma Press, 1964.

Hoebel, E. Adamson, and Llewellyn, Karl N. *The Cheyenne Way.* Norman: University of Oklahoma Press, 1941.

Howard, James. *The Ponca Tribe.* BAE Report 195 (1965).

Kroeber, Alfred L. *Ethnology of the Gros Ventre.* AMNH Anthropological Papers, vol. 1, pt. 4 (1908).

Lewis, Meriwether, and Clark, William. *Original Journals of the Lewis and Clark Expedition, 1804–1806.* 8 vols. Edited by Reuben Gold Thwaites. New York: 1904–1905.

Liberty, Margot, and John Stands in Timber. *Cheyenne Memories.* New Haven and London: Yale University Press, 1967.

Linderman, Frank B. *Plenty Coups.* Lincoln: University of Nebraska Press, 1962.

Lowie, Robert H. *The Assiniboine.* AMNH, vol. 4, pt. 1 (1909).

———. *The Crow Indians.* New York: Holt, Rinehart and Winston, 1956.

———. *Dance Associations of the Eastern Dakota.* AMNH Anthropological Papers, vol. 11, pt. 2 (1913).

———. *Indians of the Plains.* AMNH. New York: McGraw-Hill, 1954.

———. *The Northern Shoshone.* AMNH Anthropological Papers, vol. 2, pt. 2 (1908).

———. *Dances and Societies of the Plains Shoshone.* AMNH, vol. 11, pt. 10 (1915).

———. *Societies of the Arikara Indians.* AMNH, vol. 11, pt. 8 (1915).

———. *Societies of the Hidatsa and Mandan.* AMNH, vol. 11 (1913).

———. *Societies of the Kiowa.* AMNH, vol. 11 (1916).

Mails, Thomas E. *The Mystic Warriors of the Plains.* New York: Doubleday & Company, 1972.

Maximilian, Prince of Wied Neuweid. *Travels in the Interior of North America.* 3 vols. London, 1843; Thwaites edition, 1906.

McClintock, Walter. "Blackfoot Warrior Societies." *Southwest Museum Publication* 8. Highland Park, Los Angeles: Southwest Museum.

———. *Old Indian Trails.* Boston and New York: Houghton Mifflin Co., 1923.

———. *The Old North Trail.* London: Macmillan and Co., 1910.

Michelson, Truman. "Narrative of an Arapaho Woman." *American Anthropologist.* n.s., 35, 4 (1933).

Mooney, James. *The Cheyenne Indians.* Memoirs of the American Anthropological Association, vol. 1, pt. 6 (1907).

———. *The Ghost Dance Religion.* BAE Fourteenth Annual Report, pt. 2 (1892–93).

Murie, James R. *Pawnee Indian Societies.* AMNH, vol. 11, pt. 7 (1914).

Newcomb, W. W. Jr. *The Indians of Texas.* Austin: University of Texas Press, 1965.

Royce, Ernest. *Burbank among the Indians.* Caldwell, Idaho: The Caxton Printers, Ltd., 1944.

Skinner, Alanson. *The Plains Ojibway and Plains Cree Indians.* AMNH, vol. 11, pt. 6 (1914).

———. *Societies of the Iowa, Kansa, and Ponca Indians.* AMNH Anthropological Papers, vol. 11, pt. 9 (1915).

Swanton, John R. *The Indian Tribes of North America.* BAE Bulletin 145 (1952).

Trenholm, Virgina Cole. *The Arapahoes, Our People.* Norman: University of Oklahoma Press, 1970.

Wallace, E., and Hoebel, E. Adamson, *The Comanches: Lords of the South Plains.* Norman: University of Oklahoma Press, 1952.

Wildschut, William, and Ewers, John C. *Crow Indian Medicine Bundles.* Museum of the American Indian, vol. 17 (1960).

Wissler, Clark. *A General Discussion of Shamanistic Dancing Societies.* AMNH, vol. 11, pt. 12 (1916).

———. *Mythology of the Blackfoot Indians.* AMNH Anthropological Papers, vol. 2, (1908).

———. *Red Man's Reservations.* New York: Macmillan (Collier Books), 1971. Originally published as *Indian Cavalcades.* New York: Sheridan House, 1938.

———. *Societies and Ceremonial Organizations in the Oglala Division of the Teton-Dakota.* AMNH Anthropological Papers, vol. 2 (1912).

———. *Societies and Dance Associations of the Blackfoot Indians.* AMNH, vol. 2.

———. *Societies of the Plains Indians.* AMNH Anthropological Papers, vol. 11 (1913).

———. *Some Protective Designs of the Dakota.* AMNH Anthropological Papers, vol. 1, pt. 2 (1907).

———. The Whirlwind and Elk in the Mythology of the Dakota. *Journal of American Folk Lore,* vol. 19 (1905).

INDEX OF TRIBES
AND SOCIETIES

Above: *Southeastern Plains warrior wearing a horned fur cap and a grizzly bear claw necklace, both of which were styles common to that area.*

Below: *Member of the Sioux Crow-owners society with raven attached to his neck in the manner it was usually worn in war. Behind him is his shield and another view of the raven and its painted rawhide carrying case.* Right: *Member of a Sioux animal cult society wearing an ermine-covered cap adorned with buffalo horn, owl feathers and dyed eagle feathers. His war shirt has quilled bands.*

Above: *Members of a Blackfoots Brave Dog society, performing a ceremony. Their costumes are adorned with rolled ermine tails and beaded bands.*